Why I Rejected Christianity:

A Former

Apologist Explains

By
John W. Loftus

Note for Librarians: A cataloguing record for this book is available from Library and Archives
Canada at www.collectionscanada.ca/amicus/index-e.html
ISBN 1-4120-7681-1

*Printed in Victoria, BC, Canada. Printed on paper with minimum 30% recycled fibre. Trafford's print shop
runs on "green energy" from solar, wind and other environmentally-friendly power sources.*

TRAFFORD
PUBLISHING™

Offices in Canada, USA, Ireland and UK
This book was published *on-demand* in cooperation with Trafford Publishing. On-demand
publishing is a unique process and service of making a book available for retail sale to the
public taking advantage of on-demand manufacturing and Internet marketing. On-demand
publishing includes promotions, retail sales, manufacturing, order fulfilment, accounting and
collecting royalties on behalf of the author.

Book sales for North America and international:
Trafford Publishing, 6E–2333 Government St.,
Victoria, BC V8T 4P4 CANADA
phone 250 383 6864 (toll-free 1 888 232 4444)
fax 250 383 6804; email to orders@trafford.com
Book sales in Europe:
Trafford Publishing (UK) Limited, 9 Park End Street, 2nd Floor
Oxford, UK OXI IHH UNITED KINGDOM
phone 44 (0)1865 722 113 (local rate 0845 230 9601)
facsimile 44 (0)1865 722 868; info.uk@trafford.com
Order online at:
trafford.com/05-2576

10 9 8 7 6 5 4

Table of Contents

Page

Foreword by Edward T. Babinski   4
Introduction   7

PART 1: MY CHANGING YEARS

1 My Christian Conversion and Passionate Faith   9
    - 1:1 A Word About The Grounding of My Faith   16
2 Why I Changed My Mind: My Deconversion   20
    - 2:1 A Word About My Deconversion   30
3 A Letter to Dr. James D. Strauss   33

PART 2: THE CUMULATIVE CASE   37

4 The Outsider Test For Faith....   40
5 Faith and Reason   47
6 The Christian Illusion of Rational and Moral Superiority   58
7 Does God Exist?   68
8 The Problem of Unanswered Prayer   83
9 The Lessons of Galileo, Science and Religion   88
10 Science and Creation   96
11 Science and Genesis 1-11   105
12 The Strange and Superstitious World of the Bible   111
    - 12:1 Pseudonymity in the Bible   142
    - 12:2 Archaeology, the Exodus, and the Conquest   149
13 Historical Evidence and Christianity   151
14 Do Miracles Take Place?   162
15 The Self-Authenticating Witness of the Holy Spirit   172
16 Was Jesus Born of a Virgin in Bethlehem?   178
17 Was Jesus God Incarnate?   182
18 "The Passion of the Christ": Why Did Jesus Suffer?   192
19 Did Jesus Bodily Rise from the Dead?   198
    - 19:1 The Pharisees: Were They That Bad?   216
20 The Devil Made Me Do It!   219
21 Prophecy and Biblical Authority   222
22 Hell? No!   229
23 The Problem of Evil   234
24 Calvinism   257
25 The Achilles' Heel of Christianity   261

PART 3: WHAT I BELIEVE TODAY

26 Why I'm An Atheist   263
27 What is Life Without God?   268
28 What If I'm Wrong?   275

PART 4: APPENDICES

A Partial List of My Published Christian Writings   277
A Picture of Dr. Craig, Dr. Strauss, and I   278

Foreword By Edward T. Babinski.

John W. Loftus is a former conservative Christian apologist who at some point admitted that he could no longer honestly use the term "Christian" to describe his present beliefs or state of mind, since he now doubts many Christian doctrines, beliefs and Biblical interpretations he once formerly accepted as rock solid truths. His book is a clear, honest and concise summary of some of the questions he encountered along his spiritual, theological and philosophical journey. Neither is it as isolated and fearful a journey as some conservative Evangelicals may think, because many of today's top biblical archeologists and biblical scholars from William Dever to Bart Ehrman (including many professors in the Jesus Seminar) all began their own journeys as conservative Christians with few doubts, only to discover more questions and uncertainties.

Hence a diversity of opinion exists in modern day scholarship. In fact, the majority of the world's educational institutions though founded originally as conservative Christian seminaries, have also taken similar journeys to John's, when engaging the learned opinions among scholars. Within two hundred years of Calvin's death, the very College of Geneva that John Calvin founded, became open to all sorts of Enlightenment ideas and doubts concerning how literally to take the Bible, and Christian doctrines. So John's experience not only parallels that of other individuals, like Dever and Ehrman, but also seminaries once founded to promote conservative Christian views. Yale it must be remembered, was originally founded in reaction to the "theological excesses" of Harvard, yet today look at Yale!

Meanwhile, the types of institutions that continue to defend the "inerrancy of the Bible" are all relatively young institutions. In time however, if they grow and attract the brightest and the best, they will have to interact with the scholarly world and read not simply Evangelical or inerrantist publications, but engage with ongoing world-wide inter-disciplinary biblical research and questions. If a conservative Evangelical Christian pokes his nose in theology books, journals, Bible dictionaries and Bible commentaries published by Oxford, Yale, and/or Cambridge University--to name just a few (not to forget the Anchor Bible series of commentaries)--he is bound to begin running into the diversity of opinion among scholars concerning the meaning and relative importance of passages from Genesis to Revelation. Even Evangelical scholars at Wheaton like Prof. Walton are beginning to catch up with scholarly questions concerning how literally the ancient Hebrews probably understood their own "primeval history" in Genesis, and concludes we need not take them so literally today. [See the NIV Application Commentary on Genesis, (Zondervan Books, 2002)].

Another service John's book provides is demonstrating to many who are having doubts, that there are others out there like them. His book helps support others making the sometimes difficult transition, which usually involves some isolation and loneliness, since your former best friends in church have little idea why you need time away from church to read and reconsider your beliefs, or why you might not feel right about repeating the creedal affirmations aloud, or singing the old choruses.

Again, speaking as someone who has himself spent years of my former Bible-believing life trying to hold onto every word of the Bible "without error," I wonder today just what conservative Christians DO believe, or even if they themselves really know. There are probably a lot more unspoken doubts going on in the Christian world than anyone cares to personally relate. For instance, do conservative Christians imagine a literal talking serpent was "the shrewdest beast of the field God created," but then God cursed it to "go on its belly?" (Not much of a "curse" to put on a serpent, come to think of it.). Do they all believe in the story of forbidden edible fruit, and that all the natural causes of suffering on earth and throughout the cosmos including volcanoes, hurricanes, earthquakes, as well as diseases, poisonous microbes and insects were all simply the result of one human couple's disobedient hungering for a piece of fruit? Do they believe a woman named Eve was cloned directly from Adam's rib? Do Christian apologists really doubt none of those old mythological tales out of Israel's primeval history in Genesis? Do they plead that Lot's wife must have indeed turned into a literal pillar of salt? Or do some of them simply make embarrassed excuses for the tale of Noah, admitting, "it was only a local flood." Do they accept the true scientific age of the earth, regardless of what the "ages of the Patriarchs" adds up to, and regardless of the fact that Genesis states that the first light of the entire cosmos was created simply to accommodate "days/nights, evenings/mornings" as measured on one tiny planet, the earth? (How geocentric, i.e., the whole cosmos created to suit earth's "days," the time of revolution of only one planet in the whole cosmos.)

If Christian apologists do NOT imagine such things, or have even the barest of doubts concerning them, then what exactly DO they believe, and how can they tell others they are so sure? It's the old crossroads that even Christian conservatives eventually come to, either try to compress all of geology and cosmic astronomical time into the thimble-full of years of the "primeval history" portions of Genesis, whose names of patriarchs and events of their lives even Jesus alluded to, or admit that Jesus was merely repeating back the prejudices of his day just so others would understand him? But by doing so did Jesus know that he'd be legitimating today's "young-earth creationists" two thousand years hence? Can the O.T. language in the primeval history easily be interpreted to make room for a cosmos billions of years old, with the earth created later in cosmic history, with humanity appearing very late on earth geologically?

All Christians also have to face the evidence of changes in teachings over time, or explain them away as progressive revelation or "different dispensations", because the Bible's views of god, satan, the afterlife and what you needed to do to please god, changed over time, from the oldest O.T. works to later ones, and from the O.T. to inter-testamental works, and from those works to the earliest N.T. writings. There are changes internal to the Gospels themselves that can be seen when you compare and contrast stories of say, the resurrection from Paul to Mark, Matthew, Luke, John (not to forget the later Jesus tales in the apocryphal Gospels concerning the resurrection and heaven and hell, because Christians did not cease writing stories of Jesus after the four Gospels were finished, but continued composing tales).

Two thousand years and 45,000 separate Christian denominations and missionary organizations later, we have modern day "Christianity," including everything from Trappist monks and Quakers who worship in silence, and meditating Christians dialoging with eastern faiths--to hell raisers and snake handling Christians. We have damnationists--to universalist Christians, and many more groups besides. Even after the Roman Empire adopted and enforced Christian faith, Arian and Athanasian Christians rioted, killed and persecuted each other, as did Donatists and Catholics. And none of the older ideas ever fully die out, because some of the Bible verses and arguments used by Arians were much later revived and used by Deists and Unitarians, while the Donatists never gave up their fight to appoint their own priests rather than Rome, kind of like today's ultra-conservative Catholics who think the papacy is wrong but the rest of Catholicism is good. And there's many differences of opinion on everything in Christianity today from social issues to religious issues like tongue-speaking, baptism, miracles, when and how to best honor the Sabbath, what O.T. laws ought to be enforced today for the good of society, what signs to look for in the "saved," including, "short hair in men," or, using the "King James Bible" above all other translations. Meanwhile some things that the early church emphasized are little emphasized today, except among the Catholics, by which I mean clergy celibacy, as seen in the words of Jesus and Paul and the author of Revelation. Christianity continues to evolve and branch into further new rival denominations and sub-organizations as time goes on. How Darwinian of the churches!

Those like John who finally do climb off the Christian merry-go-round are indeed dizzy after leaving, and wonder why others choose to stay. There is after all something to be said for self-reliance and allowing one's inquisitive mind to ponder questions for a season, even if doubting can make one feel less secure and less ecstatic than riding the merry-go-round. At least you begin to feel more like yourself, less at the mercy of your brain which mindlessly pops out proof-texts, or fearing hell for even spending time away from church. You begin to feel more, well, "human," and hence begin to view others as having similar doubts and fears and also similar hopes and joys.

--Edward T. Babinski, author of Leaving the Fold: Testimonies of Former Fundamentalists, visit http://www.edwardtbabinski.us.

Introduction.

In his book, The End of Faith: Religion, Terror and the Future of Reason (Norton, 2005), Sam Harris argues that religious faith should no longer be given a free pass, especially since we're living in a very dangerous world; one with nuclear weapons. This book is my effort to do just that when it comes to conservative, evangelical or fundamentalist Christianity. And since I believe it has a very good chance to be correct about Christianity as a whole, by rejecting it I also reject Christianity in general.

Let me state from the outset that although I reject Christianity, I do not reject Christian people, most of whom I respect as good people. I just consider them to be deluded about their faith, like I was.

Here are some things to know about me: I was ordained into the ministry of the centrist *Restoration Movement* Churches of Christ by Jerry M. Paul, when he was at Christ's Church at Georgetown, Ft. Wayne, IN. I graduated from Great Lakes Bible (now Christian) College, Lansing Michigan, in 1977. Afterward I became the Associate Minister for the Kalkaska Church of Christ, in Kalkaska, MI, for two years. Then I attended Lincoln Christian Seminary (LCS), Lincoln, IL, and graduated in 1982 with M.A. and M.Div. degrees, under the mentoring of Dr. James D. Strauss. While at LCS I was the founding editor for the now defunct apologetical quarterly, A Journal For Christian Studies. After LCS I attended Trinity Evangelical Divinity School (TEDS), and graduated in 1985 with a Th.M degree, under the mentoring of Dr. William Lane Craig, considered by many to be the foremost defender of the Kalam Cosmological argument for the existence of God, the empty tomb of Jesus and his bodily resurrection from the grave. At TEDS I also studied with Dr. Stuart C. Hackett, the late Dr. Paul Feinberg, and the late Dr. Kenneth Kantzer. I also took classes at Marquette University in a Ph.D. program with a double major in Philosophy and Ethics, but didn't finish. At Marquette I studied with Dr. Ronald Feenstra, Dr. Daniel MaGuire, and the late Dr. Marc Greisbach.

I was a Christian apologist with several master's degrees set for the express purpose of defending Christianity from intellectual attacks. I was not afraid of any idea, because I was convinced that Christianity was true and could withstand all attacks. I have taught classes for Lincoln Christian College, Lincoln, IL, and I taught for Great Lakes Christian College, Lansing, Michigan, for the College of Lake County, in Grayslake, IL, for Tri-State University, Angola, IN, and for Kellogg Community College, Battle Creek, MI, where I still teach as an adjunct faculty member. I was in the "Who's Who Among America's Best Teachers" in 1996.

I served as an Associate Minister, a Minister, a Senior Minister, and as an interim Minister. From December of 1987 to December of 1990 I was the Senior Minister of the Angola Christian Church, Angola, Indiana. I served in the Steuben County Ministerial Association, and for a year I was its President. Before that, I had ministries in Michigan, Wisconsin and Illinois. I was in the ministry for about fourteen years, or so. There are several men in the ministry today who credit me with inspiring them to enter into it. One of them is finishing up a Ph.D. program as I write this. The Presidents of two seminaries were personal friends of mine when we were in school together, and one former professor is the President of another Christian University. I have considered many Christian college professors and a great many more ministers as my friends.

I am now an atheist. One major reason why I have become an atheist is because I could not answer the questions I was encountering. I became an atheist precisely because that's where the unanswerable questions led me. The arguments just weren't there, period. Now as an atheist, I turn that same intellectual muscle into arguing against the things I formerly defended.

In this book I'm writing to explain why I rejected Christianity. It's sincere, and it's honest. In it I present a cumulative case argument against Christianity. **I consider this book to be one single argument against Christianity.** It includes my own personal experiences with the Christian faith, along with the arguments that I find persuasive enough for me to reject that faith. My claim is that the Christian faith should be rejected by modern, educated people, even if I know many of them will still disagree. I'm just sharing the reasons that convinced me, and I think they should convince others. If someone is persuaded by the same reasons I argue for in this book, then I'm pleased. [My method is explained on pages 37-39 and on pages 55-57].

I consider the most significant sections (or subsets) of my argument to be 1) **sociological**, in *The Outsider Test For Faith*...[4], 2) **scientific**, in *The Lessons of Galileo, Science and Religion* [9], 3) **Biblical**, in *The Strange and Superstitious World of the Bible* [12], 4) **historical**, in *Historical Evidence and Christianity* [13], and 5) **philosophical**, in *Do Miracles Take Place?* [14], and especially in *The Problem of Evil* [23], which are partially summed up in *The Achilles' Heel of Christianity* [25]. These sections provide me with the control beliefs for rejecting Christianity's specific foundational miracle/doctrinal claims.

No one today can master all of the relevant issues, certainly not me. I am painfully aware of many of the objections that Christians can make to my arguments, but in the end, they don't persuade me to think differently. I have researched enough to be rationally satisfied in rejecting the Christian faith.

In this book I quote from and refer to many different resources to support and further argue for my position. If I used a book or essay in anything that I share here, then it influenced my thinking and I highly recommend you get it, and read it.

To read updates and discuss the issues in this book with me, visit my Blog on the Web: **http://debunkingchristianity.blogspot.com/**

[A big thanks goes out to **Matthew J. Green** who wrote a great review of my book by saying, "This book is one of the best introductory texts on the philosophical problems with Christianity," and for suggesting several good arguments I had initially missed. Thanks also go out to **Joe E. Holman**, who did a yeoman's job of proofreading the previous edition of this book for typographical errors, and for pointing out some stylistic changes that needed to be made. I didn't adopt them all, but he's made this a much better book].

[Revised November 2006]

1 <u>My Christian Conversion and Passionate Faith.</u>

One August in the early 90's, Greg Steere preached a sermon at the Northmen gathering on being passionate men. The Northmen is a gathering of Church of Christ men near Kalkaska, Michigan. Greg had previously attended my youth group several times at the Kalkaska Church of Christ, Kalkaska, Michigan, when I first became a youth minister after graduating from Great Lakes Bible (Christian) College (GLBC/GLCC; They later changed their name to "Christian" College). "We should be passionate men," he preached. "We should be passionate about God, and about the life God has given us." The sermon was a good one, but I couldn't help but think while he preached his first sermon at that gathering that his preaching wasn't itself very passionate. He was still a young preacher at the time.

But if there is one thing that can be said for me, it's that I am a very passionate man. When I focus on something and/or commit myself to it, I give it my all. My conversion experience was dramatic—so dramatic that it stunned everyone around me. There is no one who

> **There is no one who knew me during my early years as a Christian who would say that I was not on fire for God.**

knew me during my early years as a Christian who would say that I was not on fire for God. I burned with passion for the Lord. And for good reason, God turned my life around.

I was born in 1954 and grew up in Ft. Wayne, Indiana, in a Catholic home. I went to parochial school up until the 4th grade. It was in my youth where I heard of God's love for me, and of several Bible stories. Our family went to church but we were a nominal church going family, for the most part. I never experienced true faith growing up, but I did learn that whenever I was in need I should call out to God. And that's exactly what I did at 18 years old when I felt I had nowhere to turn for help.

I was not always a good boy, being the middle child in a home with three boys separated by 2 ½ years on both sides of me. I seemed to be in almost every fight in the household, first with my older brother, Tom, and then with my younger brother, Jim. Tom was just too big for Jim to get into many fights with him. But not me! I fought with both of them.

My mother earned a college degree and started teaching elementary school just when I was about to enter the 8th grade. But since neither my mother, nor my father would be home when we boys got home from school, they knew I would get into trouble from time to time with my brothers once school was out. So to eliminate the problem, they thought it would be good for everyone if I considered attending Howe Military School, in Howe Indiana, for 8th grade. My mother's extra income would help pay for the costs, it would help discipline me, and my two brothers would be okay at home unsupervised.

Howe was a good school and I learned for the first time that I could do well in school. I just hadn't applied myself before, for whatever reason. Howe required an hour of silence every night for doing homework, and because of this I received higher grades than ever before, B+'s and above. I also had a year long math class taught by Mr. Utz who actually taught us symbolic logic. Yes, that's right, symbolic logic! He said it was the new math. Since we didn't know any better, we thought it WAS math. I didn't realize what he had taught us until sometime after graduating from college, primarily because I never thought much about it. Later on in life I actually found myself teaching logic classes for college students!

I have never claimed to have a higher I.Q. than others, nor that I was better than others at remembering things—sometimes I lack common sense—but what Mr. Utz gave this young passionate boy was something in addition to his passion. He gave me the intellectual tools

> **Mr. Utz gave me the tools for thinking at an early age that have never left me.**

to think through arguments. When something is taught at an early age it can make you different than others simply because others were never exposed to it. If I seem to be smart, it's only because of Mr. Utz who gave me the tools for thinking at an early age.

I didn't want to go back to Howe the next year, nor did I have to. But on the first day of school in 9th grade, I found myself walking to school next to a fellow 9th grader who lit up a cigarette on the way to school. So in order to be cool I had one too. It wasn't long before I was in the wrong crowd. I also began to do terrible in Algebra class. I just barely passed with D-'s. Somehow it didn't dawn on me that the reason why was because I hadn't had 8th grade math which prepared me for Algebra. I just thought it was a higher, more advanced form of math, and I just wasn't getting it. Plus, when I started hanging around the wrong crowd, I wasn't interested in school and all of my grades plummeted.

I was a problem teenager. I had several problems that 9th grade year at Lane Jr. High School, and later got kicked out of Snider High School the next year several times for several different offenses. Then came my problems with the law. I spent many weeks in the *Wood Youth Center*, in Ft. Wayne. I dropped out of school. Most of my law breaking occurred during the time my mother and father were separated and divorced, and they found it hard to corral me in. They eventually remarried. But in the meantime, I was arrested six different times as a juvenile offender for various

> **I was arrested six different times as a juvenile offender.**

offenses! I think I just wanted to fit in. But I fit in with the wrong crowd, and I had no goals at that time.

I had hitchhiked to California twice with two different friends. On one occasion, a friend named Scott and I were taking turns hitchhiking just outside of St. George, Utah, real late at night. We only had one sleeping bag, and he was sleeping in it while I took my turn hitchhiking. I was cold, tired, hungry and very dirty. As I looked at the night sky I thought I would try a prayer, just to see what happened. So I prayed that someone would pick us up, take us to his home, feed us, let us clean up and also stay the night. If God would answer this prayer then I would know he exists. So I began counting cars, just to see how many cars would come by before my prayer would be answered, if it were to be answered at all.

The seventh car stopped, and picked us up. It was a man claiming to be a "child of God." He said he saw us up on the highway from below where he lived, and he took us to his home, fed us, let us clean up, and spend the night! In the morning we woke up and found a note that said, "I'm at work but if you're still here by lunch time I'll be back to give you a lift to the highway. Take anything you want, but please don't take my quadraphonic stereo." We just didn't know what to think. We wondered whether or not he was a cop! But he wasn't, and he came back and took us to the highway like he said. Needless to say, we didn't steal anything from him!

Eventually I began to feel as if I was possessed by some demonic being. So one night back in my home town I went over to see a woman named Cathy (aged 25 at the time, I believe), who had earlier spoken to me earlier about Jesus. She led me to accept the sacrifice Jesus made on the cross for my sins when I was 18, to repent from all of my sins, and to confess Jesus as the Christ, the Son of the living of God. I felt free and forgiven for the first time in my life. Through faith I now had a personal relationship with God the Father, and with the Holy Spirit

> **I felt free and forgiven for the first time in my life.**

I was empowered to live the Christian life. I now waited expectantly for the return of Jesus and to spend eternity in heaven. I also began evangelizing others.

On the night I first became a Christian my friend Scott was with me. As we left Cathy's house he told me he believed in Satanism. He wanted to show me the power of Satan too, so he told me he was going to make it rain that night. He asked me to pull into the carwash and he sprayed my car down with water. As we left the carwash it began to sprinkle, and then to rain! Now I didn't know anything about Jesus except what I learned as a kid, and I learned that you could call out to God and he would do things for you. So without hesitation I held my hand up to the roof of the car and said, "In the name of Jesus I command it to stop raining! And don't rain the rest of the night!" I still don't know why I said those words, but I did. And guess what? It stopped raining immediately! I was overwhelmed. "It's true," I said to myself. "It's true!" And it didn't rain the rest of the night!

Now it might appear that with such astounding experiences as these that I could never doubt the Christian faith. But people who go to Las Vegas every week win some big prize whose odds were equally astounding. It's also entirely possible that I've told these two stories so often as part of my Christian testimony during my Christian years that I have incrementally exaggerated them from what originally happened. Maybe I am merely telling these stories as I remember them, and not how they actually happened? At this point, I don't know for sure.

But my life radically changed. Here's how I later described my new life and new sense of mission in a newspaper devotional column that area ministers took turns writing every week: "I can identify with the apostle Paul who said, 'But by the grace of God I am what I am' (I Corinthians 15:10). I knew I needed help, but no one could break through to me, until I turned my life over to Jesus. Only he could save me. Only he could change me. I have totally changed due to the grace of God. When I look back on those years, it's like I'm talking about someone else. Without God I shudder where I would be today. Now, I gladly preach the message that God can change you too. Believe it. It happened in my life. Believe that it can happen to your rebellious teenager. Believe it because we serve a miracle-working God who answers prayer, and who intervenes on our behalf." Then I ended the devotional with these words: "From out of my own personal experience my heart bleeds for the victims in our society, for I know what it's like to be a victim and a victimizer. That's why I fight for the unborn, the poor and homeless, those victimized by pornography, but especially for those trapped in sin. People need the Lord." [Herald Republican, August 10, 1990].

After I accepted Jesus, I attended a youth group called the Adam 's Apple in Ft. Wayne, during the height of the Jesus Movement. It was affiliated with the Calvary Temple Church, and it was Pentecostal in nature. I got heavily involved with several Christian friends, who went street witnessing every Friday and Saturday night on Main Street where there were a couple of strip joints and one gay bar. We witnessed during a city July 4th celebration, and even after hockey games outside the War Memorial Coliseum. I would even go hitchhiking with the express purpose of witnessing to whoever picked me up. I witnessed to everyone all of the time.

> **I would even go hitchhiking with the express purpose of witnessing to whoever picked me up.**

In Ft. Wayne in 1973 it became cooler to be a "Jesus Freak" than a druggie. Being Jesus Freaks for us was rebelling against the establishment and old comforting values of our parents just as much as those who followed Timothy O'Leary's escape through drugs. We could look the same, have long hair, wear bell bottom studded jeans, and we could use the same slang when describing Jesus as a "hip" and a "cool dude." We evangelized with sound bites like "get high on Jesus," and, "turn on with Jesus."

My parents had started to attend Christ's Church at Georgetown where Jerry Paul was the minister. He eventually baptized me, preached at my ordination, and married me to my former wife, Kathy. That summer he had Brant Doty Jr. as a youth minister—my youth minister. He was attending Great Lakes Bible College (GLBC) and his dad was one of the professors, Dr. Doty. He told me that with such a passion for Christ I should consider attending there too. My parents helped me with tuition. After all, I was no longer getting arrested, and I was no longer doing drugs!

By the fall of that year, I had read completely through the Bible twice! Upon entering GLBC the incoming students take a Bible test, and I received the fourth highest score! Upon graduating from college we took that same Bible test once more, and Dr. Ely said I scored higher on that test than he'd ever seen anyone do! By that time, I had read completely through the Bible seven times, and I was busy daily memorizing Bible verses. Some students even thought I could out quote Mr. Hargrave, our Bible professor.

While at GLBC my freshman year, I took the GED test and got my high school equivalency degree so I could eventually graduate in 1977. I graduated Magna Cum Laude with the 3rd highest G.P.A.

Upon graduating, Dr. Doty told me about the Kalkaska Church of Christ, in Kalkaska, Michigan, who was in need a youth minister. I applied and started out in ministry. That's where I met Greg Steere, who actually attended his dad's church nearby, but who came to our youth group some of the time. Several years later he would be preaching to me about being passionate. Passion—it's my middle name. I've always been very passionate about the things I've been interested in, and as a Christian, I was as passionate as could be. My passion for the Christian faith led me to earn three master's degrees and a year and a half of Ph.D. work.

When in ministry I visited Israel, the "Holy Land," in 1989. I was one of nine ministers who went to Israel from Indiana, paid for by the Knights Templar organization in Angola. In another devotional written for the local <u>Herald Republican</u> newspaper (March 8, 1989) I shared what I had learned: "The stories of the beginnings of Christianity have a historical connectedness to them when contrasted with the eastern religion stories. In Christianity God reveals to man through actual historical events real answers that can be satisfying like nothing else can. For instance, Christ's claim to be 'the Way, the Truth and the Life' (John 14:6) has a real historical basis in actual time, and actual places of which I visited. I visited Bethlehem where Jesus was born. I visited Nazareth where Jesus grew up. I touched the Jordan River where he was baptized. I visited an ancient Jewish synagogue in Capernaum where Jesus had surely preached. I walked in and around Jerusalem where he ministered. I stood in the Garden of Gethsemane where Jesus prayed, 'Not my will but thine be done.' I stood on the very stones Jesus walked on the night he was betrayed. I stood in the very area where Jesus was crucified, and I visited the empty tomb from which he arose from the dead. I also stood on the Mount of Olives where he ascended into heaven:"

"There is such a close historical connectedness to the Christian faith that one is extremely hard pressed to deny Jesus' claim to be our only Savior without also denying early first century Jewish history. Its faith claims are also claims about a history that was checked by first century people of that day. Since it is impossible to deny such a historical setting for my faith, it becomes extremely difficult to deny the claims of the Christian faith. Christ is the Way, the Truth and Life—truly!"

Five years after I wrote the words above, I would find myself in the throes of doubt! But some of the seeds for my doubt had already been unwittingly sown at Lincoln Christian Seminary (LCS), which is a very good evangelical school. I went there intending to go into counseling. So I

> **Five years after I wrote the words above I would find myself in the throes of doubt!**

took a class my first semester with Dr. Paul Boatman, who is a very good Christian man. But during that semester I argued with Dr. Boatman in class over a counseling method that I thought was thoroughly Biblical at the time. [Jay Adams called it *nouthetic* counseling. I rejected it before I left Seminary]. At the end of that semester Dr. Boatman took the liberty to go around the classroom and tell each and every student what he thought about him or her. When he came to me he said, "John, you're an arrogant person." I couldn't understand why he thought he could be objective enough about who I am from class time alone to say that, and I couldn't understand what was Biblical about what he did. So I decided to change majors. What usually appears as arrogance in me, is either my confidence in what I know, even if misplaced, or the fact that I'm excited about some accomplishment I hadn't expected to attain.

At the same time I took a class with Dr. James D. Strauss, a professor with a great deal of understanding and a passion for learning. This man lit me up like a firecracker. He was what I was looking for. Following his example I became passionate for Christian studies and in defending my faith from all intellectual attacks. But he also set me on the intellectual path that would eventually lead me away from the faith. He led me to see that "all truth was God's truth." If it was true, it was of God, and truth has no fear of any question. In an essay for The Key, GLCC's quarterly magazine, I described what this meant: "There is no sacred/secular dichotomy. All subjects are religious. All truth is from God wherever you find it, for He's the God of all truth. If 2 + 2 = 4 is true, that mathematical truth is just as true as John 3:16. Both truths have been given to us by the God of truth, although they have different levels of importance and relevance. One statement is revealed generally to all, while the other is revealed propositionally in Scripture. But both are equally true. This applies to all other statements that are true in sociology, economics, psychology, science and so on. If it's true, then it is from God." (June-August 1989).

My passion for apologetics, coupled with the thinking skills I learned for the first time in the 8th grade, were ultimately the things that led me away from Christianity. I was so passionate about my faith that I sought to defend it with reason. I knew it was true—I just knew it. So I believed with all of the passion

> **My passion for apologetics coupled with the thinking skills I learned for the first time in the 8th grade, were ultimately the things that led me away from Christianity.**

within me that there is no argument that I could ever study that would ever discredit it.

After graduating from LCS, I wrote an article called, "A Christian Defense of the Gospel in a Twentieth Century Land" (Christian Standard, September 19, 1982), and later I wrote a devotional for the local Herald Republican newspaper (August of 1989) summing up and elaborating on it. I'll quote from it extensively here: "Can you prove that God exists? When asked that question what do you say? In answer to the question, you couldn't say that you believe God exists because the Bible says so. Belief in the Bible as truth only comes after one believes in God. Nor could you say that you believe because God answers your prayers. To the unbeliever this is circumstantial evidence. Nor could you say that you believe because your parents have taught you to believe. What if they're wrong? Nor could you offer the fact that God changed your life as proof that God exists. Perhaps you're deluded as to the source of the change?"

"You might want to argue that Biblical miracles prove God exists. Here the burden of proof is yours to show that such events really occurred. Yet, for someone who doesn't already believe in God, miraculous events cannot occur. Of course, the miracle of the resurrection of Christ is a powerful testimony for the existence of a God who raises the dead, but is it proof?"

"What about fulfilled prophecy in the Bible? We would first need to show that the prophecy was written before the prophesied event actually occurred. Even if it was, then we'd have to show that it wasn't just a lucky guess. The many prophecies concerning Jesus as the Messiah in the Old Testament, taken together, serve as a powerful testimony to a God who sees the future, but is it proof?"

"I think I can prove that God exists. Does that surprise you? But before I can attempt that feat, I have to know what standard of proof you are looking for. Scientists cannot prove with certainty that the sun will rise tomorrow, only that it has risen in the past. Neither can they prove with certainty that we have existed for more than one day, because every argument used to show this could be a pre-programmed memory in you. There is no proof that other minds than our own exist with whom we can converse, because it could all be in our heads. Nor could you prove that you exist as you appear to exist, rather than being brains in some future mad-scientist's vat who is causing you to experience the life you once lived all over again. Isn't that a scary thought? Now it is reasonable to believe the sun will rise tomorrow, that other minds exist, and that we have existed as we appear to have existed, even if these things are not subject to proof talk."

"In the last few centuries philosophers asked theologians to prove that God exists with a certainty that is simply not possible to attain in any field of learning, as witnessed above. Yet, because God's existence couldn't be proved by this impossible standard, people grew to believe that God's existence couldn't be supported by reason. Of course, this does not follow. For if it's reasonable to believe we are who we experience ourselves to be without proof, then it can be reasonable to believe God exists without the same kinds of proof demands."

"I can prove God exists then, only if we mean proved according to the same standards that allow us to believe we are who we experience ourselves to be. Unfortunately, to offer a proof of something doesn't mean that it's going to convince others. Most of us could offer proof that the earth is round, but there will always be people who remain unconvinced, as seen by those in the Flat Earth Society."

"God's existence can be shown to be reasonable by examining consistent sets of answers to questions concerning the basic make-up of the world and man, called 'world-views'—there are seven of them. If reasonableness is the standard, the Christian set of answers wins hands down. Christianity makes possible the standard of reasonableness without which modern science would never have arisen. Christian theism is more reasonable than any other total world-view system."

Pretty confident wasn't I? That was all to change in a few years.

1:1 A Word About The Grounding of My Faith.

When I was very young I heard the Bible stories in two Catholic churches and their parochial schools, where I attended for my first four grades. I also attended a Methodist vacation Bible school every summer.

These Church people were so sincere, and the Bible stories were all told as if they were absolutely true. These stories were amazing stories too: about Daniel in the lions den, Moses parting the Red Sea, Joseph and his coat of many colors, Jesus walking on the water, and the resurrection of Jesus. I never encountered anyone who disagreed with those stories, although I never engaged in a debate about them either. I just assumed they were true, although, since my family was just a nominal church going family, I never saw their significance for my life. I later attended a public school after the fourth grade where no one talked about their significance, either.

While I never encountered any skeptics that I could tell, I did find people who told me that God loves me and that Jesus is the one person who could help me through troubled waters. That's all I ever heard. So it seemed natural that when I was a troubled juvenile, that I would reach out to the God of the Bible and find the meaning of these Bible stories for my life.

But as you can see, I had no way to know whether or not the Bible was true. I had never investigated it with a critical mind. I just assumed it was true. When I had a dramatic conversion experience I felt forgiven and had a new sense of purpose for my life. I prayed and it seemed that God answered many of my prayers. So with this experience I began reading the Bible uncritically. I thought these were God's words, and that he was speaking to me every time I read them. It all just seemed so real.

Then I began investigating my faith. I saw a book at the bookstore by Josh McDowell, called <u>Evidence That Demands a Verdict</u>, and I read it completely through. He offered what some critics said about the Bible, and then he countered those critics with quotes from Christian apologists who argued against them. After reading that book, I thought that Christianity also passes intellectual muster. It could handle the attacks of all of the critics. I thought, "It's true! Christianity is true!"

Then I read a book by Hal Lindsey called, <u>The Late Great Planet Earth</u>. It was a popular treatment of end time Bible predictions along with the events around the world that seemed to confirm that Jesus' was going to return to the earth soon. So I once again thought to myself at the time, "It's true! Christianity is true! Jesus might return any day now."

When I first entered Great Lakes Bible College, a friend told me about Francis Schaeffer's books, and so I began reading them. I began with <u>True Spirituality</u>, then <u>The God Who Is There</u>, <u>Genesis In Space and Time</u>, <u>Escape From Reason</u>, and also <u>He Is There And He Is Not Silent</u>. With each of his books that I read, my faith was confirmed even more than before. I also read several of C.S. Lewis' books, especially <u>Mere Christianity</u>, <u>Miracles</u>, and <u>The Problem of Pain</u>. I had every reason to believe, especially since C.S. Lewis's and Schaeffer's books were philosophical in nature. There was no reason not to believe. So I thought, "It was true! It was really true!"

At this stage in my life, I probably had no doubts about my faith at all. And with good reason! I had not encountered anything at all to the contrary. It all made sense. But think about this for a minute. The confirming of my faith took place at an early age in my life. I never encountered anyone

> **At this stage in my life I probably had no doubts about my faith at all.**

who disagreed with it. I had some very powerful experiences of "God's power." Biblical prophecy seemed to be fulfilled right before my eyes. The evidence for Christianity seemed very powerful to me. Plus, there were philosophical arguments that all backed it up. With that as a background who wouldn't believe?

So with this background I began to be further informed about my faith. As I became more and more knowledgeable, I began to defend my faith. I believed there wasn't any argument that could ever disprove it. And so I proceeded with the presumption of faith to look at skeptical arguments against Christianity. Throughout most all of my Christian years I never looked critically at my faith. Oh, I considered the arguments of the liberals and skeptics, but with the faith presumption I had adopted, I just never took these arguments seriously. The arguments of the skeptics and liberals were just plain wrong, and I read them not to consider them, but to answer them. I never took an even-handed look at them—they were just wrong—because I knew my faith was right. Sometimes they even seemed laughable to me.

Later I found out that none of these initial reasons for believing had any real merit to them. Christian philosopher Thomas V. Morris, for instance, effectively dealt with Francis Schaeffer's writings, in his book: Francis Schaeffer's Apologetics: A Critique (Moody Press, 1976). And I learned that the critics of the Bible are right, not Josh McDowell. [See, The Jury Is In: The Ruling on McDowell's "Evidence," an online book edited by Secular Web founder Jeffery Jay Lowder: http://www.infidels.org/library/modern/jeff_lowder/jury/]. I am also no longer convinced by C.S. Lewis' arguments [See John Beversluis, C.S. Lewis and the Search for Rational Religion (Eerdmans, 1985)]. Furthermore, Hal Lindsey's timetable for Jesus' return has been shown to be wrong. Jesus has not yet returned to earth. Failed predictions of Jesus' return have become such an embarrassment for Christians that there is now a movement to embrace Preterism, which is the belief that Jesus returned to earth to reign from Jerusalem in a spiritual sense around 70 A.D.

I've since concluded that I believed in the Christian faith for initial reasons that were just inadequate—reasons that I have subsequently come to reject. I just did not have the ability to think through the intellectual foundations for my faith at such a time in my life. I believed what was presented to me because that's all I knew to believe, something I describe as "the accidents of birth." I didn't trust the liberals or the skeptics to help me, because they were just wrong. But I did trust other Christians to lead me to the right books to read, because I trusted them—we simply believed the same things.

So here are a couple of key questions: 1) at what point can someone say they can make an informed decision about the Christian faith? 2) What bias is the correct one when approaching the Christian faith? At what point could it be said that I had made an informed choice for my faith? In my early years I simply didn't know enough, did I? Who does? Did you? But in my later years, I continued to approach my Christian faith with the presumption I had from my early years—that my faith was correct. [This is why I'll later suggest something I call *The Outsider Test* for faith].

My initial faith was not well grounded, but as I became well grounded, I still maintained my faith, because it colored how I viewed the evidence. It wasn't until much later I began to examine why I should've started with that presumption of faith at all. Consequently, I became the atheist I am today.

[When I say that my faith wasn't well grounded here, I don't mean that my faith wasn't deep. As a Christian, I was as well grounded in the soil of Christianity as I could ever be. That is, my roots were as deep as they could be into the soil of Christianity. I lived and breathed it. But I later found out that my roots were not in solid ground at all, because Christianity itself is not solid ground.]

I just think that my conversion experience is somewhat typical in at least one regard. We first accept the Christian faith based upon personal experience, or it's something we were taught at an early age. The faith we have is usually based on where we live and the religion we are exposed to—the "accidents of birth." Very few of us decided to embrace Christianity after having first undergone years of theological studies. We embrace Christianity first, and then we investigate it. We subsequently investigate our faith with the presumption that it's true.

None of us sets out to study Christianity without some bias one way or another. A non-biased investigation of Christianity is probably psychologically impossible. We cannot start out investigating life-changing ideas (that is, faith based personal beliefs that shape our lives) without some kind of presumption one way or another. Neutrality here is practically impossible. But as is usually the case, the presumption we start out with will usually be the presumption we end up with—usually. And the presumption we start out with is usually adopted by us before we were properly informed!

> **The presumption we start out with will usually be the presumption we end up with— usually. And the presumption we start out with was adopted by us before we were properly informed!**

This is a catch-22. What I'll argue is that from the perspective of modern people living in the 21st century, the proper bias when approaching the Biblical claims of a miraculous virgin birth, an incarnate God, and a resurrected Christ, is a measure of healthy skepticism. After all, that's the same bias we have when we consider other religious faiths! [Again, see *The Outsider Test* for Faith].

But it's not always true that the presumption we start with is the one that we end with, is it? There are countless numbers of people who have approached Christianity from the perspective of a faith presumption who subsequently rejected it, like me. And while I have no statistics on this, judging by the last few centuries from the Enlightenment onward, I dare say that many more people have rejected Christianity once they accepted it, than have ever accepted it after investigating it from a skeptical bias.

I understand that there have been some people who have approached Christianity from a more or less skeptical position, and yet came to believe anyway. Here I'm thinking of Lew Wallace, the author of <u>Ben Hur</u>, Frank Morrison, who subsequently wrote the book, <u>Who Moved The Stone?</u>, which argues for the resurrection of Jesus. These are the same conversions as C.S. Lewis, G.K. Chesterton, and especially Paul the Apostle. But this is simply not the experience for most of us! And while I'll say more about Paul's conversion as evidence for the resurrection later on, what exactly does it prove that people convert to Christianity after studying it out with a more or less skeptical bias? It doesn't prove anything to me, except that people come to their own conclusions about historical claims, which is a topic I'll deal with later on. It also confirms my view of the relationship of faith and reason, which I'll say more about later on, too.

Of course, since I now reject Christianity, it appears to me that the skeptical people who investigated Christianity and then accepted it, made personal decisions based on judgments about historical questions that I take issue with. Some of these people probably read the "wrong" books. If someone wants to investigate Christianity and all they ever read are works by Josh McDowell, Paul Copan, William Lane Craig, and J.P. Moreland, then I'd say they never truly investigated Christianity.

Granting this, no one could say C.S. Lewis didn't properly investigate Christianity before he accepted it. So I'm not claiming that all of these people were just not as well informed as I am now, even if some of them were. I only claim that those who investigate Christianity, whether from the presumption of faith or one of skepticism, are dealing with historical claims that are subject to different interpretations in which a non-reducible personal element is involved. People just come to different conclusions, that's all. But if the evidence for the historical claims about Christianity is so strong, then the real problem is this: why aren't there more people who investigate Christianity from a skeptical bias who subsequently embrace it?

> **The real problem is this: why aren't there more people who investigate Christianity from a skeptical position who subsequently embrace it?**

2 Why I Changed My Mind: My Deconversion.

I was a Christian apologist set for the express purpose of defending Christianity from intellectual attacks. C.S Lewis spoke of how Christian philosophy must exist if for no other reason than that bad philosophy must be answered. That was what I desired to do, and I was not afraid of any idea, because I was convinced that Christianity was true and could withstand all attacks. A few people have said that I am too smart for my own good. I'm not at all sure what it means to say that, but when it comes to maintaining my faith against the skeptical ideas that I pondered, I wasn't smart enough to answer the critics.

> **I was not afraid of any idea, because I was convinced that Christianity was true and could withstand all attacks.**

C.S. Lewis wrote: "I have found that nothing is more dangerous to one's own faith than the work of an apologist. No doctrine of the faith seems to me so spectral, so unreal as one that I have just successfully defended in a public debate. For a moment, you see, it has seemed to rest on oneself: as a result, when you go away from that debate, it seems no stronger than that weak pillar. That is why we apologists take our lives in our hands and can be saved only by falling back continually from the web of our own arguments, as from our intellectual counters, into the reality—from Christian apologetics into Christ." [The Grand Miracle, (p. 76)].

I succumbed to this danger, and I began to doubt the very things I had previously argued for. I knew most of the arguments against Christianity, and as a philosophy instructor in a secular college I could debate both sides of most any argument. As a philosophy instructor, in many ways I am a purveyor of doubt. Too many people have a superficial faith handed down from their parents. As a teacher, my goal is to make them question much of what they believe, be it atheist or believer, or agnostic. Doing so is what's needed for them to develop a deeper faith, and it allows them to see points of view they've never considered before, thus making them more tolerant of other people's beliefs. As a philosophy instructor, I must try to eliminate from my students any smug, arrogant, simplistic or dogmatic belief system. Such beliefs are childlike and unbecoming of the adults they should become. Anyway, I could teach philosophy until I was blue in the face so long as I knew I had a loving, caring, and faithful Christian community to fall back on after my class is over. When that fell through the floor, the doubts crept in my life.

There are three major things that happened in my life that changed my thinking. They all happened in the space of about five years, from 1991-1996. These things are associated with three people: 1) Linda, 2) Larry, and 3) Jeff. Linda brought a major crisis in my life. Larry brought new information in my life. Jeff took away my sense of a loving Christian community. **These are the three things that changed my thinking: 1) A major crisis, 2) plus information, 3) minus a sense of a loving, caring, Christian community**. In the midst of these things, I felt rejected by the Church of Christ in my local area. **For me it was an**

assault of major proportions. If I still believed in the devil, I would say it was orchestrated by the legions of Hell.

LINDA- I was the founding president of Operation Shelter, (now called Turning Point) in Angola, Indiana. It was an organization that seeks to give temporary shelter to people in need. I worked day after day with the executive director, who's name was Linda. She practically idolized me. She did everything I said to do, and would call me daily to help her deal with various situations that came up from the running of the Shelter, along with her personal problems. What man doesn't want to be worshipped? I guess I did. I was having problems with my own relationship with my wife at the time, and Linda made herself available. I succumbed and had an affair with her.

There's so much more I'd like to say about this, but few people would believe me. I believe she was a con-artist, and she conned me. As a former stripper she had it in for preachers, and she took out her wrath on me. Perhaps because I was a moral crusader in town and stood against abortion and X-rated video rentals, she chose to humiliate me. Suffice it to say there are some women out there who, akin to Potipher's wife in the Bible, find it challenging to see if they can sack a minister, and she did.

> There are some women out there who, akin to Potipher's wife in the Bible, find it challenging to see if they can sack a minister, and she did.

How many sermons have you heard about Joseph and Potipher's wife where preachers wondered aloud if many men could've overcome this temptation? In order to bolster our confidence in Joseph's faith they conclude that not many men could've overcome this temptation. But when someone like me actually does succumb to such a temptation, these same preachers are quick to condemn me. There are mitigating factors here, even if I did do wrong. And I did do wrong. But until you experience a con-artist who wants to destroy you, you will never understand. This lack of understanding doubles my pain.

As far as the affair itself goes, ethicist Richard Taylor wrote a book on Having Love Affairs (Buffalo: Prometheus Books, 1982) and he discusses whose fault it is when there is an affair. I am not excusing myself here, but as he explains, there may be more to it. "Though a wife may be ever so dutiful, faultless, and virtuous in every skill required for the making of a home, if she lacks passion, then in a very real sense she already is without a husband, or he, at least, is without a wife. Similarly, a husband who is preoccupied with himself and his work, who is oblivious to the needs of his wife and insensitive to her vanities, who takes for granted her unique talents and who goes about his business more or less as though she did not exist, has already withdrawn as a husband, except in name." "What must be remembered by those persons who wish to condemn adultery is that the primary vow of marriage is to love, and that vow is not fulfilled by the kind of endless busyness exemplified in the industrious and ever generous husband or the dedicated homemaking wife...What has to be stressed is that the first infidelity may or may not have been committed by the one who is having an affair. The first and ultimate infidelity is to withhold the love that was promised, and which was originally represented as the reason for marriage to begin with."

But there is more. After a few months I decided I could no longer reconcile the affair with my faith or my family life. So I told Linda that it was over. Well, William Congreve is right, "hell has no fury like a woman scorned." She went off in a rampage and told the board of directors at the Shelter that I had raped her. She went to the prosecutor with my former associate minister and tried to press charges against me, too. They were all lies. No charges were brought against me, thankfully.

I thought everyone had heard of her accusations and that most people believed her. I received a phone call from someone who threatened my life, and it sounded like he would kill me, too. One man whom I had a great amount of respect for, had heard her accusations. I said to him, "you don't believe her do you?" He replied, "John, I don't know what to believe." This really hurt. I did some research on her and found that she was married eight times; although she told me she was only married twice. I talked with most of these former husbands and I learned she was quite the consummate liar. I dug around and found out a great deal about her, which led me to the conclusion that she had duped me about most things. But I was supposed to be smarter than that, or so I thought. How could this happen to me? How could I let her con me like that? How could I have an affair with her and sin like that against my God and family? How could I allow my reputation to be sullied by claims that I had raped her? Why did God test me by allowing her to come into my life when she did? All of this devastated me; my sin, the strange mitigating factors, the Christian people who wouldn't forgive even though I repented of this sin, the potential charge of rape, and God not seeming to care about his wayward soldier. I do thank my ex-wife, Kathy, for forgiving me and for standing by me during this period in my life. She is a wonderful woman. She understood.

I'm just being honest in revealing what changed my life. I know people will object to my behavior, but I include it anyway. Why? Because I am trying to be as honest as I can. My book is a sincere attempt to explain why I changed. You cannot dispute it either, because I write about "the good, the bad, and the ugly."

LARRY- Then while I was still feeling the devastation from Linda I carried on a correspondence debate with my cousin Larry Strawser who was a Lieutenant in the Air Force (now a Colonel) and teaches Bio-Chemistry at a base in Colorado. I handed him a book arguing for creation over evolution and asked him to look at it and let me know what he thought of it. After several months, he wrote me a long letter and a box full of articles and books on the subject. Some of them were much too technical for me to understand, but I tried to read them. While he didn't convince me of much at the time, he did convince me of one solid truth: the universe is as old as scientists say it is, and the consensus is that it is 12-15 billion years old.

Now that by itself isn't too harmful of an idea to Christian thinking, because Bill Craig believes this, but it was the first time I really considered the theological implications of it. Two corollaries of that idea started me down the road to being the honest doubter I am today. The **first** is that in Genesis chapter 1 we see that the earth existed before the sun, moon, and stars, which were all created on the fourth day. This doesn't square with astronomy. So I began looking at the first few chapters in Genesis, and as my thinking developed over time, I came to the conclusion that those chapters are folk literature—myth. You can see my studies on this later in this book. At the time I was a "concordist," in that I believed the days of Genesis represented eons of time. I just didn't know much at all by way of astronomy. I think the impact of the material from my cousin jolted me into seeing what the age of the universe really entails. It forced me to reconsider concordism like nothing I had ever read. Before that, Dr. Craig's Kalam Cosmological argument based upon a Big Bang was just seen by me as a philosophical argument to prove God exists. Isn't that strange? As an apologist I never felt the full force of these arguments. Sometimes we only see the things we want to see, and we fail to realize the implications of what we do see.

The **second** corollary for me at that time was this: if God took so long to create the universe, then why would he all of a sudden snap his fingers, so to speak, and create human beings? If time is not a factor with God when he created the universe, then why should time be a factor when it came to creating human beings? If God took his time to create the universe then why wouldn't he also create living creatures with greater complexity during the same length of time? In other words, what reason can be given for the different ways God created? Is this the same God? Why did it take God so long to create the stuff of the universe, which is less valuable and presumably less complex to create, than it did to create the most valuable and highly complex creatures to inhabit that universe? Astronomy describes the long process of galaxy, star and planet formation. It then becomes uncharacteristic of God to do otherwise with human beings. I concluded that God created human beings by the same long process he created the universe as a whole, if he created us at all.

I carried on a correspondence with Dr. Virgil Warren for about 6 months, who was a professor at Manhattan Christian College, in Kansas. I was asking him what he thought about the issues raised by the age of the universe. In a final letter to him on March 19, 1994 I wrote:

"My problem is that I earnestly desire the truth whatever the result. I do not concern myself with the results just yet,

> **"I earnestly desire the truth whatever the result."**

although I know I'll have to face them sometime. Right now I just want to make sense of it all, results be what they may. When I consider the possible results, they scare me, but that's only because they are unfamiliar to me. This is natural. The real question for me right now is the truth question. If the answers upset other cherished beliefs, then I'll have to re-examine my answers, and perhaps revise them in order to maintain those cherished beliefs. On the other hand, my answers might cause me to give up on some of these cherished beliefs—there's no way to tell at this point which way I'll go. But as time permits I am committed to finding answers that produce the least amount of tension among the things I believe."

Nearly two years later, I came to deny the Christian faith. **There were just too many individual problems that I had to balance, like spinning several plates on several sticks, in order to keep my faith. At some point they just all came crashing down.**

I personally think more than anything else, it was a deeper knowledge that caused me to leave the faith. But it was my faith that inspired me to gain that knowledge in the first place. I was so sure and so confident in my faith that I didn't believe I could learn anything that would ever cause me to doubt my faith. I believed I served a God of reason, and that "all truth was God's truth." I was not going to be afraid of any argument to the contrary. And with this assurance I sought to understand and argue against those who would debunk my faith.

It is quite ironic, really. I started with faith. That faith inspired me to understand. With more understanding, my faith increased to the point where I was confident no argument could stand up against my faith. So I proceeded to gain more and more knowledge for the express purpose of debunking the skeptics. But in so doing, I finally realized that the arguments on behalf of the Christian faith were simply not there. The skeptics were right all along. Even though everything I studied was done from the presumption of faith, and in the service of the faith, my studies ended my faith.

THE CHURCH OF CHRIST – At this point, I want to briefly describe why I left the Church of Christ in my area. The Angola Christian Church asked for my resignation in December 1990. It had nothing much at all to do with my affair with Linda, although some thought I was getting too close to her, and they wondered. I had offended John & Sybil Love, camp managers with Lake James Christian Assembly, in Angola, IN. They are decent, hard working Christian people. But they were opposed to my ministry for various petty reasons, in my opinion, so they left our church and started attending the Pleasant View Christian Church, also located in the small town of Angola. This was a church that had split off from ours a few decades back. Since the Love's had relatives and friends in our church, the pressure was on to get them back, and the church elders felt that one way to get them back was to ask for my resignation. So they did. It's not uncommon for ministers to be asked to leave a church when their effectiveness is gone. Although, at the time, I argued that doing so would not bring the Love's back, and they didn't go back, as I predicted.

When I first came to the Angola Christian Church, many local Church of Christ ministers told me that my church was hard on ministers, so I knew. But when the people I had problems with in the church were John & Sybil Love, I received little such support from those area ministers.

We didn't feel comfortable in attending church where I resigned from, so our family attended the Pleasant View Christian Church a couple of times. We sensed from the church leadership they didn't want us attending there, either, probably because that's where the Love's attended now. [The Christian Church has its *bishops* after all, despite their doctrinal position on church polity]. At this point, neither one of the Christian Churches in our area wanted me. The truth is that not enough of the right people thought I should be in ministry. Some people shouldn't be in the ministry. Maybe I was one of them. But that shouldn't be a reflection of who I am as a person.

What bothered me was that Jerry Paul, my home minister in Ft. Wayne at the time, didn't bother to call me. Somehow I couldn't call him either. I was just too embarrassed. But I needed to hear from him, and I've concluded he just didn't want to get involved. Jerry baptized me, was my ordaining minister, and married me to my wife at the time, Kathy. George Faull told me that Linda, mentioned earlier, had called Jerry Paul and told him I had raped her, etc. She was hell bent on destroying me, is all I can figure. But Jerry never called me to talk to me, or pray with me, or comfort me. When George told me that Jerry had heard from her, my heart just sank. Why? Is this what successful ministers do? They don't get involved with people who have become "hot potatoes?" Did he care? Was I just a black mark on his list of accomplishments, so that he wanted to avoid me? That's how I felt. I really don't know his reasons. Maybe he thought that if I wanted help then all I had to do is call, and he'd be right there with me all of the way. That's a nice way to do ministry, isn't it? Maybe that's just how he is, and maybe I could've gotten the encouragement I needed. But at the time, I felt rejected by someone I had respected the most. Maybe if he had just made a serious attempt to show he cared, or if the Pleasant View Church of Christ would have welcomed us, I might still be a believer today. I just don't know.

After a while, I found myself teaching classes at Great Lakes Christian College (GLCC, formerly Great Lakes Bible College). My brother-in-law at the time, Tom Spoors, became the head of the Leadership Institute. It was a degree completion program that GLCC set up and ran for a few years from about 1992-1996, I believe. I taught philosophy classes there. Shortly after beginning to teach at GLCC, Jerry Paul became the President of the College, but we never spoke about anything except those things related to my classes.

Partly because I felt the Church of Christ leadership in my local area had rejected me, but also because I tend to stretch people's minds anyway, I wrote a controversial essay on Christian baptism for Integrity (July/August 1995). The editorial board of Integrity magazine, included the late Dr. Brant Lee Doty, and Curtis Lloyd, both had been acting Presidents for GLCC in the past, and both were well respected Church of Christ people. The board said it was "thoughtful and worthy of being printed in the interests of a dialogue about the subject." But the reaction was intense. Sherman Nichols spoke at a men's meeting in the heart of Michigan and denounced that article, and me. This put the pressure on President Jerry Paul and Tom Spoors to let me go from my teaching responsibilities at the college. And they did. Jerry said that many people previously had reservations about me teaching for the college, and said this was the last straw, although Jerry also said he couldn't exactly pin point whether or not those reservations were legitimate ones. So I did the only thing I knew to do. I fired back in print with a second article on Christian baptism for (Integrity January/February 1996). One minister friend said that this second article was "superb," and another writer said that he didn't think my baptism articles could be refuted. At that point, I was done with the Church of Christ.

Several other people did encourage me at that time, including a few Bible College professors. I'm the sort of person who has a very hard time asking for help, and I was hurting badly. Even so, Curtis Lloyd, Dr. Virgil Warren, Dr. John Castelein, and George Faull all encouraged me in various ways, and I was grateful for that. But in a letter I wrote to one of them (on April 16th, 1996) I expressed an ominous threat: "I have settled down to teaching strictly secular philosophy courses at secular colleges. I actually enjoy this much more than at GLCC (where "the watchdogs of brotherhood doctrinal purity" are on the beat). I'm actually surviving quite well, and I have received some support, especially from several of my former students. I am now freed of the internal censors. I can now write as I think. **Watch out now**."

When I was cut off from the church, my doubts were unleashed, even if it took until now to fully express them. Let this book be a warning to church people to be careful how they treat others. You may turn them away from Christianity.

You'll notice that although I taught at GLCC, and was still involved in various churches, that my doubts were growing in intensity. I continued in the church because I didn't yet know where my doubts would lead. Perhaps if I had just gotten back in the ministry my doubts would've subsided, I don't know. But when GLCC cut me off from their oversight and approval, I no longer had anything to lose by expressing my doubts, especially when my livelihood no longer depended on what I believed. And my doubts took over at that point, especially after I experienced problems with my cousin Jeff at his church, a month or two later.

JEFF- The previously mentioned debate with my cousin Larry over evolution took place while I was trying to maintain my faith in the Pleasant Lake Baptist Church. As I just said, I felt rejected by the Church of Christ in my local area. After my experience with Linda, I didn't even go to church for several months. But my other cousin, Jeff Stackhouse, became the Pastor there and I said to myself, "here is a safe place to worship where I won't get hurt." So I gradually got involved. I helped wherever I could, and our family liked it very much. I taught Sunday school, preached on occasion, and eventually became an elder in that church with people who loved me and whom I loved, and I still do.

As best as I can tell, Jeff was suspicious of my motives—my own cousin! Without going into great detail, he and his wife Lurleen suspected that I was secretly trying to oust him to become the pastor there. I'm sure he felt threatened, but I didn't mean to threaten him. The farthest thing from my mind was to oust him so that I could become the new pastor. I just wanted to help. But he left the church and blamed me.

I have no ill feelings toward him and I wish him well. After all, we are just people, and people sometimes feel this way. The thing about this experience was that I had to wrestle with the question of why someone who is as close as a cousin to me could misread my intentions so badly. How could he get it so wrong? And he was wrong. From this I began to reflect on the many different interpretations people have of the Bible, and I began to ask whether it's possible to have a correct understanding of the Bible, if people as close to each other as he and I had such a misunderstanding. I began to doubt that people with our passions and living in our day and age so removed from the Bible, could properly understand that book, when people living in the same age and as close to one another as he and I couldn't understand each other.

This last thought hit home extremely hard after Jeff left the church. In his wake, he left a rift in that church between some people who liked me and some people who didn't. An elder asked me in an elder's meeting after Jeff left if I would consider being the new pastor, and I turned it down. I really didn't want to do it at all.

Soon after Jeff left the church, a problem developed between Mark, an elder, and the director of the children's program, whose name was Conny (neither of them attend there anymore). Mark didn't like Conny, or her husband, or me, and he blamed us for Jeff's having left the church. However, I thought a lot of Conny, but she had a problem with her temper and got into a confrontation with Mark. She set out a child from an activity because he was unruly, but Mark told the child to participate anyway, and did so in front of her. Well, she blew up at him.

Afterwards, a debate ensued among the elders of that church. In the first place, I disagreed totally with how they wanted to handle the problem. I argued from the Bible that the two people who had the problem should sit down and talk about it first, but few agreed with me on that point. Beyond that, there were a few of them on one side who wanted to discipline (or punish) her by removing her from her position, and there were a few elders on the other side, including me, who wanted to forgive her. The interesting thing is that both sides claimed that they were motivated by love. We all had our Bible verses to back it up, too! Again, the thought occurred to me how people living in the same day and age in the same church could have different understandings of what the Bible wanted us to do. I left that church over it, and so did most of the people involved, whom I still care for a great deal. The people of that church are just like people of any church, caring for the most part, but we can all get riled too.

But it sometimes still surprises me what people who are of the Christian faith will do with what they consider a clear conscience. I wonder to myself how these consciences can differ so widely, especially when Christianity is the only faith that claims God the Holy Spirit actually takes up residence in their being. I often ask myself why Christians don't seem to act any better than others when they alone claim to have the power, wisdom and guidance of God right there within them. Apparently, the Holy Spirit didn't properly do his job here. **This was the last blow to my faith and one of the reasons why I am an atheist today**.

> **This was the last blow to my faith and one of the reasons why I am an atheist today.**

I didn't go to church for the summer after this church experience. But our family gradually got involved with the local Fairview Missionary Church, in Angola, which is by far the largest church in our area. I taught a few Sunday School classes, preached in the evening service a few times, sang in the choir, participated in an Easter musical, several dramas on Sunday morning, the Bethlehem Marketplace, and even preached once in the AM worship service. The last sermon I ever preached was for this church, in both Sunday Morning services, February 1997. It was titled: "Moses: The Reluctant Leader."

But the damage was already done. Massive doubt crept upon me until I didn't want a part of church much at all. But something happened while I was at Fairview. I realized that my experience with Fairview was just one of a couple of pleasant church experiences I ever had in over twenty-three years! I thank Pastor Norm Fuller and his church for this. I only wish I could say I had more such experiences, although, since I know people are only human, his church probably has some of the same problems as other churches. I just didn't happen to notice any.

MY DIVORCE AND REMARRIAGE - Finally, I decided I wasn't going to live out the rest of my life not being happily married. So I left Kathy and decided I was going to find love again. I did feel somewhat guilty for this, but, neither of us was happy in our marriage. Pollster George Barna's research has shown that "a surprising number of Christians experienced divorces both before and after their conversion." [www.barna.org]. Why should it be different for skeptics when they leave their religion?

What I found was a woman who was passionate about me as I am of her, Gwen. Gwen has went with me to church whenever I have wanted to go, but she too is an unbeliever—an atheist. She's got the kind of character that most church people do not have. To a large extent, because of my divorce from Kathy and my remarriage to Gwen, I've stayed away from churches. The longer I have been away, the less I believed.

CLOSING THOUGHTS- My doubts were simmering these last few years while I've been with Gwen. I didn't think much about them. But when Mel Gibson's movie "The Passion of the Christ" came out, it made me think about them again, intensely. Plus, one day in class as I was describing, how God could've used chance as a radar beam searching the possibilities for the direction of creation, one of my students laughed at the thought. These last two events put me on a course to finally come out of the closet and tell what I think.

While the things I have just written might explain to some degree why my thinking has changed, I want to stress the fact that my thinking has indeed changed. You cannot explain away my present thinking by pointing to these experiences I've had in my life. They may be what provoked my thinking, but they don't explain away my arguments. My arguments cannot be dismissed because I'm divorced or because I had an affair, or else we can likewise reject any theory based upon how the proponent lives his life. Do you really want to reject Einstein's theory of relativity simply because he saw other women? Then don't do that with me.

I am an atheist regardless of the experiences that led up to my present way of thinking. In talking with me, you will have to deal with my arguments. Otherwise, I could point to your past experiences and explain your beliefs away as a product of what you have experienced too. People believe and doubt for a wide variety of reasons, and that's all there is to it.

For me, it wasn't just my affair with Linda that led me to reject Christianity. I could've gotten beyond the damage that had done to my faith. It was being cut off from the church, of which the affair with her was the catalyst. Taken together with the information I learned

> "It wasn't just my affair with Linda that led me to reject Christianity.

from my cousin Larry, and the subsequent church experiences I had in my cousin Jeff's church, I eventually came to reject my former faith.

Now there will be those who might say that I just wanted to live my life the way I wanted to anyway, and all of this is an excuse for my divorce, remarriage and change in my lifestyle in the past few years. Some think I chose my theology based on how I wanted to live my life. In other words, my ethics dictated my viewpoint. **But the chronological historical truth is that first my theology changed, and then I started living my life differently.** I simply started to live my life in keeping with my new set of beliefs.

Since I have intellectually landed as an atheist, some people might question why I would put out this book since it might create doubt in others. In the first place, I think this world would be better off without religious faith, as I'll argue in the "What is Life without God?" section. But there are other reasons. Consider this from Robert M. Price: "We are viewed as insidious villains seeking to undermine the belief of the faithful, trying to push them off the heavenly path and into Satan's arms. But this is not how we view ourselves at all. We find ourselves entering the field as the champions and zealots for a straightforward and accurate understanding of the Bible as an ancient text. In our opinion, it is the fundamentalist, the apologist for Christian supernaturalism, who is propagating false and misleading views of the Bible among the general populace. We are not content to know better and to shake our heads at the foolishness of the untutored masses. We want the Bible to be appreciated for what it is, not for what it is not. And it is not a supernatural oracle book filled with infallible dogmas and wild tales that must be believed at the risk of eternal peril." [The Empty Tomb: Jesus Beyond the Grave (Prometheus, 2005), p. 15].

Robert W. Funk, in his book, Honest to Jesus (p. 19) wrote: "As I look around me, I am distressed by those who are enslaved by a Christ imposed upon them by a narrow and rigid legacy. There are millions of Americans who are the victims of a mythical Jesus conjured up by modern evangelists to whip their followers into a frenzy of guilt and remorse—and cash contributions. I agonize over their slavery in contrast to my freedom. I have a residual hankering to free my fellow human beings from this bondage. Liberation from fear and ignorance is always a worthy cause. In the last analysis, however, it is because I occasionally glimpse an unknown Jesus lurking in and behind Christian legend and piety that I persist in my efforts to find my way through the mythical and legendary debris of the Christian tradition. And it is the lure of this glimpse that I detect in other questers and that I share with them."

I tried as best as I could to be a faithful Christian, and good minister. Even though I believed it was by grace that I had been saved, I almost always felt guilty that I wasn't doing enough in response to God's purported love. Whether it was spending time in prayer, evangelizing, reading the Bible, tithing, forgiving, or whether it was struggling with temptations of lust, pride, selfishness and laziness, I almost always felt guilty. It may just be because I was so passionate about Christianity that this was the case, and so it just might be my particular temperament. I never could understand how Christian people could come to church every Sunday but never get involved much in the Church's programs, because that's what believers should want to do. To be quite frank here, if Christians really believed that the non-Christian was going to hell, and that God loved them enough to send his Son to die for them on the cross, then how would they behave? How many true believers are in the churches today?

Today I am guilt free regarding the Christian duties mentioned above. I am so grateful for my present life, because I'm living life to the hilt. I just don't think anyone can live a passionate guilt free Christian life. Think about it, according to Jesus I should feel guilty for not just what I do, but for what I think about, lusting, hating, coveting, etc. I'd like every person who reads this book to experience the freedom I have found.

2:1 A Word About My Deconversion.

The way many Christians deal with ex-Christian skeptics like me is very troublesome. My present doubt is explained away both intellectually and emotionally. That is, I either was not well-grounded in what I formerly claimed to have believed, or deep down inside I still believe.

Calvinistic Christians will quote some Biblical passages that lead them to think I was never grounded in my faith, like when Jesus was explaining the "Parable of the Sower." Matthew has him say, "But since he has no root, he lasts only a short time. When trouble or persecution comes because of the word, he quickly falls away." (13:21). [Non-Calvinistic Christians dispute their exegesis of the relevant passages. I'll just let these Christians debate the issue, like they do so many issues. But the question I'll raise here is this: where is the supposed guidance of the Holy Spirit to help believers understand the Bible on this issue? In fact, there have been killings and wars between Christians down through the centuries because the Holy Spirit didn't properly do his job on these debatable issues, by offering his guidnce to Christian people. Why the lack of guidance? This is best explained by denying that there is a Holy Spirit].

People like me stand as a witness against how Calvinistic Christians interpret passages like this one, because I was indeed well rooted in my faith. And as we'll see throughout this book, there are other delusions that Christians believe too. This is only one of them. While experience is not the test for truth, our understanding of the truth must be able to explain my personal experience of having faith and then rejecting it. Those who deny

> While experience is not the test for truth, our understanding of the truth must be able to explain personal experience.

my personal experience in assessing the Bible here are throwing the baby out with the bathwater. Wasn't Paul's experience of conversion itself supposedly an argument for the truth of Christianity (Acts 9, 22, & 26), according to them? Experience has always been a check on Biblical exegesis, whether it comes to Wesleyan perfectionism, perseverance of the saints, second coming predictions, Pentecostal miracle workers, and so on. The whole science/religion discussion is an attempt to harmonize the Bible with what scientists have *experienced* through empirical observations of the universe.

I know there will be Christians who will reject the claim that I was a Christian believer at one time. So I began this book by stressing that I was truly a believer at one time—a very passionate one. I have written articles for Christian publications defending Christianity. I also have cassette and video tapes of some of my sermons, along with many church newletter articles I wrote. There are many Christian people who know of my former faith who can be consulted on this, along with the churches that I served as a minister.

Besides, when Christians judge me as never having been a Christian in the first place, aren't they doing what the Bible forbids? Matthew 7:1: "Judge not, that you be not judged." James 4:12: "There is one lawgiver and judge, he who is able to save and to destroy. But who are you that you judge your neighbor?"

Since it seems clear to people who have known me that I was a strong believer at one time, the other option is to deny that I am an honest skeptic right now. I'm in denial, one could be heard to say. **It seems as though what Christians believe takes precedence over the testimony of people, when that testimony contradicts what they believe.** That's a little bit strange when those same Christians will claim to believe the testimony of the early disciples to the resurrected Jesus, even though their testimony contradicts what we know about the regular ordered laws of nature.

> **That's a little bit strange when those same Christians will claim to believe the testimony of the early disciples to the resurrected Jesus, even though their testimony contradicts what we know about the regular ordered laws of nature.**

I don't deny there are dishonest doubters. Some of them don't know that they are being dishonest, but they are. They are dishonest to themselves. Perhaps because of a horrible accident they just refuse to believe in God, even though they know deep down inside that it wasn't God's fault. But this isn't me.

Some others know they are being dishonest, but they profess doubt anyway. It should be obvious that if someone is a dishonest doubter they must benefit from doing so in some way. Lacking any benefit in professing doubt would render such dishonest professions unnecessary. But wherever there is some benefit for doing so, then there will be dishonest doubters. But this isn't me.

I think that a better case can be made that there are more dishonest Christian believers in American society than there are dishonest atheists. Since there must be some kind of benefit to claiming something that isn't so, the question is, who stands to benefit the most by being dishonest?

Gay people need to have courage to "come out of the closet" because they fear that doing so would cause them problems with the "moral Christian majority." It's much easier to come out and declare oneself a Christian, because that's respectable in the heartland of America. Confessing Christ in our small town cultures isn't what it used to be in the early few centuries. But doing so today actually has many social benefits, in my opinion.

In small town cities across America, it takes more courage to declare oneself a skeptic or an atheist than a Christian believer, I think. And consequently, since the social benefits are clearly against minority thinking, then two things follow: 1) There are more dishonest professing Christians; and 2) Those who profess minority thinking, such as skepticism and atheism, are more likely than not being

> **In small town cities across America it takes more courage to declare oneself a skeptic or an atheist than a Christian believer.**

honest, because doing so actually denies them various social benefits. I have personally experienced this with the business that I own. If I were truly dishonest, I would turn around and profess Christian faith so that my business in this small town might thrive again.

Many Christians have walked away from their faith:

www.ex-christian.net, where you will read several ex-christian testimonies every week.

www.users.globalnet.co.uk/~slocks/decon.html, is almost encyclopedic with regard to testimonies and websites for former Christians. Steve Locks also maintains: http://www.infidels.org/library/modern/testimonials.

Edward T. Babinski, Leaving the Fold: Testimonies of Former Fundamentalists (Prometheus Books, 2003).

Dan Barker, Losing Faith In Faith: From Preacher to Atheist. (Freedom From Religion Foundation, 1992).

Joe Holman, Project Bible Truth: What Your Church Doesn't Want You To Know (Forthcoming). See www.ministerturnsatheist.org/

Ludovic Kennedy, All in the Mind: A Farewell to God (1999).

Skipp Porteus, Jesus Doesn't Live Here Anymore: From Fundamentalist to Freedom Writer (Prometheus Books, 1991).

Robert M. Price's story, From Fundamentalist to Humanist (1997) found here: http://www.infidels.org/library/modern/robert_price/humanist

Michael Shermer, How We Believe (Freeman, 2000), pp, 2-15.

Scott R. Stahlecker, How To Escape Religion Guilt Free (2004).

Charles Tempelton, Farewell To God: My Reasons For Rejecting the Christian Faith (McClelland & Stewart, 1999).

Look the following men up on the Internet and read their deconversion stories: Farrell Till, G. Vincent Runyon, Lee Salisbury, Ray Billington, Bob Hypes, Ransom L. Webster, Douglas Larson, Allan Nielsen, and Craig Cunningham.

All the members on my blog have been ex-Christians and/or ex-ministers, http://debunkingchristianity.blogspot.com/ and you can read their stories there.

For absolute must reading on the so-called unique nature of the Christian experience, see Edward T. Babinski's essay on this at the Secular Web: http://www.infidels.org/library/modern/ed_babinski/experience, in which he examines Josh McDowell's claims about this.

Those who have left conservative Christianity:

John Hick, in More Than One Way, eds., Okholm & Phillips (Zondervan 1995), pp. 29-59.

Marcus Borg, Meeting Jesus Again For the First Time (Harper, 1994), pp. 1 - 19; and The God We Never Knew (Harper, 1997), pp. 11-31.

John A.T. Robinson in Honest To God (Westminister, 1963), pp. 11-28.

James Wall, ed. How My Mind Has Changed, (Eerdmans, 1991).

Andrew Furlong, Tried for Heresy A 21st Century Journey of Faith, [http://myhome.iolfree.ie/~andrewfurlong]

My Favorite Non-Religious Songs: "Leaving to Stay," by Johnny Lang. "Dust in the Wind," by Kansas. "I Just Want You," by Ozzy Osborne. "Imagine," by John Lennon.

3 A Letter to Dr. James D. Strauss who was my mentor at Lincoln Christian Seminary, Lincoln, IL (1979-1982). This excerpt reveals the full extent of my doubt at that time, although I never sent it to him. I just didn't want to hurt him. I wrote it during the month of August 1996.

Dear Jim,

I want to share with you in bibliographic format some of the reading I've been doing to let you know where I am in my theological thinking. If you have time to comment then I'd appreciate it.

To tell you where I am, let me begin by saying that I have just finished reading John Robinson's <u>Honest To God,</u> and liked it! What has happened to me theologically? The watershed for me, and I suspect for others who have changed their assumptions, is the factual and historical reliability of Genesis 1-11. That is it. But before one can begin to seriously engage these chapters he or she would first have to be convinced that all truth is God's truth. This is something that you taught me. Arthur Holmes' <u>All Truth is God's Truth</u> says the same thing. Otherwise, people who reject this basic viewpoint will simply say that the Bible teaches something different than that--whatever "that" is.

The steps leading to a change in my thinking took place as I seriously looked at **Genesis chapter one**. Only then was I able to re-consider chapter two, and so on. I'm sending you my research on the creation accounts. So Genesis one is the key. If that chapter is mythical in genre, and late in origin, then what about the stories that follow? The question I asked myself is this: Why is it that way back in Abram's life and before, we must demand that ancient people had adopted the kind of historiography that Judeo-Christians later adopted? It's obvious that their notion of God evolved, so why not their notion of history? Anyway I had read Bernard Ramm's book <u>The Christian View of Science and Scripture</u> and knew the options for harmonizing science and Genesis. But it was Howard Van Till's book, <u>The Fourth Day,</u> which led me to see that the universe was 12-15 billion years old--it was as old as scientists say it is. From there I read Henri Blocher's <u>In the Beginning</u> and learned there were some magical statements and certainly non-historical items in Genesis 1-3, **even on a conservative account**. Blocher defends the historicity of Adam and Eve, but upon hindsight, he does so on shaky ground, once he admitted to the "wisdom" genre (as he calls it) of chapters 1-2.

In the meantime, I read <u>Four Views on Hell</u> ed. William Crockett, and came away thinking "conditional immortality" was the preferred option (defended by Pinnock). This is an important conclusion when it comes to rethinking my faith--for otherwise my questions would have been hamstrung by a fear of everlasting punishment in hell if I got it wrong. The loss of the fear of an eternal conscious punishment allowed me to pursue my doubts. Another key assumption is that faith has nothing to fear from the truth--so I pursued my questions with intensity. [I have since come to deny the existence of such a hell--conditional or metaphorical. It just doesn't square with what Freud has taught us about the depths of our subconscious motivations. Because of Freud we now know that people do bad deeds because of faulty thinking patterns and experiences that happened even before the age of accountability--we know this! Prior to Freud actions were judged <u>prima facie</u> as indicative of people's conscious deliberate attempt to be bad. We also know that once we understand these subconscious motivations and background experiences that we can find a love for people who commit evil deeds. Since God understands all of these hidden motives, past experiences, and faulty thinking patterns, then he completely understands why people do what they do. Hence, **in a post-Freudian world, we can no longer talk about a wrathful vengeful God who seeks our destruction** because we disobey our parents, shoplift a tool, or tell a lie to escape a confrontation (I use these easy examples here because examples like Jeffrey Dalmer, Hitler, Stalin, are harder for us to comprehend--but only to us, not to God, who understands all, and cannot help but love all, since religious traditions abound in teaching us that God is love).

I devoured several books and commentaries on Genesis 1-11. John Gibson's <u>Gen. 1-11</u> was read too early in my development. I rejected it. But Bernard Anderson's <u>Understanding the Old Testament</u> hit a nerve, and for the first time I understood a liberal's view on the Old Testament. There was much there that made me think. <u>The Meaning of Creation</u> by Conrad Hyers is simply a superior book--it explains many of the questions I was asking. Donald Gowan's <u>From Eden to Babel: Gen. 1-11</u> is a short book but sufficiently explained to me the origin of Cain, his wife, and the city he built. The Genesis text assumes there are other people around, Gowan explains, because just like the four gospels, which used separate pericopes to emphasize particular themes, the final editor of Gen. 1-11 wanted to emphasize the depth mankind had sunk in sin, so he drew upon that story involving Cain and inserted it here for that purpose. Claus Westerman's little <u>Creation</u> book summarizes his findings in excellent ways and sees Gen 1-11 as a unit describing man's sinfulness out of which the following chapters show God's mercy. Gordon Wenham's commentary on <u>Genesis 1-15</u>, even as a conservative one, gives up interesting ground in various ways to the liberal argument. He admitted to the presence of similar stories at least 1000 years prior to the earliest that Genesis could be written. Now, which conservative would argue that such stories could filter down that many years by ancient peoples without change? Wenham emphasizes that the CONTENT of Genesis is anti-mythical, and I definitely agree. But this doesn't win the argument, because the real debate concerns whether the first few chapters have the same genre as myth, which explicitly speaks to the issue of the factual historicity of the accounts.

Westermann simply says that the stories are myths, but he continues: "To oppose myth and history in such a way that history presents what actually happened, while myth presents fiction, is utterly unhistorical. It is much more perceptive to see that in the early period of mankind it was not possible to speak of what actually happened in any other way." (p. 13). I also devoured Ronald Youngblood's <u>The Genesis Debate</u> but found myself agreeing with the liberal side in every chapter. This book discusses several issues including: "Was Evolution Involved in the Process of Creation? [Notice here the perceptiveness of the question itself--no dichotomy here!) and "Were there People before Adam and Eve?"

Of course, I re-examined the doctrine of the Bible again. Clark Pinnock in The Scripture Principle began the quest anew. I noticed in James Dunn's Evidence for Jesus (which I used for an Apologetics class) that the Gospel book of John contains much that couldn't have come from the lips of Jesus. He showed the difference between John and the synoptic accounts both in the style of Jesus, and the content of his teaching. John often has Jesus in long discourses while the synoptic gospels have him speak in epigrams, proverbs and parables. In John the content is about himself (I am's, etc)--not the kingdom, while in the synoptic gospels he speaks often about the kingdom and little regarding himself. In John, as you taught me, "the kingdom" becomes "eternal life." Dunn defends John's Jesus but only by admitting that it is a theological elaboration of history--that the discourses of Jesus in John's gospel are meditations on a typical episode or teaching in the life of Jesus. Here he granted too much.

So I read James Dunn's article on "The Authority of Scripture According to Scripture" and his collection of essays in The Living Word (Fortress Press, 1987). After reading him I could no longer affirm inerrancy. Paul J. Achtemeier"s The Inspiration of Scripture, and even John Stott with David Edwards' Evangelical Essentials led me further away, because I was agreeing more with Edwards rather than Stott. Especially problematic was the lack of any cogent explanation of the atonement. James Barr's Beyond Fundamentalism was the clincher. I happened to be ready and primed for his discussion--a discussion with which I almost totally agreed. Barr's book ought to be mandatory reading (I haven't read his more scholarly book on the same topic).

From here I was open to the possibility that there is no personal devil, and Walter Wink's Unmasking the Powers was convincing at that point. I am planning to read The Origin of Satan by Princeton scholar Elaine Pagels.

As you can guess many things are up for grabs now. I have serious doubts about the free will defense to the problem of evil. John Hick's Irenaean Theodicy is the best I've seen so far, except he too used the free will defense in part of his argument. See Encountering Evil: Live Options in Theodicy ed. Stephen Davis.

There are other issues I am about to look into. The first concerns the destiny of the unevangelized--I lean toward universalism now. I will read John Sanders No Other Name for insight on this, and More Than One Way?: Four Views on Salvation in a Pluralistic World, eds. Okholm & Phillips [Zondervan, 1995 (with contributors Hick, Pinnock, McGrath and others)]. Another issue concerns Christology. I will look into Hick's The Myth of God Incarnate, Michael Goulder's Incarnation and Myth, and Stephen Davis' Encountering Jesus. I have read E.P. Sanders' The Historical Figure of Jesus with a great deal of agreement-- his discussion of the Nativity stories is convincing. He also disputes whether there were twelve disciples. I will read John Dominic Crossan's The Historical Jesus, and Who Killed Jesus?

All of this leads me back to Robinson's Honest to God. He said that three scholars led him away from traditional Christianity: Tillich, Bonhoeffer, and Bultmann.

I have just briefly described my intellectual journey. But there are four scholars with whom I am in agreement on many issues. Pinnock, Barr, Hick, and even Bultmann. Where Pinnock is too conservative I go with Barr, then with Hick, and even Bultmann. Concerning Bultmann, Bishop Robinson said he was wrong on three issues (p. 35), and on these issues I agree with Robinson: 1) Bultmann is too inclined to make blanket statements ("no modern man can accept..."); 2) He discredits too much of the gospels as historically expendable; and 3) His reliance on Heidegger's existentialism as a replacement is historically conditioned. But a student of Bultmann's has recently come out with a very detailed discussion of the New Testament evidence for miracles -- the book is by radical scholar Uta Ranke-Heinemann, titled Putting Away Childish Things (Harper & Row, 1994)--there is much food for thought here. Of a more general nature I am reading Robin Lane Fox's The Unauthorized Version, that discusses the whole Bible from a similar perspective, and Karen Armstrong's A History of God.

The hardest thing for me now is that of leaving friends and a conservative community behind--nearly 25 years in the making! It's a wonderful but terrible thing to grow out of a position that held you in its grip for too long.

The world-view question? That too is in a bit of flux right now. I now realize that James Sire's catalog is too simple (The Universe Next Door, IVP, 1988). There are a great deal many more world-views than he examines. There are people who argue that their world-view is consistent even though they hold to various items chosen from several different world-views as presented by Sire. You can call me a Deist if you like. I think this term fits me best -- a view of reason in which all things are judged by the light of natural revelation that is from God by the mind, conscience, and religious traditions. I can be a deist that allows for miracles, since the common denominator among deists is the belief in what's reasonable. Although, I now feel the force of David Hume like never before. By Sire's definition I am also a theological existentialist, although I reject the idea that meaning is created in the subjective world. For me meaning is objective. But I do believe that the Biblical stories and events are from God as teachings to progressively lead us to maturity in objectively seeing that God is love. At times I am also led toward panentheism or Process Theology. Arthur Peacocke in Theology for a Scientific Age, and Ian Barbour's Religion in an Age of Science (Gifford Lectures '89-91 Vol. 1) point me in that direction.

If nothing else, here lies a test case in the mystery of conversion. What makes someone change his or her mind? Although I have passed through a conversion, not even I can tell you how it happens, exactly. Perhaps it happens as a result of a crisis, plus information, minus a sense of Christian community? I'm not sure how my crisis prepared me, but I do know I was puzzled with why God allowed it, and why his people didn't seem to care.

Sincerely,
John W. Loftus

The Cumulative Case.

Now we come to the place where I make a cumulative case against Christianity. Unlike many other religions, Christianity is a historical religion in that it makes historical claims. It is based upon these historical claims, and as such, can be no truer than the probabilities of those historical claims. Christians argue that inspired Biblical authors make claims about certain miraculous events that supposedly happened in history, like Moses parting the Red Sea, the virgin birth of God incarnate, and the resurrection of Jesus from the grave. These same "inspired" authors make claims about beings that exist, like a Trinitarian God, angels (including the Devil), and places like heaven and hell. These same "inspired" authors relate prophetic utterances from the prophets, about end times, the return of Jesus, and the consummation of the ages. There is also the supposed historical continuity of the church that has existed down through the ages, which bears testimony that these claims are true.

Unless we were told of these historical claims, none of us would have known about them at all. They are all historical claims, and whether or not they are true is for us to evaluate historically.

How do we know whether these historical claims are true? To properly evaluate them we use at our disposal historical methods, which I will speak more on later. But we can also evaluate the resultant doctrinal claims by using reason, logic and modern science. That is, presuming these Christian doctrines are true, do reason and science show that these claims are implausible or inconsistent?

I will attempt to show that history, at best, cannot show us that the claims of the Bible are true. History can only give us probabilities. With the nature of any probability, it always leaves room for reasonable doubt. But even if history does somehow lead a person to believe, my position is

> **My position is that reason and modern science do not support the historical doctrinal truth claims of Christianity, and if that's true, then Christianity is not true.**

that reason and modern science do not support the doctrinal truth claims of Christianity, and if that's true, then Christianity is not true.

In short, Christians must defend their faith based upon historical grounds, which allows me to question their faith based upon logical and scientific grounds. If reason and science show Christian beliefs to be implausible, Christianity should be rejected. Since the Christian doctrinal beliefs can be questioned using logic and reason, I'll go with logic every time, especially when history cannot give anything better than probabilites, and that is the bottom line for Christianity.

My point here is that there is every reason to question both the historical consciousness of the Biblical writers, and the way these authors reasoned, which subsequently formed the basis for what later Christians came to believe, and which I will debunk in this book. I'll speak about Matthew's hermeneutical approach to the Old Testament (OT) later on. But let me offer a few examples of how much better our modern ways of reasoning are to theirs.

Look, for instance, at how **Jesus** purportedly argued on behalf of the resurrection: "And as touching the dead, that they rise: have ye not read in the book of Moses, how in the bush God spoke unto him, saying, 'I am the God of Abraham, and the God of Isaac, and the God of Jacob?' He is not the God of the dead, but the God of the living: ye therefore do greatly err." (Mark 12:26-27)

How this argument of Jesus' is suppose to lead to the belief that the dead do in fact arise, is convoluted to say the least. This OT text, taken in its original context, is merely identifying the God that was speaking to Moses from out of the so-called burning bush. No thinker today would ever conclude that God was proclaiming anything about a resurrection from the dead, even if Jesus and his contemporaries may have thought so.

Look also at how **Paul** argued on behalf of the general resurrection:

If there is no resurrection of the dead, then not even Christ has been raised.

Christ has been raised.

Therefore, there is a resurrection of the dead. (I Cor. 15:13).

This is a logically valid argument form, called *Modus Tollens*, even if I don't think it's a sound or convincing argument. Why does it follow merely from the fact that Christ rose that there shall be a resurrection of the dead? There seems to be nothing in the belief that Jesus arose that would lead me to think that there is a general resurrection. It just might be the case that Jesus arose because he's special and that's it.

The answer for Paul is that Christ is the head of those who believe, just like Adam is the head of humanity (vs. 21-22), so what is true of the head will likewise be true of his followers. But this kind of inferential argument makes no sense in today's world, no matter what Christian scholars say people believed in the past. Paul's logic is flawed here. Paul doesn't argue effectively for this. It could equally be argued from this same logic that since Jesus ascended into heaven, so will all believers, since what is true of the head will likewise be true of his followers. But of course, that logic doesn't work because even in Paul's day, some Christians had already died and didn't ascend into heaven as Jesus purportedly did from Mt. Olivet.

My position is that these ancient standards are pathetic in comparison to today's standards. Their reasoning was inadequate, their scientific testing was lame, and their understandings were infantile. So to continue believing what they tell us, when we know this about their standards, is utter foolishness. Furthermore, if we can determine from logic that the doctrines that result from their inadequate reasoning are incoherent, completely far-fetched, or even inconsistent, then their historical conclusions should be rejected.

Now here's the rub. If I misapplied an OT text, or misquoted it to make a point, or if I used *pesher*, *midrash*, typological or allegorical methods today to understand the OT, or the Bible as a whole, Christians today would be the first ones to jump down my throat based upon the grammatical historical method. Christians would not believe someone today who claimed some strange ideas about an incarnate God who rose from the dead, if the person presenting the evidence used quotations from an ancient text out of context, or their reasoning was flawed. They wouldn't, and neither do I.

Christians would say I don't have the authority to do what they did. Jesus could use the Bible this way because he was God incarnate, while Matthew and Paul could do this because Jesus authorized them to do so. But Jesus, Paul and Matthew obviously mishandled the text of the OT when judged by the more rigorous standards of today; which were learned as the result of the rise of modern science.

The bottom line is that in order for today's Christians to believe Jesus rose from the dead, they must first believe in the hermeneutical method of the New Testament (NT) writers. It cannot be reversed! The NT writers misused OT sources and subsequently reasoned as Paul did to show that Jesus was truly born of a virgin, that he was the messiah, that he atoned for our sins, and that he arose from the dead (and as we'll see, so did Matthew). None of their quotes or offered reasons supports their claims (by the way, typology is all in the mind of the beholder, like horoscope readings). Therefore, I believe there is no solid OT support for any of their claims about Jesus from the Old Testament.

But it's precisely their hermeneutical methods and reasoning here, which led them to argue the way they do on behalf of Jesus. I simply argue that if their approach is so flawed in how they argue, then we should not trust their claims at all when they go on to claim Jesus did arise from the dead. If one is flawed, then so is the other. Both stem from a faulty and inadequate way of understanding the world and of assessing the evidence for or against any historical claim, much less a miraculous one.

Against this argument, James Patrick Holding, a self-proclaimed internet apologist, said: "What happened is that they knew from fact and history that Jesus was born of a virgin, etc, and then, to normalize it for those who respected the OT as Scripture, they sought out passages that could be read typologically to verify that such events were kosher. Events called out the texts, not vice versa."

But this is the very question I'm asking. How do we know today that "events called out the texts, not vice versa?" Based on the reasoning of the NT writers, with the whole lack of a historical consciousness, it is much more likely that OT texts called out the events that were to be told, not vice versa.

The best way to understand their use of the OT is that they wrote the life of Jesus from the perspective of their understanding of the OT, and in light of their superstitious beliefs about Jesus. That is, they made Jesus' life fit the details of their flawed understanding of the OT, even if it was out of context, and even if their reasoning was flawed by today's more rigorous standards.

What Christian apologists will have to show is that early Christians were concerned in the first place, about what actually happened. For that is what's needed to prove their point. Christians might as well argue that the early Christians weren't superstitious or that they had a good grasp of science too, but I'll deal with that later.

Here's another example of what I mean: I've seen many studies that try to show that early Christians believed Jesus was God in the flesh. Even if they are correct, my question is this: "why we should believe what ancient superstitious people believed?" Why? I'll argue that the incarnation doesn't make sense on logical grounds, and those grounds are more sure to me than any historical grounds, especially when these believers exhibited such a lack of logical skills.

4 The Outsider Test for Faith...

There is a great deal of discussion among Christian apologists over Bayesian "background factors," which play a significant role in assessing the truth of Christianity in general, the likelihood of the resurrection of Jesus, the probability of miracles, and the problem of evil. But I want to take a good hard look at the most important background factor of all for cognitively assessing the truth of religious faith...one's sociological and cultural background.

I've investigated my faith from the inside as an insider with the presumption that it was true. Even from an insider's perspective, I couldn't continue to believe. Now from the outside, it makes no sense at all. Christians are on the inside. I am now on the outside. Christians see things from the inside. I see things from the outside. From the inside, it seems true. From the outside, it seems untrue.

There are many religious faiths to choose from. How does one actually choose to be on the "inside" of any of them, if from the "outside" none of them have any plausibility? Unless one is on the *inside* as an adherent of a particular religious faith, he or she cannot see. But from the *outside*, the adherents of a different faith seem blind. This reminds me of what Mark Twain said: "The easy confidence with which I know another man's religion is folly teaches me to suspect that my own is also." Believers are truly atheists with regard to all other religions but their own. Atheists just reject one more religion.

This whole inside/outside perspective is quite a dilemma, and prompts me to propose and argue on behalf of *The Outsider Test for religious faith*, the result of which makes the presumption of skepticism the preferred stance when approaching any religious faith, especially one's own. The Outsider Test is simply a challenge to test one's own religious faith with the presumption of skepticism, as an outsider. Test your beliefs as if you were an outsider to your faith. An outsider would begin her journey as a disinterested investigator who didn't think the religious faith in question was true, since there are so many different religious faiths in the world. An outsider would be someone who was only interested in which religious faith is correct, if any, and would have no intellectual affiliation with any of them at all. She would have to assume that her culturally inherited religious faith is probably false. To be an outsider would mean she would have nothing at stake in the outcome of her investigations, and hence no fear of hell (however conceived) while investigating them, beginning with her own. Threats of hell could hinder a clear-headed investigation.

Surely someone will initially object that this is a quite draconian in scope. Why take such an extreme stance? It's because that's how religious people approach all of the other religious faiths but their own. People approach other faiths this way all of the time, so why not do that with one's own religious faith? Why is there this discrepancy in how we evaluate religious faiths? For someone to object that what I'm asking is unfair, she has the burden of proof to show why her inconsistent approach to religious faith is justified in the first place. By contrast, I can offer good reasons why she should adopt such a skeptical presumption. Doing so is based upon some hard cold sociological facts.

The basis for the Outsider Test challenge can be found in a statement by John Hick: "it is evident that in some ninety-nine percent of the cases the religion which an individual professes and to which he or she adheres depends upon the accidents of birth. Someone born to Buddhist parents in Thailand is very likely to be a Buddhist, someone born to Muslim parents in Saudi Arabia to be a Muslim, someone born to Christian parents in Mexico to be a Christian, and so on."[An Interpretation of Religion (Yale Univ. Press, 1992), p. 2].

Richard Dawkins said the same thing in a much harsher tone: "Out of all of the sects in the world, we notice an uncanny coincidence: the overwhelming majority just happen to choose the one that their parents belong to. Not the sect that has the best evidence in its favour, the best miracles, the best moral code, the best cathedral, the best stained glass, the best music: when it comes to choosing from the smorgasbord of available religions, their potential virtues seem to count for nothing, compared to the matter of heredity. This is an unmistakable fact; nobody could seriously deny it. Yet people with full knowledge of the arbitrary nature of this heredity, somehow manage to go on believing in their religion, often with such fanaticism that they are prepared to murder people who follow a different one.... the religion we adopt is a matter of an accident of geography." [The Nullifidian (Dec 94)].

If you were born in Saudi Arabia, you would be a Sunni Muslim right now. This is an almost undeniable cold hard sociological and cultural fact. In today's world, if you were born in Iran, you'd be a Shi'a Muslim. If you were born in India, you'd be a Hindu right now. If you were born in Japan, you'd be a Shintoist, and if you lived in Mongolia, you'd be a Buddhist. If you were born in the first century B.C. in Israel, you'd adhere to the Jewish faith at that time, and if you were born in Europe in 1200 A.D., you'd be a Roman Catholic. These things are as close to being undeniable facts as we can get in the sociological world.

But there's more: Had we lived in the ancient Egypt or Babylon, we would have been very superstitious and polytheistic to the core. In the ancient world, we would have sought divine guidance through divination, and sought to alter our circumstances through magic. If we were a first century Christian, we would probably believe God sent illnesses and disasters to discipline and punish people for their sins, and for the first 900 years, we would have believed in the *Ransom Theory* of Jesus' atonement. As Christians in Europe during the Middle Ages, we would probably see nothing much wrong with killing witches, persecuting people of different faiths, torturing heretics, and conquering Jerusalem from the infidels in the Crusades.

There are a whole range of issues that admit of diversity in the moral and political areas as well, based to an overwhelming degree on the "accidents of birth." As Americans, we would have believed with President Andrew Jackson, in *Manifest Destiny*, our God given mandate to seize Native American territories in westward expansion. Up through the 17th century we would have believed that women were intellectually inferior to men, and consequently, we would not even have allowed them to become educated in the same subjects as men. Like Thomas Jefferson and most Americans, we would've thought this way about black people as well, that they were intellectually inferior to whites, while if we were born in the South, we would have justified slavery from the Bible.

If we were born black in today's America, we would probably still to this day believe O.J. Simpson is not guilty of murder. If we were born in the Palestinian Gaza strip, we would hate the Jews, and probably want to kill them all. If we were born in France, we would have opposed the Iraq war to oust Saddam Hussein. If we were born into a Democratic family in America in the 80's we would hate Bush and have a strong tendency to believe anything negative about him.

These kinds of moral, political and religious beliefs, based upon cultural conditions, can be duplicated into a lengthy list of beliefs that we would've had if we were born in a different time and place. For someone to claim he or she wouldn't have believed these same things is what I call *chronological snobbery*, and runs completely counter to the sociological and cultural facts. According to Voltaire: "Every man is a creature of the age in which he lives, and few are able to raise themselves above the ideas of the time."

There are so many moral beliefs we have because of "when and where we were born" that an argument is made by moral relativists based on it, and known to ethicists as the Dependency Thesis (DPT). According to the DPT "morality is not a matter of independent rational judgment but is causally dependent on cultural conditions." The DPT is one of two legs supporting cultural relativism. The DPT is the second leg supporting cultural relativism. The first leg is known as the Diversity Thesis (DVT), which states, "Moral practices and beliefs do in fact vary from culture to culture and at different times in history." Once someone acknowledges the first leg (DVT), then the second leg (DPT) offers a reason for the diversity we find around the globe. [Arthur F. Homes, <u>Ethics: Approaching Moral Decisions</u> (InterVarsity Press), 1984, pp. 15-21].

I believe that this same moral cultural relativist argument can be applied to religious faith, *qua* religious faith, with the exception that I'll not be arguing for complete metaphysical relativism. So let me introduce the **Religious Diversity Thesis** (RDVT), which states, "Religious faith does in fact vary from culture to culture and at different times in history." Based upon the RDVT, the **Religious Dependency Thesis** (RDPT) argues that "religious faith is not merely a matter of independent rational judgment but is causally dependent on cultural conditions to an overwhelming degree." The Outsider Test is based on the RDVT, and the RDPT leads us to the presumption of skepticism.

The Outsider Test challenge will have a greater degree of force against religious faiths because there are no mutually acceptable empirical tests to finally once and for all decide between them in our present world. Since this is the case, socio-political and cultural factors will play an overwhelming role in what people believe about such things.

No doubt many readers will object that no one can approach any area of learning without some presuppositions, assumptions or control beliefs, not even scientists, and this is especially true when it comes to religious faiths. They may further argue that it's demonstrably true that the presuppositions a person begins with will most always be the same ones she ends with. So what I'm arguing for is that the sociological and cultural facts strongly suggest than the adherent of religious faith should switch her presuppositions. I'm arguing that she should adopt the presumption (or presupposition) of skepticism. If she simply cannot do this, then let me suggest doing what Rene Descartes did with a methodological (or hypothetical) doubt, although I'm not suggesting his type of extreme doubt. Hypothetically consider your faith from the perspective of an outsider. At the very minimum, a believer could begin as a mere seeker of truth, who does not obstinately hold on to any prior presuppositions about any religious faith at all, and is willing to subject her faith to rigorous scrutiny by being willing to read many of the best recognized critiques of her faith. For instance, if she is a Christian, she should be willing to read this book of mine. What is more, a church should be willing to have small groups where people gather to discuss each section of it.

The Outsider Test also challenges us to examine the social and cultural conditions of how we came to adopt our particular religious faith in the first place. That is, we must ask ourselves who or what influenced us, and what were the actual reasons for adopting that faith in its earliest stages. Nearly all believers in an overwhelming number of instances simply end up believing what they were taught to believe by their parents. The reason they adopt their faith in the first place is because of social and cultural conditions. So just ask yourself if your initial experiences could be explained by a different, skeptical hypothesis, and whether the initial reasons you had for your faith were strong ones. Do what I did in "A Word About the Grounding of My Faith" (pp. 16-19). I really didn't have good initial reasons to believe. Very few of us do, as a matter of fact. We just end up believing what we were taught to believe.

Social conditions provide us with the control beliefs that we use from that moment on to incorporate all known facts and experiences. That's why they're called control beliefs...they are almost like blinders, and from that moment on you only see what your blinders will let you see, because reason is used to serve our control beliefs. Listen to Michael Shermer, a former Christian theist turned atheist, who has done an extensive study of why people believe in God and in "weird things" who concludes: "Most of us most of the time come to our beliefs for a variety of reasons having little to do with empirical evidence and logical reasoning. Rather, such variables as genetic predispositions, parental predilections, sibling influences, peer pressures, educational experiences, and life impressions all shape the personality preferences and emotional inclinations that, in conjunction with numerous social and cultural influences, lead us to make certain belief choices. Rarely do any of us sit down before a table of facts, weigh them pro and con, and choose the most logical and rational belief, regardless of what we previously believed. Instead, the facts of the world come to us through the colored filters of the theories, hypotheses, hunches, biases, and prejudices we have accumulated through our lifetime. We then sort through the body of data and select those most confirming what we already believe, and ignore or rationalize away those that are disconfirming. All of us do this, of course, but smart people are better at it..." [Michael Shermer, Why People Believe Weird Things 2nd ed., (Henry Holt and Company, LLC), 2002, pp. 283-284].

According to Robert McKim, "We seem to have a remarkable capacity to find arguments that support positions which we antecedently hold. Reason is, to a great extent, the slave of prior commitments." [Religious Ambiguity and Religious Diversity (Oxford, 2001), p. ix]. Hence the whole notion of "an independent rational judgment" is suspect, especially when there are no mutually agreed upon empirical tests to decide what to believe, even if Christian apologists, for instance, continue to defend their religious faith with reasons. These apologists, if they're good at what they do, will be smart people. But according to Michael Shermer, "smart people, because they are more intelligent and better educated, are able to give intellectual reasons justifying their beliefs that they arrived at for nonintelligent reasons."[Why People Believe... p. 299].

The Outsider Test is a thought experiment merely to help us see what the proper presumption is to approach the faith we were born into. Unlike former atheist Anthony Flew, who argued in favor of the presumption of atheism [The Presumption of Atheism (Prometheus Press, 1976), I'm arguing in favor of the presumption of skepticism. Its presumption is that when examining any religious belief, skepticism would be warranted, since the odds are good that the particular one you are investigating is wrong. **The Outsider Test is no different than the prince in the Cinderella story who must question 45,000 people to see which girl lost the glass slipper at the ball last night. They all claim to have done so. Therefore, skepticism is definitely warranted. This is especially true when an empirical foot match cannot solve the religious questions we're asking.**

For the Christian theist the challenge of the Outsider Test means there would be no more quoting the Bible to defend the claim that Jesus' death on the cross saves us from sins. The Christian theist must now try to rationally explain it. No more quoting the Bible to show how it's possible for Jesus to be 100% God and 100% man with nothing left over. The Christian theist must now try to make sense of this claim, coming as it does from an ancient superstitious people who didn't have trouble believing this could happen (Acts 14:11, 28:6). The Christian theist must not assume there is an answer to the problem of evil before approaching the evidence of suffering in our world. And she'd be initially skeptical of believing in any of the miracles in the Bible, just as she would be skeptical of any claims of the miraculous in today's world supporting other religious faiths. Why? Because she cannot start out by first believing the Bible, nor can she trust the people close to her who are Christian theists to know the truth, nor can she trust her own anecdotal religious experiences, since such experiences are had by people of all religious faiths who differ about the cognitive content learned as the result of these experiences. She would want evidence and reasons for these beliefs.

If after having investigated your religious faith with the presumption of skepticism your faith passes intellectual muster, then you can have your religious faith. It's that simple. If not, abandon it. Any God who requires you to believe correctly, when we humans have this extremely strong tendency to believe what we were born into, surely should make the correct religious faith pass the Outsider Test. If your faith doesn't stand after doing this, then the God of your faith is not worthy of being worshipped. Since it's overwhelmingly true that the presumption you begin with will be the one you will end up with, I suspect that if someone is willing to take the challenge of the Outsider Test then her religious faith will be found defective and she will abandon it. I also suspect that such a challenge could very well lead her to agnosticism and then onward to a denial of any religious faith, or atheism, like it has with me.

Answering Four Objections: One) It's objected that there are small minorities of people who choose to be Christian theists who were born and raised in Muslim countries, and that people can escape their culturally adopted faith. But these are the exceptions. Christian theists respond by asking me to explain the exceptions. I am asking them to explain the rule. Why do religious beliefs dominate in specific geographical areas? Why is that? Furthermore, if the Religious Dependency Thesis (RDPT) is correct, then religious geographical proliferation is exactly what we would expect to find in the world. The exceptions are simply that there are people who think for themselves and in so doing own a particular religious faith, rather than adopt what was taught to them. Then too, there are several social reasons for leaving the faith that a person was born into. If a person had some bad experiences at the hands of someone who taught him what to believe, this person may leave that faith for another (victims of Catholic molester-priests, for instance, or abusive fathers, or senseless suffering of any unbearable kind). If the person thinks through what her faith claims and just cannot reconcile her faith with what she learns or experiences though life, then she may leave her adopted faith. But when such a person does decide to leave her faith, and chooses another one, many times that different faith (or sect) will be one that she was already exposed to in her culture. By contrast atheism (which for our purposes is merely the non-belief in any god) can be adopted by a former believer without ever having been exposed to it, since it's simply the denial of one more god than what everyone else adheres to.

Two) Someone may argue that even if religious faiths were 100% correlated with the "accidents of birth," this wouldn't invalidate any particular one of them, for it could still be possible that it is the correct one after all. To this I answer, yes, this is possible. After all, someone can be right if for no other reason than that she just got lucky. But how do you rationally justify such luck? This is why I've developed the challenge of the Outsider Test in the first place, to test religious faiths, against such luck. If the test between religious faiths is based entirely on luck, then what are the chances, based on luck alone, that the particular sect within Christian theism that one adheres to is correct? This still favors the presumption of skepticism.

Three) Someone may ask: "Do my cultural conditions overwhelmingly 'determine' my presumption of skepticism? If so, then others don't have much of a reason to adopt the skeptical stance. If not, then why do I think I can transcend culture, but a Christian theist can't transcend her culture?" In answer I say that if it's the case that "the accidents of birth" overwhelmingly determine our religious beliefs, especially in those areas where there is no mutually agreed upon empirical tests to decide between them, then that's a sociological fact everyone must wrestle with when thinking about such matters. Let's say this is the case, i.e., that whatever we believe about the origin of this universe is overwhelmingly determined by when and where we are born. I am much more willing to accept the consequences of this than a great majority of people who have religious faith and are so dogmatic about their faith. If this is the case, then we agree that what we believe is based upon when and where we're born.

If true, this does not undercut what I'm saying at all--it supports it. I'm arguing that cultural conditions have an extremely strong influence on us to believe in a given communally shared religious faith **in a primary sense**. And although cultural influences also apply **in a secondary sense** with regard to non-communal metaphysical beliefs, if I am a skeptic because of these cultural conditions, then I'm right that cultural conditions lead us to believe these things after all. And while I might be wrong about what I believe, such an admission doesn't undercut the main reason for the Outsider Test and the skeptical presumption that goes with it based on the RDVT and RDPT. If cultural factors overwhelmingly cause us to believe what we believe, then we should all be skeptical of what we believe.

The best that could result from this admission is agnosticism. But this doesn't grant the believer any ground. For to be agnostic would again be admitting the basis for testing between beliefs that cannot be decided upon empirical grounds, and that is to be skeptical all over again, which once again is something I'm asking of believers. So I don't object to being skeptical of my own skepticism. But it's redundant from my perspective, and so it merely reinforces itself.

Four) One final objection asks whether this is all circular. Have I merely chosen a different metaphysical belief system based upon different cultural factors? Maybe it is in some sense, but it's definitely **not viciously circular**. For I have very good initial grounds for starting out with skepticism in the first place, given the RDVT and the RDPT.

Consider instead the arguments used to explain religious diversity by adherents of different religious faiths. These explanations are similar in kind to each other, if not exactly the same. They will argue that those who don't accept their particular religion are either ignorant of the truth (or willfully ignorant), unenlightened, deceived by Satan, or that God has good reasons for permitting this state of affairs. Cultural factors are downplayed or even ignored, even though I have shown they play an overwhelming role in what a person believes.

Furthermore, when actually grappling with the cultural basis of religious faith, believers will respond in the same manner against what I have been arguing for here. Whether it's a Buddhist, Muslim, Hindu, Jew or Christian, they will all argue that I have not shown their particular religious faith to be false simply because it's an overwhelming sociological fact that we believe based upon when and where we were born. Then they will proceed all over again to argue that theirs is the true faith. However, whether or not someone accepts their apologetical arguments will depend upon whether or not they are already insiders to that particular faith in the first place. Is this not circular?

Skepticism actually becomes the favored position as a result of the initial presumption, a presumption that is justified by the religious diversity around the globe. To debate this initial presumption someone would have to debate with the observed religious diversity around the globe and the explanation of this diversity given by the RDPT. **I believe skepticism of all religious and metaphysical positions leads one inexorably to agnosticism, and agnosticism can lead someone inexorably to atheism.** And atheism, in the end, is a denial of all religious faiths.

5 Faith and Reason.

In this section of the book I will briefly examine several positions on the relationship of faith and reason, and conclude with the view I have personally adopted as the best one, and how it reflects what I will attempt to do in the rest of this book.

The *Philosophy of Religion* is simply philosophy examining religious beliefs. It attempts to analyze and critically evaluate religious beliefs. It is not a branch of theology (which assumes one religious view as true). It need not be undertaken from a religious standpoint at all! Although, many of the most highly regarded scholars in the field are themselves religious believers. [Just read God and The Philosophers, ed. By Thomas V. Morris (Oxford, 1994), and Philosophers who Believe, edited by Kelly James Clark (IVP, 1993)].

Christianity and Philosophy.

Many Christians have taken an unenthusiastic view of philosophy because there are dangers in it for their faith. Paul said, "See no one takes you captive through hollow and deceptive philosophy..." (Col. 2:8). Tertullian (160-220 AD) asked: "What has Athens to do with Jerusalem?" Martin Luther called reason "the Devil's Whore." Luther argued against the *magisterial* use of reason, in which reason judges the gospel, and approved of the *ministerial* use of reason, in which reason submits and serves the gospel. William Lane Craig agrees with this viewpoint and argues, "reason is a tool to help us better understand our faith. Should faith and reason conflict, it is reason that must submit to faith, not vice versa." [Apologetics: An Introduction, (Moody, 1984), p. 21].

Jesus purportedly said: "I praise you, Father, Lord of heaven and earth, because you have hidden these things from the wise and learned, and revealed them to little children. Yes, Father, for this was your good pleasure." (Luke 10:21). **Paul** wrote: "the message of the cross is foolishness to those who are perishing, but to us who are being saved it is the power of God. For it is written: 'I will destroy the wisdom of the wise; the intelligence of the intelligent I will frustrate.' Where is the wise man? Where is the scholar? Where is the philosopher of this age? Has not God made foolish the wisdom of the world?...For the foolishness of God is wiser than man's wisdom..." (I Corinthians 1:18-25).

The truth is that anyone who engages in Christian apologetics will use reason to defend their beliefs; the Apostle Paul, Tertullian, Luther, and Craig included. The question here is this: "What role should reason play in the justification of religious belief-systems?" [See Bernard Ramm, Varieties of Christian Apologetics (Baker, 1961), Gordon R. Lewis, Testing Christianity's Truth Claims (Univ. Press of America, 1990); and Five Views On Apologetics (Zondervan, 2000)].

SETTING ASIDE FAITH: HARD RATIONALISM: "In order for a religious belief system to be properly and rationally accepted, it must be possible to prove that the belief-system is true." W.K. Clifford best exemplifies this.

W. K. Clifford was an English mathematician (1845-1879). His position is summed up with these words: "It is wrong always, everywhere, and for everyone, to believe anything upon insufficient evidence [(in "The Ethics of Belief" in Lectures and Essays, Macmillan, 1897)]. Take, for example, a ship owner who had brought himself to sincerely believe in the seaworthiness of his ship that was to carry immigrants. He came to believe in part by trusting in God's providence, but it sank to the bottom killing all aboard. The ship owner was guilty of the deaths of these people, Clifford argued, because he brought himself to believe by stifling his doubts—he did not believe based on sufficient evidence. But there's more: Had the ship not gone down, the ship owner would still not be innocent, he merely wouldn't have been found out! According to him, it is wrong to believe on insufficient grounds, to suppress doubts, or to avoid investigation. It is always right to question all that we believe. It is sinful and unethical to believe on insufficient evidence because the pleasure is a stolen one, which is in defiance of our duty to mankind. When we believe for unworthy reasons we weaken our powers of self-control, of doubting, and of fairly weighing the evidence. There is a great danger to society here, not just in believing the wrong things, but by losing the habit of testing things, and hence to sink back into savagery by becoming a credulous society. To the objection that we simply cannot check everything out, he replies, then that person should not believe anything either. What would be Clifford's opinion about a religious belief-system, given the very high standards of proof he demands? Do without them--this is thinly concealed, but there.

SETTING ASIDE REASON BECAUSE IT DOESN'T APPLY:

Alvin Plantinga. Plantinga has made one of the most sustained arguments against W.K. Clifford's position. [See "Reason and Belief in God," in Faith and Rationality: Reason and Belief in God. (Notre Dame Press, 1983), see also Nicholas Wolterstorff's Reason Within The Bounds of Religion (Eerdmans, 1984)]. W.K. Clifford's evidential challenge is this: No religious belief system is capable of meeting the high standards that believing in anything requires, so no reasonable person should accept any religious belief system.

Plantinga makes some distinctions:

Perceptual beliefs are based on what we perceive through our senses, i.e., seeing my hand in front of me. But how would you establish the truth that it is my hand that is in front of me? All your checking procedures presuppose a more fundamental belief in the general reliability of our senses. The ultimate question arises: How do we know that the whole realm of sense experience is not delusory? Trusting in the reliability of our senses can be seen as a basic belief.

Basic beliefs are those which have no evidential support for them. But they could be wrong: for example thinking someone is guilty of a crime just by looking at them.

Properly basic beliefs are basic beliefs which are reasonable to accept (for example, the past really happened).

Hard Rationalism would say all of our beliefs are either self-evident (true just by understanding them), evident to the senses (depending on experience), or incorrigible (the way things appear to me). The only evidence that is allowed is propositional evidence like an argument based upon inferences, or evidence that is provided by direct experience.

But Plantinga unveils two fatal flaws here: 1) There are countless things that we believe (and do so properly) without proof or evidence, such as the existence of other minds; that the world continues to exist even when we don't perceive it; that we have been alive for more than 24 hours; that the past really happened; that we aren't just brains in a vat; that we live in an ordered universe; that we can trust our minds and our senses about the universe; that cause and effect are universal laws of nature; that nature is uniform and intelligible, etc. 2) The Hard Rationalist position is self-defeating, for it itself is neither self-evident, nor evident to the senses, nor incorrigible!

Because of this, Plantinga thinks that the evidentialist challenge places belief in God in the wrong family of beliefs. Belief in God is among those classified as "basic beliefs," and because this belief comes from God himself, such a belief is a "properly basic belief." Belief in God and belief in other minds are in the same family of beliefs. Since belief in other minds is rational without support, so is belief in God. Religious experience, if it is to count as evidence, "is evidence that is noninferential, nonargumentative, and nonpropositional." [Ronald Nash, Faith & Reason (Zondervan, 1988, p. 100)].

According to Plantinga, "the believer is entirely within his epistemic rights in believing, for example, that God has created the world, even if he has no argument at all for that conclusion. His belief in God can be perfectly rational even if he knows of no cogent argument, deductive or inductive, for the existence of God—indeed, even if there is no such argument." [("Reason and Belief in God," (p. 65)]. He claims this because he believes God grants innate knowledge of himself to all human beings. The reason why not everyone acknowledges this is due to sin: "God has created us in such a way that we have a strong tendency or inclination toward belief in God. This tendency has been in part overlaid or suppressed by sin. Were it not for the existence of sin in the world, human beings would believe in God to the same degree and with the same natural spontaneity that we believe in the existence of other persons, an external world, or the past." ["Reason and Belief"...p. 66].

Clarifications of Plantinga's position. 1) Just because the belief in God is a properly basic belief doesn't allow for absurd beliefs to be properly basic. He participates in something called "negative apologetics" by examining and disputing the beliefs of other religious claims. 2) He doesn't deny the possibility that there may be adequate grounds for belief in God. He just claims these things are unnecessary. 3) He is claiming that a believer can be rationally justified in claiming to "know" God exists even if others do not agree—even if there are no cogent arguments for this! Proper basicality in no way guarantees the truth of the belief. His discussion is not intended to convince the agnostic or atheist. He thinks whether someone accepts the proper basic belief in God depends upon world-view considerations. "What you properly take to be rational depends upon what sort of metaphysical and religious stance you adopt. And so the dispute as to whether theistic belief is rational can't be settled just by attending to epistemological considerations; it is at bottom not merely an epistemological dispute, but an ontological or theological dispute." [Plantinga, as quoted in Ronald Nash, Faith and Reason, (p. 91). See also Plantinga's Warrant The Current Debate (1993), Warrant in Contemporary Epistemology (1996), Warrant and Proper Function (1999), and Warranted Christian Belief (2000)].

Brief Criticisms: Atheist Keith Parsons [(in Does God Exist: The Great Debate, Thomas Nelson, 1990)]: "The claim that the theist is within his epistemic rights in believing God is a rather weak claim...If theists want to claim no more than that they are within their epistemic rights in believing in God, atheists should not bother to belabor the point. After all, to say that theists are within their epistemic rights in believing in God in no way indicates that atheists are one wit less rational in not believing in God." (pp. 177ff).

John Hick in Philosophy of Religion (Prentice-Hall, 1990, 4th edition): "The argument for the proper basicality of those religious beliefs that are grounded in religious experiences must apply not only to Christian beliefs but also to those of Judaism, Islam, Hinduism, Buddhism, and so on." (p. 77).

"Voodoo followers would be able to claim that insofar as their beliefs are basic in the voodoo community, they are rational" and that Plantinga's beliefs in his Christian community are subsequently "irrational." [Michael Martin, Atheism: A Philosophical Justification, (Temple University Press, 1990, p. 272)].

[For some of my criticisms see my section, "The Self-Authenticating Witness of the Holy Spirit."]

SETTING ASIDE REASON IN THE ABSENCE OF EVIDENCE:
William James. James took issue with Clifford by espousing a faith based PRAGMATISM (1842-1910). James makes the following distinctions: A **genuine option** is living, forced, and momentous. **Living:** where we see the alternatives as serious possibilities. **Forced**: where the choice is between two exclusive and exhaustive possibilities where there is no third possibility, such as suspension of judgment (this will be one of the reasons why I cannot remain agnostic). **Momentous**: where the decision matters because it is a unique opportunity and not easily reversed. James: "Our passional nature not only lawfully may, but must decide an option between propositions, whenever it is a genuine option that cannot by its nature be decided on intellectual grounds."

To show this 1st) James insists, "Our non-intellectual nature does influence our convictions." We have a "passional nature." He also insists that most of what we believe is based upon authority. 2nd) He maintains that objective certainty is in general unattainable. 3rd) He insists that our errors are surely not such awfully solemn things. He regards the pursuit of truth as primary and the avoidance of error as secondary. Clifford's view is the opposite, where the avoidance of error is primary and the attaining of truth is secondary. Clifford's view is like "keeping soldiers out of battle forever rather than risk a single wound." In scientific matters we may suspend judgment because the options are not forced. But even here passional commitment is favorable for discovery. In moral matters we cannot wait for sensible proof.

How do these things relate to religion? Religion says 1st) that the best things are the more eternal things in the universe, and 2nd) is that we are now better off if we believe the first affirmation to be true. If someone thinks religion cannot be true by any possibility, then it is not a living option for him or her. But if there is a possibility that religion be true, then this choice is a living option for you. And as such it is also a momentous option, and a forced option.

Turning to skepticism, James faults it for vetoing faith by laying down "agnostic rules for truth-seeking." Skepticism claims "dupery through hope is much worse than dupery through fear." Yet such rules will prevent us from knowing the truth about God, if he exists. Why? "**If God exists, then we might have to meet that hypothesis halfway to see whether it is true.**" If we refused to make religious advances because of the lack of proof one "might cut himself off forever from his only opportunity of making the god's acquaintance." James claims "a rule of thinking which would prevent me from acknowledging certain kinds of truth, if these kinds of truth were really there, would be an irrational rule."

Brief Evaluation: J.L. Mackie: "This is a persuasive and powerful case." [The Miracle of Theism, (p. 207)]. J.L. Mackie: "James claims that in the absence of evidence "passion is the tie-breaker." Mackie claims, "we need a tie-breaker only where there is a tie to be broken." Also, "if faith is defended as an experiment, it must conform to the general principles of experimental inquiry....a favorable result of the experiment would have to be a series of experiences which somehow resisted psychological explanation."

John Hick "The basic weakness of James' position is that it constitutes an unrestricted license for wishful thinking." Hick: "If an idea were true, James would never come to know it by his method, a method that could result only in everyone's becoming more firmly entrenched in his or her current prejudices....It amounts to an encouragement to us all to believe, at our risk, whatever we like." [Philosophy of Religion, 4th ed. p. 60). Norman Geisler: "Of course all truth must work, but not everything that works is necessarily true." (Christian Apologetics, p. 115].

A REASONABLE WAGER IN THE ABSENCE OF EVIDENCE:

Blaise Pascal (1623-1662). Pascal lived in France, post-Descartes. People were uncritically accepting the complete ability of reason to solve their religious problems. Deism sought to judge everything in the light of reason. His problem was the smug deist, atheist and skeptic who were indifferent to the spiritual dimension. His goal was to shock these people out of their complacency, and to deal a blow to the skepticism of his time.

Pascal rejected the premise that reason is equal to the task of a rational defense of faith. He wrote: "I look on all sides and see nothing but obscurity; nature offers me nothing but matter for doubt....A hundred times I have wished that God would mark his presence in nature unequivocally.... [but] All who seek God in nature find no light to satisfy them." "Nature confounds the skeptics, and reason confounds the dogmatists...You can avoid neither skepticism nor dogmatism; but alas, you can live with neither." What then? According to Pascal the strongest proof for the existence of God is the great need felt by human beings for the sustaining presence God in an otherwise empty universe: "The heart has reasons, which reason knows nothing of." So he is satisfied to argue from our need for God to the existence of God.

He asks what is man in the midst of the infinitely huge universe and the infinitely small microscopic world. "What a chimera is man! Strange! monstrous! A chaos, a contradiction, a prodigy. Judge of all things, yet a weak earthworm." Compared to the universe, mankind is "nothing." "But were the universe to kill him, man would still be more noble than that which has slain him, because he knows that he dies, and that the universe has the better of him. The universe knows nothing of this." "Man is but a reed, weakest in nature, but a reed which thinks. A thinking reed." When Pascal contemplates the blindness and misery of man, he writes: "I fall into terror." "My terror is like that of a man who should awake upon a terrible desert island with no means of escape." Given this human condition, Pascal argues that satisfaction can only be found in God: "Man finds his lasting happiness only in God. Without him, there is nothing in nature which will take his place....There is no good without knowledge of God." And yet he realizes that this will not be enough for the skeptic.

Pascal, as the creator of probability theory, applied this theory to faith and proposed a "wager." He begins by making a distinction among people: 1) Those who have found God and serve him--happy and wise. 2) Those who have not found God but diligently seek him--unhappy, but wise. 3) Those who have not found God and live without seeking him--unhappy and fools. He has nothing but disdain for the third group. "It is an indispensable duty to seek when we are in doubt." He addresses the wager to the second group.

Blaise Pascal's Wager (No. 177). Either (a) there is a God who will send only the religious people to heaven or (b) there is not. To be religious is to wager for (a). To fail to be religious is to wager for (b). We can't settle the question whether (a) or (b) is the case, for if God exists, he is infinitely incomprehensible to us. But (a) is clearly vastly better than (b). With (a) infinite bliss is guaranteed, while with (b) we are still in the miserable human condition of facing death with no assurance as to what lies beyond. We must wager; it is not optional. So (a) is clearly the best wager: if we gain, we gain all; if we lose, we lose nothing. If we have problems in believing we must bring ourselves to believe against reason by cultivating belief—preparing ourselves morally so that God may give us the faith that we seek, praying and attending church. What do we have to lose?

Here's an Illustration: Would you bet $1 for a chance to win $1 billion if the odds are 50%? 20%? 10%? 5%? 1%? .1%? .01%? .001%? We all would! Now what are the chances that God exists and will reward your faith with an eternal bliss? The payoff is not a billion but an infinite amount, so we should wager for faith.

Some objections: 1) What if the odds that theism is true are reduced to .00001 or .000001? Since the expected payoff is infinite it doesn't matter. It's still a better bet, especially since we have to bet on something. 2) If I bet on God when God doesn't exist I've based my life on a lie with no afterlife punishment. But if one bets on atheism when God in fact exists there awaits eternal punishment. 3) Even if I love to sin--it's my whole lifestyle, how bad could a devout life be in comparison to the possible alternative of eternal punishment? Besides, religious people seem happy, fewer divorces, fewer suicides.

Could the wager be reiterated for gods who also offer infinite payoffs, thus nullifying the force of the wager? What if there is a god, Zeus, Baal, Molech, or Bali, who prepares a particularly nasty fate for devout Christians? But not all gods are as probable! Two responses: 1) There is some historical evidence that a theistic God exists, scriptures, historical reports of divine manifestations and the millions of adherents over the years. **i)** It is a better bet to go with a religion that has a long history and some claim to evidence. **ii)** One must consider the respective payoffs, other things being equal, and go for the deity that offers the more attractive afterlife and/or nastiest form of damnation. **iii)** One must go for the lowest common denominator in terms of tolerance--keeping one's faith as ecumenical as one dares, and balance this with i & ii above. 2) Anselm has provided a definition of God as the greatest conceivable being. This eliminates Zeus, Baal, Molech, and Bali. But consider Ockham's Razor: the simplest viewpoint is the best viewpoint.

Brief Evaluation: Atheist J.L. Mackie wrote: "It is clear that, given his assumptions, the argument goes through. Everything turns, therefore, on the acceptability of those assumptions." In fact, he admits, even if the odds against God's existence are close to, but not quite to infinity, one would still have the better odds in betting to believe in God's existence. For we would be betting one happy life "free of religious commitments" against an infinity of happy lives. Richard Swinburne: "A non-religious system would have to be very much more probable than the Christian system for it to be rational to adopt it." ["The Christian Wager" (Religious Studies 4, 1969)].

What about reversing the wager? James Cargile in Cahn & Shatz in Contemporary Philosophy Of Religion (Oxford, 1982), proposed a different kind of wager: Either (a) there is a God who will send you to heaven only if you commit a painful ritual suicide within an hour of first reading this, or (b) there is not. We cannot settle the question whether (a) or (b) is the case. But (a) is vastly preferable to (b), since in situation (a), infinite bliss is guaranteed, while in (b) we are left in the usual miserable human condition. So we should wager for (a) by performing the suicidal ritual.

J.L.Mackie: "**There might be a god who looked with more favor on honest doubters or atheists who proportioned their belief to the evidence, than on mercenary manipulators of their own understandings.**" Richard Dawkins concurred when he wrote, "We are talking about a bet...Would you bet on God's valuing dishonestly faked belief (or even honest belief) over skepticism?" "Pascal's wager could only ever be an argument for *feigning* belief in God. And the God that you claim to believe in had better not be of the omniscient kind or he'll see through that deception." [The God Delusion, p. 104].

Pascal's wager can be said to be a form of the adage that less proof is demanded for a higher risk situation. "The greater the risk, the less proof is required." When a bomb threat is called in, the authorities don't need much evidence to justify evacuating the building. Here, the risk is Hell, isn't it? But the risk factor is based upon the Christian historical claims, is it not? And the Christian claim is a very large one and very hard to defend from historical evidence as we'll see. So the amount of risk is mitigated by the meager evidence for the large claim. Muslims claim that you will go to hell if you don't convert to Islam too, but you cannot be a Muslim and also a Christian. Both religions offer some evidence to believe, but Christians think their faith has more evidence on its behalf than Islam, and one billion Muslims think otherwise. But according to both religions the other group is going to hell. So choose wisely. The risk is the same because a lot is at stake. Both are calling in a proverbial bomb threat. On the one hand, one claims if you stay in one building you will die, whereas a different one claims that if you leave and go into another building you will die. How Pascal's wager helps us with this quandary is itself a quandary.

Those who don't believe either of these religions just think that the historical evidence is below the threshold of proof needed to see any danger or risk in choosing not to believe. It would be comparable to someone claiming, "the sky is falling." When it comes to "bomb threats," they've heard too many of them from too many religions. Such claims are the equivalent of someone "crying wolf" way too many times.

SETTING ASIDE REASON IN RELIGIOUS MATTERS: Soren Kierkegaard (1813-1855). Kierkegaard attempted to argue that objective inquiry is totally inappropriate in religious matters. When we approach a question objectively we treat the truth as an object, whereas if we approach a question subjectively we treat the truth as a subject to which the knower is related. On which side is the truth to be found?

The objective way to pursue truth rests upon the approximation process, Kierkegaard argued, based upon Gotthold Lessing's argument that historical knowledge is insufficient grounds for the Christian faith (see my section on "Historical Evidence and Christianity"). For him, historical evidence is only approximate. So he argues we cannot base our eternal happiness on any approximation of the truth, since it will never produce the infinite personal interest demanded by religious faith. An infinite personal interest makes the greatest possible sacrifices on the smallest chance of success. Faith for Kierkegaard must be decisive. Belief excludes doubt because the conclusion of belief is a resolution--a decision. This kind of faith requires a "leap" beyond the evidence, a leap that cannot be justified by objective reasoning. "Without risk there is no faith." Moreover, one cannot have an authentic faith without being totally committed to it. On which side is the truth? Who has the greater certainty? Who has the greater faith? One who passionately takes a greater risk based on little evidence, or one who looks into the matter objectively?

The example of Socrates. Socrates risks his entire life based on 'IF' there was immortality. Kierkegaard asks, "Is there any better proof capable of being given for the immortality of the soul?"

Brief Evaluation: Something is to be said for taking risks and the commitment involved--admirable, as in the case of the patriot, or loyalty of a friend when evidence suggests you are guilty. But what about misplaced commitment and loyalty? "Given that faith is a leap, how does one decide which faith to 'jump for'?" Also, "What would we make of a religious person who calmly informs us that she is well aware that some of her beliefs are logically contradictory, or they conflict with well-known facts, yet she finds this no obstacle to holding these beliefs?" [Peterson, Hasker, Reichenbach, & Basinger in Reason and Religious Belief (Oxford, 1991, p. 40]. Robert Merrihew Adams asks the crucial question, "Whether the maximization of sacrifice and risk are so valuable in religion as to make objective improbability a desirable characteristic of religious beliefs." [Robert Merrihew Adams, in "Kierkegaard's Arguments Against Objective Reasoning in Religion," The Monist, Vol. 60, No. 2, 1977]. J.L. Mackie: "He seems to be arguing from a position, not to a position." He wants to show what Christianity is, but this means he must show it as he conceives it. He asks whether Kierkegaard thinks the only kind of commitment worthy of the name is one which accepts a paradoxical belief with no objective reasons in its favor. Hence Kierkegaard advocates "a sort of intellectual Russian roulette." [The Miracle of Theism, (Clarendon Press, 1982, p. 216). For a very interesting positive study of Kierkegaard and William James, see C. Stephen Evans, Subjectivity and Religious Belief (Eerdmans, 1978)].

FAITH AND REASON IN DIALOGUE: SOFT RATIONALISM OF William Abraham (MY VIEW): "Religious belief-systems can be rationally evaluated, although conclusive proof of such systems is impossible." [William J. Abraham, An Introduction to the Philosophy of Religion, (Prentice-Hall, 1985, pp. 104-113. See also Basil Mitchell, The Justification of Religious Belief, (Oxford University Press, 1981); Peterson, Hasker, Reichenbach, & Basinger in Reason and Religious Belief (Oxford, 1991), pp. 41-44; and C. Stephen Evans, Philosophy of Religion (IVP, 1985), pp.18-29]. Religious beliefs should be assessed only as a complete belief system, or world-view, never in stark isolation. "A world view is a set of assumptions or presuppositions which we hold about the basic make-up of our world." -James Sire, in The Universe Next Door. "A world-view is a way of viewing or interpreting all of reality--a world-view is like a set of colored glasses." –Norman Geisler & W. Watkins, in Worlds Apart, (Baker Books, 1989). A more (or less) consistent set of assumptions or presuppositions forms a world-view. Basic presuppositions answer questions about the nature of God, the world, human beings, our destiny, ethics, history, etc. A.N. Whitehead: "some assumptions appear so obvious that people do not know that they are assuming because no other way of putting things has ever occurred to them." [Science and the Modern World (p. 49)].

Here are some things to know about world-views: 1) Everyone has one; 2) They are pre-theoretical--before thought. We don't first get to them by thinking about them. Rather when we come to think about them, we find them already there, already under-girding anything we do. We don't argue to them, we argue from them, although we can argue away from them. 3) They are communal--shared by a community; caught, not taught. [See Walsh & Middleton, The Transforming Vision (IVP, 1984, pp.17ff)]. 4) They are much larger than particular religions, philosophies, and theologies. 5) While there are major outlines of world-views that many people share, world-views themselves include moral and political ways of viewing the world, so there are probably as many world-views as there are people. This book is a critical evaluation of the major tenets of a broadly evangelical Christian world-view.

William Abraham: "It should be clear that evaluating world-views will never be based on probabilistic arguments, since one cannot simply isolate one presupposition for evaluation. The case must be cumulative--a case must be built slowly." It is based upon cumulative case type arguments like "jurisprudence, literary exegesis, history, philosophy, and science." "One must be well educated in the relevant moral, aesthetic, or spiritual possibilities." But, "mastering all the relevant data and warrants needed to exercise the required personal judgment seems remote and impractical...This is surely beyond the capabilities of most ordinary mortals." "One simply has to proceed, often in an ad hoc fashion, and work through the issues as honestly and rigorously as possible."

This is exactly what I am attempting to do in this book, realizing my limitations as an ordinary mortal. William J. Abraham: "The different pieces of evidence taken in isolation are defective, but taken together they reinforce one another and add up to a substantial case. What is vital to realize is that there is no formal calculus into which all the evidence can be fitted and assessed. There is an irreducible element of personal judgment, which weighs up the evidence taken as a whole." **Therefore, I consider this book to be one single argument against Christianity, with each section as a subset of that one argument. Each section of this argument depends upon the others for its force, since no single one of them alone can bear the whole weight of showing that the Christian world-view is false. In evaluating this one argument of mine, it's proper and fitting to do so as a whole, especially since this is the only way to properly evaluate world-views.**

This book is my personal judgment as I reflect on the reasons and pieces of evidence supporting Christianity. While I am not considered a scholar on any one the issues I write about, I quote extensively from those who are considered scholars on those issues. If my arguments are considered defective in some areas, then refer to the works I quote from. As I said in the *Introduction*: "No one today can master all of the relevant issues, certainly not me. I am painfully aware of many of the objections that Christians can make to my arguments, but my arguments still hold sway over me. I have researched enough that I am very satisfied with my conclusions."

My judgment will not necessarily be yours. You may object to certain arguments of mine that are convincing to me, and you may be more informed about that objection than I am. But remember, there are people who are more informed than you are on the Jewish Holocaust who deny that it ever took place as told. It's just that when I weigh the sum total of all that I know, I believe I am rational and correct to reject Christianity. It just doesn't make sense to me. Just like any jury has difficulties in assessing the case, we must go with the position that makes the most over-all sense of everything that we know.

I consider my expertise (if I have one) in the area of the Big Picture. I learned this from Dr. Strauss at LCS. Someone has to stand back from all of the trees to see the forest and describe what it looks like. There are scholars in every field of learning that examine the specific issues in their turf and produce well-argued positions. I knew a professor once who examined the precise meaning of the word "Yaweh" in a master's thesis. I've never spent that much time doing that, have you? His answer was, "we don't know." But that's what I mean when I talk about the minutia, the specific details.

There are a whole host of minor details I have never examined in any depth at all. Many scholars do the groundwork for me. There are other scholars who will take these minutia-type conclusions and build on them to form a view of the faith of Israel, and others who will build on that to form a view of the OT itself, and still others who build on all previous work to build a theology of the OT. Other scholars will build on these conclusions to form a view of the relationship of the OT to those of NT scholars who reached their conclusions in the same way. Archeologists will step in and either confirm or deny any of these claims, which will start the whole process all over again. Philosophers will examine these theological conclusions in the light of reason and try to make sense of it all, which may cause the theologians to see things differently.

We need every level of scholarship, but we need someone who specializes in the Big Picture. But as I said no one can possibly have a scholar's grasp on every issue in this whole chain of scholarship. So in trying to view the forest, it is really tough to keep a handle on all of what goes on, but that's what I will attempt. I will attempt to see the Big Picture. Where I haven't studied something out as much as others, I will point you to those scholars who have. They argue for me.

When I first told Dr. William Lane Craig that I am now a consummate doubter, I said it was because I couldn't make any sense of my former Christian faith. Even though "faith seeks understanding," following Anselm's advice, the understanding didn't follow for me. He responded that there are many things we don't understand about quantum mechanics, but just because we don't understand it, doesn't mean we should reject quantum mechanics. [The same thing can be said about the mechanism for gravity. We can use Newton's math to predict how objects fall, but "no one has since given any machinery" for what causes gravitational attraction! [See Richard P. Feynman, Six Easy Pieces (Helix, 1995), pp. 107-113].

But it isn't the same as for quantum mechanics (or gravity, either). These things have a mathematical system to them, along with some cold hard evidence behind them. Incomprehensible for now, but since there must be a reason for this universe and its form, scientists should continue trying to figure these things out. After all, we know that we exist in this universe; so continuing to try to understand the nature of our existence is what's required. What we don't know is whether we truly experience a Trinitarian Christian God of the Bible. With such a theology the goal is to see if such a God exists, and whether or not certain miraculous events ever occurred.

I seriously question whether the Trinitarian Christian God of the Bible exists. I don't question whether this universe exists. I just want to figure out how it works. This is the difference that makes all the difference. In trying to figure out God and his purposes, we end up trying to understand something that doesn't need to be explained, because we cannot understand something that doesn't exist.

6 The Christian Illusion of Rational and Moral Superiority.

Many Christians assume a certain kind of rational and/or moral superiority over any other system of belief and thought, especially atheism. According to them, their beliefs are rationally superior in the sense that Christianity wins hands down in the marketplace of ideas. They claim that a compelling case can be made for believing in Christianity over any other system of belief and thought. Likewise, according to them, their moral foundation is also superior in the sense that Christianity provides the only sufficient basis for acting morally in life. Other moral systems either do not, or cannot, provide a sufficient basis for morality. Let me offer some brief comments about both of these assumptions, each in turn.

The Illusion of Rational Superiority. The way Christians think of atheists in general, and of ex-Christians in particular, is due to what my friend Dr. James Sennett calls, "The Illusion of Rational Superiority," in his forthcoming book: This Much I Know: A Postmodern Apologetic.

Dr. James Sennett argues against the idea that people who reject Christianity do so because they are either "ignorant," "stupid" or "dishonest with the facts." That is, he argues against the idea that a "fully rational rejection of Christianity is impossible." Dr. Sennett calls this objection the Christian "Illusion of Rational Superiority." It's simply an illusion, he claims. [Although, as a Christian philosopher he argues it is an unnecessary illusion due to the fact that even though he has a reasonable faith, it is "not rationally compelling to all."]

As an example of this illusion, Sennett quotes from Bill Bright, the late founder and president of Campus Crusade for Christ, who wrote: "During my fifty-five years of sharing the good news of the Savior ... I have met very few individuals who have honestly considered the evidence and yet deny that Jesus Christ is the Son of God and the Savior of men. To me, the evidence confirming the deity of the Lord Jesus Christ is overwhelmingly conclusive to any honest, objective seeker after truth."

As another milder example of this illusion, consider Os Guinness's book, titled: In Two Minds: The Dilemma of Doubt and How to Resolve It (IVP, 1976) Guinness discusses the main reasons why people, including Christians themselves, have doubts about Christianity: there is doubt from a faulty view of God; doubt from weak (intellectual) foundations; doubt from a lack of commitment; doubt from lack of growth; doubt from unruly emotions; doubt from fearing to believe; doubt from insistent inquisitiveness; and doubt from impatience or giving up.

Since Guinness was arguing on behalf of his Christian faith, he doesn't mention one other reason to doubt: **doubt from a lack of adequate reasons**. And he fails to note that in the above list of reasons to doubt one could just as well reverse them: believing from the need to be grateful to someone; believing from the need for a God; believing from weak (intellectual) foundations; believing from the need to be committed; believing in hopes of personal growth; believing because of unruly emotions; believing because of the fear of doubting; believing from not being inquisitive enough; and believing from giving up too soon. While Guinness isn't as blatant as others about this, we still find it here with him. There are some very solid reasons to believe, we're told, so if you doubt, it's because of some fault within you.

But Sennett argues that the Christian cannot overlook "one simple but powerful fact: most of the truly brilliant, deepest thinking, most profoundly influential movers and shakers of the last two hundred years have not been Christians. Neither Albert Einstein nor Bertrand Russell nor Sigmund Freud nor Stephen Hawking nor Karl Marx professed Jesus as lord. And the list goes on. To suggest that these people failed to believe because of ignorance or some rational defect is ludicrous." (Of course, the illusion runs both ways, Sennett claims. There is no rational superiority for unbelief, either. Atheist Thomas Nagel is quoted as saying he was made uneasy "by the fact that some of the most intelligent and well-informed people I know are religious believers").

Sennett informs us that "if there is one lesson that modern epistemology has taught us, it is that almost nothing is as rationally certain as 'the illusion' claims Christianity to be. In other words, almost nothing is so obvious that one could never rationally reject it." Furthermore, it seems possible that "one could rationally deny almost any claim, even if that claim is true." There are plenty of philosophical reasons for Sennett's argument, and many historical examples. The fact is, many scholars have indeed examined the historical evidence for Christianity and they regard that evidence as flawed. [See www.infidels.com for some examples].

This book you are reading presents a sustained case against this illusion. It's simply an illusion that Christians have a rationally superior faith. I hope to reveal this as an illusion and to further show that there are several very strong reasons to reject Christianity.

The Illusion of Moral Superiority. Many Christians will maintain they have a superior foundation for knowing and for choosing to do what is good. They claim to have objective ethical standards for being good, based in a morally good creator God, along with the best motivation for being good, which is an eternal reward in the presence of a loving God. These Christians will also claim that the atheist has no ultimate justification for being moral, much less a motivation for being good when it conflicts with their own personal self-interest. According to Christians, there is no "ultimate reason" why atheists should choose to do good or be kind to others. According to these Christians, atheists live on the memory of a Christian ethic, a borrowed ethic, because they don't have an objective basis for morality themselves. They will claim that atheists do not have a good reason to condemn murder, brutality and torture. Christians will even claim that atheists simply do not have a good reason to refrain from murdering, raping and torturing other people.

Dr. William Lane Craig quotes with approval Fyodor Dostoyevsky's character Ivan Karmazov, who said, "If God doesn't exist, everything is permissible." Dr. Craig summed up part of Dostoyevsky's defense of theism in his novel <u>Brothers Karamazov</u>, with these words: "if the existence of God is denied, then one is landed in complete moral relativism, so that no act, regardless of how dreadful or heinous, can be condemned by the atheist." [Apologetics: An Introduction, p. 37]. "If life ends at the grave, then it makes no difference whether one has lived as a Stalin or as a saint....On this basis, a writer like Ayn Rand is absolutely correct to praise the virtues of selfishness. Live totally for self; no one holds you accountable! Indeed, it would be foolish to do anything else, for life is too short to jeopardize it by acting out of anything but pure self-interest. Sacrifice for another person would be stupid." (p. 42). "In a world without God, who is to say which values are right and which are wrong? Who is to judge that the values of Adolf Hitler are inferior to those of a saint? The concept of morality loses all meaning in a universe without God. There can be no right and wrong. This means that it is impossible to condemn war, oppression, or crime as evil. Nor can one praise brotherhood, equality, and love as good. For in a universe without God, good and evil do not exist—there is only the bare valueless fact of existence, and there is no one to say you are right and I am wrong." (pp. 42-43). Craig again: "The world was horrified when it learned that at camps like Dachau the Nazis had used prisoners for medical experiments on living humans. But why not? If God does not exist, there can be no objection to using people as human guinea pigs." (p. 51). [See Francis Schaeffer's similar comments in He Is There And He Is Not Silent (Tyndale House, 1972), pp. 21-27].

The Illusion of a Superior Christian Ethical Standard. The Christian claims to have absolute and objective ethical standards for knowing right from wrong, which is something they claim atheists don't have. The Christian standards are grounded in the commands of a good creator God, and these commands come from God's very nature and are revealed to them in the Bible. There is a philosophical foundation for this claim, and then there is the case Christians present that the Bible reveals God's ethical commands. Both are illusions of superiority. It is an illusion that the Christian moral theory is superior, and it is an illusion that Christians know any better than others how they should morally behave in our world.

Here I'll focus mainly on the philosophical foundation for the Christian standard. There are two bases for grounding Christian ethical standards. The first is known as the **Divine Command Theory**. I'll deal with this theory first. The second basis is **Natural Law Theory**, which I will dispense with briefly later. I will show that neither of these bases for Christian ethics offers believers a special access to moral truth that unbelievers don't also share. Christian moral foundations are not superior ones.

The Divine Command Theory goes like this: Morality is based upon what God commands. No other reasons are needed but that God so commanded it. If God commanded it, then it is right. If God forbids it, then it is wrong. Of this theory Socrates asked a fundamental question: "Is conduct right because the gods command it, or do gods command it because it is right?" [in Plato's Euthyphro, known forever since as the *Euthyphro dilemma*].

Ever since Socrates asked this question every philosopher who has dealt with Christian ethics has commented on it. But most all commentators will admit that this theory has some huge intellectual problems to overcome. **If we say, on the one hand, that something is right because God commands it**, then the only reason why we should do something is that God commands it. It makes God's commands arbitrary, because there is no reason why God commanded something other than the fact that he did. If this is the case, God could've commanded something else, or even something contrary, or something horribly evil and simply declared it good. If God is the creator of morality like he's purportedly the creator of the universe, then he could have simply declared any act good, and there would be no moral reason to distinguish such a God from the Devil. This presents us with the "seemingly absurd position that even the greatest atrocities might be not only acceptable but morally required if God were to command them." [John Arthur, "Morality Without God" in Garry Brodsky, et al., eds,. Contemporary Readings in Social and Political Ethics (Prometheus Books, 1984)].

Furthermore, this makes the whole concept of the goodness of God meaningless. If we think that the commands of God are good merely because he commands them, then his commands are....well....just his commands. We cannot call them good, for to call them good we'd have to have a standard above them to proclaim that they are indeed good commands. But on this theory they are just God's commands. God doesn't command us to do good things, he just commands us to do things. "All that could mean is that God wants us to do what he wants us to do." [John Arthur, "Morality Without God"). And God isn't a good God either, he is just God. For there would be no standard above God for us to be able to proclaim that God is good. He is just God.

So if God were to tell us he's good, then that only means that he labels his character with the word "good." The word "good" here is merely a word God uses to apply to himself without any real definitional content, apart from the fact that God says this word applies to himself—see the circularity? The bottom line here is that if there is no moral standard for us to appeal to when we're assessing the claim that God is good, and all we have to go on is the fact that God said he was good, then we cannot assess whether or not God is good. We still haven't been given an answer to what he means by the word "good."

If we say, on the other hand, that God commands what is right because it is right, then we must ask about this higher standard of morality that is being appealed to. If this is so, then we are advocating some higher standard above God that is independent of God that makes his commands good. Rather than declaring what is good, now God recognizes what is good and commands us to do likewise. If we ask why God commands it, the answer would have to be found in some higher standard than God himself. But where did this standard come from that is purportedly higher than God? God is supposed to be the creator of the laws of nature and the moral laws we must live by.

The Divine Command theory is in such disrepute in today's philosophical circles that only modified Divine Command theories are being discussed today. Christian apologist J.P. Moreland actually claims, "I'm not a divine command theorist...this view implies that morality is merely grounded in God's will as opposed to His nature. That's not my view. I think God's will is ultimately expressed in keeping with his nature. Morality is ultimately grounded in the nature of God, not independently of God." [in Does God Exist: The Great Debate, with Kai Nielsen (Thomas Nelson, 1990), pp. 130-131; and also in Scaling the Secular City: A Defense of Christianity (Baker, 1987). After stating this, he refers to Robert M. Adam's "Moral Arguments for Theistic Belief," in <u>Rationality and Religious Belief</u>, ed., C.F. Delaney (Notre Dame Press, 1979)].

I'll take a look at Robert M. Adams' view next. But think of what Moreland is saying here. He's saying that morality is grounded in God's nature, not in his commands. **But this is a difference that makes no difference**. It does no good to step back behind the commands of God to God's purported nature at all. For we'd still want to know whether or not God's nature is good. God cannot be known to be good here either, without a standard of goodness that shows he is good. For unless there is a standard that shows God is good beyond the mere fact that God declares that his nature is good, we still don't know whether God is good. Again, God is....well....just God.

Furthermore, we usually call someone good when they make good choices. So an additional question here is whether or not God has ever made any good choices. To choose means there were alternatives to choose from. Did God at any point in the past ever choose his supposedly good nature? Christians will say he has always been good. Then when did he ever make a choice for this particular nature, which he calls "good" over-against, a different nature? At no time in the past do we ever see him doing this. But if he did choose his moral nature, then it stands to reason that the nature he chose is, by definition, good. God's nature would subsequently be called good by him no matter what nature he chose, if he ever did choose a particular moral nature. Again, all we can say is that God is....well....God, and his commands are....well....his commands.

Robert M. Adams' "A Modified Divine Command Theory of Ethical Wrongness," in Gene Outka and John P. Reeder, ed., <u>Religion and Morality: A Collection of Essays</u> (Anchor, 1973), along with Philip Quinn's, <u>Divine Commands and Moral Requirements</u> (Oxford University Press, 1978), are the best alternatives when discussing Modified Divine Command theories. The modified Divine Command theory of Robert M. Adams claims that God must properly command what is loving, or consistent with that which is loving, because that is his very nature. God is love. Therefore God's commands flow from his loving nature. God can only command what is good and loving.

The basic criticism of Adams' view has been stated adequately enough by the late Louis P. Pojman: "If we prefer the modified divine command theory to the divine command theory, then we must say that the divine command theory is false, and the modified divine command theory becomes equivalent to the autonomy thesis: God commands the Good (or right) because it is good (or right), and the Good (or right) is not good (or right) simply because God commands it. Furthermore, if this is correct, then we can discover our ethical duties through reason, independent of God's command. For what is good for his creatures is so objectively. We do not need God to tell us that it is bad to cause unnecessary suffering or that it is good to ameliorate suffering; reason can do that. It begins to look like the true version of ethics is what we called 'secular ethics.'" [Ethics: Discovering Right and Wrong 5th ed. (Wadsworth, 2006), pp. 255-56]. "If Adams wants to claim that it is goodness plus God's command that determines what is right," Pojman rightly asked, "what does God add to rightness that is not there simply with goodness...If love or goodness prescribes act A, what does A gain by being commanded by God? **Materially, nothing at all**." It is at this point where both a modified divine command ethic and a secular ethic share the exact same grounding. Why? Because then with Pojman, we must ask what difference it makes whether or not the same ethical principles come from "a special personal authority (God) or from the authority of reason?" (p. 256). For this reason Kai Nieslen argues that the Divine Command Theory in its modified forms "does not meet secular ethics head on," and consequently, "does not challenge...secular ethics." [in Does God Exist: The Great Debate, (p. 99); For a further critique of Divine Command Theory see Michael Martin's The Case Against Christianity (Temple Univ. Press, 1991), pp. 229-251].

Steve Lovell also defends this position that God's commands are rooted in His essential nature (known as the "Divine Nature Theory" or DNT), in "C.S. Lewis and the Euthyphro Dilemma" (July 14, 2002) found at, http://www.theism.net/article/29. Lovell tries to explain something about the inherent circularity of this position. "The point is that any explicit justification of my belief that God is good will be circular. But that point can be happily conceded. Circularity need not be vicious, and the kind of circularity involved here is not in any way peculiar to my position. Indeed, any theory that posits objective values will face the same problem, which is essentially a skeptical one. A fair skeptical challenge is one that does not fault a position for not answering questions that no position could be expected to answer. But no position could help us to provide explicit non-circular justifications for all of our moral beliefs, and DNT is no exception here."

But I have two questions here. One question that remains to be answered is whether he's correct that any theory that posits "objective values" will face "the same problem." If by the term "objective values" Lovell means "ultimate objective values," or "values objectively grounded in a divine being," then he is indicting his own theory all over again, and so his accusation here is true by his own concession. It would also mean Lovell is not offering a fair alternative to his own theory for comparison, since there are alternative non-ultimate objective ethical systems which do not face an infinite regress of moral standards.

The second question is whether or not the circularity that is inherent in defending the DNT reveals something metaphysical about the nature of God's existence? I personally think the inherent circularity in trying to defend the DNT points to the non-existence of God.

In an explanation to me Lovell points to an analogous case: "It might be helpful to consider the similarities of a non-moral case: trusting our senses. One theory of why we should trust our senses is that natural selection would have eliminated species whose senses weren't reliable. But why should we accept this theory? Because it's confirmed by scientific data? But that data comes to us through our senses! The justification is circular."

But is this really an analogous case for our moral faculties? We are able to justify our senses pragmatically, but that's all. They seem to help us live and work and play in our world. Can we trust our senses to tell us what is real? No. Reality is filtered through our human senses. With the senses of a dog, a porpoise, a snake, or a bird, reality would look and feel different to us. There is so much light and so much sound that we cannot see and hear it's amazing. We know there is much more to see than what we can see, and we know there is much more to hear than what we can hear. But if we saw and heard it all, it might be likened to "white noise." About the only thing we can trust our senses to tell us is that we have them and that we sense something, and therefore we conclude that something is there. So in a like manner our moral faculties merely help us live and work and play in a pragmatic sense in this world. But what Lovell needs to explain is whether or not we can trust them to tell us something about God, just like I wonder whether our five senses can be trusted to tell us what is truly real.

[I believe that the Euthyphro dilemma concerning morality also applies to logic and reason. Is something logical or reasonable because God created logic and reason, or must God adhere to the principles of logic and reason].

The second philosophical basis for grounding Christian Ethics is **Natural Law Theory**. This is the ethical system of Aristotle as adopted by Thomas Aquinas, and it has been the dominant one in the history of the church. It's an antiquated view of morals today, in that it presupposes the world has values built into it by God, such that moral rules can be derived from nature. [Modern virtue ethics are more interesting because these theories are distancing themselves from the older Thomistic view that moral rules can be derived from nature itself]. But if Natural Law theories are true, then, according to James Rachels, "This means that the religious believer has no special access to moral truth. The believer and the nonbeliever are in exactly the same position. God has made all people rational, not just believers; and so for believer and nonbeliever alike, making a responsible moral judgment is a matter of listening to reason and following its directives." [The Elements of Moral Philosophy (McGraw-Hill, 1993), p. 53].

And this is exactly my point. The foundations of Christian morality are not superior ones to atheistic morality, based upon Christian assumptions. Neither of these two bases for Christian ethics offers believers a special access to moral truth that unbelievers don't share, unless Christians are willing to grant that God could command us to do evil if he had wanted to, a conclusion that infringes on the whole notion of the goodness of God. Christian moral foundations are simply not superior ones.

Besides, there are several ethical systems of thought that do not require a prior belief in God, like Social Contract Theories, Utilitarianism, Virtue Ethics, Kantianism, and John Rawls' theory of justice. Ethical Relativism isn't the boogey man that some Christians make it out to be either, since relativism "is compatible with complete agreement on all ethical matters," whereas "ethical absolutism is compatible with wide-spread disagreement." [Michael Martin, Atheism: A Philosophical Justification (Temple, 1990), p. 9].

According to Christian philosopher Thomas V. Morris, "It has...been argued in various ways over the past century that the evolutionary process somehow provides a framework of moral reference. Basic human instincts could be cited as loci for the moral constraints needed in society. The physical, survival, functional needs of men in society or community could act as moral matrices for the guiding of moral motions...there are many possible bases or explanations for moral motions in an impersonal universe. They could easily have arisen from evolutionary or community survival needs, for example, and consequently, when identified as a human 'aspiration,' the practice of making moral distinctions could be said to be 'fulfilled' when it is successfully functional within those contexts." [Thomas V. Morris' in Francis Schaeffer's Apologetics: A Critique (Moody Press, 1976, pp. 69].

Michael Shermer makes such an interesting argument in his book, The Science of Good and Evil (Henry Holt, 2004), that "morality exists outside the human mind in the sense of being not just a trait of individual humans, but a human trait; that is, a human universal." According to him we "inherit" from our Paleolithic ancestors our morality and ethics, then we "fine-tune and tweak them according to our own cultural preferences, and apply them within our own unique historical circumstances." As such, "moral principles, derived from the moral sense, are not absolute, where they apply to all people in all cultures under all circumstances all of the time. Neither are moral principles relative, entirely determined by circumstance, culture and history. Moral principles are provisionally true—that is, they apply to most people in most cultures in most circumstances most of the time." [pp. 18-23].

Christian morality is largely in the same boat. Even if Christians did have objective moral standards, they cannot be objectively certain that they know them, or that they know how they apply to specific real life cases! Just look at Christianity's past (as we shall look at later) and you'll see what I mean. Believers will still disagree with each other on a multifaceted number of ethical issues, whether they start with the Bible as God's revelation, or the morality gleaned from a Natural Law Theory. Just take a brief tour of Church history, or read a book like J. Philip Wogman's Christian Ethics: A Historical Introduction (Westminister, 1993), to see for yourself. Willard M. Swartley's book, Slavery, Sabbath, War & Women: Case Issues in Biblical Interpretation (Herald Press, 1983) reveals how people who share the same views of the Bible can vehemently disagree with what God wants them to do. According to Sam Harris, "People have been cherry-picking the Bible for millennia to justify their every impulse, moral and otherwise." Christians use their "own moral intuitions to authenticate the wisdom of the Bible." "We decide what is good in the Good Book." [Letter to a Christian Nation, (Knopf, 2006), pp. 18, 49. As far as Biblical and Christian ethics go, see Michael Martin, The Case Against Christianity (Temple Univ. Press, 1991), pp. 62-196, and Richard Dawkins, The God Delusion, pp. 235-272].

Since Dr. Craig mentioned Hitler, Auschwitz, and Dachau, in his apologetics book, consider this: Germany was a Christian nation—the heart of the Lutheran Protestant Reformation! How could a Christian people allow these evil deeds to happen and even be his willing executioners? How? The Holocaust and the horrible things done to millions of Jews and various minorities is more a problem for the Christian ethic, because it was a more or less Christian nation that did these horrible deeds. [As to whether or not Hitler was an atheist, Michael Shermer quotes him in 1938 as saying: "I believe today that I am acting in the sense of the Almighty Creator. By warding off the Jews I am fighting for the Lord's work." Shermer argues that "Hitler and the Nazis were not atheists." (See Shermer, The Science of Good and Evil, pp. 153-154). However, it can still be argued that Hitler was "just cynically exploiting the religiosity of his audience," according to Richard Dawkins. Nonetheless, the claim that Hitler was an atheist "is far from clear." See Dawkins' discussion in The God Delusion, pp. 272-278].

The truth of the matter is that Christian religious moralists are largely in the same boat as atheists. Kai Nielsen: "The religious moralist...doesn't have any better or any worse objectivity. Because, suppose he says, 'We should love God,' and then further suppose we ask the religious moralist, 'Why Love God...Why obey his commandments?' He basically would have to say, 'Because God is the perfect good, and God with his perfect goodness reveals to us the great value of self-respect for people. He shows that people are of infinite precious worth.' But even if you accept this, you could go on to ask, 'Why should you care? What difference does it make anyway whether people are of infinite precious worth?' Faced with such questioning, you will finally be pushed into a corner, where you say that 'It is important to me that people be regarded as being infinite worth because I just happen to care about people. It means to me that people should be treated with respect. So the religious moralist as well has to rely finally on his considered convictions. So if that too is subjective ground, then both the religious person and the secular person are in the same boat." [Kai Nielsen (with J.P. Moreland) Does God Exist: The Great Debate (Thomas Nelson, 1990), pp. 107-108].

The Illusion that Atheists Do Not Have A Motivation to be Good. Many Christians will claim that atheists simply do not have an "ultimate motivation" for being good, even if they can grasp what it means to do good for the most part. What motivates an atheist to be a good and kind person? Why should we act morally? Maybe this is the crux of the problem Christians seem to be harping on. J.P. Moreland accepts the fact that atheists can and in fact do good moral deeds, "But what I'm arguing," he says, "is, What would be the point? Why should I do these things if they are not satisfying to me or if they are not in my interests? [Does God Exist: The Great Debate (Thomas Nelson, 1990), pp. 118].

C. Stephen Layman argues in a similar fashion. He points out that the main difference between secular and religious moral views are that "the only goods available from a secular perspective are earthly goods," whereas a religious perspective "recognizes these earthly goods as good, but it insists that there are non-earthly or transcendent goods." Secular ethics, he says, must pay for the individual here on earth. "By way of contrast with the secular view, it is not difficult to see how morality might pay if there is a God of the Christian type." [The Shape of the Good: Christian Reflections on the Foundations of Ethics (Univ. of Notre Dame Press, 1991)].

Before we look at the atheistic motivation for being good, let's first consider the motivation that a Christian has for acting good and not bad. Christians claim that if we disbelieve and disobey God we'll "fry in hell," as Nielsen describes it. However, obeying for this reason "is pure prudence masquerading as morality.... that is hardly a good moral reason for doing anything." [Kai Nielsen (with J.P. Moreland) Does God Exist: The Great Debate, p. 108]. It would be akin to obeying a robber who has a gun placed against your head. **The carrot and stick method of morality** due to punishment and reward is, in the end, the same motivation an atheist has, except that the carrots and sticks are those rewards and punishments we receive here on earth, which are social, internal and personal.

Besides, a Christian who desires to do wrong always has an excuse for doing whatever wrong or evil he or she wants to do. He'll simply say, "God understands, he'll forgive me." This can be the justification for doing anything he wants to do. I know, I've done this, and so has every Christian who has ever knowingly gone against their conscience. Whatever motivation a Christian may have for being good will just fly out the window if he wants to do something against what he believes to be right. How else can so many Christians maintain love affairs if they consider them to be wrong? The very fact that many of these affairs last for months and years just tells us how long they can act contrary to the Bible and still feel God understands, and that God forgives.

C. Stephen Layman is correct that with the secular view ethical choices must pay for the individual here on earth, so there is no "ultimate motivation" to do good. But it doesn't follow from the lack of an "ultimate motivation" to be a good person that the atheist doesn't have a sufficient motivational grounding for being a good person. There are plenty of motives here on earth to be a good person, and it starts with an over-all life plan.

The late Louis P. Pojman argues that it is reasonable to choose and to act upon an over-all "life plan," even though there will be many times where I may have to act against my own immediate or short-term self-interest in keeping with that plan. "To have the benefits of the moral life—friendship, mutual love, inner peace, moral pride or satisfaction, and freedom from moral guilt—one has to have a certain kind of reliable character. All in all, these benefits are eminently worth having. Indeed, life without them may not be worth living."

"Character counts," Pojman wrote, and "habits harness us to predictable behavior. Once we obtain the kind of character necessary for the moral life--once we become virtuous--**we will not be able to turn morality on and off like a faucet.**" With such an understanding "there is no longer anything paradoxical in doing something not in one's interest, for while the individual moral act may occasionally conflict with one's self-interest, the entire life plan in which the act is embedded and from which it flows is not against the individual's self-interest." [Ethics: Discovering Right and Wrong 5th ed. (p. 188). For defenses of secular morality, see Kai Nielsen, Ethics Without God (Pemberton Books, 1973), Michael Shermer, The Science of Good and Evil (Henry Holt, 2005), Richard Carrier, Sense & Goodness Without God (2005), pp. 293-348, and Richard Dawkins, The God Delusion, 2006, pp. 209-233].

Michael Shermer asks the Christian one simple question. "What would you do if there were no God? Would you commit robbery, rape, and murder, or would you continue being a good and moral person? Either way the question is a debate stopper. If the answer is that you would soon turn to robbery, rape, or murder, then this is a moral indictment of your character, indicating you are not to be trusted because if, for any reason, you were to turn away from your belief in God, your true immoral nature would emerge...If the answer is that you would continue being good and moral, then apparently you can be good without God. QED." [Michael Shermer, The Science of Good and Evil, pp. 154-155].

The bottom line here is that, "If it is highly implausible to believe in God or immortality, then a secular ethic becomes attractive...there is something to be said for a person who can hold steadily on a course without telling himself or herself fairy tales. Moral integrity, fraternity, and love of humankind are worth subscribing to without a thought to whether or not such virtues will be rewarded in heaven." [Kai Nielsen (with J.P. Moreland) Does God Exist: The Great Debate (Thomas Nelson, 1990), pp. 108-109].

7 Does God Exist?

When it comes to God's existence our choices can be reduced to these: 1) Either something has always existed--always, or 2) something popped into existence out of absolutely nothing. Either choice seems extremely unlikely--or possibly even absurd. There is nothing in our experience that can help us grasp these two possibilities. But one of them is correct and the other false. We either start with the "brute fact" that something has always existed, or the "brute fact" that something popped into existence out of nothing. A third view is that, 3) Our existence in the universe is absurd to the core.

The Christian maintains that a good personal triune Creator has always existed. The atheist maintains that the material universe either popped into existence out of nothing, has always existed, is self-caused, or it's just a brute fact. Many atheists believe there may be other universes, which have each come into existence by their own big bangs. Atheist philosopher Quentin Smith claims that our universe came "from nothing, by nothing, and for nothing," in that it caused itself to exist ["The Reason that the Universe Exists Is That It Caused Itself to Exist," Philosophy 74 (1999); 579-86].

So we can understand why both G. W. Leibniz and Martin Heidegger claim the fundamental metaphysical question is this: "Why is there something rather than nothing at all?" Think about it. We should expect that nothing at all exists--nothing. Why? Because such a state of affairs requires no explanation. The fact that something exists demands an explanation for why it exists.

In light of this problem, Blaise Pascal, one of the great French Christian apologists of the 17th century claimed, "reason can decide nothing here." He maintained, "the heart has reasons which reason knows nothing of." He then advocated making a wager for the Christian faith against atheism. With everything to gain and nothing to lose he said the best bet is for faith. William James claimed that while reason cannot decide this issue it's quite possible that God wants us to take a step toward him in faith before he will reveal himself.

Why do atheists not believe in God? We begin by attacking the notion of God as incoherent. For instance, we claim that there is simply too much intense suffering in this world for there to be a good creator. Atheists generally think Christian theism inhibits scientific progress, creates class struggles, sexism, racism, mass neurosis, intolerance and environmental disasters. Christian thinkers, however, respond that atheism cannot give sufficient reasons why human beings experience consciousness, or why people should be morally good. Fyodor Dostoevsky is reported to have said, "If God didn't exist everything would be permissible." Christians also charge atheism with not being able to sufficiently answer what Albert Camus claimed was the fundamental philosophical question. It is this: "Why not commit suicide?" That is, if we cannot find meaning in our existence, then why not just end it all? Because of this conundrum Leo Tolstoy chose to believe in God "contrary to reason," and in so doing was "saved from suicide." [See, A Confession and the Gospel in Brief (Oxford, 1921)].

Atheists have also offered suggestions why people turn to religion. Sigmund Freud claimed that religion is an expression of the longing for a father figure. Ludwig Feuerbach claimed that God didn't make man in his image, but rather we made God in our image. Karl Marx taught that religion is the opium of the working class people. It is funded and pushed by the rich class in order to numb the working class from trying to right the injustices put on them by the rich class. Religion keeps the working class focused on a hope of bliss in the hereafter. Friedrich Nietzsche claimed that religion endures because weak people need it. For Jean Paul Sartre, God represented a threat to authentic morality. If God is autonomous, in the Calvinistic sense, then human beings cannot be responsible for themselves. He argued that the rejection of God makes morality and freedom possible, for only then can people take responsibility for their own choices.

Christians answer that all of these explanations depend upon whether or not God exists. For instance, if God does indeed exist, then we need him. Christianity may be a crutch for the weak, but if it is true, then we need a crutch because we're crippled. And, if God exists, then Sartre's admonition of autonomous freedom is nothing short of rebellion against God.

What reasons do Christians have for preferring to believe that God has always existed and created the universe? There are three main categories of arguments for God's existence that I'll mention. There are Ontological Arguments, Cosmological Arguments, and Teleological (or Design) Arguments.

Ontological Arguments –

Here's a very brief history of the Ontological Argument for the existence of God: Italian Anselm originated it around the 11th century. Duns Scotus and St Bonaventure accepted the argument, but William of Ockham did not. Italian Thomas Aquinas rejected it in the 13th century. Frenchman Rene Descartes resurrected it in the early 17th century, and then Spinoza and Leibniz added their versions of it. Prussian/German Immanuel Kant refuted it in the latter half of the 17th century, but Hegel argued for it in the 19th-century. Then in the past several decades Americans Norman Malcolm, Charles Hartshorne, and Alvin Plantinga have all defended it. Criticisms and debate about it abound in almost every philosophy textbook.

It is generally agreed that the Ontological Argument never converted anyone (even though Bertrand Russell once thought it was correct, but later changed his mind). It is an amazing argument—a philosopher's delight! This is the "most famous, the most mystifying, the most outrageous and irritating philosophical argument of all time." "It remains as one of the most controversial arguments in all of philosophy." Yet, "whenever I read the Ontological Argument, I have the same feeling that comes over me when I watch a really good magician. Nothing up this sleeve, nothing up the other sleeve; nothing in the hat; presto! A big fat rabbit. How can Anselm pull God out of an idea?" [Robert Paul Wolff in About Philosophy, (pp.284ff)].

Anselm's Ontological Argument for the Existence of God:

1) On the assumption that that than which nothing greater can be conceived is only in a mind, something greater can be conceived, because

2) Something greater can be thought to exist in reality as well.

3) The assumption is therefore contradictory: either there is no such thing even in the intellect, or it exists also in reality;

4) But it does exist in the mind of the fool (i.e. the doubter; Psalm 14:1);

5) Therefore that than which nothing greater can be conceived exists in reality as well as in the mind.

Anselm argued that even those who doubt the existence of God would have to have some understanding of what they were doubting: Namely, they would understand God to be a being than which nothing greater can be thought. Given that it is greater to exist outside the mind rather than just in the mind, a doubter who denied God's existence would be caught in a contradiction, because he or she would be saying that it is possible to think of something greater than a being than which nothing greater can be thought. Hence, God exists necessarily.

One major criticism of this argument comes from whether our conceptions of the greatest conceivable being might entail attributes that involve unrecognized inconsistencies or even contractions. Anthony Kenny, in The God of the Philosophers (Oxford, 1987), examined the principal attributes traditionally ascribed to theistic God, particularly omniscience and omnipotence, and argued that there can be no such being as the God of traditional natural theology. A lot of ink has been spilled over these kinds of issues.

Many Christian theologians are presently being pushed in the direction of Open Theism, i.e., that God exists in historical time in some sense, rather than being outside of time; for otherwise, God would not be a person. [See The Openness of God, (IVP, 1994). See also my section on "Prophecy and Biblical Authority"]. However, Paul Helm claimed that "the arguments used to show that God is in time, in effect support the view that God is finite." There is such a close connection between the timelessness of God and the spacelessness of God, Helm argued, that a denial of God's timelessness is also a denial of God's spacelessness. Therefore, he claims it's possible that "the belief in God is even more incoherent than previously thought, in that it requires unintelligibilities such as a timeless and spaceless existence." Helm concluded by laying out the three options left: Someone can either a) Accept the unintelligible existence of both a timeless and spaceless God, b) Accept the consequences of a God who is both in time and finite, or, c) Supply other arguments on behalf of a God who is in time which does not also deny God's spacelessness. ["God and Spacelessness," Philosophy 55 (1980)]. I think this whole debate indicates God's existence is unintelligible, regardless of what we might conceive him to be, and hence Ontological Arguments can't even get off the ground.

Back to Anselm. The basic Kantian criticism of Anselm's argument is that someone cannot infer the extra mental existence of anything by analyzing its definition. Yet defenders reply that Anselm is not defining God into existence. He's merely asking whether we can reasonably suppose that something than which nothing greater can be conceived exists only in the intellect. Consider these statements: "No square circles exist," and "an infinite set of prime numbers exists." If we can move from concepts to statements about reality here with math, then why not with God?

But according to Toni Vogel Carey in "The Ontological Argument and the Sin of Hubris" [Philosophy Now, Dec. 2005]: "The trouble is, what it tells us is not at all what Anselm needs to show. Rather than a proof of God's existence, what emerges is a reason for doubt about claiming we have any understanding of the nature and existence of God. To see this, take a closer look at the role played by the fool. What a fool can understand, anyone can understand, fools being, by definition, deficient in candle power and wisdom. Why should we suppose, then, that a being than which none greater can be conceived by the fool is as great as a being than which none greater can be conceived, say, by a smart *Philosophy Now* reader? And by the same reasoning, why should we suppose that a being than which none greater can be conceived by you, with all due respect, is as great as a being than which none greater can be conceived by a genius like Einstein or a saint like Anselm? Finally, why should we suppose that a being than which none greater can be conceived by Einstein or Anselm is as great as a being than which none greater can logically possibly be conceived – than which none greater could be conceived even by God? For plainly this, and not merely the greatest concept of which the fool is capable, is what Anselm's argument requires."

Likewise, if we asked an Easterner what he conceives to be the greatest conceivable being, his conception will start off being different than those of westerners from the get-go. I think Anselmian arguments, including those of Hartshorne, Plantinga and Malcolm's all begin with Occidental not Oriental conceptions of God, and their western conceptions of God are theirs by virtue of the prevalence of the Christian gospel in the west. If ontological argumentation is sound, then the eastern conceptions of God will entail that their God (or the One) also exists. Since these two conceptions of God produce two mutually exclusive conclusions about which kind of God exists, then the ontological argument itself does not lead us to believe in the Christian God alone. An easterner might even start off by saying that the greatest conceivable being is the ONE, which cannot be conceived. Where do you go with the ontological argument from here?

Furthermore, John Hick argues that in Plantinga's formulation, "the reasoning looks suspiciously like an attempt to prove divine existence by definitional fiat," and he believes that the suspicion is justified. "Plantinga's argument for a maximally excellent being, if valid, would also work for a maximally evil being." [Which Hick offers in <u>An Interpretation of Religion</u> (Yale Univ. Press, 1992), pp. 78-79]. But since the ontological argument can be used to prove that two mutually exclusive beings both exist, the reasoning itself is faulty.

Cosmological Arguments:

Cosmological Arguments begin with some fact of the world and argue to a transcendent God as the best explanation of it. In the Bible there isn't a philosophical argument for God's existence. It was assumed that there was a God. The problem they faced wasn't atheism. It was polytheism. For the first thousand years Christian thinkers found the most useful philosophical framework within the philosophy of Plato. Most of the works of Aristotle were lost to Western scholars, except as known through Arabic commentators. In the mind of most Christian thinkers in the 13th century, Plato was **THE** Christian philosopher, while Aristotle was considered a pagan philosopher. But with the discovery of Aristotle's works, Thomas Aquinas (1225-75 A.D.) almost single-handedly transformed the perceptions of Aristotle, as a pagan philosopher, into **THE** Christian philosopher such that Aristotelian thought became the official doctrinal framework for the Roman Catholic church down to our own century! Nothing comparable to this intellectual feat has been done before or after.

There are three types of Cosmological Arguments:

1) **The Thomistic "Five Ways" Arguments** attempts to show that our world is dependent upon an unmoved mover for the fact of motion, an uncaused cause for our very existence, a necessary being for the universe of contingent beings, an absolutely perfect being to account for limited perfection, and a cosmic designer to account for ordered design in the universe. **These five arguments all assume the eternity of the universe.** Even an eternal universe needs a God, Thomas Aquinas argued. Aquinas did believe that the universe began at some point in time. He just figured if he could show that even granting the assumption of an eternal universe that God must exist, then how much more would it be true that God must exist if the universe had a beginning in time. When Aquinas argues against an infinite series of causes, he's not talking about a temporal series, one that stretches backwards in time, but a series stretching upward hierarchically, up the great chain of being. "That is, every moment in the universe, even if the universe has always been here, is dependent for its existence, at that moment, upon an ultimate cause." [Ed L. Miller, Questions That Matter: An Invitation to Philosophy (McGraw-Hill, 4th edition, 1984), p. 285]. The fundamental proof here is that of contingency. Defended by Brian Davies, Norman Geisler and Bruce Reichenbach, and critiqued by J.L. Mackie, Anthony Flew, and Michael Martin, to name just a few.

2) **The Kalam Argument** attempts to show that the universe must have begun at some point, which requires a timelessly existing personal God as the explanation for such a beginning. This argument states that a beginningless series of events in time is impossible, because it would demand an infinite series of events in time. But we can never have an infinite collection of anything, much less events in time. If one were to begin counting, he or his descendants would never finish counting to infinity, because it cannot be done. Therefore the universe began to exist, and since it cannot take place by events in time, it requires a personal agent, God, who is outside of time to create the universe when it began. [See Wm. Craig, The Kalam Cosmological Argument, (Macmillian Press, 1979), and J. P. Moreland in Scaling the Secular City: A Defense of Christianity (Baker, 1987)].

While the Kalam argument is fascinating, several scholars have offered critiques of it, including J.L. Mackie, in The Miracle of Theism, (pp. 92-95); Michael Martin, in Atheism: A Philosophical Investigation, (pp. 101-106), and Quentin Smith (with William Lane Craig) in Theism, Atheism, and Big Bang Cosmology (Oxford, 1993). My personal view is that even if the Kalam argument is sound, I still don't see how it follows that this universe was caused to come into existence by a personal agent, which we call God, much less the Trinitarian Christian God of the Bible. And there is nothing about the Kalam argument that tells us anything about this God, if he exists, other than that he caused it to spring into existence. There is equally nothing about the argument that leads me to think that this God is all-powerful, either, or loving. The argument at it's very best may only lead us to believe that a "god" merely created what Edward Tryon and Stephen Hawking both describe as a "quantum wave fluctuation" (Tryon in Nature, December 1973, and Hawking in Physical Review (December 1983).

But I don't consider the Kalam to be sound. Consider this, according to a fellow Blogger: "Many physicists believe the universe is 'ball-shaped.' What the theist is doing is taking a rule that is true inside the ball, where everything that begins to exist has a cause, and applying it to the conditions outside the ball. This may not, however, be the case. The outside conditions may be entirely unlike the inside conditions."

"Let me try a hypothetical. Let's say that the universe did begin, but it began inside something I will call a 'yniverse.' A yniverse is a type of meta-universe. Let's say that the physics of the yniverse are very different from the physics of our own universe. First of all, there is no indication that an yniverse had a beginning. It is like what some physicists used to call a 'steady-state' universe."

"Now, imagine that the physical laws in that yniverse allow for things to come into existence without a cause. So, in this yniverse, a universe can come into existence without any cause. If this were the case, our universe, because it is a part of another 'set' with different rules, can come about without a cause at all."

"I'm not saying that this is what I believe happened. I'm simply pointing out that just because it is the case that everything that comes into existence within the universe has a cause, that does not mean the universe itself had to have a cause. You cannot assume that a law at play within a set is true of the set itself."

While this might seem quite problematic to us, according to John Hick, the Kalam argument, like all cosmological arguments, "does not compel us to believe that there is a God. For one may opt instead to accept the universe as a sheer unexplained fact." Because "we are accordingly faced with the choice of accepting God or accepting the existence of the physical universe itself as a given unintelligible and mysterious brute fact." [John Hick, An Interpretation of Religion, p. 80].

[To read the best critique of the Kalam argument, see Wes Morriston, "Must the Beginning of the Universe Have a Personal Cause?: A Critical Examination of the Kalam Cosmological Argument" [(Faith and Philosophy Vol. 17, No. 2 (2000), 149-169.) http://stripe.colorado.edu/~morristo/kalam2.html]. See also Craig's reply: "Must the Beginning of the Universe Have a Personal Cause?: A Rejoinder":   http://www.leaderu.com/offices/billcraig/docs/morriston.html, and Morriston's counter-reply, "Causes and Beginnings in the Kalam Argument: Reply to Craig" [(Faith and Philosophy, Vol. 19, No. 2 (April 2002), 233-244: http://spot.colorado.edu/~morristo/wes2craig.html].

3) The Leibnizian Argument. (G. W. Leibniz 1646-1716). This argument attempts to show that the principle of sufficient reason, when applied to a contingent universe, leads us to believe in a Self-Explanatory Being. The Principle of Sufficient Reason (PSR) states: "There is some explanation for the existence of anything whatever, some reason why it should exist rather than not." Suppose that nothing existed--which is what we should expect to find. It would not require an explanation. But the existence of something—of anything-- does force us to ponder the question, why? We would need no reason to explain the non-existence of the world. But given the fact that the world exists, we are driven to wonder why it exists.

Richard Taylor defends this argument in <u>Metaphysics</u>, (Prentice-Hall, 1992, 4th ed.), with a thought experiment. Suppose, he asks, you were walking in the woods and you found a perfectly smooth transparent ball about your own height. This would puzzle you greatly.

Lesson 1) If you were quite accustomed to such objects of various sizes, but had never seen an ordinary rock, then upon finding a large ordinary rock in the woods you would be just as puzzled. Thus, something that is puzzling ceases to be so by its accustomed presence. Likewise, it is strange indeed that our universe exists; yet few are very often struck by this strangeness.

Lesson 2) You might not know why it is there, but you would hardly doubt that it did not appear there all by itself. Few people would entertain the idea that it might have come from nothing at all--that it has no explanation for its existence. Likewise existence requires a reason, whereas non-existence does not.

Lesson 3) It is not the fact of its having been found in the forest rather than elsewhere that renders an explanation necessary, for our question is not how it happens to be there, but how it happens to exist at all. If we annihilate the forest and everything else as well, leaving this ball to constitute the entire physical universe, and that no other reality has ever existed or will exist, we cannot for a moment suppose that its existence has been explained. Likewise, it doesn't matter what the thing in question is, or how large it is, or how complex it is--it could be a grain of sand. We do not avoid the necessity of a reason for the existence of that which exists.

Lesson 4) It is no answer to the question why a thing exists, to state how long it has existed, for the question was not one concerning age but its existence. Likewise, if the universe had no beginning at all, it can still be asked why there is a world, why there is something rather than nothing.

Some Criticisms: 1) When it comes to the PSR we atheists argue that the universe is just a brute fact—we deny the PSR, as we've seen with John Hick. Bertrand Russell said, "The universe is just there, and that's all." Maybe reason isn't something that can answer the question of our origins. After all, those who believe that God created the universe cannot offer any reasons why there should be a self-existent being that has always existed, either! For them, God is their brute fact, just like the physical universe is a brute fact for atheists.

2) Could we suppose that the universe itself contains the reason for its existence--that it is a necessary being? Reply: We find nothing about the world to suggest that it exists by its own nature, and many things that suggest that it doesn't. Every part of it suggests that it is not indestructible-- that it has a finite duration. Suppose that a single grain of sand has forever constituted the whole universe. It is quite impossible to suppose that it exists by its own nature, and could never have failed to exist. The same should be true if the world consisted not of one or two, but a million grains of sand. Yes, but what seems to be the case from our perspective, and what is actually the case might be two different things. Humans just might have the tendency to suppose these things. When it comes to the origins of reality itself we must start with a brute fact either way we look at it, and so we may have to throw all our suppositions out the window.

3) The objection: the fallacy of composition--Reasoning fallaciously from the properties of the parts to the properties of the whole. Things we experience all have causes, therefore the whole universe needs a cause. Cf. Each drink is good;

therefore a drink made of all drinks would be good. Or, individual basketball players are good; therefore a team of them would be good. Every person here weighs less than 300 lbs; therefore together we weigh less than 300 lbs.

Reply: Sometimes you can reason from the parts to the whole, sometimes you can't--the critic must show that reasoning to creation in this way is wrong. Eg's: Each block in this wall is a brick; therefore this wall is made of bricks. All the states in the U.S. are located in the Northern Hemisphere; therefore the US is in the Northern Hemisphere.

But there is no independent way to decide how we should view the universe. Is it more like a drink composed of all drinks, as just mentioned, or is it more like a wall made of bricks, mentioned in reply?

The Teleological or Design Argument.

Stated simply, the Teleological Argument argues that a designed universe demands a Designer. The modern *Intelligent Design* argument was the one argument that convinced Anthony Flew to switch to Deism from Atheism, after having been the leading defender of atheism for decades. We'll look at two areas: 1) Cosmology, and 2) Biochemical complexity. [I have been helped extensively here by L. Stafford Betty with Bruce Cordell, "The Anthropic Teleological Argument," International Quarterly, 27, no. 4 (December 1987), who argued on behalf of a designed God].

First we'll look at **1) Cosmology** and the anthropic principle: The anthropic principle claims that if the initial conditions at the Big Bang had been different from what they were, life as we know it could not have arisen. That is, human beings would not be here to wonder why it is the way it is. For instance, if gravity were significantly stronger than it is, stars would exhaust their hydrogen fuels much faster, and human life could not appear where stars die young. Or if the strong force, which binds the nuclei of atoms together, were stronger, helium nuclei would dominate the universe, and no hydrogen would be left over. Without hydrogen there would be no water, and no life, as we know it. Had the rate of expansion of the big bang been different by one million millionths no life would have been possible. If the mass of a proton were increased by 0.2 %, hydrogen would be unstable and life would not have formed. The earth is just the right distance from the sun, just the right size, with the right rotational speed, and with a special atmosphere allowing for life. The earth contains the proper amounts of metals and water-forming compounds. Other constants in the universe include the speed of light, the charge of the proton, the gravitational constant, Plank's constant, and so on. These examples can be multiplied but the point is that "with a change in any one of a number of factors" then the "universe would have evolved as a lifeless, unconscious entity." Don Page of the *Institute for Advanced Study* in Princeton, NJ, calculated the odds against the formulation of our universe. "His exact computation was 10,000,000,000 to the 124th power, a number so large that to call it 'astronomical' would be to engage in a wild understatement."

A) Atheists object that there is nothing surprising at all about the fact that we find order in the universe, for if there wasn't, then we wouldn't be around to comment on it--we could not possibly find anything else. But, theists like Richard Swinburne counter that the problem is not that we perceive order rather than disorder, but that order rather than disorder is there. Maybe only if order is there can we know what is there, but that makes what is there no less extraordinary and in need of explanation. [The Existence of God, p. 138].

The theistic answer to this objection posits a fully formed and completely ordered God as the answer to this ordered universe. This is an equally troublesome view. According to Richard Carrier in Sense And Goodness Without God (2005, p. 86-87), "Who rolled the dice that gave us our god, rather than some other god, or no god at all? Basically theism posits an extremely orderly being that just 'exists' for no reason at all." He goes on to explain how order comes from chaos, because when we roll the dice enough times, "the odds become very good that you will roll the exact orderly sequence of 1,2,3,4,5,6. The odds against such a sequence are something like one in fifty-thousand." So, he argues, "it follows that from chaos we can predict order, even incredibly complex order. But we have no comparable explanation for where an orderly god would come from, or why such an innate order would exist at all in a god, rather than a different order, or a chaos instead."

B) According to Richard Dawkins, the anthropic principle is the better alternative to the design hypothesis. "It has been estimated that there are between 1 billion and 30 billion planets in our galaxy, and about 100 billion galaxies in the universe," so "a billion billion is a conservative estimate of the number of available planets in the universe." Therefore "even with such absurdly long odds, life will still have arisen on a billion planets—of which Earth, of course, is one." Once life has arisen the principle of natural selection takes over, and "natural selection is emphatically not a matter of luck." [The God Delusion, pp. 134-141].

C) Some atheists claim there may be an infinite number of universes that co-exist alongside our own and arose out of their own Big Bangs. This is known as the "Everett Hypothesis" named after Princeton physicist Hugh Everett. He argued that when given a potentially infinite number of universes, it is not that unlikely one would come along which produced life, as we know it. Theoretical physicist Lee Smolin has argued that time didn't begin with the Big Bang but extends eternally into the past. He makes a brilliant argument for this in his book The Life of the Cosmos (1997). Smolin argues that our universe originated in a black hole from another universe. Black holes can give birth to baby universes! Smolin also argues that the fine-tuning of the universe is no accident; the fine-tuning of the universe is one that makes it possible to have many black holes and that the more black holes there are, the better are the chances that black holes can produce more baby universes like ours. Smolin believes that this is what a quantum theory of gravity will show, or what it may well show. To those who object to that such a view is an *ad hoc* hypothesis, Dawkins simply says that people who think this way "have not had their consciousness raised by natural selection." [The God Delusion, p. 146].

But consider this: what exists outside of our universe, that is, what is beyond the known order of our universe? Presumably there can be no end to that which lies beyond our universe, if we can even speak of it this way. For a lack of a better term I'll call this nothingness the VOID (with capitals). How the VOID behaves is simply not known at all, since it is nothing. We know it "exists" whatever that might mean, when speaking of nothing. But it is a well-founded supposition that the VOID is infinite—it has to be. How could it end, if we can even speak of it beginning? That thought is mind boggling to me, and if you'll take a moment to think about it then you too will be boggled by it. Never ending VOID! Infinite nothingness!

[This "Flammarion Woodcut" is of a young person peeking through the firmament of the heavens to catch a glimpse of how the universe works. It depicts my desire to know as best as possible the reason for it all...and to peer into the VOID].

We do know about the laws of our universe. But what about the VOID? Is there any law in the VOID that prohibits something coming from nothing, or prohibiting a multitude of universes from existing without beginning? Who knows? If the VOID is infinite, and we do not know its properties, then perhaps there may be up to an infinite number of universes. With such a number of universes (called a *multiverse*) other universes may have arisen just like ours inside black holes, although we are the only ones puzzled by this because it indeed looks impossible to have arisen out of blind chance, given one try. What is the possibility of our particular universe to have arisen out of an infinite VOID where there may be up to an infinite number of universes each arising out of the VOID, and where there may be no ordered laws prohibiting something coming from nothing, or something existing without beginning? Who knows?

Maybe the whole notion of God as an explanation of the universe isn't needed because there are a potentially infinite number of universes, and ours just happened to be the lucky one that resulted in us being here to wonder why we exist at all. According to Richard Carrier, "a *mutiverse* would be fundamentally causeless in exactly the same way a god is supposed to be." [To see this further argued for see Carrier's book, Sense And Goodness Without God (2005, pp. 71-95, and Paul Davies God and the New Physics (Pelican Books, 1984)].

We turn now to an even more compelling argument, **2) Biochemical complexity**. Can chance account for the jump from non-life to life? The basic assumption of Neo-Darwinists is that life originated out of an "organic soup." This soup is made of randomly generated water, ammonia, methane and other compounds, that were subjected to lightning, which produced the enzymes so critical to life. Fred Hoyle and N.C. Wickramasinghe maintain that the "usual theory of mutation and natural selection cannot produce complex biomolecules from random association of atoms"--that is, natural selection does not work where there is not already some life! They point out that there are "ten to twenty distinct amino acids which determine the basic backbone of the enzyme," and that for the enzyme to form these acids they "must be in the correct position." They calculate the odds of creating one enzyme at 10^{20}. "The trouble," they argue, "is that there are about 2000 enzymes, and the chance of obtaining them all in a random trial is only one part in $10^{40,000}$, "an outrageously small probability that could not be faced even if the whole universe consisted of organic soup." [Evolution from Space, (1981, p. 24)]. But this is only the beginning, for "nothing has been said of the origin of DNA itself, nothing of DNA transcription to RNA, and so on. These issues are too complex to set numbers to." But the chance for these biological systems being formed "through random shufflings of simple organic molecules is exceedingly minute, to a point where it is insensibly different from zero." (Ibid, p. 3).

Michael J. Behe has argued that there is an irreducible element to even the simplest bodily functions. He compares complex biological phenomena like blood clotting, to a mouse trap. If we take away any piece, like the spring, or the baseboard, the mouse trap will not work. Similarly, if any one of the more than 20 proteins involved in blood clotting is missing or deficient, clots will not perform properly. Such all or nothing systems could not have arisen incrementally, but had to be there all at once, so there must be an intelligent designer. [Behe, Darwin's Black Box: The Biochemical Challenge to Evolution (Simon & Schuster, 1996). For a theological debate over Intelligent Design and Creationism, see Three Views On Creation & Evolution, eds, J.P. Moreland & John Reynolds (Zondervan, 1999)].

The earlier defender of Intelligent Design was Phillip E. Johnson in Darwin on Trial (Regnery, 1991). [But see what Nancey Murphy said about his lame arguments in "Phillip Johnson on Trial: A Critique of his Critique of Darwin" in Perspectives on Science & Christian Faith (Vol. 45, No, 1, March 1993: 26-36]. Today there is Michael J. Behe (Darwin's Black Box) , with William A. Dembski in several books, like Debating Design : From Darwin to DNA (Eds., William A. Dembski and Michael Ruse, 2004); and The Design Revolution: Answering the Toughest Questions about Intelligent Design (IVP, 2004). Along with others.

[For some rebuttals see especially Richard Dawkins, The Blind Watchmaker: Why the Evidence of Evolution Reveals a Universe Without Design (W W Norton & Co., 1996). Matt Young, and Taner Edis Eds. Why Intelligent Design Fails: A Scientific Critique of the New Creationism. (Rutgers University Press, 2004). Mark Perakh, Unintelligent Design (Prometheus Books, December, 2003), Richard Dawkins, Climbing Mount Improbable, (W.W. Norton & Company, 1997); Daniel C. Dennet, Darwin's Dangerous Idea: Evolution and the Meanings of Life, (Simon & Schuster; 1996), and Why Darwin Matters: The Case Against Intelligent Design, by Michael Shermer (Times Books, 2006)].

In the first place, stating the odds as Intelligent Design (ID) theorists do is highly misleading. "Rarity by itself shouldn't necessarily be evidence of anything. When one is dealt a bridge hand of thirteen cards, the probability of being dealt that particular hand is less than one in 600 billion. Still, it would be absurd for someone to be dealt a hand, examine it carefully, calculate that the probability of getting it is less than one in 600 billion, and then conclude that he must not have been dealt that very hand because it is so very improbable." [John Allen Paulos, Innumeracy: Mathematical Illiteracy and its Consequences].

"DNA did not assemble purely by chance. It assembled by a combination of chance and the laws of physics. Without the laws of physics as we know them, life on earth as we know it would not have evolved in the short span of six billion years. The nuclear force was needed to bind protons and neutrons in the nuclei of atoms; electromagnetism was needed to keep atoms and molecules together; and gravity was needed to keep the resulting ingredients for life stuck to the surface of the earth." Victor J. Stenger, at www.talkorigins.org.

"Behe's colossal mistake is that, in rejecting these possibilities, he concludes that no Darwinian solution remains. But one does. It is this: An irreducibly complex system can be built gradually by adding parts that, while initially just advantageous, become - because of later changes - essential. The logic is very simple. Some part (A) initially does some job (and not very well, perhaps). Another part (B) later gets added because it helps A. This new part isn't essential, it merely improves things. But later on, A (or something else) may change in such a way that B now becomes indispensable. This process continues as further parts get folded into the system. And at the end of the day, many parts may all be required." ["Darwin v. Intelligent Design (Again)" by H. Allen Orr, in the Boston Review, (Dec/Jan 1997; http://bostonreview.mit.edu/].

Natural selection is the organizing principle for evolution, where the environment selects those species and mutations that can survive in their given environment. Cesare Emiliani, in The Scientific Companion (New York; Wiley & Sons, p. 149) illustrates how efficient natural selection can be: "Imagine that you want to have the entire Bible typed by a wild monkey. What are the chances that such a monkey, typing at random, will come up with the Bible neatly typed without a single error? The English Bible (KJV) contains about 6 million letters. The chances of success, therefore, are 1 in 26 to the 6 millionth power, as there are 26 letters in the English alphabet. This is equal to 10 to the minus 8,489,840. I wouldn't exactly wait around. Suppose, however, that I introduce a control (the environment) that wipes out any wrong letter the monkey may type. Typing away at one letter per second and assuming an average of 13 errors per letter (half of 26), the monkey will produce the Bible in 13 x 6,000,000 seconds = 2.5 years. Not only that, but you are mathematically sure that the monkey will produce the Bible within that time and without a single error. What is utterly impossible has suddenly become not only possible but certain."

Richard Dawkins argues: "It is often said that natural selection makes God unnecessary, but leaves his existence an open plausibility. I think we can do better than that. When you think it through, the argument from improbability, which traditionally is deployed in God's favor, turns out to be the strongest argument against him. The beauty of Darwinian evolution is that it explains the very improbable, by gradual degrees. It starts from primeval simplicity (relatively easy to understand) and works up, by plausibly small steps, to complex entities whose genesis, by any non-gradual process, would be too improbable for serious contemplation. **Design is a real alternative, but only if the designer is himself the product of an escalatory process such as evolution** by natural selection, either on this planet or elsewhere. There may be alien life forms so advanced that we would worship them as gods. But they too must ultimately be explained by gradual escalation. Gods that exist *ab initio* are ruled out by the argument from improbability, even more surely than are spontaneously erupting eyes or elbow joints." [*The Root of All Evil?*]. Therefore, "God, or any intelligent, decision-taking, calculating agent, would have to be highly improbable in the very same statistical sense as the entities he is supposed to explain." [The God Delusion, p. 147].

"If we assume that Behe is correct, and that humans can discern design, then I submit that they can also discern poor design (we sue companies for this all the time!). In Darwin's Black Box, Behe refers to design as the 'purposeful arrangement of parts.' What about when the 'parts' aren't purposeful, by any standard engineering criteria? When confronted with the 'All-Thumbs Designer' - whoever designed the spine, the birth canal, the prostate gland, the back of the throat, etc, Behe and the ID people retreat into theology. [I.e., God can do whatever He wants, or we're not competent to judge intelligence by God's standards, or being an intelligent designer does not mean being a good or perfect designer.]" ["A Central Illinois Scientist Responds to the Black Box," Karen Bartelt, http://www.reall.org/newsletter/v07/n12/index.html]. According to Sam Harris, "Examples of unintelligent design in nature are so numerous that an entire book could be written simply listing them." [Letter to a Christian Nation (Knopf, 2006, p. 78).

John Hick has objected, "when we look past ANY event into its antecedent conditions, their improbability multiplying backwards exponentially towards infinity, the event appears as endlessly improbable." [An Interpretation of Religion, (Yale, 1992, p.89]. Whether or not such an event is improbable is purely notional, not objective. "There is no objective sense in which this is either more or less probable than any other possible universe. The only reality is the actual course of the universe, with ourselves as part of it." Given any event it is improbable that it occurred at all when one considers the antecedent conditions required for its occurrence. "The antecedent improbability of an individual being conceived who is precisely me is thus already quite staggering--truly astronomical." My great great grandparents had to meet and marry, and one sperm penetrated one egg to form one of my parents who met and married their spouse, who raised me the way they did plus all of the experiences and thoughts that make up who I am today. Hick: "And the same kind of calculation applies to everyone and everything else in the universe." So for any two people who meet and have a conversation, the odds of them meeting and speaking the exact words they do to one another, being dressed as they are is quite literally impossible from the standpoint of just 100 years ago. But it happened!

Richard Swinburne claims that in a typical argument there is certain phenomenon that calls for an explanation. If a scientific (non-personal) explanation fails to do justice to the phenomena, it is natural to conclude that we must seek an explanation in terms of the intentional action of some rational agent; i.e., God in this case. [See his The Existence of God, Clarendon Press, 1979, p. 20]. But a personal explanation in a self-existent eternal triune God of the Bible doesn't do justice to the phenomena in question at all, so it's not time to give up on a scientific explanation for it all.

The Design argument is supposed to lead us to a universal creative intelligence, known as God. But as I've suggested, even if this argument does leads us to believe in a God, and there is plenty of room for doubting this, then such a conclusion doesn't lead us to the specific view of the Trinitarian God of the Bible. Many other arguments must be made to connect the conclusions of the design argument to such a Christian God. This argument does nothing, for instance, to indicate that such a God still exists, or is good, since there is a great amount of evil in the world. And it certainly says nothing about a virgin birth or a resurrection from the dead, either.

Who Made God? Dr. Paul Copan answers the atheist question, "If God Made the Universe, Who Made God?" [in "That's Just Your Interpretation" (Baker, 2001), pp. 69-73]. Who says that someone cannot write a philosophically astute answer to such a deep question as this in just a few short pages? Paul Copan has. Let's take a brief look.

His main argument is that "the theist does not claim that whatever exists must have a cause, but whatever begins to exist must have a cause." "We must begin with a non-question-begging starting point" and this "does just that." Such a starting point, he says, "does not automatically entail that God created the universe," for then the question to explore is "whether the cause is personal or impersonal." But without such a starting point, he argues, the skeptic is "assuming what one wants to prove." It's like arguing that "all reality is physical; therefore God can't exist."

Atheists have two responses here. 1) They can argue that theists are begging the question as well. Why? Because it's question begging to assume that something can exist without ever having a beginning, especially a fully formed complex eternally uncaused self-existent three-in-one theistic being. Then they can simply argue that this universe popped into existence out of nothing, or that it's just a brute unexplainable fact, not unlike how the theistic God is accepted as a brute unexplainable fact. 2) They can agree with Copan's non-question begging starting point that everything that begins to exist has a cause, but turn around and argue with Lee Smolin that baby universes are born out of black holes within other universes in a process that stretches back into infinity, as absurd as that might seem [see his book, The Life of the Cosmos, 1997].

The God of the Bible. One thing is sure to me. The triune God in the Bible simply cannot be describing the God who exists. I find it implausible to believe that a Triune (3 persons in 1?) God has always and forever existed without cause and will always and forever exist (even though our entire experience is that everything has a beginning and an ending) as a fully formed being (even though our entire experience is that order grows incrementally) with all knowledge (and consequently never learned anything), with all power (but doesn't exercise it like we would if we saw a burning child), and who is present everywhere (and who also knows what time it is everywhere in our universe even though time is a function of movement and bodily placement).

Paul Copan tries in vain to answer how God can be three *and* one by arguing that the three persons of the Trinity are "each centers of consciousness, responsibility, and activity" with three separate wills, and therefore "distinct from one another." But since they all share the same divine nature they all form one God. ["That's Just Your Interpretation" (Baker, 2001), pp. 121-126]. I fail to see how with three separate consciousnesses we have one Being—God. Maybe there are three divine consciousnesses who always agree with each other and have all existed forever, but what sense can be made of three separate consciousnesses, three separate wills, but just one metaphysical Being? There had better be very strong historical evidence for such a strange claim.

Regardless, that God is a hateful, racist and sexist God. Consider the following things: In the Flood story we're told God wanted to destroy all mankind. In Moses' day God wanted to destroy all of the Israelites. In Joshua's day God wanted the Israelites to kill all of the inhabitants of the *Promised Land*. Saul was purportedly told by God to obliterate the Amalekites (I Sam. 15:3), while later we find God is pleased with anyone who would dash Babylonian babies against the rocks (Psalms 137:9). According to Jonah, God was going to destroy the people of Nineveh. God also destroyed and scattered the northern tribes of Israel because he was displeased with them. God allowed Satan, the accuser, to destroy Job's health and family life just to win a "bet." In the New Testament, God will destroy all unbelievers in the lake of fire. He's a pretty barbaric God, if you ask me. This God is simply the reflection of ancient barbaric peoples.

Christians think Militant Muslims are wrong for wanting to kill free loving people in the world, and they are. But the only difference between these Muslims and the Biblical God is that they simply disagree on who should be killed. They both agree people should be killed; they just disagree on who should die.

God decreed that a man who picked up sticks on the Sabbath day was to be stoned to death (Numbers 15:32-36). God commanded that anyone who curses his father or mother was to be put to death (Exodus 21:17). Witches, and those of differing religious views were to be killed (Ex. 22:18, 20). These are pretty stiff punishments, eh? This God declares that a slave is the property of another man (Exodus 21:21). God commanded men to divorce their foreign wives for no other reason but that they were not God's people (Ezra 9), and women were helpless if they weren't married in those days.

God asked Abraham to kill and sacrifice his son Isaac. If we heard a voice today telling us to do that, we would not think this voice was God's, although Abraham wasn't horrified at the suggestion. *Enough!*

Ludwig Feuerbach is surely right; God did not make us in his image, human beings made God in their image. The ancient people of the Bible constructed their views of God based upon their own ancient, barbaric nature.

There Have Been Four Cosmological Displacements:

1) The Copernican theory of the heliocentric universe defended by Galileo. (1600's). Man was no longer the center of our particular solar system.

2) The discovery that our solar system is not central to the Milky Way galaxy, but located on the periphery; out on a spiral arm. (c. 1900). Man was not even central in his own galaxy.

3) The discovery that our galaxy is only one of billions of galaxies. (c. 1930's). Man isn't even central to the universe as a whole. We are insignificant.

4) The possibility that there are an infinite number of universes, called a *multiverse*. God is no longer needed.

8 The Problem of Unanswered Prayer.

I'm not a stranger to unanswered prayer. When I was a young Christian I prayed daily for several years that Elton John would become a Christian and record Christian songs. I finally gave up. I also prayed for years that I would be a full time Bible College professor. Some are even as skeptical of prayer as the late Carl Sagan, who wrote: "We can pray over the cholera victim, or we can give her 500 milligrams of tetracycline every 12 hours...the scientific treatments are hundreds or thousands of times more effective than the alternatives (like prayer). Even when the alternatives seem to work, we don't actually know that they played any role." [The Demon Haunted World, (Random House, 1996, pp. 9-10)]. Voltaire said: "Prayer and arsenic will kill a cow."

The problem of unanswered prayer is particularly vexing when many Biblical promises of answered prayer seem unqualified (Matthew 7:7; John 14:13; 15:16; and 16:23). The problem is that our experience teaches us otherwise. We all know of someone who has died even though believers had prayed. This is true even of those we deem spiritual giants.

When we seriously reflect upon it, a recipe for disaster would be for God to simply give us whatever we ask. Whenever we experience the slightest suffering, answered prayer would rescue us. Yet suffering teaches us to have a deeper faith, we are told, which brings more glory to God (James 1:2-4; I Peter 1:6-7). According to the Bible it's God's will that sometimes we suffer (Job). Sometimes it may even be God's will that we fail in an endeavor. For only through pain and failure can we learn of God's grace and truth in our lives in a way that makes future ministry more effective. (See Acts 7:23-36; Luke 22:31-32; John 21:15-19).

Several Biblical examples of unanswered prayer are discernible. They include Jesus' request to avoid the cross (Matthew 27:39; Luke 22:42); Jesus' prayer for Christian unity (John 17:20-22); Paul's request to remove a "thorn in the flesh" (II Corinthians 12:7); and Paul's request that he would be delivered from unbelievers in Jerusalem (Romans 15:31; compare Acts 21). While it may be true that both Jesus and Paul sought "Thy will not mine" their expressed desires went unanswered as intended.

INADEQUATE SOLUTIONS-- Three solutions are inadequate for this problem. **One)** Some Christians simply deny that prayer ever goes unanswered if prayed in faith. This is a radical view and has given rise to the "name it claim it" theology. But this view leads to intense guilt if prayers go unanswered, and forces some to paradoxically claim that God healed them even when the symptoms remain! **Two)** Others believe God always answers prayer, but that sometimes his answer is "No." But think about it; how is it possible that a negative answer is not considered an unanswered prayer? Someone who says an answered prayer is one in which God could sometimes say "No", is merely saying God has responded in some way. But for us to say that prayer was answered we really want to know whether the request was granted or not. A denied request is one that goes unanswered, and a request granted is one that is answered. If someone wants to maintain that all prayers are answered, then we merely need to ask them whether God says, "yes" to all prayers, and God clearly doesn't do this. That's the whole reason why unanswered prayer is a problem in the first place, and it is a problem. **Three)** Still others rationalize things away so that they can still say God answered their prayer even though God didn't do as they requested. One church prayed for a cancer patient who died. The minister subsequently claimed God had answered their prayer because he said they were praying for her release from the hospital. Since she died, she was in fact released from the hospital and went to be with God. But that was not what they meant when they prayed. While it may be true to say God gives us what is best, that doesn't mean he gives us exactly what we asked him.

SOME OTHER SOLUTIONS— Several other solutions are offered to help explain the problem of unanswered prayer. They demand that we see the promises of answered prayer as qualified ones. **My question here is whether the Biblical promise of answered prayer "dies the death of a thousand qualifications," so to speak.** Depending on how one categorizes them, I've discovered several qualifications to answered prayer. [I've been helped to some degree by William Lane Craig's book, No Easy Answers, although, as you can tell, I will draw different conclusions].

ONE) Sin in our lives. God is under no obligation to answer the specific prayers of one tangled in sin. (Psalms 66:18; Isaiah 59:1-2; James 5:16; I John 3:21-22). This includes all of the outward and inward sins in the Bible, plus not treating family members right (I Peter 3:7), and not growing as a Christian (John 15:15-16; Galatians 5:22-23). But a problem surfaces here. Since Christians are washed in the blood of Jesus, God supposedly sees no sin in them. How can God see our sins if we are already washed clean? But if somehow God can see our sins, and if that means seeing inside our filthy hearts, then no one is clean enough to expect anything from God when we pray.

TWO) Wrong motives in our prayer. God is under no obligation to answer selfish prayers. (James 4:3). Conversely, God is under no obligation to answer prayers that fail to give glory to God. (John 14:13; II Corinthians 12:9-10). We may not even know what would bring God the most glory. (John 9:3). But there are some very strong arguments that indicate there is nothing a human can do or say that are completely free of selfish motives. *Psychological Egoism*, for instance, is the theory that everything we do, even if in some small degree, benefits us the most. Even if we don't take that extreme stance, and I don't, most all of what we do is done from motives that benefit ourselves first. Most all of our prayers contain some selfish motives. Even the preacher who prays that his church mature and grow can also be wanting a bigger paycheck, more power, some recognized fame, and fewer problem people as they mature in their Christian faith. So which prayers qualify to be answered when many, if not most of them, are prayed from selfish motives?

THREE) Lack of faith in prayer. God is under no obligation to answer the prayers of someone who doesn't believe he will. (Mark 11: 24; James 1:6-8; 5:15). This faith must show itself to be persistent and earnest in prayer. (Matt. 7:7; Luke 11:5-8; 18:1-8). Jesus does talk as if all you need is faith and God will intervene for you. He makes it sound easy. All you should have to do is say to that mountain to move over there, and it shall be done. But it doesn't move. So you blame yourself. Something must be wrong with your faith, is the conclusion. Then that failure is a memory and you don't step out so far on the limb next time. And when you fail in faith again, then you hesitate to step out on that limb again. This happens until you find yourself clinging to the tree trunk for fear of stepping out on faith much at all. So you feel guilty about this all over again. Then you hear a good sermon and try again, and when your faith fails you are back to the tree trunk again. So you feel guilty again. It's simply impossible for adults to have childlike faith because we are no longer children. We've had too many experiences that temper our faith—too many tragedies, too many unanswered prayers, too many setbacks. And all of these things have taught us that believing doesn't always work. So we simply don't believe like we think we should. So we feel guilty, and we struggle some more. And we feel guilty some more for struggling, etc.

This goes on until all that we can do is to 1) offer up non-falsifiable prayers that can't be tested to see whether or not God actually did anything as a result of our prayers ("God, be with them." "Help them."). And, 2) offer up self-fulfilling prayers, that are fulfilled because we are the ones praying ("Give me strength." "Give me wisdom to know what to do." "Please encourage me." "Help me stay on the narrow road that leads to you."). I blame the Christian faith for causing this guilt and for these lame, modern, non-falsifiable, and self-fullfilling prayers. My view doesn't produce guilt because I no longer have such expectations.

FOUR) It must be according to God's will. God is under no obligation to answer the prayer that is ignorant of God's will. (I John 5:14-15: Matthew 27:39-41; Luke 22:42; John 14:13-14; 15:16; 16:23). Likewise, God is under no obligation to answer a prayer that brings any injustice on others. (Lk. 18:7-8).

Why would God answer the prayers of a slave owner who asked that none of his slaves would run away, or the prayers of the KKK for white supremacy, or the prayers of those who want a man standing accused of a crime to be found guilty, if in fact he is innocent? Unjust prayers have no assurance God will answer them. But there are so many ethical and social issues in our world today. How can we really claim on every issue that we really know the mind of God enough to pray for what we think should be done? Most of history is the history of human errors.

It is said that we may be praying for an end to AIDS, poverty, teenage pregnancy, and so on, but God doesn't do much to change the situation because as a nation we have to repent first. But I cannot see how it's not God's will that more people be saved, and yet the Christian faith is losing ground in the world today. Jeff, my cousin, told me once that he doesn't think God wants everyone to be saved. Of course, he's a good Calvinist and thinks God wills or decrees everything that happens. But the problem of evil resurfaces here. It takes more faith than I will ever have to say that it was God's will for Hitler to start WWII, or for terrorists to fly planes into the World Trade Center's Twin Towers in New York, or for good churches to fight and split up, or for children to die prematurely, or for people to starve to death. Calvinists believe God decrees those things to happen, and non-Calvinists simply believe that Christians are the ones blamed for not praying enough.

FIVE) It must be within God's power to grant the request. Sometimes believers are praying for contradictory things. It's like two fellows both praying for the romantic affections of one girl, two athletes on opposite teams both praying to win a certain ball game, two people praying for the same job, or the farmer who prays for rain while the vacationer is praying for sunshine, and so on. Then too, what about mothers who are praying for the lives of their sons on opposite sides of a battle during the Civil War, or WWII? Or, what of a convicted criminal who prays for a judge to be lenient in his sentencing versus the victim who prays the criminal receives the maximum penalty allowed by law? God cannot answer all prayers because to do so would be to do what is logically impossible. **This qualification alone may cause hundreds of thousands of prayers to go unanswered.**

SIX) Biblical history teaches us that when praying for certain things God is under no obligation to answer our requests in our lifetime. We are told we must have patience because of God's timetable. Think of the prayers offered during the long Israelite Egyptian slavery (Exodus 2:23-25), or the Babylonian Captivity (Lamentations 1-5). There were Jews who prayed for the coming of the Messiah, and for the many Christians down through the centuries who have prayed for the return of Jesus. There are surely other requests that just don't fit into God's timetable, we are reminded, because we just don't know God's plan for earth. But in the meantime we wonder why God doesn't help and/or rescue us when we hurt so badly.

SEVEN) Certain other requests must eventually be denied no matter how often we pray for them. Death, sickness, pain, hard work and strained relationships are part of the curse placed upon humankind because of the supposed fall into sin. (Genesis 3:8-19). Prayer can lessen the effects of the Fall but it cannot eliminate them. We will eventually die. We cannot avoid getting sick from time to time. There will be strained relationships, and work will nearly always be hard. So if we prayed every day to be healthy, we'd still get sick from time to time, and if we prayed every day not to die, we know that such a prayer will not always be answered.

EIGHT) There is the additional problem of human free will (for non-Calvinists). There seems to be the admittance throughout the Bible that human beings have been given free will and that some choose to reject God ("whosoever will, may come"). Given this fact, one must wonder how much change we can expect by praying for an unrepentant person. I recall a conversation Pastor Norm Fuller had with me, as I was becoming a skeptical person:

Pastor: John, my prayer for you is that you come to your senses before you go off the deep end.

John: Well, if that's your prayer and if prayer works, then I won't go off the deep end, will I?

Pastor: But it will depend upon whether or not you have a receptive heart.

John: Well, if it depends upon my heart, then why bother to pray for me?

Had my Pastor responded further by saying he will begin praying that I have a receptive heart, I could've responded as I did at first. I could've replied, "Well, if that's your prayer and if prayer works, then I will be given a receptive heart, won't I?" [Sometimes I'm just cantankerous].

If Christians want to maintain that God doesn't curtail our free human actions, then how does prayer get answered at all? When we pray for safety as we leave our house, how does that prayer have even a remote chance of being answered, if there is a predator out there who is going to meet up with us? If God does not stop this predator's free choices, or anyone else's for that matter, how can any prayer that involves free human choices have a remote chance to be answered?

Of course a Calvinist must admit that God has decreed that I should be a doubter and that I should write this book that will lead others into becoming doubters like me—even though the Bible tells us God desires all people everywhere to be saved! (See II Peter 3:9).

THREE MORE THOUGHTS—First) Just because there are several qualifications for prayer we are chided for not being persistent in prayer. In Hebrews 4:16 we are encouraged to come confidently before God's throne of grace. Even when we are unsure what to pray for we are assured that God can read the thoughts of our hearts (Romans 8:26-27). But with all of the qualifications, this is extremely hard to do. **Second)** When it comes to petitionary prayer, why should we even ask God to do things? **Shouldn't God do the right thing even if we never prayed? Third)** Prayer is not just asking God for things. There is also praise, thanksgiving, and intercession (I Timothy 2:1). We can always ask for strength to endure, power to obey, love to share, insight to know God's will, and peace in the midst of turmoil. We can pray for a renewed sense of God's forgiveness, for a grateful heart, for joy unspeakable, and so on. I think these are the things that Christians should focus on, and for an atheist like me, it's not much different than positive thinking.

Two scientific tests of petitionary/intercessory prayer: 1) The American Heart Journal (April 2006) reported on a scientific study of patients who had heart by-pass surgery who were separated into three groups. Group 1 received prayers and didn't know it. Group 2 received no prayers and didn't know it (the control group). Group 3 received prayers and did know it. Groups 1 & 3 were prayed for by different congregations throughout America. The results were very clear. There was no difference between the patients who were prayed for and those who were not prayed for. Moreover, the patients who knew they were being prayed for suffered significantly more complications than those who did not know they were being prayed for.

2) **Why won't God heal amputees?** If God answers prayers and heals people, then why are there no reports that he made amputated limbs grow back? This would be observable and it could be easily documented and tested. There is a website that makes this challenge. See **http://whydoesgodhateamputees.com/**: "For this experiment, we need to find a deserving person who has had both of his legs amputated. Now create a prayer circle. The job of this prayer circle is simple: pray to God to restore the amputated legs of this deserving person. Pray that God spontaneously and miraculously restores the legs overnight. If possible, get millions of people all over the planet to join the prayer circle and pray their most fervent prayers. Get millions of people praying in unison for a single miracle for this one deserving amputee. Then stand back and watch."

9 <u>The Lessons of Galileo, Science and Religion</u>

The French *Philosophes*, or social critics, used the trial of Galileo for propaganda purposes showing the conflict between science and Christianity, and it was. It was a conflict of sciences that the church as an *institution* got caught up in. The church had taken a stand on Aristotelian science and was not prepared to let the new science progress. And yet there was more to it. [See Diogenes Allen, <u>Christian Belief in a Postmodern World</u>, (Westminster Press, 1989].

The problem for astronomers in this era was to explain the retrograde motion of the planets. [The word "planet" in the Greek literally means, "wanderer," and in the New Testament the word means "deceiver."] In the night sky the planets seem to back up and then go forward again as the weeks go by, rather than move in one direction across the sky. This observed motion is actually because the earth revolves around the sun along with the other planets. All of the planets pass each other in their yearly cycles. But since "the ancients viewed the celestial realm as the residence of the gods, the planets were defying the perfect symmetry of the realm of the gods." [<u>The Passion of the Western Mind</u>, (Ballantine Books, 1991), by Richard Tarnas, (p. 49)]. The retrograde motion of the planets seemed to contradict the perfect divine order of the universe, thus endangering human faith in the divinity of the universe.

The philosopher's task, in Plato's words, was to "save the phenomena"--to redeem the apparent disorder of the empirical heavens. The Pythagoreans actually suggested a stationery sun, and Aristarchus posited a heliocentric theory! Yet the obstacles were formidable to such viewpoints: there was no observable stellar parallax (described later) because they lacked a telescope. There was also the common sense notion that a moving earth would force people on earth to be knocked about. Plus the ancients believed in the terrestrial-celestial separation between the realm of the gods and of humans. They believed that the heavens operated by a different set of laws than on earth!

The reason this was a problem is because Aristotelian cosmology led to the conclusion that the earth was the center of the universe. Aristotle's viewpoint is teleological. He concluded there were **four causes** for everything that exists: 1) Formal cause; "What is its form?" 2) The material cause; "What is it made of?" 3) The efficient cause; "What made it?" and 4) the fourth is most significant: **the final cause; "**<u>What purpose does it serve</u>?" According to Aristotle rocks fall to earth because they seek their rightful place. And heavier ones fall faster because they have more potentiality, he said. This is a purpose-oriented answer, but completely untrue when falling in a vacuum. "Why does water freeze faster when it's hotter?" Because hot water has more potentiality, he said. It doesn't freeze faster! "Why is there wind?" Aristotle claimed the wind is the result of the earth breathing! These are purpose oriented answers. He talks as though nature is a consciously operating organism. This teleological viewpoint led to the idea that the earth was the fixed center of the universe. Why? Because all objects fall to earth, their rightful place. Therefore the earth is the center of the universe. According to Aristotle teleological explanations are ultimate explanations for why something happens.

Ptolemy (100-178AD) outlined the answer to the problem of the planets that held sway until Copernicus. It was very complicated and involved the notion that planets revolved around certain circular points in the universe called **epicycles**, thus explaining why the planets were brighter during the retrograde cycle. [By the way, Ptolemy argued convincingly for a spherical earth!] "When the Aristotelian-Ptolemaic cosmology was embraced by the Christian poet Dante (1265-1321 AD) in the <u>Divine Comedy,</u> the ancient cosmological view fully entered the Christian psyche." –Richard Tarnas, (p. 194). [See Dante's "Universe" p. 95, from <u>Dante</u>, in <u>Great Books of the Western World</u>, ed. Mortimer Adler].

Nicholas Copernicus had come to regard the Ptolemaic system as a "monster" which still failed to account for or to predict observed planetary positions with reliable accuracy. (Tarnas pp. 248ff). Copernicus believed that "the divine creator, whose works were everywhere good and orderly, could not have been slipshod with the heavens" (Tarnas, p. 249). With him the appearances were saved with greater conceptual elegance. He saw his work fully published on the last day of his life, 1543 AD (<u>The Revolutions of the Heavenly Spheres</u>). Yet "for most who heard of it, the new conception was contrary to experience and so patently false, as to not require serious discussion." (Tarnas, p. 251).

The Trial of Galileo (1633 AD). By Galileo's day in the early 17th century the Catholic Church felt compelled to take a definite stand against the Copernican hypothesis (the Protestants had done this much earlier). Why? Dante harmonized religion and science by "poetically uniting the specific elements of the Christian theology with the equal specific elements of classical astronomy. The Aristotelian geocentric universe thus became a massive symbolic structure for the moral drama of Christianity. All of the Ptolemaic planetary spheres took on Christian references, with specific ranks of angels and archangels responsible for each sphere's motion. Every aspect of the Greek scientific scheme now was imbued with religious significance. If, for example, a moving earth were to be introduced into that system, the effect of a purely scientific innovation would threaten the integrity of the entire Christian cosmology." (From Richard Tarnas, pages 195-6).

"If the earth truly moved then no longer could it be the fixed center of God's Creation and his plan of salvation. Nor could man be the central focus of the cosmos. The absolute uniqueness and significance of Christ's intervention into human history seemed to require a corresponding uniqueness and significance for the Earth. The meaning of redemption itself, the central event not just of human history, but also of universal history, seemed at stake. *To be a Copernican seemed tantamount to atheism.*" (Richard Tarnas, pp. 253-254).

According to Diogenes Allen, the Aristotelian/Ptolemy view "included values as part of the very fabric of the universe...obligations and rights...are confirmed and supported by the physical order of the cosmos itself....it seemed to threaten the very foundations of the social, political, and moral order." [<u>Christian Belief in a Postmodern World</u>, (John Knox Press, 1989, p. 41, 42)].

The invention by Galileo of the telescope changed the debate. It destroyed several Ptolemaic conceptions: A) They believed that the spheres of the universe were perfect, yet Galileo noticed the moon has craters; B) They believed everything rotates around the earth, yet Galileo discovered Jupiter had four moons; C) They believed the heavenly bodies were eternal, yet Galileo discovered sun spots indicating that the sun was decaying. He defended the Copernican system with observations, and thus began the rise of experimental science! He showed by experiment (contrary to Aristotle) how heavier rocks do not fall faster than lighter ones. He conceptualized tying a string from a heavier rock to a lighter one, thus making them one object! But would the combined rock now fall faster than either one, or would the lighter one drag? Such problems plagued the older view.

But look at how Galileo's views were answered by Florentine astronomer Francesco Sizzi: "There are seven windows in the head: two nostrils, two eyes, two ears, and a mouth. So also in the heavens there are two favorable stars, two unfavorable, two luminaries, and Mercury alone undecided and indifferent. From all this, and from other such natural phenomena, such as seven metals, etc., all too pointless to enumerate, we can conclude that the number of planets is necessarily seven." "Furthermore, the alleged satellites of Jupiter are invisible to the naked eye, and therefore can have no influence on earth, and therefore would be useless, and therefore do not exist." "Besides all this, the Jews and other ancient peoples as well as modern Europeans have always divided the week into seven days and have named them after the seven planets. Now if we, like Galileo, increase the number of planets, this whole and beautiful system falls to the ground." [Francesco Sizzi, _Dianoia Astronomica_, 1611]

What must be understood about the trial: 1) There was real debate about the geo-centric system--but it was to be regarded as a "hypothesis not fact." 2) Copernicus and Galileo's systems contained ideas that were "hopelessly inaccurate," and there was no evidence yet for things that should be noticed. For instance **a)** the proper planetary orbits were not known yet--they were arguing for more complete circles revolving around the sun, also, **b)** There was "no observable stellar parallax"—individual stars should appear at different points in the sky when the earth is at its two farthest distances in its cycle around the sun. Either the stars were immensely more distant, which we now know is the case, or the earth didn't move. Thus, the Copernican system was not yet established on scientific grounds! 3) The Pope, Urban VIII, felt personally betrayed by Galileo, a former friend, because he thought one of the incompetent speakers in the Dialogue of Two Chief World Systems was intended to represent him.

The belief that the universe operates uniformly by the same consistent pattern of laws is firmly established as fact. Scientists will not, cannot, and should not give in on this. Any theory that contradicts this viewpoint should be judged on scientific grounds to be in gross error, which rejects Biblical literalism.

The Relationship of Science to Religion. Ian Barbour, in Religion in an Age of Science, (Harper & Row, 1990) presents four ways of relating science and religion: 1) **Conflict**. Scientific materialism vs. biblical literalism. Both positions seek to reign over the other. **Scientific materialism** makes two assertions: 1) the scientific method is the only reliable path to knowledge; 2) matter is the fundamental reality of the universe. The first one is an epistemological assertion. The second one is a metaphysical assertion, yet it's a conclusion based upon the first assertion, which has been shown to be very reliable through the centuries. **Biblical literalism** claims that a literal interpretation of the Bible sets the limits for science. It claims that a universal flood explains geology, and a seven-day creation explains the origin of the universe. Biblical literalism was the problem in

Galileo's day. As shown in his day it is a very untrustworthy approach to science, and so it is rejected by educated people today.

2) **Independence**. Science and religion are totally independent enterprises, and separated into watertight compartments. They have contrasting methods, and differing languages. The rest is merely deciding who reigns over which area--turf wars. However, "if religion deals with God and the self, and science deals with nature, who can say anything about the relationship between God and nature, or between the self and nature?" Furthermore, if religious beliefs have an independent status there must be ways of establishing religion on its own grounds, and that is something I'm arguing against in this book. Unless someone can propose a mutually agreed upon test to show that religion is a legitimate domain of knowledge on its own merits, it doesn't have any independent status.

3) **Dialogue**. There are some methodological parallels between the two and some differences. Religious beliefs interpret and correlate experience, much as scientific theories interpret and correlate experimental data. Beliefs can be tested by criteria of consistency with experience, as with scientific theories. But personal involvement is more total in the case of religion, since the primary goal is the reformation of the person. Science sets limits within which accounts of meaning can work. Science explains but religion reveals, science informs but religion reforms.

Donald MacKay: "both science and theology gives different kinds of explanations--with different methods and aims--about the same objects. Both explanations of the same event can be true and complete on their own levels. But the methods differ greatly." [See Brain, Machines & Persons, (Eerdmans, 1980, p.19f)]. Both of these explanations can be correct and are not mutually exclusive. Compare how an artist, poet, theologian or astronomer might view a sunset. They can all be correct from their perspective, even if they disagree with one another. MacKay would argue that there is no incompatibility in claiming that the formation of the universe as we know it is the result of natural processes, and that "the cosmos is God's creation." Each explanation is from a particular conceptual framework, and can be true from that framework. Howard Van Till argues: "When scientists make statements concerning matters of origin, governance, value or purpose of the cosmos, they are necessarily stepping outside the bounds of scientific investigation and drawing from their religious or philosophical perspectives....[similarly]...when theologians make statements or conjectures about geological processes or thermodynamic phenomena or cosmic chronology, they are necessarily stepping outside the bounds of scriptural exegesis and into the domain of modern natural science." [The Fourth Day (Eerdmans, 1986), (pp. 197-198), see also Van Till, Young, & Menninga, Science Held Hostage: (IVP, 1988)].

However, unless someone can propose a mutually agreed upon test to distinguish between competing religious claims, scientists don't know which one of them to dialogue with. Furthermore, Richard Dawkins in The God Delusion (2006) makes a passionate and thoughtful case that science does not need to dialogue with religious views since they don't have a reliable method like scientists do. He writes: "Why shouldn't we comment on God, as scientists? And why isn't Russell's teapot, or the Flying Spaghetti Monster, equally immune from scientific skepticism?...a universe with a creative superintendent would be a very different kind of universe from one without. Why is that not a scientific matter?" (p. 55). It is said that "science concerns itself with *how* questions, but only theology is equipped to answer *why* questions. What on Earth *is* a why question? Not every English sentence beginning with the word 'why' is a legitimate question. Why are unicorns hollow?...What is the color of abstraction? What is the smell of hope? The fact that a question can be phrased in a grammatically correct English sentence doesn't make it meaningful, or entitle it to our serious attention." "Perhaps there are some genuinely and meaningful questions that are forever beyond the reach of science...But if science cannot answer some ultimate question, what makes anybody think that religion can?" (p. 56).

Religion is used by people of faith to explain the gaps in our knowledge, but science has been filling those gaps one by one. After surveying several times when theologians have retreated in the face of the progress of science, Richard Carrier wrote, "theologians have been wrong every time so far. Why keep betting on them?" [Sense and Goodness Without God, 2005, pp. 87-88].

4) **Integration.** The content of theology and science can be integrated. A) Natural theology asserts that understanding nature can give rise to and support theology: Aquinas, Swinburne. B) Theology of Nature asserts that our understanding of the general characteristics of nature will affect our models of God's relation to nature. Religious beliefs and scientific theories should be in harmony, such that some adjustments or modifications are called for. Arthur Peacocke, Theology for A Scientific Age, and Teilhard de Chardin, Phenomenon of Man. Teilhard de Chardin argues from evolution to the existence of God, and that at some point humans will achieve convergence to an "Omega Point." C) Panentheism, or Process Theology. Paul Davies, Alfred North Whitehead, Charles Hartshorne. "The World is God's Body." D) Deism.

If there is any integration taking place, religious beliefs are always the ones that have been forced to integrate with science and not the other way around, so why not just admit science sets the boundaries for what we believe? While science has its assumptions, they can be tested empirically, whereas there is no mutually agreed upon test to establish religious beliefs. [The one scientific test that was done on prayer actually showed the opposite, see page 87].

The Origins of Experimental Science. Christians claim that "The fully amplified Judeo-Christian view of creation was, historically, a very significant factor in the rise of science...furthermore, it appears that no other historic views had the same fruitful logic and suggestiveness that could give science momentum." "Science makes sense only in a certain kind of world--the kind that was in fact first envisioned by Christian theism." [Peterson, Hasker, Reichenbach & Basinger, in Reason and Religious Belief (Oxford, 1991) pp. 212, 214. See also the works by Stanley Jaki, Science and Creation (Scottish Academic Press, 1974), The Origin of Science and the Science of its Origin (Regnery, 1978); and The Road of Science and the Ways to God, (U. Of Chicago, 1978)].

However, Richard Carrier (http://www.richardcarrier.blogspot.com/) and others disagree. He is doing his doctoral dissertation on the history of science and Christianity. According to him, to say "'our concept of science is an outgrowth of Christian theology' is no more true than 'our concept of science is an outgrowth of pagan theology.' Modern science grew up in a Christian context, but only by re-embracing ancient scientific values against the grain of the original Christian mindset. In turn, those ancient scientific values grew up in a pagan context. As with Christianity, that's not causality, it's just circumstance." Moreover, "most Christians were uniformly hostile to the whole system of scientific values, condemning them as vain, idolatrous, arrogant, and unnecessary, if not outright dangerous. It took a long, gradual process to finally change minds on that score." In the end, Carrier argues, "Christianity was bad for science. It put a stop to scientific progress for a thousand years, and even after that it made science's recovery difficult, painful, and slow." [John Hick argues for the same thing in An Interpretation of Religion, p. 327-329].

Let me put it this way. There are many theological views in our world today, so the odds are quite likely that science would have arisen because one of them would get lucky to have the right ingredients that allowed for it. Besides, the very fact that creative science proceeds without Christian assumptions shows that science does not need them. A scientist could be an atheist, pantheist, Deist, or Satanist.

What motivated Newton to quantify the movements of objects? The history of scientific notions about motion itself reveals various ideas, depending a great deal upon religious and philosophical views, beginning with Parmenides and Zeno who denied there was motion! Ockham simply believed there was no need to posit the existence of motion since the simpler explanation is that things just reappear in a different place! And yet Ockham, Zeno and Parmenides all saw the same things we do today! There would have been no possible experiment you could show them that would convince them otherwise, as with those who believed in the ubiquitous and nebulous concept of Ether! So for them to see things differently, people had to adopt different philosophical assumptions. Without a change in these assumptions science would never have arisen, this is true. The question is whether they came from Christian theism or not.

There are four "assumptions" of science: 1) "The belief in an external world independent of the perceiving subject is the basis of all natural science."--Albert Einstein. [Einstein, by the way, did not believe in the supernatural. See Richard Dawkins, The God Delusion, pp. 13-19]. 2) The intelligibility of nature—that we can understand nature. 3) The uniformity of nature--that nature is ordered according to patterns we generalize into laws, and that these laws operate uniformly throughout the whole universe. 4) The adequacy of scientific language and math to adequately describe the world. "Humans invent abstract mathematics; basically making it up out of their imaginations, yet math magically turns out to describe the world." Newsweek, "Science Finds God" (July 20, 1998).

Michael Polanyi in Personal Knowledge, and Ian Barbour in Religion in an Age of Science and Issues in Science and Religion, and even Karl Popper in The Logic of Discovery all examine the art of scientific discovery. It's definitely more than one fact built upon another. The philosophical and religious "assumptions" had to be in place for there to be discovery, even though occasionally some discoveries caused a change in their assumptions--a surprise discovery! Perhaps it's just a two way street, both changing the other in tandem. And with today's science we simply do not need metaphysical assumptions, if by this we mean scientists don't have any evidence for the foundational things they believe. They do. At bottom line, if nothing else, science justifies itself pragmatically. In fact, many metaphysical assumptions hamper and stall the progress of science. We needed some assumptions to help get science off the ground and to jettison the superstitions that held us back from discovering it. But now those assumptions are known as the bedrock of science because, if for no other reason, it produces solid results. Pragmatic justification may alone be all we need! To reach the moon we must do *thus and so*. We did *thus and so* and we reached the moon. Therefore doing *thus and so* gets us to the moon. Why would we need a worldview to see this? And the results of science are breaking down superstitions around the globe too. So in a way, as science progresses its tearing at the heart of religious beliefs everywhere.

Methodological Naturalism best describes my view on this whole matter. Methodological naturalism assumes that for everything we experience there is a natural cause. [For discussions of this see "Methodological Naturalism?" by Alvin Plantinga, which can be found at: www.arn.org, "Justifying Methodological Naturalism" by Michael Martin, and "Methodological Naturalism and the Supernatural," by Mark I Vuletic, to be found at www.infidels.org/library]. We who live in the modern world operate on this assumption ourselves everyday. This assumption is the foundation of modernity. We now know how babies are made and how to prevent them; we know why it rains; why nations win and lose wars; why trees fall; why most people get sick and how to cure most of them, etc. In previous centuries we either praised God for the good things that happened to us, or we wondered why he was angry when bad things happened in our lives. If we lost a war, there was sin in the camp. If someone got sick, it was because of sin in his or her life, and so on. Now we have scientific explanations for these things, and we all benefit from those who assumed there was a natural cause to everything we experience.

Many mainstream scientists believe that methodological naturalism has had so many successes in the past that it will prove fruitful in understanding how we humans got here on planet earth too—that there is a natural explanation for it all—even if there are many problems to work out yet. Creation scientists believe that there are too many problems to work out and that a supernatural explanation is needed to explain human life. Many mainstream scientists think that creation scientists have given up way too early in the game on an assumption that is rock solid throughout history. Creation scientists stress that methodological naturalism is only a method and not a final statement on how the world works, whereas many mainstream scientists think that the reason the method works so well is because nature alone must be the final reality.

Two things are very clear to me here. On the one hand, I am personally thankful for every thinker who ever adhered to this assumption, for it has brought in modernity and jettisoned superstition. It is what defines us as modern people. So I'm thankful for those who seek an understanding of how we humans got here. On the other hand, it is clear to me that as yet there is no repeatable experiment that can show that nature is ultimate. However, it isn't beyond the realm of possibility, and there are some very good conceptual schemes for how it may have taken place. [For a naturalistic account of the beginning of this universe, see Paul Davies book <u>Superforce</u> (1984)].

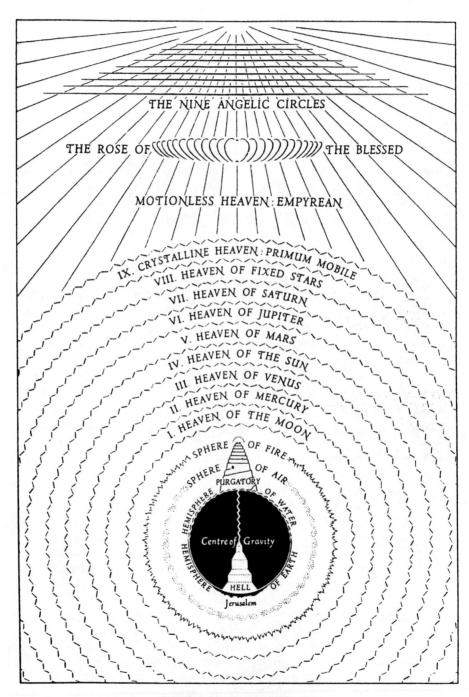

THE NINE ANGELIC CIRCLES

THE ROSE OF (((((((((((((((((((((((((((((((((THE BLESSED

MOTIONLESS HEAVEN : EMPYREAN

IX. CRYSTALLINE HEAVEN : PRIMUM MOBILE
VIII. HEAVEN OF FIXED STARS
VII. HEAVEN OF SATURN
VI. HEAVEN OF JUPITER
V. HEAVEN OF MARS
IV. HEAVEN OF THE SUN
III. HEAVEN OF VENUS
II. HEAVEN OF MERCURY
I. HEAVEN OF THE MOON

SPHERE OF FIRE
SPHERE OF AIR
PURGATORY
HEMISPHERE OF WATER
Centre of Gravity
HEMISPHERE OF EARTH
HELL
Jerusalem

>> · THE UNIVERSE · <<

10 Science and Creation.

SOME PRELIMINARIES, when speaking to Christians from their perspective: 1) An omnipotent God could probably create instantaneously, by fiat. We merely want to know whether he did. He supposedly has the power to do a great many things but chooses not to use his power that often. 2) There is nothing about the concept of creation itself that leads us to conclude God must create by fiat. Arthur Peacock argues that God could use chance as his radar beam searching for the possibilities. Desirable results are then locked in place like a ratchet wrench. God loads the dice so to speak, so the results are his. [See Theology for a Scientific Age, (Fortress Press, 1993, pp. 115-121, 156)]. 3) Someone could still hold to the authority of the Bible even if Genesis doesn't speak to the issues of modern science. He or she could maintain that the Bible is authoritative on every issue it speaks about. 4) Phillip Johnson: "Evolution contradicts creation only when it is explicitly or tacitly defined as fully naturalistic evolution--meaning evolution that is not directed by any purposeful intelligence. Similarly, creation contradicts evolution only when it means sudden .creation, rather than creation by progressive development." [Darwin on Trial, (Regnery, 1991, p. 4)]. 5) The universe operates uniformly by the same consistent pattern of laws. Any creation theory that denies this is to be rejected.

One scientific fact seems to be agreeable to many (but not all) atheists and Christians: the Big Bang Theory. There are four scientific models of the universe: 1) The Big Bang, where this universe exploded into existence; 2) The Pulsating (Oscillating) Universe where the universe endlessly explodes and then implodes over and over again; 3) The Steady State model, in which the universe creates new stars as older stars burn out—that the universe continually recreates itself in a steady state of equilibrium. 4) In his book, The Life of the Cosmos (Oxford, 1999), Lee Smolin argues that our universe originated from a *Black Hole* from inside another universe, and that universes give rise to baby universes as *Black Holes* explode into them from a Big Bang. According to Ian Barbour, "today big bang theories have clearly won the day" [Religion in an Age of Science, (p. 129)]. Of the pulsating model, Stanley Jaki says, "There simply is no evidence for this."[In Science and Creation: From Eternal Cycles to an Oscillating Universe (Scottish Academic Press, 1974]. In fact, the Astronomical Society met in the summer of '97 and heard some major scientists claim they now "know" there isn't enough matter in the universe for gravitational attraction to bring the universe back in on itself.

Confirmations of the Big Bang: a) Hubble's law (red shift) which shows the universe is expanding because light, like sound, changes as it moves away from you from blue to red (much like the sound of a car horn as its sound passes you).; b) Background microwave radiation temperature is constant throughout the universe indicating the residual energy from a big explosion; c) the Curvature of Space resulting from Einstein's $E=MC^2$ equation; and, d) Öblers Paradox shows the universe is finite, otherwise the night sky should be all lit up at night with starlight from an infinite number of stars that have existed from eternity. e) The presence of elements in the universe that cannot be made in stars, like deuterium, helium 3, and lithium 7. The only plausible theory is that the universe began in a big bang. [See Richard Morris, Cosmic Questions (Wiley & Sons, 1993)].

What does astronomy tell us about the age of the universe? Astronomy's foundational assumption is that the universe operates by one set of laws. This was a theistic assumption because one God created the universe. It allowed for the origin of modern astronomy in the first place. Using a spectroscope astronomers can determine the actual brightness, know the chemical elements, size and temperature of a star from its "fingerprint." We can even know it's projected life cycle. We can also tell how far away it is, and how fast it is moving. The distance is measured in light years, which is also a measurement of time. The nearest Galaxy, Andromeda, is 2.5 million light years away, which means the universe must be at least that old if that galaxy truly exists! The universe as a whole is judged to be 12-15 billion years old. But if Genesis 1-2 is taken literally, then nearly all the starlight we see in the sky does not come from any existing stars. This means there is just starlight in the sky unconnected to the stars it supposedly represents. There wouldn't have to be any stars that sent the light because the universe would have to be about 12-15 billion years old for light from many of the stars to actually reach us. If however, the earth is only 4,000 to 10,000 years old then only light from stars within that time frame could actually come from existing stars. And of course, it would also undermine the fundamental assumption of astronomy that was fought and won by Copernicus and Galileo that the universe operates uniformly by the same consistent pattern of laws. (See Howard Van Till, The Fourth Day, (Eerdmans, 1986, pp. 95-277).

What exactly does the Bible say with regard to creation?
In the first place, there four models of creation found in the Bible, not just one. Genesis 1: **Creation by Word**. God speaks, "Let there be..." and there is. Chapter 2: **Creation by Action**. God "planted a garden" which he later walked in (3:8); he brought the beasts to Adam for him to name; he took a rib from Adam and created Eve. Here God is shown to be working, and it made sense that after working he rested on the 7th day. We also see **Creation by Birth** Gen. 2:4; 5:1; 6:9 (toledot or "generate") and **Creation by Theomachy or Divine Conflict** (cf. Isaiah 51:9-10; Ps. 74:13-14; 89:10-12; Job 26:7-13). The reason why there are so many models of creation in the Bible is because it doesn't claim to tell us how God created, only that he did. When it comes to creation by divine conflict (the fourth model), whom was God fighting?

Theories to harmonize Science with Genesis 1-2: [See Bernard Ramm, The Christian View of Science and Scripture, (Eerdmans, 1954), and Henri Blocher, In the Beginning (IVP, 1984)].

One) Local Creation. Genesis 1 speaks only about a localized creation in a garden of Eden in Mesopotamia, not the whole earth. But how can this be when God created the sun, and the stars on the fourth day? How can they be localized?

Two) Ideal Time; (vs real time), where God creates with the appearance of age. That is, God created Adam and Eve with age--16 years, 18 years or 21 years old? Applied to geology and the starry heavens, this means that they too were created with the appearance of age. Proposed by Philip Henry Gosse. He claims that the evidence of fossils and geological strata are simply testimonies to the perfection of which God made the world and universe to appear with age. But the lessons of Galileo show us that the universe operates uniformly by the same consistent pattern of laws. It would be treating geological history as unreal and unreliable, and astronomy as a sham. This is to say that the universe of starlight was created without any connection at all to actual existing stars and galaxies, since astronomy tells us that the universe is 12-15 billion years old. Ramm: "Such a scheme, clever as it is, is a tacit admission of the correctness of geology." (p. 134). Someone would have to be very sure of his or her interpretation of the Bible here before rejecting the sum total of knowledge gained from astronomy and geology.

Three) <u>**Creation Revealed in Seven Days**</u>--not performed in seven days—one of Ramm's views. But there is nothing in the text to indicate this at all, and as we will see, there is a better alternative.

Four) <u>**The Reconstruction Theory**</u> **(or the Gap Theory)**. Between Gen. 1:1 and 1:2 is a huge time gap to account for geological the data. First proposed by Thomas Chalmers (1780-1847). According to Henri Blocher, this theory "Invented in order to please the scientists, it has had considerable difficulty satisfying them." (p. 42). It presupposes three radical phases of life on earth, but there are two insurmountable difficulties: 1) "And the earth BECAME" is an inadmissible Hebrew translation. Compare the same word used in Genesis 3:1 "Now the snake <u>was</u>..."). 2) It also requires that the verb "made" be given the meaning "remake." (cf. 1:31; 2:2f; Ex. 20:11). According to Blocher, the verdict on the whole theory must be "quite impossible."

Five) <u>**The Concordist Interpretation**</u>--each day in Genesis 1 is a very long period of time. (cf. Ps. 90:4). First proponent was Hugh Miller (1869 AD). It was meant to harmonize science and the Bible, but it does no such thing. In the Bible, trees (day 3) precede marine life (day 5), and birds (day 5) precede insects (day 6); scientists think the opposite. But the biggest objection is the fourth day—the creation of the sun, moon, stars after the earth and its vegetation and trees! To say God revealed the sun, moon and stars on the fourth day is an *ad hoc* theory. You cannot turn the word "made" into "reveal"(1:16). Genesis has a perfect word for "appear" when it needed to use it (1:9). "On this reef the concordist boat is wrecked." [Blocher, (p. 45)]. According to Genesis, God first created the earth, and only later, on the 4th day, did he create the universe of stars. This conflicts with astronomy, and the battle won in Galileo's day.

Six) <u>**The Literal View**</u> - God created in six literal days. This view receives support from earliest of times and has the majority of scholars throughout church history. But Blocher reminds us that, "The rejection of all the theories accepted by scientists requires considerable bravado. One must be sure that the text demands the literal interpretation. It must not be adopted out of loyalty to the past." [Blocher, p. 48]. In the first place, it's obvious that the term "day" (YÔM) for earth-dwellers means the 24-hour time period it takes for the earth to revolve around the sun. But the sun wasn't even created until the 4th "day"!

Additionally, there are some huge differences between modern science and Genesis 1 that must be acknowledged (next page):

Modern Science	**Genesis 1**
First the universe of stars existed, then the earth was was formed.	First the earth was formed, then the universe of stars was created.
Rain comes from clouds.	Firmament holds back. the water.
Stars are extremely far away.	Stars in the Firmament.
Sun exists before vegetation.	Vegetation before the sun.
Marine life before vegetation.	Vegetation exists before marine life.
Insects exist before birds.	Birds exist before insects.
Classifies life by biological complexity & structure.	Classifies life by habitat and the environment.

The Hebrew Universe: The ancient Hebrews viewed the universe much like their contemporaries. There is some disagreement with the sketchy details we have in the Bible itself. But they had contact with Babylonia (Abraham came from there); Egypt, the Canaanites (whom they fought with), and other nations around them. It's not likely they would have described the universe totally different from them, except that God created it all. (See Genesis 1:6; 7:11; Job 37:18; Isaiah 40:22; Psalms 19:4-6; 78:23-24; 104:2-4; II Kings 7:2; Amos. 9:6).

According to the Harper's Bible Dictionary, "The ancient Hebrews imagined the world as flat and round, covered by the great solid dome of the firmament which was held up by mountain pillars, (Job 26:11; 37:18). The blue color of the sky was attributed to the chaotic waters that the firmament separated from the earth (Gen. 1:7). The earth was thus surrounded by waters above and below (Gen. 1:6,7; cf. Psalms 24:2; 148:4, Deut. 5:8). The firmament was thought to be substantial; it had pillars (Job 26:11) and foundations (2 Sam. 22:8). When the windows of it were opened, rain fell (Gen. 7:11-12; 8:2). The sun, moon, and stars moved across or were fixed in the firmament (Gen. 1:14-19; Ps. 19:4,6). It was also the abode of the birds (Gen. 1:20; Deut. 4:17). Within the earth lay *Sheol*, the realm of the dead (Num. 16:30-33; Isa. 14:9,15)."

[See "Genesis Knows Nothing of Scientific Creationism: Interpreting and Misinterpreting The Biblical Texts" by Conrad Hyers, and "Biblical Views of Creation" by Frederick E. Greenspahn, at the National Center for Science Education: http://www.ncseweb.org/resources/articles. Edward T. Babinski: "Evolving Interpretations Of the Bible's 'Cosmological Teachings": http://www.edwardtbabinski.us; See also the Anchor Bible Dictionary entry "Cosmogony, Cosmology"].

[The following diagram (on the next page) of the Hebrew Universe is from James L. Christian, Philosophy: An Introduction to the Art of Wondering (Harcourt, p. 512), 1994]:

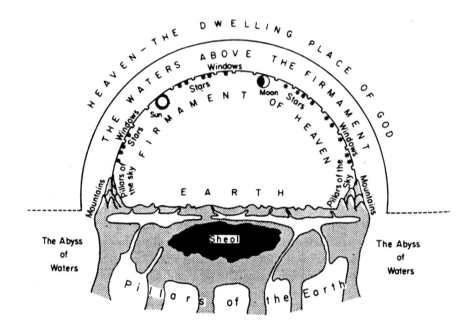

Based on these many facts alone, the literal theory has no basis to stand on. The Biblical writers could not have written about how God actually created the universe, because the Hebrews didn't even have an adequate understanding of the universe.

Ignoring these insurmountable problems, young earth literalists will go on to claim that Noah's flood can account for the geological age appearance of the earth. Until the rise of geological science and Biblical criticism most interpreters of the Bible assumed that the story of Noah's flood was about a worldwide flood. Only Noah and his family survived—along with pairs of the earth's animals—in a huge ark that came to rest in the region of Mt. Ararat. (Genesis 6-9). But, both Biblical criticism and geology have now totally undercut this assumption. [See my next section on this].

The Age of the Earth. "The signs favoring a 'young earth' belong to a class of facts which are still not properly understood or explained; they do not carry enough weight to counterbalance the much more numerous signs of a great age for the earth." "A young earth could never have borne the vegetable mass necessary to create the deposits of coal." "There are 600 meters of stratification in the Yellowstone Park which reveal eighteen forests which were covered over by lava one after another, each successive layer which engulfed its predecessor." A young earth simply cannot account for these layers of forestations and volcanic eruptions! [Henri Blocher, In The Beginning (IVP, 1984, 218-219)].

Davis A. Young takes on the young earth advocates in a chapter titled, "Was the Earth Created a Few Thousand Years Ago?" (in Ronald Youngblood, ed. The Genesis Debate (Baker, 1990, pp. 56-85). He examined evidence from sedimentary rocks, igneous rocks, metamorphic rocks, along with radiometric evidence, and concluded: "Geological evidence accumulated over the past three hundred years overwhelmingly indicates that the planet had experienced a dynamic history measurable in billions of years." (p. 79-80)

Davis A. Young with Howard Van Till and Clarence Menninga in their book, Science Held Hostage: What's Wrong with Creation Science AND Evolutionism? IVP, 1988) have also investigated the so-called evidence for a young earth. Suffice it to say, neither the legend of the shrinking sun, the recent decay of the earth's magnetic field, nor the level of dust on the moon, nor the salt levels in the salty sea, nor the claim of missing rock in the Grand Canyon supports the youth earth theory at all. The young earth theory is maintained despite the overwhelming geological and astronomical evidence simply because of a particular theory about the literalness of the Bible. But not even the Bible claims to be literal in its descriptions of the creation or the flood. With such evidence abounding, it's time to abandon the theory in total! [See also the debate in Three Views on Creation and Evolution eds. J. P. Moreland & John Mark Reynolds (Zondervan, 1999)].

7) Textual Creationist Model of John Sailhamer. [See his book, Genesis Unbound: A Provocative New Look at the Creation Account (Multnomah, 1996)]. The essence of Dr. Sailhamer's book is that Genesis 1:1 describes the creation of the universe during an indeterminate amount of time, while Genesis 1:2-2:4a describes the preparation of the land (the Garden of Eden/Promised Land) over six literal days. Sailhamer claims that ancient Jewish readers would naturally understand the land of Genesis 1 as referring to the *Promised Land* (p. 52). This is a implausible claim indeed, considering that none of the Talmudic writers understood Genesis 1 in this way. Sailhamer's interpretation involves many other far-fetched ideas, such as a belief that the sky was still empty of life on Day 2 (p. 122). But this is preposterous if birds had been flying around for millions of years as he previously claimed. Since Sailhamer believes the universe, including the sun, was created "in the beginning" (verse 1), when God said, "Let there be light" (Genesis 1:3) it refers to the advent of sunrise. But if the sun had been continuously rising every day for billions of years prior to that day, then what is so noteworthy about this particular sunrise such that it deserves any mention at all? The Biblical text is against this model in so many ways.

8) The Literary Interpretation—My View. Historical chronology is entirely absent. Advocated by M.J. Lagrange in 1896 AD, and adopted by other Evangelicals such as N. Ridderbos, B. Ramm, M.G. Kline, & D. Payne. I go farther and say that it is *mythic folklore*.

Consider two facts: **a)** At the start of the older second account of creation (2:4) we find that the absence of vegetation is explained by the lack of rain and humans to work the land (2:5). This would be a strange explanation if the first account described literal 24-hour days, for it presupposes the regular activity of nature for plant growth. In Genesis 1 we already had vegetation (1:11-12)! The author connects these two accounts without clearing up this glaring difficulty indicating that he didn't think the days of creation were literal ones. **b)** The omission of the words "evening and morning" on the 7th day. The natural conclusion: That day is not literal—it was never finished! It is still continuing., Jesus makes an argument that he has the right to work on the Sabbath because God works on his Sabbath (John 5:16-19). His reasoning is sound only if the Father works during his Sabbath. If so, the Son has the same right.

Comparing the widely recognized fact that Genesis 1 and 2 are two different literary accounts of creation we can better see the truth of the literary interpretation. [See also Ronald Youngblood, ed. The Genesis Debate (Baker Book House, 1990). Compare the following differences:

Genesis 1	Genesis 2
God alone creates.	God & man in creative harmony
Begins with watery chaos in which dry land is made to appear.	Begins with not enough water in which water is introduced.
In six days.	In one day.
Creation by divine fiat.	Creation by action.
Vegetation before sun & stars.	Sun & stars before vegetation.
Man created after plants & animals.	Man created before plants & animals.
Adam and Eve created together.	Eve created after Adam.

Claus Westermann: "This separation of the two Creation accounts into two literary sources is one of the most important and most assured results of the literary-critical examination of the Old Testament" [cf. Creation, p. 6]. **Scholars believe Genesis 2 was composed earlier with Genesis 1 much later, reflecting a more pronounced monotheism. Both were combined in one narrative. Genesis 1 reflects civilizations that inhabited river basins and seas, while Genesis 2 is drawn from the imagery of shepherds in semiarid fringes of the fertile plains.**

The Overall Structure of Genesis 1. See Conrad Hyers, The Meaning of Creation, (John Knox Press, 1984, p. 69). In verse 2 we see three problems: darkness, watery abyss, and a formless earth. Then on days 1-3 God prepares his creation for the kinds of things that will populate it in days 4-6, thus solving the three initial problems:

Problem (vs.2)	Preparation (days 1-3)	Population (days 4-6)
darkness	**1a** creation of light (day) **b** separation from darkness	**4a** creation of sun **b** creation of stars
watery abyss	**2a** creation of firmament **b** separation of waters *above* from waters *below*.	**5a** creation of birds **b** creation of fish
formless earth	**3a** separation of earth from sea **b** creation of vegetation	**6a** creation of animals **b** creation of humans

Why Seven Days? **Are numbers to be taken in a literal sense in the Bible?** Conrad Hyers writes: "In the modern world numbers have become almost completely secularized, but in antiquity they could function as significant vehicles of meaning and power. It was important to associate the right numbers with one's life and activity and to avoid the wrong numbers." [cf. The Meaning of Creation, p. 79]. "The symbolic meaning of the number seven and of seven days harks back to the lunar calendar which in Mesopotamia had quite early been divided into four phases of seven days each, followed by the three day disappearance of the moon, thus equaling thirty days." (p. 76). "The symbolism of the number of seven was also reinforced in antiquity by association with the seven visible planetary bodies, which had become important in Mesopotamian astrology.... Seven has the numerological meaning of wholeness, plenitude, and completeness. This symbolism is derived, in part, from the combination of the three major zones of the cosmos as seen vertically (heaven, earth, underworld) and the four quarters and directions of the cosmos as seen horizontally. Both the numbers three and four in themselves often function as symbols of totality, but a greater totality results from the combination of vertical and horizontal planes. Thus the number seven (adding three and four) and the number twelve (multiplying them) are recurrent biblical symbols of fullness and perfection: seven golden candlesticks, seven spirits, seven words of praise, seven eunuchs, seven churches, the seventh year, the forty-ninth year, the seventy elders, forgiveness seventy times seven, etc." (p. 76-77; cf. also Daniel 9:24).

According to C. Cassuto's A Commentary on the Book of Genesis, Vol. 1 [Jerusalem Magnes Press, 1992] the Genesis account is highly structured using the symbolic numbers three, seven, and ten. For instance, the first verse contains 7 Hebrew words, the second verse has 14 Hebrew words (twice 7) and the first section of Genesis is divided into seven sections. This symbolism is undeniable since in Genesis 1 there are at least nine creative acts squeezed into God's six day work week: 1) light, 2) firmament, 3) land, 4) vegetation, 5) sun, moon & stars; 6) birds; 7) fish; 8) animals; 9) humans.

The Theology of Genesis 1-2. "The crucial question in the creation account in Genesis 1 was polytheism vs. monotheism.... For most peoples in the ancient world, all the various regions of nature were divine. Sun, moon, and stars were *gods*. There were sky gods and earth gods and water gods, gods of light and darkness, rivers and vegetation, animals and fertility.... In light of this historical context, it becomes clearer what Genesis 1 is undertaking and accomplishing: a radical sweeping affirmation of monotheism vis-à-vis polytheism, syncretism, and idolatry.... On each day of creation another set of idols is smashed." [Hyers, The Meaning of Creation, (pp. 44-45)]. There thus runs through the whole Genesis cosmology "a conscious and deliberate anti-mythical polemic'" [Heidel, Babylonian Genesis, (p. 91)]. The question for us today is whether we should believe this polemic, since it was written by a superstitious people who argued for their superstitious view over against other superstitious views.

Creation myths were abundant in the ancient world. There are Sumerian, Babylonian, Egyptian, and Levantine creation myths. According to Gordon Wenham in his commentary on Genesis 1-15, Genesis could not have been put into final literary form before 1250 B.C. (the events all had to have occurred first; i.e. Jacob's death in Egypt, and the Exodus). Yet, this Babylonia epic, along with the Atrahasis epic, the Adapa myth, and Sumerian flood story, were known in the ancient world and dated about 1600 B.C. or earlier. Wenham: "We believe therefore that the final editor of Genesis had before him an outline of primeval history, an abbreviated version of our present Gen. 1-11, which he reworked to give the present form of the text." (p. xli). According to Bruce K. Watke, "The biblical writers borrowed their imagery, not their theology." They were written "consciously to exclude mythological elements." ["Creation Myths" in the Baker Encyclopedia of the Bible]. Gordon Wenham: "Most likely the Biblical authors were conscious of a number of accounts of creation current in the Near East of their day, and Genesis 1 is a deliberate statement of the Hebrew view of creation over against rival views." (p. 9).

Just look at the parallel accounts of creation between the older account in the Babylonian "Creation Epic" (*Enuma Elish*), and the Genesis account. It seems readily apparent that they both got their views from out of the mythical stories of their day. These stories were merely shaped by them for their own religious purposes.

Babylonian "Creation Epic"	Genesis 1 Creation Account
1. Divine spirit and cosmic matter are coeternal.	1. Divine spirit creates cosmic matter and is independent of it.
2. Primeval chaos: *Tiamat* enveloped in darkness.	2. The earth a desolate waste, with darkness hovering over the deep (*têhŏm*).
3. Light emanating from the gods.	3. Light created.
4. The creation of the firmament.	4. The creation of the firmament.
5. The creation of dry land.	5. The creation of dry land.
6. The creation of the luminaries.	6. The creation of the luminaries.
7. The creation of the human race.	7. The creation of the human race.
8. The gods rest and celebrate.	8. God rests and sanctifies the seventh day.

The similarities here are very striking, although Paul Copan points out some differences, like the Babylonian epic's co-existence of divine spirit and cosmic matter, the successive rival deities, and polytheism. [See Paul Copan, "That's Just Your Interpretation" (Baker, 2001), pp. 149-150]. But these differences are merely the ones that the idea of God gradually gained in the Hebrew mind over time.

The Phenomenal *Language of Appearances*? Christians will argue that God revealed creation to the Biblical writers in "the phenomenal language of their day," given that we still talk about the "sun rising," and so forth. But along with everything else I argue for in this book, it's more likely that the Bible merely reflects ancient views of cosmology based upon a mythic non-historical consciousness. We see this same kind of thing when it came to prophecy, divination, blessings & curses, dreams, magic (for which see sections 12 and 21), and slavery (see page 237), so why not here as well? **In fact, the Bible does not contain one single statement that could not have been written by a person living in that time period.** What best explains this? If God exists, what was so wrong to tell these ancient people about the true age and vastness of the universe, or in giving them the knowledge of penicillin right from the start, or by unambiguously condemning slavery? By not doing so, God has produced many unbelievers who don't see any true divine revelation in the Bible!

11 Science and Genesis 1-11.

John Hick admits that the picture of a fall from grace by angelic beings and then by humanity in Adam and Eve cannot, strictly speaking, be disproved. The reason is obvious, he wrote, "because those who believe the Bible also believe God can do these things." But it "is fatally lacking in plausibility. For most educated inhabitants of the modern world regard the biblical story of Adam and Eve, and their temptation by the devil, as myth rather than as history." [See "An Irenaean Theodicy" in Encountering Evil (John Knox, 1981), p.40-41].

Scientific problems with Genesis 1-11.

1) The order of creation depicted in chapter one is totally out of sync with what cosmology teaches--in Genesis the earth existed first, then the universe of stars; there was plant life before the sun, that a fully formed man existed before there was a female, etc.

2) Evolutionary theory describes death as something natural to plants, animals, & human beings--not the result of a particular act of punishment by God for human sin.

3) Mythical elements like serpents that talk, trees that have magical powers to confer eternal life, and the supposed ages of human beings; i.e., Adam lived 930 years.

4) The idea that brothers married sisters and produced children is very disturbing, if they actually did.

5) The origin of different races among humanity is not sufficiently explained in Genesis.

6) A universal flood that covered every mountain would upset the earth's orbit and not dissipate in the time allotted.

7) That every species of animal life could be gathered in Noah's ark lacks plausibility (dinosaurs?).

8) The origin of languages at the Tower of Babel is counter to how linguists view language development—Chinese? African languages? Australian Outback?

9) That human beings could cohabit with angels to produce children is simply rejected, if that is what is meant.

10) Astronomy, Geology, and Anthropology show that the universe, the earth and humanity are much older than it allows.

Options with regard to Adam and Eve in the Garden of Eden:

1) Literal/historical. The stories are actual historical events.

-- **Francis Schaeffer** in reference to the serpent in Gen. 3 wrote in Genesis in Space and Time (Inter Varsity Press, 1972): "The Bible is a book for fallen man. Whenever it touches upon anything, it does so with true truth, but not exhaustive truth. That is, where it speaks of the cosmos, science, what it says is true. Likewise, where it touches history, it speaks with what I call true truth, propositional, objective truth." (p. 78).

2) Quasi-Literal/historical. These stories are merely based on actual historical events.

--**John Stott** in Evangelical Essentials (Inter Varsity Press, 1988), writes: "I have long held and taught that [Gen 2-3] contain figurative or symbolic elements, so that we should not dogmatise about the snake and the trees. But I cannot agree that the Adam and Eve story is myth, whose truth is purely symbolical. Adam's body may well have evolved from hominids. But alongside this continuity with the animal creation, he enjoyed a radical discontinuity, owing this to his having been created in God's image. (p. 96.)

--**Henri Blocher's** book In the Beginning (Inter Varsity Press, 1984), states: "The presence of symbolic elements in the text in no way contradicts the historicity of its central meaning.... The real problem is not to know if we have a historical account of the fall, but the account of a historical fall." (p. 155-157).

--**Gordon Wenham** in Genesis 1-15 (Word Biblical Commentary, 1987): "To affirm that Gen 2-3 is a 'factual report' is not to say it is history, at least history in the normal meaning of the term." Some have suggested 'pre-history,' and 'mytho-historical' (p. 54) but Wenham thinks "the story offers a protohistorical account of man's origins and his sin." (p. 91).

--**Derek Kidner** in his commentary on Genesis (Inter Varsity Press, 1967) states: "nothing requires that the creature into which God breathed human life should not have been a species prepared in every way for humanity, with already a long history of practical intelligence, artistic sensibility and the capacity for awe and reflection. On this view, Adam, the first true man, will have had as contemporaries many creatures of comparable intelligence, widely distributed over the world. Yet it is at least conceivable that after the special creation of Eve, which established the first human pair as God's vice-regents and clinched the fact that there is no natural bridge from animal to man, God may now have conferred his image on Adam's collaterals, to bring them into the same realm of being. Adam's 'federal' headship of humanity extended outwards to his contemporaries as well as onwards to his offspring, and his disobedience disinherited both alike." (p. 29).

--**Clark Pinnock** in The Scripture Principle (Harper & Row, 1984): "it is not necessary to understand the story of the fall of Adam as a historical, eyewitness account, which it could not have been." (p. 67). "The literary genre... is figurative rather than strictly literal...the hints are very strong that it is symbolic: Adam (which means 'Mankind') marries Eve (which means 'Life'), and their son Cain (which means 'Forgerer') becomes a wanderer in the land of Nod (which means "Wandering')!" (p. 116). He still maintains: "It makes sense to think of the Fall as being historical. There must have been a moment when the decision was first taken and a new direction was first chosen...Such a turning point would have had to be posited had the Bible not reported it."--Unbounded Love (Inter Varsity Press, 1994), (p. 62).

--**Donald Gowan** in From Eden to Babel: Genesis 1-11 (Eerdmans, 1988): the stories of Genesis 1-11 can only be misunderstood if they are "thought to be a historical account of what happened to two people who lived long ago in a world utterly different from ours." Instead, they "lie somewhere between a purely imaginative story and straightforward accounts of historical events." So he rejects labeling them as "saga" "legend" and "tale" but chooses to call them "archetypal stories" in that their experiences are to be seen as "archetypal, repeated in each of us." (pp. 35-36.)

3) Non-historical/mythical stories. They are divinely inspired parabolic stories. They are not historical stories at all, but they teach us spiritual truths about the universe in which we live and our place in it. The stories are told by human beings (men) who tried to explain why the world and society operates the way it does. This is my view except that these stories are not divine ones.

--**H. Wade Seaford** argues that "the ecological and cultural data contained in Genesis 1-4, if compared to established archeological knowledge, places the events somewhere between ten thousand and two thousand years ago" (egs. iron metallurgy and domesticated food), that is, "at the dawn of the Neolithic Age." But "there is overwhelming, staggering evidence that humans inhabited the world millennia before the Neolithic/Iron Age setting of the creation story." So he asks: "Can we understand the Genesis account as an allegory, written by persons who used the ecological setting with which they were acquainted to tell the story of human alienation from God and of God's redemptive purpose? If we wish to claim Adam and Eve as symbolic progenitors of the entire human race, we must consider them as representing an event occurring thousands or millions of years before the setting in which the text of Genesis places them. Unfortunately...the paleontological record thoroughly establishes that one population is always preceded by another, making the idea of a single pair of humans procreating an entire species unthinkable." The Genesis Debate (Baker 1990, pp. 154-162). [For a response see Millard Erickson, Christian Theology (Baker, 1984) Vol. 2, p.486f.]

--**Conrad Hyers** in The Meaning of Creation: Genesis and Modern Science (John Knox Press, 1984) that "Genesis 2-3 is mythical in form." (p. 125). Myths account for "why snakes have no legs like other reptiles, why they 'eat dust,' why there is special 'enmity' between snakes and humans, why humans and not animals are embarrassed by their nakedness and wear clothes, why there is pain in childbirth. Other, more substantial features of existence are also accounted for in like manner: the relationship between male and female, between animals and humans, and between humans and God, as well as the sources of toil, suffering, and death." (p. 126).

--**Alan Richardson** in A Theological Word Book of the Bible (SCM Press, 1957): "The time element in the myths of the Creation and Fall (as in all biblical myths) must be discounted; it is not that ONCE...God created man perfect and then fell from grace. God is...eternally making man...so the 'Fall' is an ingredient of every moment of human life; man is at every moment 'falling', putting himself in the centre, rebelling against the will of God. Adam is Everyman." (p. 14.)

--**John C.L. Gibson** in Genesis (Westminister Press, 1981): "There never was a place as the Garden of Eden, nor was there ever a historical person called Adam who lived in it and conversed with snakes and with God in Hebrew...animals only speak in fables..." The garden is a garden of the mind, a garden of 'men's' dreams, the kind of place they would like this world to be, the kind of place indeed they know this world ought to be. And Adam is each one of us, he is Everyman.... Each and every day Paradise beckons us, but each and every day we eat the forbidden fruit and are banished from it." (pp. 100-101, 121-125).

Case in Point One: The Story of Cain (Gen. 4:1-25):

God's judgment upon Cain for killing his brother Abel was to be a wanderer. Cain is deathly afraid of this and says: "whoever finds me will kill me." So God places a mark on him so that "no one who found him would kill him." (v.14). Now who is Cain afraid of here? Supposedly the only people on earth were his mom and dad, and a few sisters. Then it says, "Cain lay with his wife." (v.17). Where did he get a wife? Nothing was said about that, but presumably the author isn't interested in such matters. Why? It's because the author of chapters 3-11 was stressing the sinfulness of human beings. God created the world good, but look how his highest creation behaves—he behaves very very badly. Human beings are very sinful beginning with Adam and Eve's disobedience, to Cain killing his brother, to the flood where God destroyed everyone but Noah and his family, to the tower of Babel. Human beings are very sinful and ungrateful for what God has done. To try to make sense of where Cain got his wife is to miss the point of these chapters. It has the feel of a story with a point, not a statement about marrying sisters. Then it says when Cain's wife gave birth to his firstborn, Enoch, Cain was in the process of "building a city." (v.17). If we try to make sense of this we simply cannot do it. Cain is banished from his parents and marked so that no one who finds him will kill him. He gets a wife and starts to build a city, and while doing so Enoch is born. None of this makes much sense given the whole setting. A city? Instead, maybe it should have read, "Cain was building a house." But a whole city? Do fugitives build cities?

It doesn't make sense to think there was a massive amount of incest going on, producing babies. Even then the text would still be incorrect, for Cain should've said: "any of my brothers or sisters who finds me will kill me." And since this whole problem is obvious, the author/editor surely would've cleared it up, if he considered it to be something that needed to be cleared up at all.

According to *Donald Gown* this whole scenario "seems to presuppose a different background from that provided by chapters 2-3, one in which Cain and Abel live in an already well-populated world. Furthermore, the genealogy at the end, leading to the founding of guilds of cattle-raisers, musicians, and metallurgists, seems strangely irrelevant when we realize that all the descendants of these people will be wiped out by the flood. Originally, then, the story of Cain and Abel was probably told as a self-contained narrative, without having any relationship to the stories of the garden or the flood." [From Eden to Babel: Genesis 1-11 (pp. 62-63)].

This should surprise no one. Even the Gospels do not present the same chronology of events in the life of Jesus or stress the same things about him. The events in the life of Jesus were arranged by each of the four authors to stress certain distinct things in the life of Jesus, and very few, if any N.T. authorities think otherwise. [See almost any scholarly introduction to the Gospels for this].

But with the story of Cain we have an additional problem. If so many things in this story are inserted without the need to correct the setting, like his wife, the people he fears, and the city he is building, then when the editor/author earlier said that "Eve would become the mother of all the living" (Gen. 3:20) we can see it for what it really is. It is just a folk story with a point, like one of Jesus' parables. *John Gibson*: "Genesis is essentially folk literature. The vast bulk of it consists of stories which still carry about them the marks of having been composed to entertain and to instruct ordinary folks." "In effect we are treating this and other opening chapters of Genesis as imaginative stories, approaching them as we would a modern short story or, to use a Biblical parallel, one of our Lord's parables." [Genesis 1-11, (pp. 2, 11)].

This view undercuts what both Jesus and Paul purportedly thought about Adam & Eve, Cain and Able too. Either they were both wrong to think of them as real historical people, or they thought these were imaginative folk-tales.

Case in Point Two: the Flood Story of Genesis 6-9:

The first thing to notice in the story is that there is a great deal of repetition. We are told that Noah is commanded by God to make an ark, load it with food and animals, and then board it. Afterward it says Noah "did everything just as God had commanded him." (6:14-22). But after doing all of this once, God repeats similar instructions to Noah, and once again it says Noah "did all that the Lord had commanded him." (7:1-5). Did Noah make two arks and board them twice? But we're not done yet. It goes on to say Noah and his family boarded the ark again (7:7-9), and again (7:13-16). There are also discrepancies in these chapters. In 6:14-22 God is referred to as "Elohim", and only one pair of each species of animal was put in the ark, whereas in 7:1-5 the word for God is "Yahweh" and Noah is told to put in the ark seven pairs of clean animals and one pair of unclean animals. There are also discrepancies with how long the flood lasted: 40 days (7:17), 150 days (7:24), or one year (compare 7:11 with 8:13)?

Biblical scholars now see the way the flood is presented here as reflecting two ancient sources that were combined into one account. This was done by "following a very conservative principle of keeping virtually everything from both sources, even though that produced considerable repetition" and, I might add, discrepancies. [Donald Gowan, From Eden to Babel: Genesis 1-11 (Eerdmans, 1988, p. 89)]. The closest stories we find to the flood story in the Bible are from Mesopotamia: the Epic of Gilgamesh, and Atrahasis. According to Gordon J. Wenham the Epic of Gilgamesh was written about 1600 B.C. and it "may be based on the flood story told in Atrahasis." These stories have several striking similarities, including a flood hero, an ark, a universal worldwide flood because of man's disobedience, and even a dove! [See "Ancient Parallels to the Flood Story," in Gordon Wenham's book, Genesis 1-15 (Word, 1987, pp. 159-166). "These texts are evidence for the transmission of a very popular story from century to century and from people to people; among the recipients of this tradition were the Greeks and the Hebrews." [Gowan, (p. 91)].

If this is the case, then the flood story in the Bible is taken and reshaped to fit the purposes of the final editor of Genesis 1-11. And if we consider prior sources to be the more authentic sources (and historical scholars consider this to be the case in every other historical investigation), then the true account of the flood (if there is one and it reflects something that historically happened) is to be found in Atrahasis along with the Epic of Gilgamesh! Genesis 6-9 is very late and therefore unreliable, historical analysis would reveal. Atrahasis and the Epic of Gilgamesh would be our primary sources for information about a great universal flood that covered the whole world. And in them neither a person named Noah, nor a God named "Yaweh," are to be found!

How much of the flood story that we find in the Bible can be regarded as historical, if it is based upon ancient superstitious polytheistic folk-tales which were handed down throughout the centuries?—tales which have been told by almost every ancient culture except most of Africa, and in central and eastern Asia? [To read 97 pages of summaries of these tales see Sir James G. Frazer's book, Folklore in the Old Testament]. Textual analysis cannot really lead us to think all of these tales speak of the same event. Rather, these tales are told based upon local devastating floods (notice the absence of Egypt!) which most ancient cultures believed were sent by the gods to punish people for their disobedience. We now know why floods take place, and it isn't because of our sins, but because of atmospheric, and oceanic conditions.

Problems Connected to the Flood Story. Bernard Ramm's critical analysis of a universal flood (while dated a half century ago) is still one of the best summations of the evidence. [See Bernard Ramm's book, The Christian View of Science and Scripture (Eerdmans, 1954, pp. 163-169). 1) "There is no known geological data to support those who defend a universal flood." Gowan sums up the evidence with these words: "Not only have all archeological excavations failed to uncover any such evidence (for a universal flood), the record of the earth's history discovered by geology virtually rules out the possibility that anything of that sort has ever happened." (p. 89). [There is a recent discovery by Robert Ballard that the Black Sea shoreline increased by 60,000 square miles around 7,500 years ago. But he admits this could have been the result of an earthquake, a massive storm, or perhaps the sheer weight of the ocean waters, none of which demands a worldwide flood (See U.S. News & World Report "Mysteries of the Bible, November 2004)]. 2) "The problems in connection with a universal flood are enormous." a) "It would have required eight times more water than we now have." b) The mixing of salt water and fresh water along with the pressure of the waters would have been devastating to marine life. Fresh-water fish would die in salt water and salt-water fish would die in fresh water. The pressure of the water six miles high (to cover the Himalayas) would crush to death the vast bulk of marine life that lives within the first fifty fathoms in the water. c) Getting rid of such a vast amount of water would be impossible—think of it! d) "The astronomical disturbances caused by the increase of the mass of the earth would have been significant." e) There are improbabilities with regard to the animals involved. How did Noah get them all into the ark? Bringing them from all four corners of the globe would take considerable time. How did they get along in the ark? Some are carnivorous and would be prone to eating the other animals, while others would have vegetarian diets. Where did the food come from to feed all of these animals from around the world? How could a few people care for them all in the ark? Some animals need a moist climate, and others a dry one; some need it very cold, while others need it warm. f) After the flood how did these animals all migrate back to their original lands, like the kangaroo, from Australia? **There was no universal flood to account for the geological evidence that leads scientists to believe the earth is billions of years old.** According to the Anchor Bible Dictionary, "Scholars are agreed that archaeological evidence for a universal flood in the historical past is wanting," and this admission comes from Christian scholarship on the issue!

12 The Strange and Superstitious World of the Bible.

In the Bible we find a strange world. Karl Barth wrote an essay titled "The Strange New World Within The Bible." To the question of what lies within the world of the Bible, Barth gives this answer: "Within the Bible, there is a strange, new world, the world of God." [The Word of God and the Word of Man (Harper, 1928), p. 33]. And it is indeed strange to us today—very strange.

We find a world where a snake and a donkey talked, where people could live 800-900+ years old, where a woman was turned into a pillar of salt, where a pillar of fire could lead people by night, where the sun stopped moving across the sky or could even back up, where an ax-head could float on water, a star can point down to a specific home, where people could instantly speak in unlearned foreign languages, and where someone's shadow or handkerchief could heal people. It is a world where a flood can cover the whole earth, a man can walk on water, calm a stormy sea, change water into wine, or be swallowed by a "great fish" and live to tell about it. It is a world populated by demons that can wreak havoc on earth, and also make people very sick. It is a world of idol worship, where human and animal sacrifices pleased God. In this world we find visions, inspired dreams, prophetic utterances, miracle workers, magicians, diviners and sorcerers. It is a world where God lived in the sky (heaven), and people who died went to live in the dark recesses of the earth (*Sheol*).

Today's Christians believe the Bible accurately describes this world, and that the events depicted in it really happened, depending on how they interpret it all. Others think that such a world is so strange to their ears that it simply must be a recorded reflection of very superstitious people.

New Testament scholar Rudolph Bultmann just calls them "myths" and gets his point across by exaggerating his case: "The cosmology of the N.T. is essentially mythical in character. The world is viewed as a three-storied structure, with the earth in the center, the heaven above, and the underworld beneath. Heaven is the abode of God and of celestial beings—angels. The underworld is hell, the place of torment. Man is not in control of his life. Evil spirits may take possession of him. Satan may inspire him with evil thoughts. It is simply the cosmology of a pre-scientific age. To modern man...the mythical view of the world is obsolete. It is no longer possible for anyone seriously to hold the N.T. view of the world. We no longer believe in the three-storied universe. No one who is old enough to think for himself supposes that God lives in a local heaven. There is no longer any heaven in the traditional sense. The same applies to hell in the sense of a mythical underworld beneath our feet. And if this is so...we can no longer look for the return of the Son of Man on the clouds of heaven. It is impossible to use the electric light and the wireless and to avail ourselves of modern medical and surgical discoveries, and at the same time to believe in the N.T. world of spirits and miracles. The same objections apply to the doctrine of the atonement. How can the guilt of one man be expiated by the death of another who is sinless?" [R. Bultmann, in Kerygma & Myth, (pp. 1-7)].

Ancient People Weren't Stupid, Just Superstitious –

Ancient people were not stupid people. After all, they built great walls, roads, buildings, cities, temples and empires, along with weapons and military strategies to defend themselves. But many Christians think ancient people were just as skeptical as we are today, and/or that modern people today are just as superstitious as they were. The main difference, according to them, is that the events described in the Bible really happened, that's all. However, if the Biblical people were very superstitious in comparison to ours, it would greatly weaken their claims, because then it could be claimed by skeptics that ancient people did not have solid evidence to believe. It could then be argued that extremely superstitious people will tend to believe most any wondrous story if it was told by a sincere and devoted person. This will be my point here.

My contention is that ancient people weren't stupid, just very superstitious. While I'll admit that our day and age still contains a lot of superstitious people, more thoughtful and scientifically literate people in today's world have different standards—higher standards--for the evidence needed to believe. Carl Sagan was right when he subtitled his book, The Demon Haunted World, with these words: Science As a Candle in the Dark. Our standards have been adopted as the results of modern science, where we know how babies are born, what makes it rain, why nations win wars, and what makes people sick, for the most part. Even Christians look for natural causes, for these things, for the most part. Why else would they go to fertility doctors, or any doctors at all? Why would they listen to the weatherman on TV? Or, why seek guidance from American generals about Iraq and Afghanistan? It's because even Christians today have accepted the same standards from modern science as the rest of us.

Let's define *Superstition*, using Microsoft Encarta: "Superstition, a belief or practice generally regarded as irrational and as resulting from ignorance or from fear of the unknown. It implies a belief in unseen and unknown forces that can be influenced by objects and rituals. Magic or Sorcery, witchcraft, and the occult in general are often referred to as superstitions. Examples of common superstitions include the belief that bad luck will strike the person in front of whom a black cat passes or that some tragedy will befall a person who walks under a ladder. Good luck charms, such as horseshoes, rabbits' feet, coins, lockets, and religious medals, are commonly kept or worn to ward off evil or to bring good fortune."

"The question of what is or is not superstitious, however, is relative. One person's beliefs can be another's superstitions. All religious beliefs and practices may be considered superstition by unbelievers, while religious leaders often condemn unorthodox popular practices as a superstitious parody of true faith." [Emphasis mine]

As the last paragraph indicates, there are problems in defining "superstition." But this is true of many words. Would you please define pornography? What is a "normal" human being? What is beautiful? We may not always be able to specify what we mean, but "we know it when we see it," don't we? And this is usually an acceptable answer, even though it's a person-related answer too. All I'm arguing here is that ancient people believed a great many things that modern eductated people today would say are superstitious, and that's good enough.

I can propose scientific tests for what I consider superstitions. I can compare what a meteorologist says about the weather with someone who plans to do a rain dance, and test to see who's right more often. That's science. The results of reason and science have jettisoned a great many superstitions. Testing and comparing results. That's science. I can do the same for the superstitious practice of blood-letting, for exorcisms, for people who claim to predict things based on palm reading, or tea leaves, or walking under a ladder, or breaking a mirror, or stepping on a sidewalk crack. I can even test the results of someone who gets a shot of penicillin when sick with the person who refuses this and prays instead. That's science. And we modern people are indebted to science for these things. It's what makes us different from ancient people.

Ancient People Definitely Were Very Superstitious One way to examine whether or not ancient people were very superstitious is to examine historical documents to see what these people were doing and thinking at that time. Richard Carrier has done this in "Kooks and Quacks of the Roman Empire: A Look Into the World of the Gospels" which can be found at www.infidels.org/library, or see his Sense And Goodness Without God, Part IV, "Not Much Room For the Paranormal" (2005), pp. 209-252. According to him, the ancient NT age was one "of fable and wonder, where magic, miracles, ghosts, and gods were everywhere and almost never doubted." [The Empty Tomb (Prometheus Books, 2005), p. 171)].

But I think there is another way to see how superstitious the ancients were. I decided to re-read portions of the Bible just like fundamentalist and evangelical Bible believing Christians do. That is, I took the Bible at face value without utilizing the results of higher critical Biblical scholarship regarding the true nature of the dates, sources and time periods of the Biblical documents. [For two excellent books revealing the results of higher critical scholarship, see Who Wrote the Bible? by Richard E. Friedman (HarperSanFrancisco, 1997), and Robin Lane Fox The Unauthorized Version: Truth and Fiction in the Bible (Knopf, 1992]. What I wanted to find out is whether the Bible, taken at face value, leads us to think other surrounding cultures were superstitious by our standards today. If the Bible is believed to be the word of God, and the Bible tells us that the peoples of that time were superstitious, then it will lead us to think that even the Israelites and Christians were superstitious too, especially if it shows that they regularly were "led astray" to practice the same beliefs. After all, "Every man is a creature of the age in which he lives, and few are able to raise themselves above the ideas of the time." –Voltaire.

What I found was that there were so many superstitious beliefs by the Gentile nations at every period of time in the Bible that superstition reigned in those ancient days. I don't think any modern person should be able to conclude anything other than that. The beliefs of these nations were so prevalent that God's people in the Bible regularly joined in the same practices and worship of these gods and goddesses. **So my question here will be this: if these nations were so superstitious that Israel regularly joined them in their beliefs, then how do we know that the beliefs of the Israelites, and later the Christians, didn't base their religious beliefs upon superstitions too?**

Every surrounding culture had a plethora of gods and goddesses, along with priests, magicians, sorcerers, astrologers, and diviners. This is very easily documented. [On Canaanite divinities see the entry in <u>Baker Encyclopedia of the Bible</u> (Baker, 1988). On Egyptian mythology see Anthony S. Mercatante, <u>Who's Who in Egyptian Mythology</u> (Crown, 1978). On Babylonian and Assyrian mythology see Gwendolyn Leick, <u>A Dictionary of Near Eastern Mythology</u> (Routledge, 1991). On Greek and Roman mythology see Catherine Avery, <u>The New Century Handbook of Greek Mythology and Legend</u> (Appleston, 1972), and Michael Grant, <u>Myths of the Greeks and Romans</u> (Dutton, 1989)].

These myths of gods and goddesses were believed by the peoples of those days, and these people had a great deal of contact with the Jews of the Old Testament and the Christians in the New Testament. After all, Abraham came from the Babylonian area, and was brought up by his father who served other gods (Joshua 24:2). Abraham traveled to Palestine by means of the Fertile Crescent, and he lived in Egypt for a time during a famine. The Fertile Crescent was used as a heavily traveled trade route for the near-eastern peoples of Assyria, Babylonia, Asia, and Egypt, which met midway in Palestine. So they had to have a great deal of contact with other cultures throughout Biblical times.

Furthermore, the Israelites lived in Egypt, the Bible says, for about 400 years, and then they settled in and among the Canaanites. Later they were destroyed and/or carried away into Babylonian captivity for 70 years, before being able to return home. First century A.D. Jews and Christians lived under Roman rule. How could they not be influenced by these great cultures, is the question I pose. **And since people of every era are unavoidably "children of their times," the burden of proof is on those who say that the Jews and Christians are the exceptions to this rule.** Even though it can be shown they had distinctive beliefs and practices, whereby every culture distinguished itself from the others, they all shared a fundamental superstitious outlook on the world.

We who live in the modern world of science simply don't believe in a god of the sun, or moon, or harvest, of fertility, or rain, or the sea. We don't see omens in an eclipse, or in flood, a storm, a snakebite, or a drought, either. That's because we understand nature better than they did, by using science. We don't see sickness as demon possession, nor do educated thinking people believe in astrology to get an insight into the future. Nor do we think we are physically any closer to God whether we're up on a mountaintop rather than down in a valley. But every nation did in ancient days. Most all of the kings of those days believed these things, even if it can be accurately pointed out that there were many people who did not believe in the myths of their day. For example, Socrates (5th century B.C.) was charged with not believing the Greek gods, and consequently condemned to die for corrupting the youth. But remember, he was condemned to die by the superstitious people of his day, too, so he's merely an exception.

<u>**Old Testament Examples-**</u>As I looked at the O.T. I took the Bible at face value to see how it describes the beliefs and practices of other peoples, including apostates. **There is the purported Tower of Babel (Genesis 11:3-9):**

> *3 They said to each other... "Come, let us build ourselves a city, with a tower that reaches to the heavens, so that we may make a name for ourselves and not be scattered over the face of the whole earth." 5 But the LORD came down to see the city and the tower that the men were building. 6 The LORD said..."Come, let us go down and confuse their language so they will not understand each other." 8 So the*

LORD scattered them from there over all the earth, and they stopped building the city."

The implication here, although not expressly stated, is that God wanted to stop them from building a tower to "heaven." Among the ancients this would be clearly understood that God didn't want these people to approach him where he lived, so God stopped them from doing so. Gordon Wenham: "It was a commonplace of Babylonian thought that temples had their roots in the netherworld and their tops reached up to heaven." "It seems likely that Genesis views it as a sacrilege. For the sky is also heaven, the home of God, and this ancient skyscraper may have been another human effort to become like God from what is said here (cf. 3:5; 6:1-4)." [Genesis 1-15 (Word, 1991), pp. 237-239].

Furthermore, ancient people would also consider that this God, like the other gods, had a pantheon of gods with him who helped him (hence the words, "let us"). No one would have considered the idea of a triune God here. It was something Christians read back into the O.T. stories of creation and the tower of Babel. Gordon Wenham: "Christians have traditionally seen this verse as adumbrating the Trinity. It is now universally admitted that this verse was not what the plural ("let us") meant to the original author." [See his discussion of this in Genesis 1-15, pp. 27-29].

There are three mythical beasts that God defeated. There is "Rahab." According to Harper's Bible Dictionary: This is "the mythical chaos dragon whom God killed in battle and thus made an orderly creation possible (Job 26:7-14; Isa. 51:9; Ps. 89:10)." **There is "Leviathan."** According to the Harper's Bible Dictionary: "Leviathan, a great, mythological monster. In Ugaritic mythology, Leviathan (appearing by the name 'Lothan') is one of the primeval sea monsters who battles against Baal on the side of Mot (the god of the underworld) and who is ultimately defeated. This mythological tradition was adopted and transformed in the Bible where God appears as the victor over the sea monsters (Ps. 74:13-14, cf. Job 3:8; 26:12-13; 41:1-34; Ps. 104:26). The references to God 'playing' with Leviathan (Ps. 104:26; Job 41:5) are explainable on the basis of God's omnipotence which reduces this mighty rebellious dragon to a plaything....The future and final destruction of Leviathan becomes a symbol in Isaiah (27:1) for the death of the wicked, to be succeeded by the redemption of Israel (26:20-21; 27:2-13)." How can God defeat mythical beasts that do not exist? **There is "Behemoth"** (Job 40:15). It has been claimed, "Behemoth and Leviathan denote respectively the hippopotamus and the crocodile. However, they are probably instead chaos monsters. The description of neither Behemoth nor Leviathan corresponds to any known creature, and certainly not the hippopotamus and crocodile. It seems fundamental to the argument in Job 40–41 that the beasts in question can be captured by God alone, otherwise Job might have replied that he could have captured them, and then God would lose the argument!" [The Anchor Bible Dictionary].

A Brief History of Superstition in Israel.

When Moses confronted the Egyptian Pharaoh of his day we read: *"Aaron threw his staff down in front of Pharaoh and his officials, and it became a snake. Pharaoh then summoned wise men and sorcerers, and the Egyptian magicians also did the same things by their secret arts: Each one threw down his staff and it became a snake."* (Exodus 7:10-12). Never mind for the moment that we're told that Aaron's staff swallowed up their staffs, because whether or not this happened is in question. We're told that the Egyptian magicians were able to turn a staff into a snake, turn water into blood (Exodus 7:19-22), and duplicate the plague of frogs (Exodus 8:18), just as Moses did. And the Egyptian sorcerers weren't surprised at doing so. They weren't surprised at all? Not even Moses nor Aaron were surprised by this, nor was the writer of this account, nor the ancient people who believed such a story. That's very strange to modern ears, that these sorcerers weren't surprised at doing this. But we would be if we heard such a tale.

After just being rescued out of Egyptian slavery, we read, that the people *"have made themselves an idol cast in the shape of a calf. They have bowed down to it and sacrificed to it and have said, 'These are your gods, O Israel, who brought you up out of Egypt.' "I have seen these people,"* the LORD said to Moses, *"and they are a stiff-necked people."* (Exodus 32:7-9).

This took place "on the third month after the Israelites left Egypt," plus forty days and nights (Exodus 19:1; 24:18). So four months and ten days later these people ("all the people," Exodus 32:3) wanted to worship a golden calf that Aaron said, "brought you out of Egypt." How could they so quickly abandon the God of Moses? If the events all took place as described in Exodus, I doubt very much if anyone would dare take the risk to worship this calf against the God of Moses. If I was there I know I wouldn't! This leads me to the conclusion that the reason they could so quickly abandon the Biblical God of Moses is that their history was itself built upon non-historical myths. But because they did, Moses had the Levites kill "his brother and friend and neighbor," 3000 of them (Ex. 32:27-29)! It looks like Moses just intimidated the people to believe against their wills. They knew who delivered them out of Egypt—it was the gods of Egypt who revolted against the Egyptians themselves, allowing the Israelites to escape.

It just seems more likely to me that the Pharaoh of Egypt was himself superstitious. And because there were some strange natural phenomena going on in the land at the time, which he would have viewed as omens, he would've sent these foreigners away, while Moses received the credit for it all. So when Moses didn't come down from Mt. Sinai, the Israelite people simply gave credit to the true god that had given them their freedom, in their minds. "The calf was probably similar to representations of the Egyptian bull-god Apis." [Ronald Youngblood & Gleason Archer, in the <u>NIV Study Bible</u>]. They knew who had released them from Egypt, but Moses threatened them with death if they disagreed.

When the Israelites were camped along the Jordon river before entering the Promised land, we read: *"Balak son of Zippor, who was king of Moab at that time, sent messengers to summon Balaam son of Beor, who was at Pethor, near the River, in his native land. Balak said: 'A people has come out of Egypt; they cover the face of the land and have settled next to me. Now come and put a curse on these people, because they are too powerful for me. Perhaps then I will be able to defeat them and drive them out of the country. For I know that those you bless are blessed, and those you curse are cursed.' The elders of Moab and Midian left, taking with them the fee for divination. When they came to Balaam, they told him what Balak had said."* (Numbers 22:4-7, 24:1) And even though Balak took Balaam to three "high places," which were believed closer to where God lived in heaven, we're told Balaam couldn't curse the Israelites.

Ancient people like Balak and Balaam believed that curses could actually help defeat an enemy. And it's recorded in the Bible because we're told God would only allow Balaam to bless the Israelites. Blessings cause good events to happen. The Biblical author believed the same thing as Balak did about curses and blessings; it's just that Balaam couldn't curse the Israelites. So let me ask you this: How would that go over today if our President did that with the approval from the House and Senate to curse the militant Muslims? What would the media say about doing this? What would you say?

The reason the story about Balak is even recorded here is because of the importance the Israelites placed on blessings and curses--something we find throughout the O.T. [Note especially Genesis 12:2-3; 27-28; 49; Deut. 27-28; 33; and Judges 5]. The Patriarchs blessed their children, but notice that Isaac cannot reverse what he has promised to Jacob (Gen. 27:33-37). Notice also that when Jesus cursed a fig tree, it withered and died (Mark 11:12-23).

Even though Balaam couldn't curse Israel but blessed them instead, some of the Israelites were seduced by Moab: *"While Israel was staying in Shittim, the men began to indulge in sexual immorality with Moabite women, who invited them to the sacrifices to their gods. The people ate and bowed down before these gods. So Israel joined in worshiping the Baal of Peor. And the Lord's anger burned against them. So Moses said to Israel's judges, "Each of you must put to death those of your men who have joined in worshiping the Baal of Peor."* (Numbers 25:1-5). More people died who disagreed with Moses! **It would seem that many people followed their cult hero, Moses, out of fear, not true belief**.

After Israel settled in the land promised we're told, *"the LORD raised up judges, who saved them out of the hands of these raiders. Yet they would not listen to their judges but prostituted themselves to other gods and worshiped them. Unlike their fathers, they quickly turned from the way in which their fathers had walked, the way of obedience to the LORD's commands. Whenever the LORD raised up a judge for them, he was with the judge and saved them out of the hands of their enemies as long as the judge lived…But when the judge died, the people returned to ways even more corrupt than those of their fathers, following other gods and serving and worshiping them."* (Judges 2:16-19, also Judges 10:6). It just didn't take the people of Israel very long at all to worship other gods, especially if God provided miraculous manna to eat, gave them water from rocks, and didn't let their shoes wear out for forty years!

Judge Jephthah sacrificed his daughter to "God" (Judges 11:39). Was God pleased at that? Micah had a shrine, some idols, and even a priest (Judges 17:5,10). When Samson lost his strength the Philistines praised their god for this (Judges 16:24). Yep, the Philistines believed their god helped them.

The people of God were tempted with the religious beliefs and practices of their neighbors throughout all of the Old Testament. The first King of Israel, King Saul, resorted to necromancy when *"the Lord did not answer him, either by dreams, or by Urim, or by prophets,"* and he had to consult the medium of Endor to bring up Samuel for him (1 Sam. 28).

At the beginning of King Solomon's reign we find that *"The people…were still sacrificing at the high places, because a temple had not yet been built for the Name of the Lord. Solomon showed his love for the Lord by walking according to the statutes of his father David, except that he offered sacrifices and burned incense on the high places."* (1 Kings 3:2-3). Even though Solomon built a temple to the God of Israel, he married 700 foreign wives for political gain, but these foreign marriages brought foreign religions. So we read, *"As Solomon grew old, his wives turned his heart after other gods, and his heart was not fully devoted to the Lord his God, as the heart of David his father had been. He followed Ashtoreth the goddess of the Sidonians, and Molecha the detestable god of the Ammonites. So Solomon did evil in the eyes of the Lord; he did not follow the Lord completely, as David his father had done. On a hill east of Jerusalem, Solomon built a high place for Chemosh the detestable god of Moab, and for Molech the detestable god of the Ammonites. He did the same for all his foreign wives, who burned incense and offered sacrifices to their gods."* (1 Kings 11:1-8).

After the kingdom divided between Israel to the north and Judah to the south, we see little change. In the northern kingdom of Israel we are told that King Ahab *"did more evil in the eyes of the Lord than any of those before him. He not only considered it trivial to commit the sins of Jeroboam son of Nebat, but he also married Jezebel daughter of Ethbaal king of the Sidonians, and began to serve Baal and worship him. He set up an altar for Baal in the temple of Baal that he built in Samaria. Ahab also made an Asherah pole and did more to provoke the Lord, the God of Israel, to anger than did all the kings of Israel before him."* (1 Kings 16:30-33). Queen Jezebel herself practiced sorcery (2 Ki. 9:22), and had a personal war with Israel's prophets by attempting to kill them off (I Ki. 18:4).

At times Judah to the south ended up being worse than the nations they destroyed when possessing their land: *"Manasseh led Judah and the people of Jerusalem astray, so that they did more evil than the nations the LORD had destroyed before the Israelites."* (II Chronicles 33:1-9)   Listen to the prophet Isaiah here: *"O house of Jacob, come, let us walk in the light of the LORD. For thou hast rejected thy people, the house of Jacob, because they are full of diviners from the east and of soothsayers like the Philistines, and they strike hands with foreigners. Their land is filled with idols; they bow down to the work of their hands, to what their own fingers have made."* (Isaiah 2:6-8). Filled with idols? That's what it says. [Since Isaiah speaks about the Philistines here, see what they once did in I Samuel 6].

When Israel was destroyed by Babylonia, here are the stated reasons why: *"They followed worthless idols and themselves became worthless. They imitated the nations around them although the LORD had ordered them, "Do not do as they do," and they did the things the LORD had forbidden them to do. They forsook all the commands of the LORD their God and made for themselves two idols cast in the shape of calves, and an Asherah pole. They bowed down to all the starry hosts, and they worshiped Baal. They sacrificed their sons and daughters in the fire. They practiced divination and sorcery and sold themselves to do evil in the eyes of the LORD, provoking him to anger. So the Lord was very angry with Israel and removed them from his presence."* (II Kings 17:14-18). *"Only the tribe of Judah was left, and even Judah did not keep the commands of the Lord their God. They followed the practices Israel had introduced."* (II Kings 17:18-19).

According to Robin Lane Fox, when the Jews were defeated by Babylonia in 587 B.C. "a realistic response to the fall of Jerusalem would have been to accept that the God of the Jews was in fact less strong than his neighbors." But the "Jews whose writings survive did not take that route: they interpreted events in defiance of the facts. The authors do not blame Yahweh; they blame the Jews' own sins." They "had brought ruin on themselves." [The Unauthorized Version: Truth and Fiction in the Bible (Knopf, 1992, pp. 71-71.)].

When we look at Israel's history we see how quickly Israel can follow the God of Moses during the lifetime of a "good" king, and then when an "evil" king arises, turn and follow other gods and goddesses and their worship practices. This happened in both the divided monarchies of Israel and Judah. How could they so easily reject their "history," unless there was no real history to reject? I'm suggesting that much of their history rested on the same foundations as all the other nations. It rested on myths, legends, and superstitions.

Take for instance, the development of the Hebrews' notion of God. Isaiah 40-55 most likely shows the culmination of God's teaching to the Israelites that he alone is God (monotheism vs. henotheism). However, the word for God, *elohim*, is plural, "gods." And, in Genesis 1:26, God says: "Let **us** make man in our image." [Christians were able to use this to argue for the doctrine of the trinity, but as Alan Hauser argues, "the concept of the trinity could not have been in the mind of the writer or the writer's audience." And, "'wind,' not 'spirit,' is the best translation of *ruah* in Genesis 1:2." [See, The Genesis Debate, ed. Ronald Youngblood (Baker, 1990, pp. 110-129)]. In some of the Psalms we read only that he is the "God of the gods" (Ps. 86:8; 95:3; 96:4,9; 135:5; 136:2; 138:1). Why didn't the text deny the existence of any other gods at this point? Either the authors of the Psalms didn't quite get it yet, or God was still in the process of teaching them the whole story. It certainly looks as if the Hebrews started out believing in a plurality of gods, which was progressively brought down to the belief in just one God. [See Jonathon Kirsch, God Against the Gods: The History of the War Between Monotheism and Polytheism (Viking, 2004)].

Christians might object that America has changed drastically in 200+ years, too. Someone might say, "If we observed just the last 200+ years of our history in this part of the world, we'd be a different nation." But consider this. Look for yourself how long a judge ruled in the book of Judges to see how quickly, in terms of a few short years, the people of Israel went back and forth between gods. The same thing goes for "good" kings and "evil" kings throughout the monarchies of both Israel and Judah. And yes, we've changed in America in the last 200+ years, but some things we still all agree on, like democracy is the worst form of government until you compare it with all the others. Our changes have been significant because of the rise of globalization and the results of science and the electronic media. A better comparison would be the minimum changes in the medieval society lasting over a thousand years before the rise of science. The Medieval world didn't change that much, so why did Biblical Israel change back and forth and back and forth between the God of Moses and the gods and goddesses of the neighboring nations?

Magic, Divination, and Dreams. When Jews were held in captivity in Babylonia, King Nebuchadnezzar had a dream. Never mind for a minute that it's claimed Daniel told him the dream and he also interpreted it, because whether he did this or not is what's in question here. I want us to consider the religious culture surrounding the ruler of a great empire. We read, *"In the second year of his reign, Nebuchadnezzar had dreams; his mind was troubled and he could not sleep. So the king summoned the magicians, enchanters, sorcerers and astrologers to tell him what he had dreamed. When they came in and stood before the king, he said to them, "I have had a dream that troubles me and I want to know what it means."* (Daniel 2:1-3). Nebuchadnezzer believed that dreams came from the gods as divine communication. And he had magicians and sorcerers that he depended upon to advise him and help run his whole country (see Daniel 5:7). How would that go over today, if the President had such advisors? But it was acceptable to the ancient people whom Nebuchadnezzer ruled over. And to treat our

President's advisors as if they were the equivalent of magicians and sorcerers is historical nonsense. Modern Presidential advisors think through the problems and try as best as possible to come up with reasoned answers. But what if one advisor were to say, "I read my tea leaves today and they say we should attack Iraq"?

Since Daniel himself was appointed by king Nebuchadnezzer to be in charge of his "wise men" (Daniel 2:48), which included the magicians, enchanters, astrologers and diviners (Daniel 5:11), let's take a look at two of these practices, and ask ourselves how he could be in charge of them when they practiced the arts of **magic** and **divination**.

According to Harper's Bible Dictionary, "**Magic** is the means by which humans attempt to secure for themselves some action or information from superhuman powers. Magic is an attempt by human beings to compel a divinity, by the use of physical means, to do what they wish that divinity to do."

"A host of intermediary beings called demons exist between gods and humans. Depending on their proximity to the gods, demons possess divine power in diminishing measures. Those closest to the gods have bodies of air; those closest to humans, bodies of steam or water. Because of this descending order, the unity of the cosmos can be preserved. Otherwise, human and divine would be irreparably separated and no communication between the two would be possible. Everything is connected through the demons who mediate between the divine and the material. Magic rests upon the belief that by getting hold of demons in physical objects, the divinity can be influenced. The magician's art is to find out which material (metal, herb, animal, etc.) contains which divinity and to what degree. Thus magic can achieve either blessing or curse. The magician knows the secret and knows how to use it in the correct way with the best results."

Biblical people themselves practiced magic. Rachel used mandrake plants in order to bear a child (Genesis 30:14-24), and the text doesn't say they didn't help her to conceive. Jacob made his flock of speckled or spotted sheep to increase over Laban's sheep by pealing branches from poplar and almond trees and placing them in the water troughs so that when the flocks mated in front of the branches they bore young that were speckled or spotted. (Genesis 30:25-43). What? How? Where is the science in that? Samuel's pouring out water to induce a storm, 1 Sam. 7:6, is often thought to denote sympathetic magic. Samson's long hair gave him strength. There are some stories from all parts of the world in which the soul or the strength of someone resided in his hair. Job asked that the day of his birth should be cursed by those who curse the day, who are ready to rouse up Leviathan, a mythical beast (Job. 3:8). Here might be a reference to magicians who were thought to rouse up a dragon to swallow the sun at an eclipse. Then there is the Magical power of blessings and curses, already mentioned when we discussed Balaam.

Harper's Bible Dictionary ("Magic and Divination"): "It was believed that great power rested in those holy men who were in close proximity to God. Physical contact with such a person would have beneficial consequences." We see this with Elijah (1 Kings 17:17-24); Elisha (2 Kings 4:31-37); and Jesus (Matt. 8:14-15; Matt. 9:29). "Anything in connection with such holy men absorbed and transmitted a portion of their power. Elijah's mantle parted the waters of the

Jordan, and when Elisha put it on, Elijah's spirit rested on him (2 Kings 2:8-15). The garment of Jesus radiated and transmitted healing power (Mark 5:28-29), as did the handkerchiefs and aprons that people carried away from the body of Paul (Acts 19:11-12). Some believers even attributed beneficial properties to the shadow of Peter (Acts 5:15)."

What about divination? Pagan diviners are also mentioned in 1 Sam. 6:2; Isaiah 44:25; Ezekiel 21:22, and in Acts 16:16 a girl has a spirit of divination. According to Harper's Bible Dictionary: "With divination, in contrast to magic, one does not seek to alter the course of events, only to learn about them. The ancient world developed many devices by which the veil of secrecy covering future events could be lifted." Divination may take many forms, according to the New Bible Dictionary ("Divination"). The following forms are mentioned in the Bible: "One) **Rhabdomancy.** Ezk. 21:21. Sticks or arrows were thrown into the air, and omens were deduced from their position when they fell. Two) **Hepatoscopy.** Ezk. 21:21. Examination of the liver or other entrails of a sacrifice was supposed to give guidance. Three) **Teraphim.** Household gods associated with divination in 1 Sam. 15:23; Ezk. 21:21; Zech. 10:2. Four) **Necromancy**, or the consultation of the departed (Deut. 18:11; 1 Sam. 28:8; 2 Ki. 21:6). Five) **Astrology** draws conclusions from the position of the sun, moon and planets in relation to the zodiac and to one another. The wise men (Magi) who came to the infant Jesus (Mt. 2:9) were probably trained in Babylonian tradition which mixed astronomy with astrology. Six) **Hydromancy,** or divination through water. Here forms and pictures appear in the water in a bowl, as also in crystal-gazing. The gleam of the water induces a state of light trance, and the visions are subjective (Gen. 44:5, 15)."

Even among God's people we see divination through the **Casting of Lots**. In the OT the lot was cast to discover God's will for the allocation of territory (Jos. 18–19, etc.), the choice of the goat to be sacrificed on the Day of Atonement (Lev. 16), the detection of a guilty person (Josh. 7:14; Jonah. 1:7), the allocation of Temple duties (1 Chr. 24:5), the discovery of a lucky day by Haman (Esther 3:7). The Urim and the Thummim are lots used to make important decisions where the answer was either yes or no (1 Sam. 14:41; 28:6; Exod. 28:29; Deut. 33:8; Lev. 8:7; Num. 27:21). In the NT Christ's clothes were allocated by lot (Mt. 27:35). The last occasion in the Bible on which the lot is used to divine the will of God is in the choice of Matthias (Acts 1:15–26). Can you imagine any judges today casting lots to divide up land or to make any decisions?

Dreams. Dreams in the ancient world were believed to be communication from God. Dreams were thought to convey messages from God or the gods. (See Genesis 20; 21:32; 24; 31:24; 40-41; Judges 7:13-14). Pharaoh had two dreams and demanded that someone interpret them, and it's claimed Joseph accurately interpreted them for him (Genesis 41); Solomon had a dream where he asked and received his request for wisdom (I Kings 3:5-15); Matthew records five dreams in connection with the birth and infancy of Jesus, in three of which an angel appeared with God's message (Mt. 1:20; 2:12–13, 19, 22). Later he records the troubled dream of Pilate's wife that Jesus is innocent, and this dream was considered by Matthew as at least enough evidence of Jesus' innocence to mention it (27:19). On occasions there is virtually no distinction between a dream and a vision during the night (Job. 4:12f; Acts 9:10; 10:10, 30; 16:9; 18:9f.). There is a very close connection between dreams and visions and prophecies: "And afterward, I will pour out my Spirit on all people. Your sons and daughters will prophesy, your old men will dream dreams, your young men will see visions." (Joel 2:28 & Acts 2:17, cf. Numbers 12:6) [On dreams see A. L. Oppenheim, The Interpretation of Dreams in the Ancient Near East, 1956].

Today's modern educated people simply don't accept that view of magic, divination, blessings, curses or dreams. Dreams, for instance, are the combined product of memory and sensation running wild, as the rational part of our brains is unconscious. CAT scans and probes tell us which parts of our brains are "asleep" and which parts are awake when we are sleeping. Dreams open the window of the mind. Dreams give us a glimpse of a person's unconscious self. The Bible contains far too many things that people living in our day and age simply cannot accept any longer. It is irrational and superstitious, in the light of brain science, to consider dreams as any communication from God, gods, or the dead.

The OT Prophets– The Old Testament prophets had to battle with the Israelite tendency to worship other gods, spoken of earlier, in both the northern and southern kingdoms (Isaiah 47:11; Jeremiah 27:16-16; 29:8-9; Ezekiel 13:2-9; 14; 22:28; Micah 3:6-7; Zech 10:2; Malachi 3:5), and beyond to other nations.

For what I consider a typical look at the evidence of a prophetic word, **take a look at the prophetic story in Jonah**. Although I do not believe there is a shred of historical evidence for this story, let me treat it as if it were historical in every detail. Try to put yourself in the shoes of each of the characters involved, including Jonah, the sailors, the police in Tarshish, the king of Ninevah and his people. Read the story as if you are each of these characters respectively. What would you think and do?

Prophets received their prophecies by means of dreams and visions (Numbers 12:6). Several of the prophetic books claim to be based upon visions (Isaiah 1:1; Ezk. 1:1; Obadiah 1:1; Nahum 1:1), while most all of the rest of them start out either with "the word of the Lord came to me," (Jonah 1:1) or simply, this is "an oracle." I have known Christian people in the Pentecostal tradition who will claim a word from God too. One lady "prophesied" to a group of us that we'd start a Christian rock band (I played the drums) and we'd name it "Walk By Faith Not Sight." Such a band never came about. (Maybe it could still happen?). She was wrong.

In the O.T. there were many prophets (I Sam. 10:10-13), and they sought guidance from God in dreams and visions. So how did any of them know for sure their prophecies were truly from God? They had a dream. They saw a vision (which probably is indistinguishable from a dream like state anyway). I take it that Jonah was upset at the corruption in Ninevah, much like Christians today are upset at the corruption in America, and had a dream about it, and just felt certain about it.

There were lots of prophets in the land, false ones, and prophets for other gods. They all felt certain their prophecies were of divine origin; all of them. The tests of the prophet laid down in Deut 13, and 18 merely demand that they spoke in God's name, and if they prophesied about the future the things prophecied should come to pass.

When God purportedly called Jonah to preach against the city of Nineveh he tried to flee from God by sailing to some place called Tarshish (v.3). Even though Jonah felt certain about the prophecy, he didn't like it, because he didn't want to warn the Ninevites of their impending destruction, because as later explained he thought they might repent and escape God's judgment. But the kind of God he believed in when he fled was a tribal, localized god, and certainly not the later monotheistic omnipotent creator God.

1:4 Then the LORD sent a great wind on the sea, and such a violent storm arose that the ship threatened to break up. 5 All the sailors were afraid and each cried out to his own god. And they threw the cargo into the sea to lighten the ship.

Of course, any sailor back then would blame the gods for the wind and the storm, but this is also Jonah's belief, since this is supposedly his writing, that his God sent this storm because he was running away from him. Is that what we do today?...blame ourselves or someone else for a storm?

1:5-6 But Jonah had gone below deck, where he lay down and fell into a deep sleep. The captain went to him and said, "How can you sleep? Get up and call on your god! Maybe he will take notice of us, and we will not perish."

The captain didn't care which god Jonah prayed to, so long as no god was left out of their prayers. This is true polytheism.

1:7 Then the sailors said to each other, "Come, let us cast lots to find out who is responsible for this calamity."

They cast lots and the lot fell on Jonah. This is a form of divination. Do you want to cast lots to see who's to blame for any hurricanes that come our way? Jonah accepted the results too.

1:8 So they asked him, "Tell us, who is responsible for making all this trouble for us? What do you do? Where do you come from? What is your country? From what people are you?" 9 He answered, "I am a Hebrew and I worship the LORD, the God of heaven, who made the sea and the land." 10 This terrified them and they asked, "What have you done?" (They knew he was running away from the LORD, because he had already told them so.)

Jonah expresses a view of God here that is at odds with his running away from God earlier. It's hard to reconcile the fact that he thought he could run away from God with his belief that the God is a "God of heaven, who made the sea and the land," except that Jonah may have truly realized this for the first time in the storm itself. But he states this as if he thought this all along.

With the casting of lots and the fact that he was running away from this kind of God, it terrified these sailors. These things would not terrify us today. Does God zap people who disobey him today? Like Ananias & Sapphira? Uzzah? Lot's wife? What if the lot had instead fallen on some follower of Zeus who was running away from him, or fighting against him, like Odysseus in the Odyssey? These sailors would still respond in the exact same way, because the proof was in the casting of lots, and the storm, and the story. They didn't need any other proof or evidence. Does this type of gullibility describe any **thinking** person today?

1:11 The sea was getting rougher and rougher. So they asked him, "What should we do to you to make the sea calm down for us?" 12 "Pick me up and throw me into the sea," he replied, "and it will become calm. I know that it is my fault that this great storm has come upon you."

Yep, that's what Jonah concluded. Kill me and it'll be okay for you. We learn at the end of this book that he was suicidal anyway, so there's no difference expressed in this attitude of his. Jonah believes the storm is his fault. Have you ever blamed yourself because of a storm? Does God or nature act that way?

1:13 Instead, the men did their best to row back to land. But they could not, for the sea grew even wilder than before. 14 Then they cried to the LORD, "O LORD, please do not let us die for taking this man's life. Do not hold us accountable for killing an innocent man, for you, O LORD, have done as you pleased."

Here they faced an ethical decision. They "know" Jonah is to blame for the storm, but does Jonah's God really demand they kill him? If they kill him, will Jonah's God be more upset with them for doing so? But Jonah eased their minds, because he himself says that's what they should do.

1:15 Then they took Jonah and threw him overboard, and the raging sea grew calm. 16 At this the men greatly feared the LORD, and they offered a sacrifice to the LORD and made vows to him.

These sailors should be tried for attempted murder. Surely they had a list of the people on board. And when they docked to a port someone would notice him missing. What would the police in Tarshish do then? Anything comparable to what our police would do? What would these men say to the police? Would their story hold up in today's courts? Absolutely not!

1:17 But the LORD provided a great fish to swallow Jonah, and Jonah was inside the fish three days and three nights.

Hmmm. With a person like that telling the first part of this story, I doubt that he can be trustworthy telling the rest of the story. And if people were superstitious enough to believe God caused a storm to stop Jonah in his tracks without any evidence but nature and the story itself, then they would also believe he was swallowed by a fish simply because he told them it happened. If no evidence is required to believe the first part of the story, then no evidence is required to believe the last part.

At the end (chapter 3) after the fish puked him up we read,

1 Then the word of the LORD came to Jonah a second time: 2 "Go to the great city of Nineveh and proclaim to it the message I give you." 3 Jonah obeyed the word of the LORD and went to Nineveh. Now Nineveh was a very important city—a visit required three days. 4 On the first day, Jonah started into the city. He proclaimed: "Forty more days and Nineveh will be overturned." 5 The Ninevites believed God. They declared a fast, and all of them, from the greatest to the least, put on sackcloth.

Jonah obeyed his vision or dream, and preached the message he felt certain about, that "Forty more days and Nineveh will be overturned."

That's what he said. Remember this.

3:6 When the news reached the king of Nineveh, he rose from his throne, took off his royal robes, covered himself with sackcloth and sat down in the dust. 7 Then he issued a proclamation in Nineveh: "By the decree of the king and his nobles: Do not let any man or beast, herd or flock, taste anything; do not let them eat or drink. 8 But let man and beast be covered with sackcloth. Let everyone call urgently on God. Let them give up their evil ways and their violence. 9 Who knows? God may yet relent and with compassion turn from his fierce anger so that we will not perish."

In the first place, what evidence did the king of Ninevah have for believing Jonah? We are simply not told. Presumably none was needed because of the supposed fame of the Hebrew God. But if that's the case then why didn't they already believe in this God? Even with the supposed fame of the Hebrew God, how would the King know that Jonah was his true prophet? That's a fair question, isn't it? Even Moses supposedly had wondered how the Pharaoh would know he was sent from God, didn't he?

Still, how would America react to the same prophetic message by none other than Billy Graham: "Forty more days and America will be overturned." The laugher would be constant. Jay Leno and David Letterman would have a field day with this. That's because we today would demand some evidence. And there have been some prophets of doom in America too. Just listen to Jack Van Impe. But for the last 30 years or more Van Impe has always been wrong, and he's still getting donations to stay on the air!

I just don't see Ninevah repenting simply because the Ninevites probably didn't think they were doing that much wrong. And I see no further reason to suggest that at Jonah's preaching they would've turned and believed in the Hebrew God either, since they were polytheistic to the core.

3:10 When God saw what they did and how they turned from their evil ways, he had compassion and did not bring upon them the destruction he had threatened.

WHAT? WHAT? WHAT? I'm sure I read somewhere that the test of a prophet was that what he said was to come to pass (Deut. 18:22). Didn't he say Nineveh would be destroyed? Did he or didn't he? Answer the question. But it wasn't destroyed after all, was it? What if Billy Graham used this excuse to explain why America wasn't destroyed? Laughter again. What would you say about Jonah then? After all there were a great many prophets running around proclaiming that God spoke to them too. If what he prophesied didn't come to pass, then is there any evidence at all that he was really called to speak God's word? And how should we now think about Jonah? After all, his prophecy failed the test of a true prophet! But yet his book is in the Bible. [For more on this see my section: "Prophecy and Biblical Authority."]

What's missing in this story is evidence. No evidence was offered for any claim, except that Jonah said it was true. Without a doubt no Christian today would believe the same type of story told in the modern era, unless there was some pretty hard evidence.

Is there any evidence that Nineveh became monotheistic and righteous? If they remained polytheistic and failed to worship the Hebrew God, that wouldn't be enough for Jonah's God, would it? If it was just about their moral behavior, then cities and countries all go through some cycle of "revival" from time to time, so it might be that Jonah was taking credit for something that happened on its own anyway. And where's this purported fish, anyway? The ancients had the superstitious belief that mythical beasts and fish lived in the seas, likened to the Loch Ness Monster, like "Rahab," "Behemoth," and "Leviathan."

This is what I mean by superstition. Little or no evidence is required, just a good story, based in fear, along with the storms of life.

Who Spoke For God? - The Old Testament prophets argued for their God over the gods and goddess worship which vied for the attention of the Israelites. Christians claim that anyone who worshipped these other gods were just doing wrong. After all, Moses and the prophets warned Israel to stay away from these beliefs and the practices that went with them, like sorcery, magic, witchcraft, and divination (e.g. Lev. 19:26; 20:27; Deut. 18:10–14). However, my question is that if God condemned these things over and over again, why did the people practice them over and over again? Why did they? My suggestion is that with a history mixed with so many myths, Israel was engaged in a battle over the correct message of the divine will, and the correct methods for discovering it. It was a constant battle over the hearts and minds of the people, precisely because the so-called history from Genesis through Joshua contained far too many non-historical myths to be reliable enough evidence as to their origins. On the one side you had magicians, sorcerers, and diviners, and on the other hand you had the prophets, all vying for the people's hearts. Even among the prophets themselves there were many who were called false prophets by the other group of prophets.

Who was it in the first place that said idol worship and sorcery were wrong? The prophets said so, whom the so-called "faithful" believed, from Moses, to Samuel, to Isaiah, to Malachi. In my opinion the Biblical prophets simply forbad all other methods but their own for knowing God and his will. They gained their prophecies by means of "visions" and "dreams" (Numb. 12:6) being formerly called "seers" (I Samuel 9:9), and they forbad all other ways of gaining divine knowledge, because that's how they did it. There is power in advocating that how you do things is the way they should be done, isn't there? No wonder then, that Queen Jezebel attempted to kill off the prophets (I Kings 18:4, cf., Jeremiah 20:1-2). It was a power struggle over who could know the divine will and which methods were appropriate for this, since she practiced sorcery (2 Kings 9:22), and she worshipped Baal.

There were many prophets in the land (I Samuel 10:5), as I've said, but only the ones who gained a following were highly regarded (ex. Samuel was highly regarded as such, I Samuel 3:20). The other ones were just regarded as false prophets by the others. **One person's false prophet was another person's true prophet of God, and vise versa** (Jeremiah 23:9-40; 26:7-9). There were also many challenges between prophets to see who was a true prophet of God (I Kings 18; Jeremiah 28). The reason was because people didn't automatically know the true ones from the false ones. [See "Prophet" in the <u>Anchor Bible Dictionary</u>].

Elijah on Mt .Carmel - I Kings 18:16-40:

18:16 So Obadiah went to meet Ahab and told him...summon the people from all over Israel to meet me on Mount Carmel. And bring the four hundred and fifty prophets of Baal and the four hundred prophets of Asherah, who eat at Jezebel's table."

Jezebel was Ahab's wife, who was the "daughter of Ethbaal king of the Sidonians." It was a political marriage done to stave off war and to save lives. Ahab *"began to serve Baal and worship him. He set up an altar for Baal in the temple of Baal that he built in Samaria. Ahab also made an Asherah pole and did more to provoke the Lord, the God of Israel, to anger than did all the kings of Israel before him."* (1 Kings 16:30-33). Queen Jezebel practiced sorcery (2 Kings 9:22). She amassed herself with many prophets of Baal and Asherah. They had 850 prophets. Why so many? Where did they work and live? They practiced sorcery, magic, divination, and probably astrology. That's a great number of prophets, and for each one of them there were many people went to them for guidance and knowledge. I'm sure these prophets would've warned the people not to be misled by the other prophets, so the people had a great deal of difficulty knowing whom to believe, didn't they? Most Christians would say they wouldn't have had a hard time with this at all; they would've just rejected Baal. But that's claiming to be more intelligent than these ancient people were, and I never said they were stupid, just superstitious. It's always easier to decide which prophet was the true prophet after the war is over, that is, if you consider success the key characteristic of which god was the true god like they did, and that's probably all they had to go on.

Just think if our President did what Ahab did, and amassed for himself prophets who practiced sorcery in Christian America? Wouldn't the Christian majority rise up against such a thing as one, both liberals and conservatives of every shape and size? That's because Christians claim to have evidence for their beliefs—whether they do or not is the question here.

Who are these gods that Ahab accepted? Harper's Bible Dictionary: "**Baal** is a weather god associated with thunderstorms. Baal was said to appoint the season of rains. Clouds were thought to be part of his entourage. Lightning was his weapon, and it may have been his invention. The windows of Baal's palace were thought to correspond to openings in the clouds through which rain flowed. Rain was important to Canaanite agriculture, and Baal was consequently a god of fertility—a prodigious lover as well as the giver of abundance."

"The gods are regarded as the children of **Asherah** and El. Her relationship with Baal is perplexing. Baal's assault on the offspring of Asherah is once narrated, yet Asherah advocates for Baal the role of king and judge among the gods."

And here we have many people in Israel believing this? Was there any evidence for this? I cannot think of any since we know something about rain, and lightning and thunderstorms. So why did they believe this? If there was any solid evidence for the God of Moses and what he supposedly had done, then why would the Israelites so easily believe these other myths? Unless, of course, as is my contention, the stories told about the God of Moses were on an equal playing field—that there was no evidence for believing those stories either.

20 So Ahab sent word throughout all Israel and assembled the prophets on Mount Carmel. 21 Elijah went before the people and said, "How long will you waver between two opinions? If the LORD is God, follow him; but if Baal is God, follow him." But the people said nothing. 22 Then Elijah said to them, "I am the only one of the LORD's prophets left, but Baal has four hundred and fifty prophets. 23 Get two bulls for us. Let them choose one for themselves, and let them cut it into pieces and put it on the wood but not set fire to it. I will prepare the other bull and put it on the wood but not set fire to it. 24 Then you call on the name of your god, and I will call on the name of the LORD. The god who answers by fire—he is God." Then all the people said, "What you say is good."

Now let's think about some challenge like this occurring in the modern world. Would anyone even show up to see it? Would any Christian issue such a challenge? If challenged, would any Christian accept this challenge? Not at all. So I ask why?

Elijah said: "I am the only one of the LORD's prophets left." Boy that sure sounds like a minority of one here. So again, how is it possible that the people of Israel had so fully rejected the God of Moses to the point where there was only one faithful prophet of God in the northern kingdom of Israel? The answer is that they were a very superstitious people who were swayed very easily to believe stupendous mythical stories that lacked evidence. That is, there was no evidence either way, just religious experiences and stupendous stories. These stories competed for the hearts and minds of the people because there was no historical evidence either way between them.

25 Elijah said to the prophets of Baal, "Choose one of the bulls and prepare it first, since there are so many of you. Call on the name of your god, but do not light the fire." 26 So they took the bull given them and prepared it. Then they called on the name of Baal from morning till noon. "O Baal, answer us!" they shouted. But there was no response; no one answered. And they danced around the altar they had made. 27 At noon Elijah began to taunt them. "Shout louder!" he said. "Surely he is a god! Perhaps he is deep in thought, or busy, or traveling. Maybe he is sleeping and must be awakened." 28 So they shouted louder and slashed themselves with swords and spears, as was their custom, until their blood flowed. 29 Midday passed, and they continued their frantic prophesying until the time for the evening sacrifice. But there was no response, no one answered, no one paid attention.

Apparently these prophets thought they were up to the challenge, so they tried and they tried. That's what it says. These prophets really believed they could do it, so they tried. Would you have tried? And even if it was for show, to save face, how long would you try? And look how they tried, by shouting and slashing themselves "as was their custom" and prophesying. There is every indication here that they thought they could do it. If I was back then and I was challenged by Elijah, I would simply say, "I don't think it will work, so you go ahead and show me." That's because I am not superstitious by their standards. I live in the modern world of science where lightning is a meteorological event produced in a thunderstorm.

30 Then Elijah said to all the people, "Come here to me." They came to him, and he repaired the altar of the LORD, which was in ruins.....Elijah stepped forward and prayed: "O LORD, God of Abraham, Isaac and Israel, let it be known today that you are God in Israel and that I am your servant and have done all these things at your command. 38 Then the fire of the LORD fell and burned up the sacrifice, the wood, the stones and the soil, and also licked up the water in the trench. 39 When all the people saw this, they fell prostrate and cried, "The LORD—he is God! The LORD—he is God!"

If this truly happened, then I would fall on my face and worship God as well. But I'm trying to establish that such an age as theirs was highly superstitious, and hence unreliable as a testimony to understand what actually happened. Just look at any introduction to I Kings and you'll know that at best, this account was compiled no earlier than 180 years after it supposedly happened. Even in a modern society we have developed myths surrounding our heroes, like Paul Revere's Ride, George Washington and the cherry tree, Abe Lincoln walking for a mile to return someone's penny. And these myths are small ones among less superstitious people, but think about the myths that could be generated in 180 years surrounding the Mt. Carmel event by superstitious people. Probably the same kind of myths that surrounded Samson and his great strength. Remember here, we're dealing with a superstitious people who may just believe any good story and embellish it as it goes, adding to it some very stupendous things.

David L. Edwards wrote that when it comes to Elijah and Elisha, "the story-telling has become fanciful...the stories are so colorful that we cannot tell exactly what took place in the time of Elijah and Elisha." [(p. 179), in <u>Evangelical Essentials: A Liberal--Evangelical Dialogue </u>(Inter Varsity Press, 1988)].

40 Then Elijah commanded them, "Seize the prophets of Baal. Don't let anyone get away!" They seized them, and Elijah had them brought down to the Kishon Valley and slaughtered there.

It's no wonder that Jezebel waged war against the other prophets who claimed to speak for the God of Moses. She had a personal war with Israel's prophets by attempting to kill them off (I Kings 18:4). A lot of killing was going on, depending on which religion you practiced. And it was indeed a war; the war of the prophets. And this story ends with 850 prophets dying at the hands of Elijah's new converts.

Furthermore, since I Kings was compiled either at the time of Jerusalem's demise or afterward, the people finally concluded that the prophets of Baal and Asherah were the false prophets, so their whole history was written and compiled from hindsight with this lesson in mind. Why did they conclude that those "false" prophets were wrong? Here's why: since the worship of these other gods was blamed by the "true" prophets for why they were destroyed as a people and sent into captivity, then those gods were the false gods and those prophets were the false prophets. Nations believed in the gods that brought them victory, and rejected the gods that didn't. History would have been written differently, from the perspective of the prophets of Baal and Asherah, had it turned out differently. [For more on this see Canaanite Myth and Hebrew Epic, by Frank M. Cross (Harvard, 1997), Ancient Israel, by Hershel Shanks (Prentice Hall, 1999), and by G.E. Wright, The Challenge of Israel's Faith (Chicago, 1956), and The Faith of Israel (Abindon Press, 1952).

The New Testament Period. Now we turn to the various events and superstitions we find in the New Testament. In the NT, miracles themselves are sometimes seen as the result of magic. The pagan world certainly regarded many miracles as magic (Acts 8:9–11), and on at least one occasion Jesus used magic when he put mud in a man's eyes to heal him of blindness. In John 9:6-7 we read: *"Having said this, he spit on the ground, made some mud with the saliva, and put it on the man's eyes. "Go," he told him, "wash in the Pool of Siloam" (this word means Sent). So the man went and washed, and came home seeing."* For the magical properties of the "pool of Siloam" look at John 5:1-7: *"Now there is in Jerusalem by the sheep gate a pool, which is called in Hebrew Bethesda, having five porticoes. In these lay a multitude of those who were sick, blind, lame, and withered,* **[waiting for the moving of the waters; for an angel of the Lord went down at certain seasons into the pool and stirred up the water; whoever then first, after the stirring up of the water, stepped in was made well from whatever disease with which he was afflicted.]** *A man was there who had been ill for thirty-eight years. When Jesus saw him lying there, and knew that he had already been a long time in that condition, He said to him, "Do you wish to get well?" The sick man answered Him, "Sir, I have no man to put me into the pool when the water is stirred up, but while I am coming, another steps down before me."* [NASB] The part in brackets was pseudonymously added by a later Christian to explain why these people were there. A "multitude" of them believed in the magical properties of this pool, when it's stirred. Where is a pool like that today? It sounds to us like the mythical "fountain of youth."

Demon Possession in the NT.

In the gospels we often read that Jesus' opponents say he is demon possessed: (cf. Matt 9:32-34, Matt. 12:24). Sometimes Jesus is called demon possessed simply because he says things that seemed to his hearers just plain crazy: *"'Has not Moses given you the law? Yet not one of you keeps the law. Why are you trying to kill me?' 'You are demon-possessed,' the crowd answered. 'Who is trying to kill you?'"* (John 7:20). *"At these words the Jews were again divided. Many of them said, "He is demon-possessed and raving mad. Why listen to him?"* (John 10:19-20, also John 8:48-51). Even John the Baptist was thought to be demon possessed. (Matt. 11:18). It was easy to claim someone was possessed in those days. Whenever Jesus acted contrary to what was normally expected, or his teaching sounded strange or weird, they concluded he was a demon-possessed person, much like someone today might say, "you're crazy."

Look how Jesus responded to these charges: *"Jesus knew their thoughts and said to them, 'if I drive out demons by Beelzebub, by whom do your people drive them out? So then, they will be your judges.'"* (Matt 12:27). There were lots of Jewish exorcists and lots of demon possessed people in those times, and Jesus didn't deny what these exorcists could do. *"Teacher," said John, "we saw a man driving out demons in your name and we told him to stop, because he was not one of us." "Do not stop him," Jesus said. "No one who does a miracle in my name can in the next moment say anything bad about me, for whoever is not against us is for us."* (Mark 9:38-40). *"Some Jews who went around driving out evil spirits tried to invoke the name of the Lord Jesus over those who were demon-possessed. They would say, "In the name of Jesus, whom Paul preaches, I command you to come out." Seven sons of Sceva, a Jewish chief priest, were doing this. One day the evil spirit answered them, "Jesus I know, and I know about Paul, but who are you?" Then the man who had the evil spirit jumped on them and overpowered them all. He gave them such a beating that they ran out of the house naked and bleeding."* (Acts 19:13-16).

There were also many sorcerers too, in Samaria (Acts 8:9-11) and in Paphos on the island of Cyprus there was a sorcerer "who was an attendant of the proconsul, Sergius Paulus." (Acts 13:6-8, see also Rev. 21:8; 22:15).

Look at the close connection between healing and exorcism: *"The Twelve were with him (Jesus), and also some women who had been cured of evil spirits and diseases: Mary (called Magdalene) from whom seven demons had come out."* (Luke 8:1-2). *"Jesus said, 'Go tell that fox, "I will drive out demons and heal people today and tomorrow, and on the third day I will reach my goal."'"* (Luke 13:32)   *"Philip went down to a city in Samaria and proclaimed the Christ there. When the crowds heard Philip and saw the miraculous signs he did, they all paid close attention to what he said. With shrieks, evil spirits came out of many, and many paralytics and cripples were healed. So there was great joy in that city."* (Acts 8:5-8).

Today we just don't think sick people are demon possessed. With the advent of modern medicine we treat the physical causes, and with psychology we treat the mental causes of illnesses the best that we can. And while it can be argued that Luke was a "physician" (Col. 4:14) and that he knew the difference, we simply have to consider how much of the science of medicine he knew in his day. As a child of his times it would seem reasonable to suppose that those illnesses he couldn't cure with the medicine he had at his disposal would be thought of by him as demon possession too. <u>Harper's Bible Dictionary</u>: "As with other ancient cultures, there was in Israel no necessary conflict between belief in divine, demonic, and/or human causation of illness or between requests for divine assistance and the application of practical therapy." ["Physicians"].

All I can say here is what a mixed up world it must have been to live in such a superstitious age as the first century! Formerly epilepsy was viewed as demon possession. But now we know some of the causes and can minimize the effects. Mental disease also has its known causes, and some specialists can help with brain surgery. So there is a whole lot less demon possession today simply because of modern science.

Some Christians will argue from the book of Revelation (20:1-10) that Satan is bound and cannot hurt us like that anymore. But if Christians believe this then it also says that Satan will be bound for a 1000 years. When did those 1000 years start so that I may know when they end? If they say that the 1000 years is not literal, then how can they take a literal view of Satan being bound at all? [As far as Satan and the demons go, see my section "The Devil Made Me Do It!"]

Visions in the NT. From the New Bible Dictionary: **"VISION.** The borderline between vision and dream or trance is difficult, if not impossible, to determine. This is reflected in the biblical vocabulary of 'vision'. The NT uses two words in this connection: *horama* (Acts 9:10, 12; 10:3, 17, 19) and *optasia* (Luke 1:22; Acts 26:19; 2 Cor. 12:1). They signify 'appearance' or 'vision'." [Later on this will have some significance with the resurrection appearances of Jesus].

"The circumstances in which the revelatory visions came to the seers of the Bible are varied. They came in men's waking hours (Daniel 10:7; Acts 9:7); by day (Acts 10:3) or by night (Genesis 46:2). But the visions had close connections with the dream-state (Num. 12:6; Job 4:13)." "In the NT Luke manifests the greatest interest in visions. The supreme set of visions in the NT is that in the book of the Revelation."

Luke's usage of the word group for "vision." Zechariah, John the Baptist's father, didn't actually see angels, he saw a vision. (Luke 1:22). The women who went to the tomb of Jesus said they didn't see angels, just a vision. (Luke 24:23). According to the Prophet Joel, and Peter the Apostle, and Luke who records it, dreams, visions, and prophecies have a close connection with each other. "'*In the last days, God says, I will pour out my Spirit on all people. Your sons and daughters will prophesy, your young men will see visions, your old men will dream dreams.* (Acts 2:17).

Ananias saw visions and followed them to speak to Saul/Paul: "*In Damascus there was a disciple named Ananias. The Lord called to him in a vision, 'Ananias!'*" (Acts 9:10) "*So Ananias departed and entered the house, and after laying his hands on him said, 'Brother Saul, the Lord Jesus, who appeared (i.e., gave a vision) to you on the road by which you were coming, has sent me so that you may regain your sight and be filled with the Holy Spirit.'*" (Acts 9:17)

At Caesarea there was a man named Cornelius who was "a centurion in what was known as the Italian Regiment." He received a vision "one day at about three in the afternoon," and followed it. (Acts 10:1-3). Then the Apostle Peter himself had one and learns from it that "God has granted even the Gentiles repentance unto life." (Acts 11:5-6,18). That's an educated way to learn something, isn't it?

Luke also tells us Peter received his "vision," while "in a trance." A trance? A trance? Paul himself received a vision while in a trance (Acts 22:17). Ancient people, especially those considered prophets and priests (and apostles too), would put themselves in a trance to gain divine knowledge. How often did Peter and Paul do that? Enhanced Strong's Lexicon: "Trance" = Ecstasy, "throwing of the mind out of its normal state, alienation of mind, whether such as makes a lunatic or that of a man who by some sudden emotion is transported as it were out of himself, so that in this rapt condition, although he is awake, his mind is drawn off from all surrounding objects and wholly fixed on things divine that he sees nothing but the forms and images lying within, and thinks that he perceives with his bodily eyes and ears realities shown him by God." [On "trance" in the OT, see also Daniel 8:18, 10:9].

Paul's missionary journeys are said to be directed by visions, which happened in the night (hence, dreams). *"And a vision appeared to Paul in the night; There stood a man of Macedonia, and prayed him, saying, Come over into Macedonia, and help us. And after he had seen the vision, immediately we endeavored to go into Macedonia, assuredly gathering that the Lord had called us for to preach the gospel unto them."* (Acts 16:9-10. [See also Acts 18:9 where it is said that Paul was once again in a trance]. Paul even seems to equate his Damascus Road conversion experience to a vision: *"So, King Agrippa, I did not prove disobedient to the heavenly vision."* (Acts 26:19). Was his vision of Jesus just another dream?

Acts 14:8-20, Paul in Lystra of the Galatians.
8 In Lystra there sat a man crippled in his feet, who was lame from birth and had never walked. 9 He listened to Paul as he was speaking. Paul looked directly at him, saw that he had faith to be healed 10 and called out, "Stand up on your feet!" At that, the man jumped up and began to walk.

I know that this is difficult to dispute, since the story is written by Luke, "the Physician." What I do know is that such things are claimed by Benny Hinn's followers all of the time, as well as Oral Roberts. I also know that Luke was a believer and he wanted to tell a story that would cause other people to believe. So I reflect back and remember how Christians would regularly inflate their claims of healing too, and wonder if this is what Luke did. But the bottom line is that I require more evidence to believe something like this than a mere report by someone in the past who lived and breathed among people who were wildly superstitious. Anyway, are there any other clues here?

11 When the crowd saw what Paul had done, they shouted in the Lycaonian language, "The gods have come down to us in human form!" 12 Barnabas they called Zeus, and Paul they called Hermes because he was the chief speaker. 13 The priest of Zeus, whose temple was just outside the city, brought bulls and wreaths to the city gates because he and the crowd wanted to offer sacrifices to them.

The crowd? Greek: *οχλοι* noun, masculine, plural, nominative, "a multitude, the common people." Not the educated classes, but we are hardly ever talking about the educated classes in the N.T. It's almost always, unless specified, the common average classes, or lower classes that Jesus and Paul reached. And so far, those classes of people seemed overwhelmingly superstitious. Moreover, there doesn't seem to be any case that can be made that they were motivated by money here, either.

Wait a minute? "The gods have come down to us in human form!" What? They believed it was possible for the gods to come down in the human forms of Paul and Barnabas? Isn't that also what Paul and Barnabas believed about Jesus? Hmmm. And they wanted to offer sacrifices to Paul and Barnabas? This is all so strange to us today.

14 But when the apostles Barnabas and Paul heard of this, they tore their clothes and rushed out into the crowd, shouting: 15 "Men, why are you doing this? We too are only men, human like you. We are bringing you good news, telling you to turn from these worthless things to the living God, who made heaven and earth and sea and everything in them. 18 Even with these words, they had difficulty keeping the crowd from sacrificing to them.

Paul did a great miracle and yet the people had a hard time believing what these two gods said? That too is very strange. If I thought someone was god, I'd listen to what he said. But they were in a frenzy.

19 Then some Jews came from Antioch and Iconium and won the crowd over. They stoned Paul and dragged him outside the city, thinking he was dead. 20 But after the disciples had gathered around him, he got up and went back into the city. The next day he and Barnabas left for Derbe.

How would it be possible for the Jews to have "won the crowd over" after what Luke just told us that Paul had done? The usual response of rational people would be to reject what the Jews said, rather than what Paul said, since they already believed Paul was a god. And Jews? This polytheistic crowd listened to Jews? My how quickly they were swayed back and forth and back and forth, according to Luke's own account. And Luke wants us to believe him? That's very strange too.

They stoned Paul? The only reason they might have listened to what the Jews said is that they claimed Paul and Barnabas were demons or demon-possessed. But Paul and Barnabas would be right there denying it. So whom would you believe? Paul supposedly did a great miracle, and the next moment they stoned him. Maybe the miracle wasn't so great after all? And it shows once again that the people Paul spread the gospel to were superstitious to the core. No evidence was needed. They just believed the person who had the best story. And they were ready to kill Paul too.

Why would they turn Paul over to the Jews to kill him, or attempt to kill him themselves? Again, it's because they were fearful that with these two demons in their midst, the gods would be displeased with them and not send rain, or not allow their women to bear children, or send fire from the sky instead. No wonder the message of Paul spread. It was quite literally the best story out there. Nothing could top it. But the evidence? Who needs that when you're dealing with superstitious people like this? All you had to be concerned about, was being stoned.

Acts 17:16-31: Paul In Athens –

16 "While Paul was waiting for them in Athens, he was greatly distressed to see that the city was full of idols."

Athens was full of idols? These people were overwhelmingly superstitious people. There are rites and sacrifices that go with each idol. There are priests and diviners, sorcerers and magicians that go with each one, and there are even temples that go with each one.

17 "So he reasoned in the synagogue with the Jews and the God-fearing Greeks, as well as in the marketplace day by day with those who happened to be there. 18 A group of Epicurean and Stoic philosophers began to dispute with him. Some of them asked, "What is this babbler trying to say?" Others remarked, "He seems to be advocating foreign gods." They said this because Paul was preaching the good news about Jesus and the resurrection."

Of course whoever writes the story frames the discussion. Paul "reasoned" with them, it says. Did they not reason with him too? They had to. I's just that the author considered Paul's arguments much more reasonable. But look at how some of them responded: "He seems to be advocating foreign gods." They were referring to the god "Jesus" and the god "resurrection" here. They were so polytheistic that they couldn't understand what Paul was even talking about. But they were concerned about these two "foreign gods." They liked their own gods and may have felt threatened by the missionary who wanted to advocate other foreign gods.

19 "Then they took him and brought him to a meeting of the Areopagus, where they said to him, "May we know what this new teaching is that you are presenting? 20 You are bringing some strange ideas to our ears, and we want to know what they mean." 21 (All the Athenians and the foreigners who lived there spent their time doing nothing but talking about and listening to the latest ideas.)"

By the way, verse 21 has to be such an exaggeration that it's quite simply false, and hence a lie. "All the Athenians"...."spent their time doing nothing but talking..." What? They didn't work, or wash clothes, or cook? Such a demeaning attitude toward Athens is just that, demeaning. And even taking into consideration that it is an exaggeration, which we would quite naturally do, as an exaggeration it's still false, stupid, and a lie. What if the your local newspaper prints: "All the people in Chicago and all of its visitors spend their time doing nothing but talking about and listening to the latest ideas"? At first glance we'd shake our heads. Then we'd read the story and ask ourselves what the people of Chicago would say in response, because the story is obviously biased. Then we'd say that such a report is so grossly unfair and exaggerated that the editor should be fired. Since we already know this report in Acts is a gross exaggeration, we have to start asking what would the people in Athens say in response to this account, as well as the rest of the book of Acts.

22 "Paul then stood up in the meeting of the Areopagus and said: "Men of Athens! I see that in every way you are very religious. 23 For as I walked around and looked carefully at your objects of worship, I even found an altar with this inscription: TO AN UNKNOWN GOD. Now what you worship as something unknown I am going to proclaim to you."

This was the milieu of Athens. The KJV uses the words "very superstitious" instead of "very religious" here. "Very religious" or "Very superstitious" (KJV), it doesn't matter. They were so superstitious that they even had an idol "TO AN UNKNOWN GOD." Apparently they didn't want to offend any god at all!

24 "The God who made the world and everything in it is the Lord of heaven and earth and does not live in temples built by hands. 25 And he is not served by human hands, as if he needed anything, because he himself gives all men life and breath and everything else. 26 From one man he made every nation of men, that they should inhabit the whole earth; and he determined the times set for them and the exact places where they should live. 27 God did this so that men would seek him and perhaps reach out for him and find him, though he is not far from each one of us. 28 'For in him we live and move and have our being.' As some of your own poets have said, 'We are his offspring.'"

Of course, Paul here really misunderstands the nature of idols. The truth is that these idols *represent* the gods. They are images of the gods. This analysis can be borne out, I think. But still, look at what their own poet said: 'We are his offspring.' Very religious, and very superstitious.

29 "Therefore since we are God's offspring, we should not think that the divine being is like gold or silver or stone—an image made by man's design and skill. 30 In the past God overlooked such ignorance, but now he commands all people everywhere to repent. 31 For he has set a day when he will judge the world with justice by the man he has appointed. He has given proof of this to all men by raising him from the dead."

The ignorance Paul refers to may be his own, about the divine nature being like gold or silver or stone—an image made by man's design and skill. I grant that any image of any god can be mistakenly worshipped, and Paul's point here isn't that far off the mark. Those adherents who were educated about their idol worship would know the difference. But the fact that many people in Athens may not have is itself telling on their level of understanding. How much more superstitious are these people who think the man made idol is itself the god!

All I point out here is the nature of the people in Athens at the time of the spreading of Paul's gospel. Superstitious people like the ones described here in Acts do not need evidence for their beliefs. They just need to hear a believable story by sincere people, and have some corresponding religious experiences.

Acts 19:23-41: The Riot in Ephesus.

23 "About that time there arose a great disturbance about the Way. 24 A silversmith named Demetrius, who made silver shrines of Artemis, brought in no little business for the craftsmen. 25 He called them together, along with the workmen in related trades, and said: "Men, you know we receive a good income from this business. 26 And you see and hear how this fellow Paul has convinced and led astray large numbers of people here in Ephesus and in practically the whole province of Asia. He says that man-made gods are no gods at all. 27 There is danger not only that our trade will lose its good name, but also that the temple of the great goddess Artemis will be discredited, and the goddess herself, who is worshiped throughout the province of Asia and the world, will be robbed of her divine majesty."

Who's Artemis, anyway? While it's probably an exaggeration to say that this goddess "is worshiped throughout the province of Asia and the world," certainly most all people in and around Ephesus did. There were undoubtedly many people throughout the known world who did.

From Microsoft Encarta: "Artemis, in Greek mythology, one of the principal goddesses, counterpart of the Roman goddess Diana. She was the daughter of the god Zeus and Leto and the twin sister of the god Apollo. She was chief hunter to the gods and goddess of hunting and of wild animals, especially bears. Artemis was also the goddess of childbirth, of nature, and of the harvest. As the moon goddess, she was sometimes identified with the goddesses Selene and Hecate."

"Although traditionally the friend and protector of youth, especially young women, Artemis prevented the Greeks from sailing to Troy during the Trojan

War until they sacrificed a maiden to her. According to some accounts, just before the sacrifice, she rescued the victim, Iphigenia. Like Apollo, Artemis was armed with a bow and arrows, which she often used to punish mortals who angered her. In other legends, she is praised for giving young women who died in childbirth a swift and painless death."

28 "When they heard this, they were furious and began shouting: "Great is Artemis of the Ephesians!" 29 Soon the whole city was in an uproar. The people seized Gaius and Aristarchus, Paul's traveling companions from Macedonia, and rushed as one man into the theater. 30 Paul wanted to appear before the crowd, but the disciples would not let him. 31 Even some of the officials of the province, friends of Paul, sent him a message begging him not to venture into the theater."

Even though the text attributes financial motive to Demetrius, the overwhelming reaction is that the initial crowd overwhelmingly believed in Artemis.

32 "The assembly was in confusion: Some were shouting one thing, some another. Most of the people did not even know why they were there. 33 The Jews pushed Alexander to the front, and some of the crowd shouted instructions to him. He motioned for silence in order to make a defense before the people. 34 But when they realized he was a Jew, they all shouted in unison for about two hours: 'Great is Artemis of the Ephesians!'"

Even if some of these Ephesians hadn't known why they were there, they did know what they believed--with fanaticism! Two hours!

35 "The city clerk quieted the crowd and said: "Men of Ephesus, doesn't all the world know that the city of Ephesus is the guardian of the temple of the great Artemis and of her image, which fell from heaven? 36 Therefore, since these facts are undeniable, you ought to be quiet and not do anything rash. 37 You have brought these men here, though they have neither robbed temples nor blasphemed our goddess. 38 If, then, Demetrius and his fellow craftsmen have a grievance against anybody, the courts are open and there are proconsuls. They can press charges. 39 If there is anything further you want to bring up, it must be settled in a legal assembly. 40 As it is, we are in danger of being charged with rioting because of today's events. In that case we would not be able to account for this commotion, since there is no reason for it." 41 After he had said this, he dismissed the assembly."

Here's a pragmatic clerk in the midst of fanaticism. But can you imagine any town clerk in America dealing with the same problem...and admitting the things he did: "these facts are undeniable." That's the difference between them and us today, I think. These people were definitely overwhelmingly superstitious, and had no evidence for the existence of Artemis, except religious experiences which can be interpreted according to their own beliefs. These people would believe any good story if told sincerely, wouldn't they? And so it would seem that the competition among religious truth claims would be in who had the best story, wouldn't it, even if old beliefs die hard, like in Ephesus. The Christian story had to win, because it couldn't be topped! And Paul established a church there.

Paul in Malta, Acts 28:1-6:

"Once safely on shore, we found out that the island was called Malta. 2 The islanders showed us unusual kindness. They built a fire and welcomed us all because it was raining and cold. 3 Paul gathered a pile of brushwood and, as he put it on the fire, a viper, driven out by the heat, fastened itself on his hand. 4 When the islanders

saw the snake hanging from his hand, they said to each other, "This man must be a murderer; for though he escaped from the sea, Justice has not allowed him to live."

I'm not sure the incident occurred as reported. "Fastened on his hand;" later he "shook it off." Most snakebites are very quick. And if it was quick maybe the venom wasn't enough to kill or even hurt Paul? Even if otherwise, who actually was there to see it happen? How many actually saw it? Maybe Paul merely told them what happened? Or maybe one other person saw something and told the others. So when it says the "islanders" saw it, how many people does that mean? And if it actually means most or all of them, then the rest of the islanders believed it because it was merely told to them. And if the snake fell into the fire afterward, who knew exactly which kind of snake it was that bit him?

They concluded that Paul was a murderer and that the god "Justice" has not allowed him to live. A murderer? Why not a rapist? Or a thief? I tell ya, I could get these people to buy a piece of property in the Land of Oz. Bad things happen because of the gods. That's just stupid.

5 But Paul shook the snake off into the fire and suffered no ill effects. 6 The people expected him to swell up or suddenly fall dead, but after waiting a long time and seeing nothing unusual happen to him, they changed their minds and said he was a god.

They changed their minds? All of them? Back and forth and back and forth. If a bad thing happened, then god was angry. If a good thing happened, a god was pleased, or the person himself was a god. This is much too fickle for me, and we've seen this before. But my point is to see how these people reached conclusions that few educated modern people today would reach. I tell you I could go back in time and with a slight bit of hand, I could convince them I was a god and have a pampered life. I could also convince them that Jesus arose from the dead too.

The NT "War of the Teachers."

In the NT, like the OT we see numerous warnings against false prophets, teachers, and ministers <u>This warning is from Jude:</u>

3 Dear friends, although I was very eager to write to you about the salvation we share, I felt I had to write and urge you to contend for the faith that was once for all entrusted to the saints. 4 For certain men whose condemnation was written about long ago have secretly slipped in among you. They are godless men, who change the grace of our God into a license for immorality and deny Jesus Christ our only Sovereign and Lord.

<u>This warning is from II Peter 2:1-3:</u>

But there were also false prophets among the people, just as there will be false teachers among you. They will secretly introduce destructive heresies, even denying the sovereign Lord who bought them — bringing swift destruction on themselves. 2 Many will follow their shameful ways and will bring the way of truth into disrepute. 3 In their greed these teachers will exploit you with stories they have made up. Their condemnation has long been hanging over them, and their destruction has not been sleeping.

The author says, "with stories they have made up." This is spoken from the authors' perspective, of course. But apparently many people did make up stories back then, didn't they?

My questions here are threefold: **1) Since we already know that prophets received their prophecies by means of dreams and visions (Numbers 12:6), how did any of them know for sure their prophecies were truly from God?**

Just go back and read Jonah. The only way they could tell whether a "vision" was from God or not was whether something they did afterward corresponded to it, much like self-fulfilled prophecies, or horoscope reading, or Chinese fortune cookies. If something didn't correspond with their vision they merely concluded they misunderstood it, or this particular vision wasn't from God after all. But it wouldn't stop them from considering future dreams and trance-like states as visions. And given the numbers of superstitious people in the ancient world, many people considered their dreams as visions, so some of these "visions" will turn out, if for no other reason but the odds themselves.

2) Why are there so many warnings about false teachings in the N.T. if these people had solid evidence to base their faith upon, and they were not like their contemporaries who would believe most any good story? Why the many warnings? Along with the threats? It seems obvious that many Christians were led astray, beginning with Ananias & Sapphira (Acts 5). Many in the Corinthian church rejected Paul's apostleship, tolerated immorality in the church, doubted the resurrection of Jesus, accepted "false apostles," and the list goes on and on. They doubted the resurrection of Jesus? That's right! (I Cor. 15)

And if we have trouble with these questions, then **3) How did the authors of the Bible know they themselves were teaching divine truths?** There are many apocryphal books that were written back then. Just go to www.EarlyChristianWritings.com, to see for yourself. But again, the winner of the N.T. "war of the teachers" decided which books went into the canon.

When an outsider looks at Christian history he will find so many disagreements down through the years between different denominations and inside of each one of them that it becomes quite a tangled mess to figure out which branch of Christianity adheres faithfully to the spirit and/or beliefs of the first Christians. Even the earliest Christians, including the apostles themselves, had internal debates about what beliefs and practices were truly Christian ones, along with who their true leaders were. [See Paul's debates over accepting Gentiles into the faith (Acts 15, and Galatians); and see Paul's answers to Chloe's household (in I Corinthians). There were people in the early church that wanted to discredit Paul (II Corinthians), and so on].

According to James D.G. Dunn, "earliest Christianity was quite a diverse phenomenon. The Christianity established by the first apostles was little different from Christianity since then—the same sorts of tensions and differences, even divisions, such as we know all too well today!" [Evidence for Jesus, (Westminster Press, 1985), p. 99]. There were three branches of early Christianity which vied for dominance: "Catholic," "Jewish," and "Gnostic." Concerning Gnostic Christianity Dunn acknowledges that "much of the 20th century scholarly debate about Christian beginnings has focused on the question of whether Gnosticism was already in full flower before Christianity and whether Christianity borrowed its ideas about Christ as heavenly redeemer from Gnosticism, rather than the other way around."(p. 97). One thing seems likely, according to Dunn, most of the evidence and documents from Gnostic churches were suppressed and/or destroyed as Catholic Christianity gained in popularity. [For more on this see

John Dominic Crossan, The Birth of Christianity: Discovering What Happened in the Years Immediately After the Execution of Jesus (Harper, 1998), L. Michael White, From Jesus to Christianity (Harper, 2004), and Bart Ehrman's, Lost Christianities].

Four Last Objections. **Objection 1)** Someone might claim that modern people are just as superstitious as the ancients, with the major exception that we have less to be superstitious about because of modern knowledge. That is to say, some modern people still read their horoscopes, have a lucky rabbit's foot, or are worried about seven years of bad luck if they break a mirror.

Okay, so let's assume that there were 10,000 things to be superstitious about in the ancient world, but because the ancients lacked accessible scientific knowledge the most superstitious among them believed in all 10,000 of them, while the more knowledgeable believed in only 9,000 of them. Among modern educated westerners let's say there are now only 100 things to be superstitious about, and the more superstitious among us will believe all 100 of them, while the more knowledgeable will believe 5-10 of them. This describes the "god of the gaps" epistemology, and there are far fewer gaps with our knowledge today.

But my whole point is about the number of superstitious beliefs ancient people had when compared to ours. If someone wants to maintain that modern people are just as superstitious as the ancients, with the major exception that we have less to be superstitious about because of modern knowledge, then what does that gain him in terms of what I'm claiming here? The whole reason I'm discussing this is because I'm questioning the knowledge claimed by the Biblical writers and early Christians. I'm saying that their knowledge was largely based upon ancient superstitions, which even modern Christian's would reject if those same things were claimed by someone today. I'm arguing that Christians have a non-historical double standard when they evaluate the superstitious knowledge claims of people in our day in comparison to how they evaluate the knowledge claims of Biblical writers. And even though a majority of skeptics think that all religious people today are superstitious doesn't help the Christian's case here, either, because these same skeptics will agree that the modern educated religious people of today are by far less superstitious than those people of the ancient past.

Objection 2) A second objection is that modern scientifically educated people have their own myths: Rationality comes from irrationality, order comes from chaos, morality comes from amorality, life comes from non-life, complexity comes from from simplicity. But these beliefs are the result of weighing all of the religious and non-religious alternatives—these beliefs are the result of the process of thinking and weighing evidence, not from reading Tarot cards.

A point of clarification might help here. There are several different ways to view modern science and it's relationship with philosophy and/or theology. Ian Barbour in Religion In An Age of Science (Harper, 1990), deals with these relationships. There are several branches of scientific study: The "Philosophy of Science" is the area where science and philosophy interact the very most, because in this branch of study, the whole question is this: "What Constitutes Science?" There is a branch of science called "Theoretical Physics" which is almost completely mathematics. But the branch of science I'm mostly referring to here is "Applied Science," along with its implications for modern people. We can see how applied science has impacted us (in no particular order) in the areas of medicine, biology, earth science, computer science, engineering technology, zoology, geology, electricity, botany, genetics, dental technology, rocket science, astronomy, forensics, meteorology, chemistry, laser surgery, hydraulics, X-rays, Plasma Physics, increased the number of elements in the Periodic Table of Elements, understanding the nervous and muscular system, brain science, the whole notion of friction, etc, etc. [See the popular treatments in New York Public Library's Science Desk Reference, or the Encyclopedia of Science and Technology, ed. James Trefil, (Routledge, 2001)].

Compare the above scientific disciplines with such things as divination, casting of lots, dreams, visions, trances, magic, exorcisms heal people, astrology, necromancy, sorcery, prophets· for every religion, idol worship, gods and goddesses for every natural phenomena, human and animal sacrifices, priests, omens, temples, festivals, sacred writings, and the Pseudepigrapha. We live in a much different world than the ancients, primarily because of Newtonian science.

Objection 3) It's claimed from original letters and the writing of the educated classes that Rome was not that superstitious in Paul's day. The Roman government (and usually Rome itself) was "atheistic" in that the gods were used in order to manipulate those either in Rome or outside of Rome (typically the latter). Roman (not Greek) religion was all about enhancing the power of the state. Belief was irrelevant as long as one sacrificed to the statue of *Roma*, which was done to show or maintain citizen status. Thus what mattered was an outward action that showed service to the state. Many of the different Greek gods were adopted (under Latin names) into the Roman pantheon for the purpose of conquering through diplomacy rather than arms. If a group joins the Roman Empire, their god(s) were often honored by adoption under a different name into the Roman gods. Then the goddess *Roma* would then be added to their major temple.

So what does this prove? Rome was adoptionistic in practice, and as a political system among superstitious people, it worked very well. How is that exactly different than in America, except for the so-called separation of church and state? American people are very religious, but our government is democratic, allowing us all to practice our faith as we may. This doesn't automatically make Rome atheistic anymore than it makes America atheistic. We are just not a theocracy. I'm don't see how the political structure of Rome and how they handled the various religions shows anything non-superstitious about the nature of the ancient people of that day that Paul reached with his Christian message.It only reveals the Roman political system, which dealt with superstitious people. Christianity converted mostly the lower classes of people, and they are the ones who were overwhelmingly superstitious.

Objection 4) Some might say that I am a intolerant when I harshly judge superstitious thinking people. In reply let me mention just one example: Consider the witch trials the church "investigated." [Carl Sagan does a great job of this in The Demon Haunted World]. Once accused by some priest who should know, there was nothing that could get the accused off the hook. And they looked for the "signs" of a witch, like a birthmark, that was unusual (put there as Satan's brand mark). And the woman was stripped and examined by "celibate" priests who could rape her and claim she was lying when she told anyone about it. Anything she claimed differently was meant to deceive the "investigators." And anyone who came to her defense was being deceived by her. So the only thing to do was to force her to confess and burn the demon out of her.

This kind of superstitious thinking is very dangerous. It is what I strongly object to. Since I believe this is the kind of thinking the Bible is based upon, this is the stuff I reject. So I don't feel maligned when someone calls me intolerant, if being intolerant is condemning superstitious ways of thinking that can be used to convict people of crimes they didn't commit without any evidence. It goes against educated, logical, and scientific reasoning.

Conclusions: Throughout this brief study we find that the Gentile pagans believed and practiced many superstitious things. This is undeniable from the Bible itself. My contention here is that ancient people weren't stupid, just very superstitious. We also see many hints that God's people in the Bible were heavily influenced by such beliefs and practices. If these Gentile nations were so superstitious, whom God's people had so much contact with, then it seems clear that the beliefs of the Israelites, and later the Christians, are on the same level. Much of Israel's history rested on the same foundations as all the other nations, it rested on myths, legends, and superstitions. This explains how they could so easily reject their "history"—there just wasn't a real history to reject. Most superstitious people like the ones described in the Bible would probably believe any good story if told sincerely. And so it would seem that the competition among religious truth claims would be in who had the best story. The Christian story had to win, because it couldn't be topped!

The Christian Big Picture assumes that ancient people were just as superstitious as people are in our day, and yet that flies in the face of the results of modern science. Moreover, their Big Picture has a double standard when looking at the ancients, too. Their Big Picture assumes that the "faithful" people in the Bible were different than their contemporaries—that they were not as superstitious as their contemporaries. Their Big Picture acknowledges how many people in the ancient past claimed divine knowledge, and yet they arbitrarily choose to accept the divine knowledge claims of the "faithful" people in the Bible. Their Big Picture doesn't see how prevalent the Pseudepigrapha was in ancient times and how it crept into the Bible, even given some very clear examples, like Isaiah, the additions in the LXX of versions of Esther and Daniel; also the Letter of Jeremiah [next section]. **I merely want to know why they apply a double standard here.**

Modern Christians would absolutely hate living in the ancient first century AD. They'd hate it with a passion! They'd hate the superstitions, and the religious rites. They'd want to reason with these people and asking them for evidence for their religious claims, and the ancients might simply brush them off with a wave of their superstitious hands.

[For a very accessible recent book describing the war between pagans and the people described as "faithful" in the Bible, you must read Jonathon Kirsch's, God Against the Gods: The History of the War Between Monotheism an Polytheism (Viking Compass, 2004), and Robin Lane Fox, Pagans and Christians (Alfred Knopf, 1987)].

12:1 **Pseudonymity in the Bible**

If I am correct that there was a war of the prophets and that the history of Israel and of Christianity was written and rewritten from the perspective of the winners of each of these wars, then we'd expect to see some evidence of this in the Bible itself. This is where Biblical criticism comes into play. We've already seen where there were two creation accounts in Genesis 1-2 (with the first one written much later to reflect more of a monotheistic belief), the story of Cain (which was originally a self contained folk-story), and how that the Flood story in Genesis 6-9 has several sources from which it was drawn. Now I just want to indicate that there is indeed evidence of rewriting in the Bible itself, that is, up until the canon of each testament was declared "closed."

Scholarship has shown that Moses did not write what is now known as the first five books of Moses, known as the Pentateuch. According to James D.G. Dunn, **"it would be flying in the face of too much evidence and good scholarship to deny this basic affirmation: that the Pentateuch is the product of a lengthy process of tradition**." [The Living Word (Fortress, 1987), p. 71]. Here's just some of the evidence:

1) Deuteronomy tells where Moses is buried and states "no one knows his burial place to this day." This indicates that this was written some time after Moses' death because it is remarkable that no one knows to this day--i.e. in a time far removed from his death. Even conservatives admit that Moses didn't write this. Usually, they say it is Joshua, but that really wouldn't make sense of the "to this day" comment. **2)** In Genesis 14, it states that Abraham chased his nephew's captors to the city of Dan. The problem is that Dan wasn't a city until the time of Samson (Judges 18:27) some 331 years after Moses died. Moses could not have known about Dan. This one is better. Was it a different Dan in the same location 300 years before it was renamed "Dan"? Unlikely. **3)** In Genesis 36:31 it lists some kings of the other countries "before any king reigned over the Israelites." In Moses' life there were no kings in Israel. This didn't happen until Saul, hundreds of years after Moses died. And the fact that they say any king implies that there have been at least more than one before this passage was written. Moses couldn't have written this. This is pretty difficult to get around. Sure, Moses was a prophet, but the fact that this statement is said so matter-of-factly is notable. One wonders why Samuel wouldn't have brought it up when the people were calling for a king hundreds of years later. **4)** Exodus 16:35 reads, "The Israelites ate manna forty years, until they came to a habitable land; they ate manna, until they came to the border of the land of Canaan." Moses was dead before the Israelites reached the border. Hmmm. Doesn't sound like a "prophecy" to me. Sounds like a statement of fact. **5)** In trying to prove the existence of giants, Deuteronomy 3:11 says, "Now only King Og of Bashan was left of the remnant of the Rephaim. In fact his bed, an iron bed, can still be seen in Rabbah of the Amorites." In this passage, this bed is already an ancient relic that can still be seen in Rabbah (a city which was not even conquered until King David ruled over Israel). This is much too late for Moses to write.

When could the Pentateuch have been written? In 2 Kings 22:8-13, there is this interesting story. Israel had long been divided into two kingdoms. Josiah had just come to be king of Judah. He wanted to repair the temple and told the priest to go through all the stuff and see how much money they had. While the high priest was looking, he found the "Book of the Law" and gave it to a secretary who read it to Josiah. When Josiah heard it, he tore his clothes because he realized that they had not been obeying God.

Scholars think that instead of "finding" the Law (another way of saying the first five books of the Bible) here, this is when it was actually compiled and/or much of it written. Most of the Hebrew Bible was actually written at a time in the divided kingdom of Israel when Josiah wanted to control the people he was ruling. It was written to keep a crumbling kingdom together as a system of control, and it was claimed that Moses wrote it. That's what scholarship leads us to think. [See Who Wrote the Bible? by Richard E. Friedman (Harper, 1997)].

But there is more. Take a look at the **Book of Isaiah**. It has been long accepted that the present book of Isaiah was compiled by at least two authors, and probably three. From the Anchor Bible Dictionary, "Isaiah": "The historical context of chaps. 40–55 differs entirely from that of chaps. 1–39. The enemy of Israel is the Neo-Babylonian Empire (626–539 b.c.; cf. chaps. 46; 47; 48:20–21), not the Neo-Assyrian Empire of Isaiah (935–612 b.c.; cf. chaps. 10; 14:24–27), which collapsed with the destruction of Nineveh in 612 b.c. The gentile king in chaps. 40–55 is Cyrus of Persia (fl. 560–530 b.c.; cf. 41:2–3, 25; 44:24–45:13; 48:14), not the Assyrian king of Isaiah (10:5–19). The people are in Babylon, not in Isaiah's 8th-century Jerusalem; the message is to leave Babylon, cross the desert, and return to Zion." "**That a 6th-century author, name unknown, wrote chaps. 40–55, and another author or authors, also anonymous, wrote chaps. 56–66, is now accepted by all but a scholarly minority, who hold out for the unity of Isaiah.**"

Conservative professor R.K. Harrison in his Introduction to the Old Testament: "Whereas the earlier sections of the prophecy [of Isaiah] spoke of the divine majesty, later chapters described His uniqueness and eternity. As contrasted with the emphasis found in the first thirty-nine chapters, where Jehovah was exalted above all other gods, the remaining chapters of the prophecy denied their very existence, and instead discussed the concept of God as the sole deity. In the first portion of Isaiah, the remnant was held to constitute the faithful left behind in Jerusalem, whereas in the later part of the work it was thought of as the faithful exilic group about to be brought back to Palestine. Finally, the messianic king of chapters 1-39 was to have been replaced by the concept of the Servant in chapters 40-66." (p. 775).

The main reason why the unity of Isaiah was accepted for so long despite the problems with the different historical contexts was because of a predisposition to believe in the verbal inspiration of the Bible as a whole, modeled on the prophetic paradigm (which I appraise in a later section). But eventually, with the rise of historical consciousness, scholars challenged this assumption with the facts of Isaiah itself." Professor James D.G. Dunn: "we can speak of an overwhelming consensus of biblical scholarship that the present Isaiah is not the work of a single author. **It is not simply a question of whether predictive prophecy is possible or not. It is rather that the message of Second Isaiah would have been largely meaningless to an 8th century Jerusalem audience.** It is so clearly directed to the situation of exile. Consequently, had it been delivered a century and a half before the exile, it would be unlike the rest of Jewish prophecy..." [The Living Word (Fortress, 1987), p. pp.73-74].

This re-writing is true of many, if not most of the books in the Bible. The **Book of Daniel** clearly had pseudepigraphal additions to it. The book contains sections of Hebrew and sections of Aramaic languages. Anchor Bible Dictionary: It is probable that "the two languages reflect the history of composition. Chapters 2–6 (and probably chap. 1) were composed in Aramaic and chap. 7 was added in the time of Antiochus Epiphanes (c.a. 175–164 B.C.). Then either the same author or others of the same circle composed chaps. 8–12 in Hebrew (possibly because of nationalistic fervor). Chapter 1 was either translated from Aramaic or composed in Hebrew in order to form a Hebrew inclusion around the Aramaic chapters." ["Daniel"]

Anchor Bible Dictionary: "**The Additions to Daniel (Adds)** consist of three extended passages in the Greek Septuagint which have no counterpart in the canonical text of Daniel: (1) "**The Prayer of Azariah and the Hymn of the Three Young Men**," consisting of 66 verses and located between what would correspond to vv 23 and 24 of the third chap. of canonical Daniel; (2) "**Susanna**," consisting of 64 verses; and (3) "**Bel and the Snake**," consisting of 42 verses, the latter two Adds usually appearing after the canonical chaps. of Daniel. All three Adds have their setting in Babylon and describe how some Jew who trusted in the Lord God of Israel was delivered from certain death through the intervention of an angel." "Evidently never a part of the Jewish canon (neither the one probably established by ca. 150 B.C.) nor as it existed in Josephus' day in the 1st century A.D., the Adds were regarded as part of the Christian canon of the Western Church until the time of the Protestant and Catholic movements, at which time they were rejected by Protestants and were termed "apocryphal" while the Roman Catholic Church at its Council of Trent in 1546 reaffirmed them and termed them "deuterocanonical." ["Additions of Daniel"]

The Prevalence of Pseudonymity. That there might be more than one author of the Pentateuch, Isaiah, Daniel or many of the books in the Bible itself, introduces us to the whole idea of pseudonymity in the Bible, and the Pseudepigrapha. The books known as Pseudepigraphal are considered by scholars to be works that are false, by today's standards. They are either purported to be authored by a famous person of the past, or they contain material claimed to have been from a famous person of the past. And there are many such Old Testament examples: works: *1 Enoch, Questions of Ezra, 2 Enoch, Revelation of Ezra, 3 Enoch, 2 Baruch, Treatise of Shem, 3 Baruch, Apocryphon of Ezekiel, Apocalypse of Abraham, Apocalypse of Zephaniah, Apocalypse of Adam, The Fourth Book of Ezra, Apocalypse of Elijah, Greek Apocalypse of Ezra, Apocalypse of Daniel, Vision of Ezra, Testaments of the Twelve Patriarchs, Testament of Moses, Testament of Job, Testament of Solomon, Testaments of the Three Patriarchs (Abraham, Isaac, and Jacob), Testament of Adam, More Psalms of David, Prayer of Joseph, Prayer of Manasseh, Prayer of Jacob, Psalms of Solomon, Odes of Solomon,* and so on.

Some of the New Testament examples are: **Documents falsely attributed to Paul**: *3 Corinthians, the Epistle to the Alexandrians, the Epistle to the Laodiceans, the Epistles of Paul and Seneca, the Apocalypse of Paul, the Vision of Paul, the Acts of Paul, the Martyrdom of Paul, and the Martyrdom of Peter and Paul.* **Documents falsely**

attributed to Peter: *the Apocalypse of Peter, the Gospel of Peter, the Preaching of Peter, the Acts of Peter, the Acts of Andrew and Peter, and the Martyrdom of Peter (also II Peter!)*. **Documents of Mary the mother of Jesus**: *The Birth of Mary, the Gospel of the Birth of Mary, the Passing of Mary, the Questions of Mary, the Apocalypse of the Virgin, the Assumption of the Virgin, and the Coptic Lives of the Virgin.* [See Bart Ehrman, Lost Scriptures: Books That Did Not Make It Into The New Testament].

The Meaning of Pseudepigrapha Authorship. According to

Pseudepigraphal scholar, James H. Charlesworth, "The Pseudepigrapha poses a perplexing problem for many readers: Why did the authors of these writings attribute them falsely to other persons? These authors did not attempt to deceive the reader. They, like the authors of the Psalms of David, the Proverbs of Solomon, the Wisdom of Solomon, and the additions to Isaiah, attempted to write authoritatively in the name of an influential biblical person. Many religious Jews attributed their works to some biblical saint who lived before the cessation of prophecy and who had inspired them. Also, the principle of solidarity united early Jews with their predecessors who, in their eyes, had assuredly been guided by God himself. It is also conceivable that some of the apocalyptic writers had dreams or visions in which they experienced revelations given to Enoch, Abraham, Elijah, Ezra, Baruch, and others." ["Pseudepigrapha" The Anchor Bible Dictionary. See Charlesworth, The Pseudepigrapha and Modern Research with a Supplement, and The OT Pseudepigrapha and the NT].

James D.G. Dunn: "In the Septuagint there are expanded versions of Esther and Daniel; also the Letter of Jeremiah; and not to mention the reordering of the chapters of Jeremiah. Here we see a willingness to make substantial additions to earlier writings. There was evidently no sense that a document once written was complete and closed, that no additions to it would violate its character or the integrity of the original author. And certainly talk of deception and forgery would be inappropriate. What we have rather is a sense that earlier traditions can be expanded and elaborated in a way wholly appropriate to that tradition, so that the elaborations and expansions can be retained within that tradition, continuous with it, part of a larger integrated whole which can be regarded as belonging to the original author's corpus without impropriety." Dunn goes on to argue this happened with regard to the Pentateuch, the Psalms, I Samuel through II Chronicles, and NT writings like the Pastoral letters and II Peter. [The Living Word (Fortress, 1987), p. 69-70. For further treatment see David G. Meade, Pseudonymity and Canon (Tübingen, 1986)].

Along with the overwhelming number of scholars who have studied this out, I just don't think that anyone "tried to get away with it" when they wrote their pseudepigraphal works or placed pseudonymous comments inside other books. Perhaps the authors just thought that the spirit of Isaiah, Moses, Ezra, Baruch, Solomon, or David, etc, was speaking through them, or more than likely, they believed historical and prophetic truth could be revealed directly to them by God. That's most likely what they thought, whether the whole book was purportedly written by those men of antiquity, or they quoted them within their work. That's why the second author of Isaiah had no problem adding and reworking the original Isaiah's work. God was still speaking Isaiah's message, or rather, that he was a prophet "like unto" Isaiah-- a "second Elijah."

Richard Carrier claims that the empty tomb story of Matthew and Luke was a legendary expansion of Mark's original metaphorical empty tomb. But Carrier says, "This does not mean these authors must be considered liars. Just as Paul can find 'hidden meaning" in the Old Testament Prophets...so could the Gospel authors *CREATE* narratives with deeper, hidden meanings under a veil of history. It was honest work then, even if it disturbs us today." [The Empty Tomb (Prometheus Books, 2005), p. 156, emphasis his].

My point is about the very presence of the pseudonymous writings and what they tell us about ancient Jewish thinking. It tells us that the written product was able to be amended, because, according to Dunn, the authority was not "a closed authority, but a living authority which could be and WAS (his emphasis) expanded and elaborated as new insights emerged and which could be and evidently was adapted and modified as circumstances changed." [The Living Word (Fortress, 1987), p.p. 71]. They just wrote and rewrote their history from the conclusions of hindsight.

Clear examples of pseudonymity appearing in the NT. First, let's consider the most obvious examples of pseudonymity in the Bible. The most obvious cases are **Mark 16:9-20; John 5:3-4; Acts 8:37; John 7:53-8:11; and I John 5:7-8**. Just compare these passages in the KJV the NIV, NASB or NRSV. Notice them missing in later translations? These are obvious cases. How did they get in the text in the first place? Who wrote them? Why were they accepted as Scripture for way too long? **Revelation 1:11**: The phrase "I am Alpha and Omega, the first and the last" (KJV) was not in the original Greek texts. The Alpha Omega phrase "is not found in virtually any ancient texts" nor is it even mentioned in a footnote in modern versions. [For a discussion of these and other texts, see Bruce Metzger A Textual Commentary on the Greek New Testament, (United Bible Societies, 1994), see also Bart Ehrman, Misquoting Jesus: The Story Behind Who Changed the New Testament and Why].

Jude 14: *"Enoch, the seventh from Adam, prophesied about these men: "See, the Lord is coming with thousands upon thousands of his holy ones."*

Enoch, the "seventh from Adam" didn't say this, because the *Book of Enoch* was written in the 2nd century B.C. and couldn't have come from Enoch himself! About this text, listen to what James Barr said in his book After Fundamentalism (pp. 42-50): "The letter of Jude quotes from the Book of Enoch with all the air of accepting it as a fully authoritative religious book. It is not just a minor allusion, or the borrowing of a few words as a matter of style. It is the fullest and most explicit use of an older sacred text within the letter. It is aligned with a series of references: to the exodus from Egypt (v. 5), to Sodom and Gomorrah (v.7), to an incident involving the body of Moses, an incident not related in the Old Testament (v. 9), to Cain, Balaam and Korah (v. 11), and to 'predictions of the apostles of our Lord Jesus Christ' (v. 17). It is clearly intended to carry the strongest weight within the argument of the letter....Enoch is regarded as having 'prophesied', just as Moses or Elijah or Isaiah had done. As all true prophets were, he must have been inspired. The citation of Enoch had, for the purposes of Jude's argument, just the same validity and the same effect as the citation of the scriptures which came later to be deemed canonical....He quoted Enoch because it was an authoritative utterance of a prophet of ancient times, accepted as such in the church. To say...Enoch's book 'was not scripture' would have been unintelligible to Jude."

While Jude's use of Enoch is an explicit quotation, there is a great deal of implicit acceptance of the OT apocryphal and pseudepigraphal writings in the NT. According to Barr: "Much of the impact of ancient authoritative writings on the New Testament comes not through explicit quotation but through tacit or implicit acceptance of their doctrine or their emphasis. In this respect the thinking of a book like the *Wisdom of Solomon* can be traced with high probability in various parts of the New Testament: **in fact such a book, though it counts as 'apocryphal' in Protestantism, very likely exercised more influence than some portions of the now canonical Old Testament**.....The New Testament did not confine itself strictly to what is said in the canonical texts, but also included embellishments of Jewish tradition....Paul uses the Genesis story as mediated through the sort of tradition that Wisdom represents." About the *Wisdom of Solomon*, Marcus Borg informs us: "This remarkable book has been more important in the history of Christianity than the non-canonical status given it by Protestants would suggest. Augustine, for example, refers to it almost 800 times." [Meeting Jesus for the First Time (1994) p. 113, note 21].

Consider for example, the Pauline argument from sin and death (Rom 5:12): "Therefore as sin came into the world through one man and death through sin, and so death spread to all men because all men sinned," which clearly stresses a stress on sin and death much greater than we actually find in the story of the supposed Fall of Adam and Eve (Gen 2-3). James Barr: "We simply do not find anywhere in the OT where the origin of evil and sin is traced back to the transgression of Adam and Eve in the Garden. It is only from later interpretation, especially in the apocryphal and pseudepigraphal writings that we find this stressed as the central lesson of the story. Thus, in the *Wisdom of Solomon* (2:23f), we read, 'For God created man for incorruption, and made him in the image of his own eternity, but through the devil's envy death entered the world, and those who belong to his party experience it.'"

Claus Westermann claims: "the teaching of the Fall and of original sin rests on the late Jewish interpretation (of Edras 7.118). It has no foundation at all in the narrative." He claims Paul's interpretation of Genesis 2-3, which reached its full development in Augustine's doctrine of original sin doesn't accord "with the intention of the narrator at the beginning of the Bible." "This interpretation rests on a misunderstanding; it has failed to realize that the whole course of events here is meant to be a primeval happening, and so something quite separate from our own history." [Creation, Fortress Press, 1974, (p. 108-109)].

2 Tim. 3:8-9: *"Now as Jannes and Jambres withstood Moses, so do these also resist the truth: men of corrupt minds, reprobate concerning the faith. 9 But they shall proceed no further: for their folly shall be manifest unto all men, as theirs also was."*

"Though the Jannes and Jambres tradition probably arose on Palestinian soil and in a Semitic-speaking environment, there is no indication that the original language of the book was other than Greek. The date of origin of the tradition can hardly be much later than the 2nd century B.C.E., while the book was written probably at least as early as the 2nd century C.E." [Charlesworth "Pseudepigrapha," Anchor Bible Dictionary]. The names of these two men are historically unknown!

Other examples: There is the detail that the prophets 'were sawn in two' (**Hebrews 11:37**), which is probably from the *Martyrdom of Isaiah,* and the story that: 'the archangel Michael, contending with the devil, disputed about the body of Moses (**Jude 9**), which is not to be found anywhere in the OT, but once again, a Jewish legend, and used by Jude as a matter of fact to make an important point.

The whole **Gospel of Matthew** itself is a work finished by a pseudonymous author (or a school of authors). "All scholars now admit that the author of this gospel simply cannot have been an eyewitness of the ministry of Jesus, since he employs secondary sources (Mark & Q), themselves patchworks of well-worn fragments. It is inconceivable that an eyewitness apostle would not have depended upon his own recollections." [Robert M. Price, The Empty Tomb, eds. Price & Lowder, (Prometheus Books), 2005, p. 88]. This is especially true when this gospel tells of the calling of Matthew by Jesus into discipleship. Why would he copy almost word for word Mark's account of this calling if the author were actually the disciple Matthew (Matt 9:9-13, Mark 2:14-17)?

I Cor. 15:3-11 is a disputable case, but where a plausible case is made by Robert M. Price. He argues that there are several statements which are interpolations of Pauline pseudepigraphy. The burden of proof is on those who think it's not pseudonymous since it was so rampant in those ancient days. Why would Price claim this since there is no textual evidence for it? It's because I Corinthians 15:3 says that as Paul "received" his gospel he delivered it to them. The language used is the technical language for the handing down of rabbinic tradition. But in Galatians (1:1; & 11-12) Paul says with an oath that he did not" receive" his gospel "from man." Price: "If the historical Paul is speaking in either passage, he is not speaking in both." (p. 74). [The Empty Tomb (Prometheus Books, 2005)].

II Peter is also pseudonymous: "The strong consensus among scholars is that 2 Peter is also pseudonymous and may well be the last NT book to be composed, perhaps in the first decades of the 2nd century." [The Anchor Bible Dictionary]. "If any document in the NT is pseudonymous it is this one. Its language and style is so very different from that of I Peter. It is clearly post-Pauline and reflects an anxiety over the delay of the *parousia* which would be unlikely were Peter himself still alive. And its difficulty in gaining acceptance into the canon points firmly to the same conclusion." [James D.G. Dunn, The Living Word, p. 83].

So in the war of the OT prophets, and even in the war of the NT teachers, we find that not even the inspired writers themselves knew what a true prophetic voice from God was! And we can see this in the continued early church discussions of the canon, which can be called the "war over the canon." [For which see James Barr, Holy Scripture: Canon, Authority, Criticism, (Westminster 1983]. Again, for probably the best single, one volume accessible work on the writing and re-writing of the Biblical accounts see Robin Lane Fox, The Unauthorized Version: Truth and Fiction in the Bible (Knopf, 1992).

There is also a widely recognized pseudonymous interpolation in Josephus's work by a later Christian author too, which claims that Jesus was the Christ, and that he arose from the dead. [Antiquities of the Jews, Book 18:3,3]. Not even conservative scholars think Josephus made these claims, because he was not a Christian.

12:2 Archaeology, Exodus, and the Canaanite Conquest.

Assuming the story of the Exodus is correct there should be some archaeological evidence for the Exodus, the crossing of the Red Sea, their camping at Sinai, their wilderness wanderings, and their Canaanite conquest that should correspond to the Biblical account. After all, the plagues described in Exodus would have wiped that nation out; the numbers of slaves they lost, (over 3-4 million of them!), loss of crops, cattle, soldiers, and first-born children.

The plagues would have devastated the Egyptian country (cf. Exod. 8:20; 9:6, 25; 10:7, 15; 12:29-30). This is actually what we are led to believe from the text. The crops had all been destroyed, their cattle were all killed (on three separate occasions: 9:6, 9:25,11:5), the infrastructure severely damaged, culminating in the death of every firstborn male in the country. Finally, we're told that the entire army had perished in the "Red Sea." We should expect to find some indication of this in archaeological digs and in the Egyptian hieroglyphic texts, no matter how embarrassing it may have been to their pride.

According to William G. Dever, Professor of Near Eastern Archaeology and Anthropology, University of Arizona, Tucson, AZ: "As is often observed, there is no direct archaeological evidence that any constituents of later Israel were ever in Egypt." ["Archaeology and the Israelite Conquest", in the Anchor Bible Dictionary]. See the article for more details, or see his book, Who Were the Early Israelites and Where Did They Come From? (Eerdmans, 2003), or William H. Stiebing, Out of the Desert? Archaeology and the Exodus/Conquest Narratives (Prometheus Books, 1989).

If God actually did do what the book of Exodus claims, then why is it so hard to even date the Exodus? There should be some archaeological evidence for this cataclysmic event that would show one date over the other. According to K.A. Kitchen, Professor of Egyptology, Oriental Studies, University of Liverpool, Liverpool, England, "The lazy man's solution is simply to cite the 480 years ostensibly given in 1 Kings 6:1 from the Exodus to the 4th year of Solomon (ca. 966 B.C.) and so to set the Exodus at ca. 1446 B.C. However, this too simple of a solution is ruled out by the combined weight of all the other biblical data plus additional information from external data. Kitchen concludes by saying, "the Exodus, the sojourn in the wilderness, and the entry into Canaan can reasonably be limited to within ca. 1279–1209 B.C., a maximum of 70 years; or if within about 1260–1220 B.C., very nearly 300 years before the 4th year of Solomon (966 B.C.)." [Exodus, The, in The Anchor Bible Dictionary].

Why is it so hard to identify the Red Sea that these 3-4 million people crossed on dry land? The Egyptian soldiers with their armor and chariots all died there, so where is this evidence? Surely there should be chariots and shields and spears to find. Scholars are debating the actual place of the crossing, but there is not a shred of evidence for any conclusion. [Once again, see the Anchor Bible Dictionary, "Red Sea"].

The unheard of numbers of Israelites that supposedly were let go from Egypt presents all sorts of problems. The Israelites emerged from Egypt numbering three to four million. Using only the biblical text, which was all that was available to him, Hermann Samuel Reimarus (1694-1768) in his Apologie (book 3, ch. 2 "Uber den Durchgang der Israeliten durch das Rohte Meer"), made a number of interesting calculations.

The livestock to support the Israelites would have been numerous. They lived in Goshen because they raised livestock (Gen. 46:31-34). Their cattle were said not to suffer from the plague that killed the Egyptian cattle (Exod. 9:1-7). When they supposedly left Egypt, Moses had wanted Pharaoh to allow them to take all of their livestock (Exod. 10:24-26; 12:32,38; cf. Num. 11:21-22).

Dr. Lester L. Grabbe of the University of Hull Grabbe wrote a detailed essay about this for Biblical Interpretation, 8½ (Koninklijke Brill NV, Leiden, 2000), where he tells us that Reimarus asked some tough questions about the text. He asked "about the amount of time required for such a large group to exit the country. Taking the figures of three million people, 900,000 animals [300,000 beef cattle and 600,000 sheep and goats, based on Exodus 9:1-7; 10:24-26; 12:32,38; cf. Num. 11:21-22)] and 10,000 wagons (Num. 7:3, 6-8), he calculated how long the traveling column would be. Naturally, that would depend on how wide the column was. He estimated fifty people marching abreast (which he thought was too many), with the space of three steps taken up by each row of people." "It would surely have taken at least a week to cross the 'Red Sea!'"

The crucial issue is "the refusal of cooperation by the Edomites and the Transjordanian tribes, and the resistance by the Canaanites," which "are practically inexplicable. They make little sense, for two reasons: first, the size of the Israelite forces, and, second, the reputation that must have accompanied this group which had lived in the wilderness for 40 years. Suppose you are king of a small nation, such as Edom or Midian, which can be defeated by an army of 12,000 (d. Num. 31:6-8). So when a nation with a potential army of 600,000 men in their prime, who have been living on miraculous provisions falling from heaven, asks to move peacefully through your land, you say no?"

Furthermore, when the Bible speaks of the conquest of Canaan, archaeology presents a different picture. William Dever, in The Anchor Bible Dictionary concludes: "Clearly, from our discussion the conquest model is ruled out. The founders of the Iron I villagers do not appear to have been newcomers to Palestine, much less settlers displacing Canaanites in the urban centers by military force. The few sites actually destroyed ca. 1200 B.C. were destroyed either by the Philistines, or by unknown agents; and none is resettled within a reasonable time by people who could be implicated in the destruction, or could otherwise be identified as "Israelites."

"The peasants' revolt (or "internal conquest") model seems more compatible with current archaeological data and theory than any other. This model presumes that the early Israelite movement was made up of various dissident elements of late bronze age Canaanite society, mostly dispossessed peasant farmers, who colonized new areas in the hinterland and there adopted a less stratified social order better suited to an agrarian economy. [From "Archaeology and the Israelite Conquest," Anchor Bible Dictionary].

13 Historical Evidence and Christianity.

Here I will examine whether or not the historical evidence for Christianity is enough to lead someone in today's world to believe. I will claim that it isn't. **If God revealed himself in history, then he chose a very poor medium to do so.** I start with German critic Gotthold Lessing's (1729-1781) argument with regard to historical knowledge, personal experience, and the necessary truths (or conclusions) of reason when it comes to the Christian faith.

"Miracles, which I see with my own eyes, and which I have opportunity to verify for myself, are one thing; miracles, of which I know only from history that others say they have seen them and verified them, are another." "But...I live in the 18th century, in which miracles no longer happen. The problem is that reports of miracles are not miracles....[they] have to work through a medium which takes away all their force." "Or is it invariably the case, that what I read in reputable historians is just as certain for me as what I myself experience?"

Lessing, just like G.W. Leibniz before him, distinguished between the contingent truths of history and the necessary truths of reason and wrote: Since "no historical truth can be demonstrated, then nothing can be demonstrated by means of historical truths." That is, "the accidental truths of history can never become the proof of necessary truths of reason."

He continued: "We all believe that an Alexander lived who in a short time conquered almost all Asia. But who, on the basis of this belief, would risk anything of great permanent worth, the loss of which would be irreparable? Who, in consequence of this belief, would forswear forever all knowledge that conflicted with this belief? Certainly not I. But it might still be possible that the story was founded on a mere poem of Choerilus just as the ten year siege of Troy depends on no better authority than Homer's poetry."

Someone might object that miracles like the resurrection of Jesus from the dead, are "more than historically certain," because these things are told to us by "inspired historians who cannot make a mistake." But Lessing counters that whether or not we have inspired historians is itself a historical claim, and only as certain as history allows. This, then, "is *the ugly broad ditch* which I cannot get across, however often and however earnestly I have tried to make the leap." "Since the truth of these miracles has completely ceased to be demonstrable by miracles still happening now, since they are no more than reports of miracles, I deny that they should bind me in the least to a faith in the other teachings of Christ." ("On the Proof of the Spirit and of Power," [Lessing's Theological Writings, (Stanford University Press, 1956, pp. 51-55)].

Christianity is a historical religion, unlike most eastern religions. It asks the faithful to believe certain historical events took place, like the prophesied virgin birth of Jesus, his reputed miracles, his teachings as told to us by "inspired historians," his death on the cross, his resurrection from the dead, and his ascension into heaven. From these historical claims we are further asked to believe he was God incarnate, that he died on the cross "for our sins," that he will physically return to earth, and that he will reward the faithful and punish the unfaithful eternally. With this belief we are asked to surrender everything we have in service to the demands of such a faith, and to "forswear forever all knowledge that conflicted with this belief."

Gotthold Lessing asks us to consider whether Christianity should be believed based upon history alone, over against his own personal experiences. That is, can this history be demonstrated in the same way that his own experiences can be demonstrated? And his answer is an emphatic "No!" Why? Because just like it might be false that Alexander conquered almost all of Asia, then it might also be false that the aforementioned historical events in the life of Jesus didn't happen either. And if these supposed events in the life of Jesus cannot be historically demonstrated, then even more so it cannot be demonstrated he is God incarnate who died for our sins and will reward or punish us in the hereafter, either. This then, he says, is the "ugly broad ditch which I cannot get across, however often and however earnestly I have tried to make the leap."

Lessing did, however, claim to believe in the faith of Jesus based upon other grounds. He believed, he said, because of the teachings of Jesus themselves. But of course, today there are many historical questions about what Jesus actually taught. So Lessing's faith is actually undercut by his own skepticism over historical knowledge. Since history teaches us about what Jesus taught, then Lessing too had no basis to believe--but he probably saw that. [See Henry Chadwick's "Introductory Essay" to Lessing's Theological Writings]. According to Henry Chadwick: "In one sense, it could be said that Lessing spent his life hoping that Christianity was true and arguing that it was not." [The Encyclopedia of Philosophy, (Macmillan, 1967) "G.E. Lessing"].

Lessing's argument influenced existentialist Sören Kierkegaard, who regarded historical knowledge as completely insufficient grounds for the Christian faith. In C. Stephen Evan's words, Kierkegaard believed that "there is an incommensurability between the evidence supplied by historical research and the decision to become a Christian. The historical evidence attains at most a certain level of probability. The decision which I must make on the other hand carries with it an infinite risk—eternal happiness or eternal damnation may be the result. No amount of probability could be sufficient to base such a decision upon." [Subjectivity and Religious Belief (Eerdmans, 1978), p. 83.]

The Problems of Historical Research.

Any historian will tell you the problems he faces when researching into the past. The historian attempts to write an accurate report of what happened in the past given the hindsight implications of that past for his day and age. That's the goal. Writing this historical record cannot be divorced from the hindsight implications for his era, for some events in the past may not have been viewed by the people of the past as importantly as they are viewed in his own day. Conversely, the people of the past may have viewed other events more importantly than they are considered at the time of the historian. That's why historians have to continue re-examining the past to see how it needs to be re-written. History is written from the perspective of the historian, and it's unavoidable to do otherwise. The question here is whether or not the perspective of the people in the past is preferable to the perspective of the present day historian. This is where the historian's values unavoidably enter into the picture.

Consider the claim that Columbus "discovered" America. Certainly that was big news to the European people of the past, and likewise to present people today, for it did change the world to a very large degree, but depending on your perspective the change may not have been good. Columbus called the inhabitants of the Americas, "Indians," because he thought he had reached the coasts of India. This on hindsight we know to be false. But it took a hindsight perspective to see this, so history has a way of correcting how we view the past. Another claim is that he "discovered" the Americas. Did he? Well it depends upon your perspective, doesn't it? If Native Americans were writing that history they would say he didn't discover America. They did! Europeans wrote about that great "discovery" and what it gained for them by bridging the two worlds, but Native Americans would have described how it destroyed their civilization with diseases, land grabbing, massive Buffalo slaughter, and the subsequent westward expansion of these foreigners.

In a book called Patterns of History: A Christian View (IVP, 1979), D.W. Bebbington (Ph.D., Cambridge) describes the problem of the historian: "The historian's history is molded by his values, his outlook, his world-view. It is never the evidence alone that dictates what is written. The attitudes that a historian brings to the evidence form an equally important element in the creation of history. The bias of a historian enters his history. The historian himself is part of the historical process, powerfully influenced by his time and place. The problem of the historian himself nevertheless dictates that two historians presented with the same evidence are likely to reach different conclusions. This is true of people living in the same period; it is more true of people living in different periods. That is why each age writes history that reflects its own concerns." (Pp. 5-8)

According to E. Schillebeeckx, "Historical objectivity is not a reconstruction of the past in its unrepeatable factuality, it is the truth of the past in the light of the present." [God, the Future of Man, p. 24]. Albert Nolan has argued this point with regard to Jesus: "To imagine that one can have historical objectivity without a perspective is an illusion. One perspective, however, can be better than another, [but] the only perspective open to us is the one given to us by the historical situation in which we find ourselves. If we cannot achieve an unobstructed view of Jesus from the vantage point of our present circumstances, then we cannot achieve an unobstructed view of him at all." [Jesus Before Christianity (Orbis Books, 1978), p. 4].

Of course, this historical problem is compounded further when we understand that the evidence the historian considers is the stuff of the past, and the past is not immediately available for investigation. Time separates the historian from his subject matter. The historian "cannot conduct opinion polls on the dead." And there is a "paucity of evidence" for a great part of the past. According to Bebbington, "Our knowledge of the earlier middle ages depends on a tiny number of written sources that can be eked out by such supplementary material as place-names and coinage."(p. 3). Furthermore, the evidence is not always reliable. According to Bebbington, "forgeries and misrepresentations, whether from good or bad motives, litter the world's archives. The historian, therefore, develops a skeptical turn of mind. Original documents may themselves mislead; and what books about the past claim is much more likely to be wrong. History demands a critical frame of mind."(p. 4) Because of these problems Bebbington states the obvious: "Written history cannot correspond precisely with the actual past." (p. 8) "To write a value-free account of the past is beyond the historian's power. (p. 12).

One school of thought headed up by Leopold Von Ranke actually sought to do this. Their goal was to write history "free from prejudices," and in so doing write the events of the past "as they actually happened." But most all modern historians think this is impossible to do. In A History of Historical Writing (Dover, 1962, pp. 266-271), Harry Elmer Barnes argues against this possibility. In the first place, modern psychology has completely undermined total historical objectivity by showing that "no truly excellent piece of intellectual work can be executed without real interest and firm convictions." In other words, total objectivity in a subject is impossible. Secondly, Barnes reminds us that each historical event is essentially unique never to be repeated in its entirety. Hence, "no one can ever entirely recreate this historical entity...it is manifestly impossible to create the past 'as it actually happened.'"

Some thinkers like Carl Becker have gone so far as to deny that we can know the past with any objectivity at all—that historical facts only exist in the mind, and they advocate a historical relativism with regard to the events of the past. ["What are Historical Facts?" in The Philosophy of History in Our Time, ed. H. Meyerhoff (Doubleday, 1959), pp. 120-39].

At least three Christian apologetics books address this issue: In Defense of Miracles: A Comprehensive Case for God's Action in History (Douglas Geivett and Gary Habermas, eds., InterVarsity Press, 1997) "History and Miracles" by Francis J. Beckwith; William Lane Craig's Reasonable Faith: Christianity and Apologetics (Crossway, 1994), formerly, Apologetics: An Introduction (Moody Press, 1984), pp. 126-150; and Norman Geisler's Christian Apologetics pp, 285-304 (Baker, 1976). [Geisler's discussion follows a summary of William Lane Craig's master's thesis]. And yet the meager conclusion from reading Craig and Geisler's comments is that objective knowledge of history is possible. According to Craig, "first, a common core of indisputable historical events exists; second, it is possible to distinguish between history and propaganda; and third, it is possible to criticize poor history." (p. 145-146). Craig concludes: "neither the supposed problem of lack of direct access to the past nor the supposed problem of the lack of neutrality can prevent us from learning something from history." (p. 149). The goal is to "obtain probability, not mathematical certainty."

But such a conclusion is indeed a meager one; that knowledge of the past is possible. Even if true, and I think it is, there is a lot of doubt for any supposed historical event, especially momentous ones.

Consider the following historical questions: How were the Egyptian pyramids made? Who made them? Why? Was Shakespeare a fictitious name for Francis Bacon? Exactly how was the Gettysburg battle fought and won? What was the true motivation for Lincoln to emancipate the slaves? What happened at Custer's last stand? Who killed President John F. Kennedy? Why? Who knew what and when during the Watergate scandal that eventually led to President Nixon resigning? Why did America lose the "war" in Vietnam? Did George W. Bush legitimately win the 2000 election? Did President Bush knowingly lead us into a war with Iraq on false pretenses? What about some high profile criminal cases? Is O.J. Simpson a murderer? Who killed Jon Bene Ramsey? Is Michael Jackson a pedophile?

There are also many problems inside the Bible itself that Biblical scholars who believe are trying to figure out. How many times did Paul visit Jerusalem? What was Jesus crucified on? A stake or a cross? What day was Jesus crucified on? What is the date of any specific book in the Bible? Who wrote the first five books in the Bible? Who wrote the book of Hebrews? How many times did Jesus "cleanse the temple"? And so on....

The Historian and Miracles.

Is it any wonder then, why Lessing and Kierkegaard both questioned the reliability of historical knowledge to lead one to believe in Christianity with its miraculous claims? History itself is fraught with many difficult problems when one comes to understand the events of the past. According to Bebbington again, "Any historical account is, in strict logic, open to doubt. It is not just remarkable events long ago like Biblical miracles that are not logically certain. (p. 8). But if non-supernatural events in the past are open to doubt, then how much more so is it the case with supernatural claims of events in the past, like Biblical miracles! Just as historical scholars disagree with each other on any number of non-supernatural historical events, they disagree even more so over supposedly supernatural "historical" events.

One of the claims made by William Lane Craig, when arguing that knowledge of the past is possible, is that both the historian and the scientist seek systematic consistency by using the "hypothetical-deductive model": "we should accept the hypothesis that provides the most plausible explanation of the evidence."(p. 147). Since he brings up science as an analogy to historical understanding, let's revisit exactly how science has brought in the modern world.

Science wasn't content to accept the notion that epilepsy was demon possession, or that sicknesses were sent by God to punish people. Nor was science content with the idea that God alone opens the womb of a woman, nor that God was the one who sent the rain. If someone got sick, it was because of sin in his or her life. If it rained, God was pleased with them, if there was a drought God was displeased, and so on, and so on. Now we have scientific explanations for these things, and we all benefit from those who assumed there was a natural cause to everything we experience. Now we have some control over the natural processes of life, because we seek to understand the forces of nature. We can predict the rain; we know how babies are created; and how to prevent a host of illnesses.

Modern scientists operate based upon "methodological naturalism," which assumes that for everything we experience there is a natural cause. We who live in the modern world operate on this assumption ourselves everyday. This assumption is the foundation of modernity. It is what defines us as modern people. In previous centuries we either praised God for the good things that happened to us, or we wondered why he was angry when bad things happened in our lives. But by scientifically investigating into the forces of nature we can better run our own lives, and we know how to make life easier for ourselves, with fewer diseases.

In scientific fields methodological naturalism is a way to gain the truth about nature, and it has astounding results. Some scientists go so far as to claim that since it works, then nature must be ultimate, but that doesn't follow, for the later conclusion is beyond the scope of science; it is a metaphysical claim. [For discussions about this see "Methodological Naturalism?" by Alvin Plantinga, which can be found at: www.arn.org, "Justifying Methodological Naturalism" by Michael Martin, and "Methodological Naturalism and the Supernatural," by Mark I Vuletic, to be found at www.infidels.org/library]. Still, if such an assumption has had so many successes in science, then why not apply that method to history as well? And modern historians have done just that. When looking into the past they assume a natural explanation for every historical event. They are taught to be critical of the past, as we've just mentioned. As historians they must. That is the standard for what they do as historians, to be skeptical of the past record, especially claims of the miraculous.

According to I. Howard Marshall in I Believe in the Historical Jesus (Eerdmans, 1977) "many historians—the great majority in fact—would say that miracles fall outside their orbit as historians. For to accept the miraculous as a possibility in history is to admit an irrational element which cannot be included under the ordinary laws of history. The result is that the historian believes himself justified in writing a 'history' of Jesus in which the miraculous and supernatural do not appear in historical statements. The 'historical' Jesus is an ordinary man. To some historians he is that and no more. To others, however, the possibility is open that he was more than an ordinary man—but this possibility lies beyond the reach of historical study as such." (p. 59). (Marshall defends Christianity, but he has an excellent summary of the problems of the modern historian for his faith, from which I use in what follows).

Three lines of evidence incline "the great majority" of historians to take this stance. **One) Our knowledge of Jesus comes almost exclusively from those who believed Jesus was the one and only savior of the world, and they were convinced he was God's Messiah.** They sought to convert others to this same belief. They were committed men. But the historian asks how reliable their record can be when they wrote the books of the New Testament? They were simply not impartial with regard to what they wrote. And if these authors were dependent upon other committed believers for their information, doesn't this call into question their reliability? It does in every other area of historical research. Marshall again, "How can we be sure that the whole story has not been colored by the pious imagination of the earliest Christians who saw the story of Jesus in the light of the religious position which they ascribed to him after his death? If the Evangelists had been scientific historians, disinterested recorders of what happened, then there is some chance that they might have avoided displaying such bias. But this is not what they were. They were writers of Gospels, works intended to convert the outsider and strengthen the believer. They were not writing history but religious propaganda." (p. 54) Did they check their sources? Did they cross-examine their witnesses? Or did they have a predisposition to believe what was told to them?

Two) It can be pointed out that many similar stories of the miraculous were told by all kinds of respected people in ancient times. According to R. Bultmann, an impressive list of miraculous stories can be found from the same age and environment of Jesus and first century Christians. [See <u>The History of the Synoptic Tradition</u> (London, 1968, pp. 218-244)]. The Jews had similar stories about some of their rabbis that claimed they had the power to heal. It was also claimed that the Roman Emperor Vespasian had the ability to heal. Richard Carrier has also documented these stories in "Kooks and Quacks of the Roman Empire: A Look Into the World of the Gospels" which can be found at www.infidels.org/library. Here is what he concluded: "From all of this one thing should be apparent: the age of Jesus was not an age of critical reflection and remarkable religious acumen. It was an era filled with con artists, gullible believers, martyrs without a cause, and reputed miracles of every variety. In light of this picture, the tales of the Gospels do not seem very remarkable. Even if they were false in every detail, there is no evidence that they would have been disbelieved or rejected as absurd by many people, who at the time had little in the way of education or critical thinking skills. They had no newspapers, telephones, photographs, or public documents to consult to check a story. If they were not a witness, all they had was a man's word. And even if they were a witness, the tales above tell us that even then their skills of critical reflection were lacking. Certainly, this age did not lack keen and educated skeptics--it is not that there were no skilled and skeptical observers. There were. Rather, the shouts of the credulous rabble overpowered their voice and seized the world from them..."

So the modern historian can ask two questions about these similar kinds of stories. 1) To today's Christians who believe in miracles, he will ask whether the other miraculous stories about other great men in the first century occurred? Why should we believe one set of miraculous stories and not another set? The evidence for both kinds of stories seems to be the same, so why do Christians just accept one set of stories and reject the other set? 2) If miraculous stories were being told about other great men during their day, then wouldn't early Christians be tempted to tell similar kinds of stories—and even greater stories— about Jesus, to prove he was greater than the others? In an environment where a great man is known by his great and even miraculous deeds, then early Christians would be faced with the choice of telling even bigger deeds for their Jesus, or not gaining the attention of those who believed Jesus wasn't that great of a man.

Three) The modern historian lives in the modern world, a world where miracles and supernatural events simply don't take place. At least, that is his experience, as well as my own experience. I have never personally seen a miracle even in my days as a former Christian and minister in the Christian faith. But if this is true for us, then it must be true among ancient people as well. As historians it's extremely difficult, if not impossible, to step outside what one has learned and experienced in his own day and time, and not see the past from that same perspective. There should be no reason to suppose that ancient historical people experienced anything different than what we experience today. They were perhaps just superstitious, that's all, and they lived in a world where there was nothing known about nature's fixed laws—just their belief in a God who expresses his will in all events. So when confronted with a miraculous story the modern historian assumes a natural explanation, or that the story became exaggerated in the telling, or the cure was a psychological one, or it may simply be a legend to enhance the reputation of the miracle worker.

The Christian Framework for Viewing History.

Ronald A. Wells, who teaches at Calvin College, wrote a book called <u>History Through The Eyes of Faith</u>. Wells provides the meaning of history through the eyes of Christian faith starting with Jesus and Christianity down through to the 20th century. It's history as interpreted by means of the Christian framework. In the first chapter he admits that, "the facts of history simply do not speak for themselves; historians speak for them from an interpretive framework of the ideas they already hold." (p. 8). He merely suggests that over-against the secular view of history as a two dimensional world (space & time) Christians "insist that there is a third dimension—spirit—and that a whole view of the world must be three dimensional." (p. 11). This, he claims, is the proper way to view history.

But this isn't the only framework for viewing history. David Bebbington, in <u>Patterns In History</u>, speaks of five different philosophies of history, Christianity being just one of them. The other four are briefly as follows: 1) the ancient and oriental cyclical view of history in which history is a pattern of cycles; 2) the idea of progress, in which there was confidence that the future will be better than the past with human beings as the sole actors, not God; 3) historicism, which regards each nation as having a distinctive culture, and that history is the story of the growth of each culture from within each culture; and 4) Marxism, in which the historical process is created by man as he labors to satisfy his basic needs, with ideas about God hindering that process. There are also Feminist views too!

However, in order to read history in light of Christianity, one must have sufficient reasons for this Christian framework; otherwise doing so is circular. The Christian looks at history using the Christian framework (or world-view) to do so. The question is whether or not that framework is the proper way to view all of history, especially Bible "history." Think about the circular nature of this for a while. Using the Christian framework the Christian views all of history, especially Biblical "history," from that perspective. So when the Christian examines Biblical "history," he or she will more than likely believe its miraculous claims, because that's what the Christian framework dictates in the first place. And yet, Christians claim that this same Biblical "history" provides them with the framework to view that "history" as believable in the first place. What? How is it possible to gain the Christian framework for viewing Biblical "history" from that same "history," unless there are reasons for viewing it as such? Conversely, how is it possible to view Biblical "history" as real history unless one already approaches it with the Christian framework for viewing it as real history?

It's this conundrum that forces me to ask God for more evidence to believe today, like Lessing. I need evidence to believe for today. Yesterday's evidence no longer can hold water for me, for in order to see it as evidence I must already believe in the framework that allows me to see it as evidence. In other words, in order to see yesterday's evidence as evidence for me, I must already believe the Christian framework that allows me to see yesterday's evidence as evidence.

I. Howard Marshall's answer to this vexing problem is to argue that our particular framework (worldview, or set of presuppositions) and the historical evidence "stand in a dialectical relationship to one another." "We interpret evidence in light of our presuppositions, and we also form our presuppositions in the light of the evidence. It is only through a 'dialogue' between presuppositions and evidence that we gain both sound presuppositions and a correct interpretation of the evidence. The process is circular and unending. It demands openness on the part of the investigator. He must be prepared to revise his ideas in the light of the evidence, for ultimately it is the evidence which is decisive." Now I don't deny that he's right about this. This is the best that a human being can do. **But even Marshall admits that while the Christian should be prepared to let his worldview be altered by the evidence, "his world view is part of the evidence, and cannot be simply laid aside."** And while he argues that a modern day personal experience of "the risen Lord" is a "relevant factor" in assessing the historical facts regarding the resurrection of Jesus, "if a person fails to have a personal experience of the risen Lord, this may prove to him that the biblical evidence does not support belief in the resurrection of Jesus." [I Believe in the Historical Jesus (Eerdmans, 1977), pp. 98-101.)]

Historical Knowledge and Our Eternal Destiny.

Let me ask one final question. It's this: **How can our eternal destiny be at stake if it is based upon historical knowledge?** Let's say, for instance, that in order to gain an eternal reward in heaven you must know what the primary cause was for the Protestant Reformation in the 16th century, or whether or not II Peter was actually written by the apostle Peter, or why America lost the "war" in Vietnam, or whether or not Michael Jackson is a pedophile. These are all historical questions. I suppose, if our eternal destinies were at stake then we'd certainly study such things out, as much as possible, because our lives would be at stake. However, even if this were the eternal threat, there would still be people who disagreed with each other on these issues. The main reason isn't because we wouldn't want to know the truth for fear of a lifestyle change, because we would be desperate to know the truth. It would be because we have different ways of looking at the facts. We have different presuppositions about what is even considered a fact. That's the nature of human understanding, and that is the nature of historical investigation.

But if we ended up being wrong, God would be heard to say, "I'm sorry, you got it wrong. Off you go into eternal damnation." That wouldn't be fair would it? That is, unless there was an overwhelming case on behalf of any of these issues, and even that wouldn't be fair, because an overwhelming case is still not a case that is certain, is it? A sufficient, but not certain case, is insufficient, when our eternal destiny is at stake, wouldn't you think? But that's exactly the situation we face when it comes to believing the truth about Christian history, isn't it? People who get it wrong will be punished forever, according to the Christian faith. Now I know that Christians will respond that getting Biblical history wrong isn't what condemns people to hell—their sins send them to hell. But the way to be saved from eternal condemnation, according to them, is to get biblical history right—that is, they must believe certain Biblical historical claims.

When it comes to history, especially the miraculous "history" represented in the Bible, there can never be a sufficient case for accepting it—much less a certain one—because it depends on the particular framework we use to view history in the first place. This is, in my opinion, circular reasoning. There is simply no way to tell for sure that a historical religion like Christianity is true based upon history, and there is likewise no way that God can judge us for all of eternity if we get it wrong. Lessing is surely right. What we need is some incontrovertible evidence for Christianity for us living in today's world.

Three Objections To This Conclusion. Let me mention and briefly argue with three anticipated objections to what I've written.

ONE—**The origin and the historical continuity of the church from the earliest days up until now, even if somewhat fragmented, provides sufficient evidence for the claims made about Jesus. That is, the history of the church provides sufficient evidence to believe in the New Testament documents of the church.**

But how can the history of the church provide sufficient evidence for the history about Jesus? History provides evidence for history? Lessing would say, whether or not we have an accurate history of the earliest days of the church is itself a historical claim, and only as certain as history allows. How one sees the origin of the church is a historical question fraught with all of the same problems mentioned earlier in this essay. Quite simply there are various accounts of the origins of the church. [For two accounts of the earliest days of the church see John Dominic Crossan's The Birth of Christianity: Discovering What Happened In The Years Immediately After The Execution Of Jesus (Harper, 1998); and L. Michael White, From Jesus to Christianity (Harper, 2004)].

It's just false to say that history provides justification for viewing history. Islam, another historical religion, has a long history to it too. Does that history justify their faith? Well, it depends upon whether you approach Muslim history from a Muslim framework, doesn't it? The Mormons have a history to their faith too, howbeit not as lengthy as Islam or Christianity. Does that history justify their faith? Again, it depends on whether you approach the Mormon history from a Mormon framework.

TWO—**Jesus said that some people wouldn't believe even if God raised a man from the dead. Even after Jesus was raised from the dead they still didn't believe. Likewise, some people today would not believe even if God provided a glowing cross in the sky for all to see.**

The word "some" here needs to be unpacked when it is said, "some people today still would not believe." How many does the word "some" mean? Who knows? But let's think about the numbers of others who would believe. That's the whole point. Millions of people would believe if there was a glowing cross in the sky, and yet all that some Christians can do is to object that there will still be "some" who don't believe? Every Christian cares more for the lost than God purportedly does, for they would do whatever they could to see that the lost were saved. And if a Christian had died for the sins of the world (the greater deed), he would certainly do other things to help people accept that salvation by providing more evidence to believe (the lesser deeds).

Let's say I die and I go to hell. Then God grants me my wish to come back and tell my friends and relatives to avoid hell. They were at my funeral, and they got stuck with all of my funeral bills. I would be able to convince everyone who was at my funeral and anyone who saw me die, for starters. And so this is the whole reason God doesn't raise anyone else up from the grave to warn others today? He doesn't do this because he proclaims it wouldn't do any good? That's a lame excuse if I ever heard one.

I think it's demonstrably false to say that most people wouldn't believe if the evidence were overwhelming, because God carries a big stick—he'd send you to hell if you don't believe. With that big stick God carries around, coupled with the overwhelming evidence of a glowing cross in the sky, people would turn to Christianity by the millions. How could one say otherwise? People all over the world are looking for answers, in every continent across the globe. Most of them agonize over the truth. It's frustrating not to know who they are, why they are here, and where they are going. They would be greatly relieved to find the answer. And the answer Christianity gives, that God loves them and sent his Son to die for them is the most wonderful story of them all! There is no other story to compare with that one--none. It is such a fulfilling and satisfying answer to the perplexity of life that with overwhelming evidence, and the threat of hell, there would only be a small minority of people who refused to believe.

THREE—The reason people don't believe the historical evidence is because most people reject the gospel for the same reasons people rejected Jesus during his ministry: pride and pleasure. People want answers that won't cost them anything -- as in repentance.

Really? People all over the world in various non-Christian religions are taking Draconian measures to live up to their faith. In some of them it costs them everything, as in a Tibetan Monk. And what about militant Muslims who are willing to become suicide bombers to kill American infidels? And they don't believe in Christ because it'll cost them something? Just study these other religions. It costs them as much or more to believe what they do than Christianity does, as evidenced by even the most committed Christian. People will commit everything they have for something they can really believe in, Americans included, although I think Americans are just soft on commitment with regard to any faith they believe in. People want something big enough to commit themselves to. It's just that few people find something they can believe in that will cause them to be totally committed. And how do Christians first convert? They are relieved to find the answers that Christianity offers. It was grand to believe in a God who loves and forgives me. Surely that's enough motivation to change lifestyles. Repentance isn't too hard to try when you come to believe in the Christian message. Repentance is something we would willingly, joyfully do, if the message were believed. It's not the change of lifestyle that is feared, for that comes naturally. It's whether or not the message is true. If it's true it's worth the lifestyle change. But why change if it's not true? Why bother at all?

[For some further references on the historian's craft, see: Gilbert J. Garraghan, A Guide to Historical Method, Fordham University Press: New York (1946). Louis Gottschalk, Understanding History: A Primer of Historical Method, Alfred A. Knopf: New York (1950). Martha Howell and Walter Prevenier, From Reliable Sources: An Introduction to Historical Methods, Cornell University Press: Ithaca (2001). C. Behan McCullagh, Justifying Historical Descriptions, Cambridge University Press: New York (1984). R. J. Shafer, A Guide to Historical Method, The Dorsey Press: Illinois (1974)].

14 Do Miracles Take Place?

"The Biblical view of miracles is something different from our conception of miracle as a disruption of natural law. As a matter of fact, the Biblical writers had no conception of 'nature' as a realm for which God has ordained laws. Rather, God himself sustains his creation, and his will is expressed in natural events, whether it be the coming of the spring rains or the birth of a child....God is constantly active. His will is discernible in every event." [**Bernard W. Anderson** in Understanding the Old Testament (Prentice-Hall, 1957), (p. 43)].

Scientific problems with Miracles in the Bible:

1) Some miracles are based on an outmoded cosmological viewpoint in which: a) heaven is above the firmament which holds back water and in which the stars are said to reside; b) the flat earth is supported by fountains of water beneath it; and, c) hell is the abode of the dead which is in the belly of the earth. Here we have problems with descriptions of the flood, the placement of created stars, the sun stopping in its place for Joshua, and also backing up for Hezekiah. There are also problems with a star which led Magi to the city of Bethlehem, the ascension of Jesus into heaven, and the promised return of Jesus from heaven.

2) Some are additionally problematic to the natural sciences: having an ax-head float; walking on water; creating bread and fish to feed over five thousand people, changing water into wine; immediately calming the wind and the waves, cursing a fig tree which withers on the spot.

3) Some are problematic to the biological sciences: the blind, deaf, and lame being instantaneously healed on the spot; a virgin birth; and the dead being raised back to life.

4) Others seem just strange to modern people today: exorcisms of demonic beings which caused sicknesses; people speaking unlearned foreign languages; both Balaam's donkey and a serpent spoke; Daniel was thrown into a hungry lion's den, yet not eaten; Daniel's friends are thrown into a fire pit, yet not harmed; or being healed by shadows, handkerchiefs or the stirred waters of the *Pool of Siloam*.

"The problem of myth in the NT is that the NT presents events critical to Christian faith in language and concepts which are often outmoded and meaningless to 20th century man. **1)** Many of the NT metaphors and analogies are archaic and distasteful to modern sensibilities (e.g. blood sacrifice); **2)** In the first century world the activity of divine beings is often evoked as the explanation for what we now recognize as natural and mental processes (e.g. epilepsy as demon possession); **3)** Out of date conceptualizations determine certain traditionally important expressions of NT faith about Christ--in particular, the problem that 'ascension' and parousia [Christ's return] 'in clouds' 'from heaven' were not merely meant as metaphors or analogies but were intended as literal descriptions which derive from and depend on a first century cosmology which is impossible to us." (p. 300). [James D.G. Dunn in

"Demythologizing--The Problem of Myth in the New Testament" in New Testament Interpretation ed. I. Howard Marshall (Eerdmans, 1977)].

--E.P. Sanders in The Historical Figure of Jesus (Penguin Books, 1993) offers five rational explanations for Jesus' reputed miracles: 1) "More or less all the healings are explicable as psychosomatic cures or victories of mind over matter:" 2) "It may be thought that some miracles were only coincidences;" 3) "It has been suggested that some miracles were only apparent;" 4) "Group psychology has often been used to explain the feeding miracles;" 5) Some miracle stories may be historicizing legends." (p. 158).

Deism (Latin "deus", god) began with Herbert Cherbury in England during the 17th century and went through several different stages in several different countries. It is basically seen as a natural religion where knowledge is acquired solely by the use of reason, as opposed to the Bible or the church. Its adherents held only beliefs that could be supported by reason. The final stage is largely of French origin where God is seen merely as the creator of the universe. God created it and set it in motion, but he does nothing to intervene in its affairs. The analogy for Deists was the technological marvel of their time—the pocket watch. What would we think, Deists would ask, if the watchmaker had to constantly intervene to fix or repair the watch? Their conclusion was that an inferior watchmaker would have made the watch. Likewise, when it comes to God creating the universe, for him to intervene with miracles means he didn't do a good job of creating it in the first place. It would be an admission that God's original creation was flawed. After Darwin's publication of his 1859 Origin of the Species book that accounted for the ascent of human beings on earth through natural selection, Deism quickly moved in the direction of atheism.

David Hume's Argument against miracles: "even if...but in fact." He argues first that miracles could never be identified in principle, *even if* they took place, *but in fact* there can't be enough evidence to believe they took place. Hume never said miracles couldn't occur, he only argued that it is not rational to believe that a miracle took place unless it would be more "miraculous" that it didn't. The wise man proportions his belief based upon what is most likely to be the case.

Hume Defines Miracles as Violations of Natural Laws. We couldn't argue that a miracle is just a surprising event that was timed right, or a psychosomatic healing, because then what right do we have to assert that it is a miracle at all? We couldn't argue that a miracle is an event that occurs outside the knowledge and control of natural law as available to the miracle worker *at that time*. Then the problem resurfaces, maybe people believed for less than adequate reasons? Hume's definition of miracles as "violations of natural laws" might seem too strident of a definition, however. What does it mean to violate natural law? While miracles must have a cause that lies outside natural law itself, they wouldn't violate the principle of cause and effect—miracles would just have a supernatural cause. Still, Dr. Eric Mascall insisted that a miracle signifies "a striking interposition of divine power by which the operations of the ordinary course of nature are overruled, suspended, or modified. "Miracles" in Chamber's Encyclopedia. We can define it no better than that, although I know of many good attempts to define them. William Lane Craig merely asks whether an event can occur "that has neither physical nor human causes." [Apologetics: An Introduction, (p. 114); see Richard Swinburne, The Concept of Miracle (Macmillian, 1970, and his Miracles (Macmillian, 1989), along with Basinger & Basinger, Philosophy and Miracle: The Contemporary Debate (1986)].

Hume argues that the probability of a miracle happening (that is, violation of natural law) will always be lower than the probability that a miracle has not occurred (that is, that natural law was not violated). Why? Because "there must be a uniform experience against every miraculous event, otherwise the event would not merit that appellation." Hence, the wise person should not believe a miracle occurred unless it is more "miraculous" not to believe it occurred, than to believe that it did. And in the modern world we have a strong presumption in favor of natural law, based on science as opposed to the miraculous, as Anthony Flew explains: "a strong notion of the truly miraculous can only be generated if there is first an equally strong conception of a natural order. Where there is as yet no strong conception of a natural order, there is little room for the idea of a genuinely miraculous event as distinct from the phenomenon of a prodigy, of a wonder, or of a divine sign. But once such a conception of a natural order has taken firm root, there is a great reluctance to allow that miracles have in fact occurred, or even to admit as legitimate a concept of the miraculous." "Exceptions are logically dependent upon rules. Only in so far as it can be shown that there is an order does it begin to be possible to show that the order is occasionally overridden. The difficulty (perhaps an insoluble one) is to maintain simultaneously both the strong rules and the genuine exceptions to them." "Miracles" in the Encyclopedia of Philosophy. Critical Biblical scholar David F. Strauss agreed with this and wrote: "We may summarily reject all miracles, prophecies, narratives of angels and demons, and the like, as simply impossible and irreconcilable with the known and universal laws which govern the course of events." [In his Life of Jesus].

Hume Offers Four "but in fact" Arguments. **1)** Miraculous claims are mainly made by uneducated superstitious people who lack common sense, integrity, or a good reputation. **2)** There are many instances of forged miracles, which prove the strong propensity of mankind to believe a wondrous and extraordinary story, and then exaggerate it when they retell it. **3)** Miracle claims originate among tribes who are uncivilized, ignorant and barbarous. Hume asks, why is it that "such prodigious events never happen in our days?" **4)** Competing religions support their beliefs by claims of miracles; thus these claims and their religious systems cancel each other out. That is, any miracles that count for one religion cancel out the miracles of the other, and vise versa.

The late Ronald Nash said the strongest of these four arguments is the 4th one. [Faith & Reason, p. 238]. Richard Swinburne criticized Hume by arguing that competing religious claims only cancel each other out if the proclaimed miracles of each religion did in fact occur, and if these purported miracles are used to establish the truth of each of these separate religions (since there is nothing prohibiting God from doing a miracle out of kindness to anyone of any faith). [The Concept of Miracle, 1970, (pp. 60-61)]. But listen to what Hume actually said: "This argument...is not in reality different from the reasoning of a judge, who supposes that the credit of two witnesses, maintaining a crime against anyone, is destroyed by the testimony of two others, who affirm him to have been two hundred leagues distant, at the same instant when the crime is said to have been committed." [An Enquiry Concerning Human Understanding, Section X]. For Hume this is an epistemological problem, and a credibility problem. Against Swinburne the question in Hume's mind is how he can even know whether or not both miracles occurred, since the credibility of both is suspect. And as far as two purported miracles being used to establish the truth of two separate religions go, how about the claim that Muhammad was miraculously inspired to write the Koran (where it states Jesus did not rise from the dead), and compare that with the Christian claim that Jesus did rise from the grave? Hence, the Muslim faith does indeed "cancel out" the credibility and epistemological significance of Christianity, and vice versa.

Hume concludes: "Therefore we may establish it as a maxim that no human testimony can have such force as to prove a miracle, and make it a just foundation for any such system of religion." Should a miracle be ascribed to a system of religion, we are obliged "to compare the instances of the violation of truth in the testimony of men, with those of the violation of the laws of nature by miracles, in order to judge which of them is most likely and probable. As the violations of truth are more common in the testimony concerning religious miracles than in that concerning any other matter of fact; this must diminish very much the former testimony, and make us form a general resolution, never to lend any attention to it, with whatever specious pretence it may be covered." [Enquiry Concerning Human Understanding, (chapter 10)].

Can You Refute Hume? I remember sitting down and talking with my former professor, William Lane Craig, at an apologetics conference. Craig is one of the leading defenders of the miracle of the resurrection of Jesus, and in his popular book, Reasonable Faith: Christianity and Apologetics (Crossway, 1994), he devoted a full chapter to the problem of miracles. While we were talking he said to me "Hume has been refuted years ago." To which I replied, "I didn't know Hume could be refuted because he merely said that the wise man proportions his belief based upon what is most likely to be the case." To which Bill admitted, on second thought, that I was right, "You're right, Hume cannot be refuted." But he argued that we could believe in miracles in spite of Hume, and I agreed. But Hume makes a great deal of sense. I have about a dozen books that take issue with Hume's argument, showing that it's still possible in spite of Hume to believe in miracles. But again, Hume never said miracles cannot occur, only that there is no reason he knows of to believe in any of them.

Stephen T. Davis wrote an essay in the journal, Faith and Philosophy, which is produced by the Society of Christian Philosophers. While Davis thinks Hume "overstates his case," he wrote: "Hume is not the sort of philosopher one can dismiss with a casual wave of the hand. Much of his argument, I believe is beyond reproach...He is surely correct that rational people will require very strong evidence indeed before they will believe that a miracle has occurred." ["Is it Possible to Know That Jesus Was Raised From the Dead," April 1984 issue].

What's Wrong With This Kind of Skepticism Anyway? Michael Shermer, a former Christian turned skeptic wrote a book titled: Why People Believe Weird Things (2002). There are a great many weird things that people believe took place in history. How do you decide what happened? Whether you know it or not, when it comes to the apparent unexplainable event, you apply Hume's standards, *especially* when it comes to the miraculous claims of religions you don't accept. Likewise, adherents of those religions, apply Hume's standards to the miracles you accept.

Michael Shremer calls skepticism a virtue: "Skepticism is a virtue and science is a valuable tool that makes skepticism virtuous. Science and skepticism are the best methods of determining how strong your convictions are, regardless of the outcome of the inquiry. If you challenge your belief tenets and end up as a nonbeliever, then apparently your faith was not all that sound to begin with and you have improved your thinking in the process. If you question your religion but in the end retain your belief, you have lost nothing and gained a deeper understanding of the God question. It is okay to be skeptical." [In How We Believe: The Search for God in an Age of Science, (W.H. Freeman, 2000, p. 23)]. The late atheist Carl Sagan listed some "tools for skeptical thinking" which he called his "baloney detection kit," [in The Demon Haunted World: Science as a Candle in the Dark (Random House, 1996, pp. 210-18)]. Here are a few of them: 1) "Whenever possible there must be independent confirmation of the facts;" 2) "Encourage substantive debate on the evidence by knowledgeable proponents of all points of view;" 3) "Spin more than one hypothesis;" 4) "Try not to get attached to a hypothesis just because it's yours;" 5) "Always ask if the proposition can at least in principle be falsified," and so on.

Two Major Objections to Hume's Argument:

The major objection with Hume's main argument against miracles is that he begs the question of whether miracles have in fact taken place. By defining a miracle as a violation of natural law, it then automatically follows that a miracle is less probable, as it must be for it to be classified as a miracle. Based upon this understanding Hume claims that a wise man should not believe in miracles because by definition they are less probable. C.S. Lewis: "If there is absolute 'uniform experience' against miracles, if in other words they have never happened, why then they never have? Unfortunately we know the experience against them to be uniform only if we know that all reports of them are false. And we know all the reports to be false only if we already know that miracles have never happened." [Miracles (p. 105)]. William Lane Craig: "To say that uniform experience is against miracles is to implicitly assume already that miracles have never occurred. The only way Hume can place uniform experience for the regularity of nature on one side of the scale is by assuming that the testimony for miracles on the other side of the scale is false. And that, quite simply, is begging the question." [Apologetics: An Introduction (p. 121)]. Or to put it another way, just because it's very improbable that a miracle has actually occurred doesn't mean that it didn't. By saying a wise man shouldn't believe in a miracle begs the question of whether or not a miracle occurred.

Hume does overstate his case somewhat when he indicates that a wise person "shouldn't believe" a miracle occurred because of our confidence in the regular order of the laws of nature. But there's nothing wrong with Hume when he argues that the preponderance of historical, physical, testimonial and circumstantial evidence should outweigh our confidence in the laws of nature. He could still admit the possibility of a miracle but yet deny that there is enough evidence to lead him to believe one has occurred. And yet, he did say that. He said that it is not rational to believe that a miracle took place unless it would be more "miraculous" that it didn't.

Hume is surely right that we should be skeptical of any claim of a miracle. As I said before: When it comes to the apparent unexplainable event, you apply Hume's standards, *especially* when it comes to the miraculous claims of religions you don't accept. Likewise, adherents of those religions apply Hume's standards to the miracles you accept. So the issue of question begging can be turned back on both C.S Lewis and Craig, who defend the truth of the Christian faith. Since they both believe in Christianity then they won't believe any miracles that attest to the major truth claims of other religions. Which one of them, for instance will take seriously the claim that God spoke "miraculously" to Muhammad so that the Koran is his word? Conversely, since they believe in Christianity, they do not approach the Biblical miracles with the same kind of scrutiny or skepticism they use to judge miracles outside of their faith. They have a very strong presumption in favor of Christian miracles, just like Hume—a Deist—has a very strong presumption that miracles shouldn't be believed. If Hume begs the question, then in practice so does Craig and C.S. Lewis when it comes to the miraculous claims of religions they reject.

Another objection has to do with the possibility that Hume commits the logical fallacy of hasty generalization. This fallacy occurs when someone makes a generalization hastily based upon a small sample of experiences or tests. John King-Farlow and William Niels Christensen ask us to imagine a container hidden from sight so we don't know how large it is. From this container we draw out nothing but red marbles, every time. Based on our limited sampling we conclude that the container has nothing but red marbles in it. But since we don't know how large the container is it may actually contain more blue marbles than red ones, because it's extremely huge. In the same way, events that seem miraculous to us might prove in the end to be more probable after all. Judging things as Hume does might prove to be too hasty of a conclusion before all experience is in. [Faith and the Life of Reason, 1972 (p. 50)]. This could be true, if there is a God. And just because we today don't experience miracles doesn't mean that throughout the history of mankind God has done a plethora of them, and will do so again when the time is right in the future too.

King-Farlow and Christensen are asking us to believe against the overwhelming present day experience of nearly all modern people that things might turn out differently than we now experience. Is this impossible? No, not at all. But we must still ask whether this is probable given our present day confirmations of natural law. The only basis for asking us to consider whether events that seem to be miraculous to us might prove in the end to be more probable after all, is the existence of God. As C. Stephen Evans writes: "The defender of miracles may claim that whether miracles occur depends largely on whether God exists, what kind of God he is, and what purposes he has." [Philosophy of Religion (IVP, 1985, p. 113)]. Evans is surely right here: it depends on whether God exists, who he is, and his goals for us.

What if, as Alvin Plantinga has argued, that the belief in God is properly basic for human beings? [See my "Faith and Reason" section]. Does this properly basic belief in God contain the ideas that Jesus was God incarnate born of a virgin in Bethlehem, or that Jesus bodily rose from the grave? These are historical questions of miracles that must be believed additionally. **So here's the catch-22**. For someone to believe the evidence for the foundational Christian miracle claims, as I'll call them, then as Evans admits, he must first believe in the Christian God. He cannot bring himself to believe those miracles if he begins by first believing in Allah, as we've seen, because then he will apply Hume's standards to those miracle claims. But in order to believe in the Christian God, as opposed to Allah, he must first have some pretty strong historical, physical, testimonial and circumstantial evidence to believe in the foundational Christian miracle claims. Think about this. We either start with the Christian God, or the evidence must be very strong. From where comes this starting point? People born into different religions have a different starting point, as we've seen. So we're left with just the evidence. But evidence alone cannot convince someone otherwise!

There are Christian evidentialists, like Gary R. Habermas, who think otherwise and argue that the evidence for one particular Christian miracle, the bodily resurrection of Christ, can be strong enough to convince a rational skeptic to believe in Christ and the Christian world-view. However, Stephen T. Davis argued convincingly against Habermas in a debate on the resurrection of Jesus in Faith and Philosophy (April 1984, & July 1985). Davis: "The non-believer's position is probably convincing to the non-believer not primarily because of the evidence or arguments in its favor but because it is entailed by the world-view he or she accepts. Similarly, the believer's position is probably convincing to the believer not primarily because of the evidence or arguments in its favor but because it dovetails with the world view he or she accepts." "There is no such thing as bare uninterrupted evidence or experience, and so the way one evaluates the evidence one see depends to a great extent on one's world-view, i.e., on whether or not one thinks miracles are possible or probable." [April 1984, p. 154-155]. "All people interpret their experience within a certain philosophical framework. For many people, their philosophical assumptions exclude God's existence and the possibility of miracles. The odd thing is that a decision a person makes whether to believe in the resurrection is usually made on some basis other than the evidence pro and con. Those who believe in Christ believe in the resurrection; those who accept naturalism do not. There is a curious circularity here," but it is "not an instance of committing the fallacy of circular reasoning," (i.e., it's not "viciously circular"). Some episodes of circularity are "unavoidable." [July 1985, p. 306].

Norman Geisler stated this problem much stronger: "The mere fact of the resurrection cannot be used to establish the truth that there is a God. For the resurrection cannot even be a miracle unless there already is a God." "The real problem for the Christian apologist is to find some way apart from the mere facts themselves to establish the justifiability of interpreting the facts in a theistic way." "No fact, event, or series thereof within an overall framework which derives all of its meaning from the framework can be determinative of the framework which bestows that meaning on it. For no fact or set of facts can of and by themselves, apart from any meaning or interpretation given to them, establish which of the alternative viewpoints should be taken on the fact(s)." [Christian Apologetics, Baker, 1976 (pp. 94-98)].

J.L. Mackie's Argument Against Miracles.

The late J.L. Mackie in his book, The Miracle of Theism (Clarendon Press, 1982) argues against the belief in miracles, along with Hume. Let me quote from him: "The defender of a miracle...must in effect concede to Hume that the antecedent improbability of this event is as high as it could be, hence that, apart from the testimony, we have the strongest possible grounds for believing that the alleged event did not occur. This event must, by the miracle advocate's own admission, be contrary to a genuine, not merely supposed, law of nature, and therefore maximally improbable. It is this maximal improbability that the weight of the testimony would have to overcome." "Where there is some plausible testimony about the occurrence of what would appear to be a miracle, those who accept this as a miracle have the double burden of showing both that the event took place and that it violated the laws of nature. But it will be very hard to sustain this double burden. For whatever tends to show that it would have been a violation of a natural law tends for that very reason to make it most unlikely that is actually happened."

Mackie then distinguishes between two different contexts in which an alleged miracle might be considered a real one. First, there is the context of two parties in which "already both have accepted some general theistic doctrines and the point at issue is, whether a miracle has occurred which would enhance the authority of a specific sect or teacher. In this context supernatural intervention, though *prima facie* ("on the surface") unlikely on any particular occasion, is, generally speaking, on the cards: it is not altogether outside the range of reasonable expectation for these parties." The second context is a very different matter when "the context is that of fundamental debate about the truth of theism itself. Here one party to the debate is initially at least agnostic, and does not yet concede that there is a supernatural power at all. From this point of view the intrinsic improbability of a genuine miracle...is very great, and that one or other of the alternative explanations...will always be much more likely—that is, either that the alleged event is not miraculous, or that it did not occur, or that the testimony is faulty in some way." Mackie concludes by saying: "This entails that it is pretty well impossible that reported miracles should provide a worthwhile argument for theism addressed to those who are initially inclined to atheism or even to agnosticism." (From chapter one).

Why is it that someone like Hume has had such a great influence over us, and yet William Lane Craig could say at one point that "Hume has been refuted"? Why is it that I can accept much of J.L. Mackie's argument against miracles, while William Lane Craig can say in the introduction to the Truth Journal that "Mackie's critique of miracles is *particularly shockingly superficial*" (emphasis mine)? Is it because people who see things a different way are less intelligent? Not at all! Mackie's arguments are not superficial.

Craig said this when commenting on Alvin Plantinga's critique of Mackie's book, The Miracle of Theism (Clarendon Press, 1982). So I reread Plantinga's essay, "Is Theism Really a Miracle?," in Faith and Philosophy, [April 1986]. And as I was doing so, I thought to myself that this was superficial too. Really! It's obvious that Plantinga critiques Mackie from a theistic perspective. He even says so. Plantinga refers repeatedly to the phrase "to me," "my evidence," "my experience," or "our evidence." Take for example this sentence: "as a matter of fact it could be that what is in fact a violation of a law of nature (a miracle) not only wasn't particularly improbable with respect to *our evidence* (emphasis mine), but was in fact more probable than not with respect to it." What kind of evidence is he speaking to that is specifically his? He's debating Mackie from within a viewpoint Mackie doesn't accept. That is, he totally ignores Mackie's distinction between the two contexts in which an alleged miracle might be considered a real one. Mackie's debate is inside the second context where it's a "fundamental debate about the truth of theism itself." Plantinga asks the following question: "why should we think it is particularly improbable that a law of nature be interfered with?" "I have no reason to suppose that the world is not regularly interfered with. Why couldn't interferences with nature be the rule rather than the exception?" But to people who disagree with Plantinga, that's not a very bright question at all. How often has anyone ever seen a real miracle? **Science has progressed on the assumption that miracles don't occur in the laboratory. Plantinga debates with modern science here. Now to those of us who question the believability of miracles, that just seems superficial to us.**

Miracles and Invisible Chairs.

How exactly is it that a spiritual God (John 4:24) can act in a material universe? Can he pick up a material box? Humans are material beings, so we have no trouble picking up a box, because our bodily matter makes contact with the matter inherent in the box, and up it goes. How does something that is Spirit make contact with something that is matter, unless there is some point of contact between them that they both share?

Take for example the idea of ghosts that can walk through walls, etc. How does a being like that actually move matter, unless there is some point of contact between such a ghost and what they move on earth? Likewise, how can God speak audibly and be heard by sound waves to our ears, unless he can move sound waves--that is, unless there is once again a point of contact between a Spirit being and the material waves in the air?

Imagine an existing chair located in the same room you are in now. It is invisible to your eyes because it's in another dimension, or parallel universe. It really exists there, but you cannot see it or touch it because it's not a material chair in your universe. Now sit on it. Try to kick it around. Pick it up and throw it as far as you can. Go ahead, experiment all you like. Then report back your findings. Conversely, can that chair act in your world? Let's say it grows a brain, for a minute. And it wants to pick you up and kick you around a while. Can it? How? You couldn't, so how can it?

God, being "spiritual" is like that invisible chair. There can be no physical interaction with an invisible chair, and there can be no action in the world of physical objects by invisible entities, whether they are chairs, ghosts or God-- unless, Christians can specify for me what that point of contact might actually be.

Can you precisely describe for me how spirit and matter are the same so they can interact, and yet how they are also different? Analogies are weak, like ghosts and invisible chairs, I suppose. But the question remains, "how can the two interact?" How? Logically they cannot interact, unless they both share a quality or something that they both have. Are spirit and matter two poles of the same reality?: then welcome to **panentheism, or process theology.** Are they one and the same: then welcome to **pantheism** (all is "spirit"), or **atheism** (all is matter). Idealism proclaims there is no material universe. You could go that way, I suppose, like George Berkeley. But then what exactly did God create? Ideas? We don't exist with bodies? Then exactly where do we exist? Do we exist at all? Maybe we are only "dreams" that God is having?

If a spiritual God can act in this universe, then give me some reasons to believe that God can do this by showing how it is possible for two different types of, for lack of a better word, "substances" can interact. Energy is after all, matter. Gasses like air are all matter too! And if spirit and matter are not different substances, then what are they? How are they different? How are they the same? [J.P. Moreland defends "substance dualism," in his book Scaling the Secular City (pp. 77-104), but he doesn't answer this question. Paul Copan basically argues that such interactions aren't logically impossible, and switches the discussion to the problem of consciousness for atheists, in "How Do You Know You're Not Wrong" (Baker Books, 2005) pp. 115-122. For great discussions on this whole issue, see Gilbert Ryle's classic book, The Concept of Mind (1949); Arthur Peacocke's, Theology For a Scientific Age, (Fortress Press, 1993), (pp. 135-189), Daniel Dennet's Consciousness Explained, (1991); Francis Crick's, The Astonishing Hypothesis: The Scientific Search for the Soul (Scribner's 1994); and Jaegwon Kim's, Philosophy of Mind, (Westview, 1996)].

What If A Miracle Could Be Shown to Have Occurred?

If Christians can show how Biblical miracles took place then there is an additional problem. What if believers can actually show exactly how a Biblical miracle took place? Then doesn't it take all of the force out of the miracle? I have seen a two-tape video series called "Mysteries of the Ancient World" (Sun-Pko Productions, 1993) which is narrated by Dennis Weaver, and purports to show how several of the miracles in the Bible can be shown to be believable. Take for example the segment about Shadrach, Meshach, and Abendego being saved out of the firey furnace (Daniel 3). The tape tries to show how it all happened naturalistically by quoting from various scholars! Yes, that's right. The tape wants us to see how that the furnace had compartments and the fire was underneath these men in a separate compartment, allowing for pockets of cooler air where they were thrown. But by "proving" this happened, exactly as they claim it did, it takes all of the miraculous out of the event. Robert M. Price noted this when he wrote: "If you can offer scientific proof for the Star of Bethlehem, as popular apologists do every Christmas season, claiming it corresponds to some ancient supernova or planetary alignment, you have thereby evacuated the phenomenon of all its miraculous character. Whatever you prove this way can never transcend the framework of the criteria you try to employ." [The Empty Tomb (Prometheus Books, 2005), p. 13-14].

15 The Self-Authenticating Witness of the Holy Spirit.

In light of the **catch-22** mentioned in the previous section, Dr. Craig argues that Christians should start with faith in the Christian God. Why? "We know Christianity to be true by the self authenticating witness of God's Holy Spirit." What does he mean by that? "I mean that the witness, or testimony, of the Holy Spirit is its own proof; it is unmistakable; it does not need other proofs to back it up; it is self-evident and attests to its own truth." Hitchhiking on the philosophical work of Alvin Plantinga's defense of a properly basic belief in God, and citing the Bible (Gal. 3:26; 4:6; Rom. 8:15-16; I John 2:20, 26-27; 3:24; 5:7-10), Craig writes: "I would agree that belief in the *God of the Bible* (emphasis mine) is a properly basic belief, and emphasize that it is the ministry of the Holy Spirit that supplies the circumstance for its proper basically. And because this belief is from God, it is not merely rational, but definitely true." [Apologetics: An Introduction, (pp. 18-22)].

Bill claims that there is a distinction between **knowing** Christianity is true from **showing** Christianity is true. He believes that he knows Christianity is true by the inner witness of the Holy Spirit, period. Such a witness for him is self-authenticating, and needs no intellectual arguments on its behalf.

When it comes to showing Christianity is true, his arguments can only show probabilities and plausibilities. By offering them up on the table as an apologist, he hopes the Holy Spirit will use his arguments to speak to those who haven't made a commitment to Jesus. But if his arguments don't convince anyone, he still has done the best he could do, because at best, that's all he can expect.

At the end of his debate with Gerd Ludemann on the historicity of the resurrection, Craig provides us with an example of what he means: "So if you ask me why I believe Christ is risen from the dead, I would not only point to the historical evidence, but I would reply in the words of the old hymn, 'You ask you I know he lives? He lives within my heart!' Now somebody might say I'm deluded. But that's where the historical evidence comes in. In the absence of any good, compelling historical reason to deny the fact of the resurrection of Jesus, it seems to me that it's perfectly rational to believe in Christ on the basis of his living in my life." [Jesus' Resurrection: Fact or Figment?, p. 65].

Craig defends Christianity by the **Classical Apologetical Approach**, not the **Evidential Approach**, as best seen in the book, Five Views On Apologetics, ed. by Steven B. Cowan (Zondervan, 2000). This approach is a continuation of his former mentor, Norman Geisler in his book Christian Apologetics, and it is definitely known as Thomistic, or Classical. When it comes to showing Christianity true, Craig begins by defending the existence of God through the Kalam Cosmological Argument. After defending the probability that God exists, he then argues for the bodily resurrection of Christ, which validates the revelation found in the Bible.

Gary Habermas distinguishes his own **Evidential Approach** from Craig's **Classical Approach**: "Instead of having to prove God's existence before moving to specific evidences (Craig's Classical Approach), the evidentialist treats one or more historical arguments as being able both to indicate God's existence and activity, and to indicate which variety of theism is true." (p. 92).

In a way, Craig is a presuppositionalist, in that this is how he knows Christianity is true, except he claims to know it's true by experiencing the Holy Spirit. But he is not when it comes to his methodology, where he shows Christianity is true. He argues that presuppositionalism as an apologetic methodology "commits the informal fallacy of begging the question, for it advocates presupposing the truth of Christian theism in order to prove Christian theism." (p. 232).

I myself wasn't an evidentialist; that apologetic is doomed to failure because evidence can never justify how to view that evidence. Hence in my opinion, it doesn't even offer an apologetic, that is, an overall defense of the evidence. And a presuppositionalist apologetic assumes what needs to be proved. I am a proponent of the **Cumulative Case Method** of the late Paul D. Feinberg, also a former professor of mine. Craig, however, admits that when it comes to showing Christianity true, he finds himself "largely in agreement with the conclusion of Paul Feinberg. A successful apologetic for the Christian faith should be in an appropriate sense a cumulative case." (p. 173). This same **Cumulative Case Method** is the one I use when debunking Christianity in this book too. While my beliefs have changed from believer and former apologist to atheist, the method I use to justify my beliefs is still a cumulative case.

There is always reciprocity and a dialectic between evidence and presuppositions in historical and scientific investigations, so why should it be different in theological investigations? No matter what methodology one *CLAIMS* to have when coming to believe a religious or metaphysical set of control beliefs, the case is always going to end up being a cumulative one. This explains, in part, why there can be no "smoking gun" type of an argument that will convince believing Christians who disagree with me about their faith.

When arguing that he knows Christianity is true based on the self-authenticating witness of the Holy Spirit, Dr. Craig stands in the steps of some great Christian thinkers like Augustine, Anselm, and even Barth and Bultmann. According to Wolfart Pannenberg, "the basic presupposition underlying German Protestant theology as expressed by Barth and Bultmann, is that the basis of theology is the self-authenticating Word of God which demands obedience." [Revelation as History (p. 9)]. Unlike some of these theologians though, the basis for Craig's faith is in the inner witness of the Holy Spirit alone, who may use the Bible, evidences or nothing at all to create faith in the believer.

Does Dr. Craig mean to say that he cannot be wrong? Yes! He knows Christianity is true. With this understanding he has insulated himself from any and all objections to the contrary. Dr. Craig knows he's right because he knows he's right, and that's the end of the matter. Since he knows he's right, Christianity is true.

Mark Smith (of www.jcnot4me.com) set up the following scenario for Craig: "Dr. Craig, for the sake of argument let's pretend that a time machine gets built. You and I hop in it, and travel back to the day before Easter, 33 AD. We park it outside the tomb of Jesus. We wait. Easter morning rolls around, and nothing happens. We continue to wait. After several weeks of waiting, still nothing happens. There is no resurrection- Jesus is quietly rotting away in the tomb."

Smith asked Craig, given this scenario, if he would then give up Christianity, having seen with his own two eyes that Jesus did not rise from the dead. Smith wrote: "His answer was shocking, and quite unexpected. He told me, face to face, that he would STILL believe in Jesus, he would STILL believe in the resurrection, and he would STILL remain a Christian. When asked, in light of his being a personal eyewitness to the fact that there WAS no resurrection, he replied that due to the witness of the 'holy spirit' within him, he would assume a trick of some sort had been played on him while watching Jesus' tomb. This self-induced blindness astounded me." Like Smith I am stunned. There is no way that the witness of the Holy Spirit can in any way, shape, or form, be more reliable than his own two eyes!

But it's this view in mind that allows Dr. Craig to write: "A believer who is too uninformed or ill-equipped to refute anti-Christian arguments is rational in believing on the grounds of the witness of the Spirit in his heart even in the face of such unrefuted objections. Even such a person confronted with what are for him unanswerable objections to Christian theism is, because of the work of the Holy Spirit, within his epistemic rights—nay, under epistemic obligation—to believe in God." [Five Views on Apologetics (Zondervan, 2000, p. 35)].

Even though Muslims and Mormons also claim to have the witness of God in their hearts, Dr. Craig denies that other conflicting faiths have this exact same self-authenticating witness of the Holy Spirit, or that their claims are even relevant to the witness he has in his heart. With William Alston, he can suggest that their claims are partially true because the people holding to different faith commitments may have had "a vertical experience of God as the Ground of Being on whom we creatures are dependent, or as the Moral Absolute from whom values derive, or even as the loving Father of mankind." [Five Views on Apologetics (p. 36)].

But this is a very large claim for him to make when we consider the number of people who believe otherwise, who believe based on the "accidents of birth." Why is that? And where is the self-authenticating witness of the Christian Holy Spirit among the non-Christian people of the world, over 4 billion of them? Michael Martin: "To accept Craig's thesis one must believe an outrageous and outlandish hypothesis: namely, that billions of people now and in the past were not telling the truth when they claimed that they never had such an experience." ["Craig's Holy Spirit Epistemology," at www.infidels.com].

These other religions could respond in a similar fashion and claim that what Dr. Craig experiences is not relevant to their experiences, and they too can claim that Dr. Craig's claims are partially true because the people holding to different faith commitments may have had "a vertical experience of God as the Ground of Being on whom we creatures are dependent, or as the Moral Absolute from whom values derive, or even as the loving Father of mankind." Sounds like an impasse to me.

In a debate with Dr. Corey Washington Dr. Craig offers up an analogy: "Suppose you are accused of a crime that you know you didn't commit, and all the evidence stands against you. Are you obliged to believe that you're guilty because the evidence stands against you? Not at all; you know better. You know you're innocent, even if others think that you may be guilty. Similarly, for the person who has an immediate experience of God, who knows God as a personal, living reality in his life, such a person can know that God exists, even if he's not a philosopher and doesn't understand all of these arguments, and so forth. God can be immediately known and experienced, Christ can be immediately known and experienced in your life today, and that is true even if you've never had the chance to examine the evidence." [http://www.leaderu.com/offices/billcraig].

But what if you woke up one morning to police officers who arrested you for murder? The case against you is that there were two witnesses who saw you at the scene of the crime, you had no alibi, you had a motive for murder, your blood and hair were found under the victim's fingernails with corresponding scratches on your back, and the victim's blood was found on your shoes next to your bed? But you "know" you didn't kill anyone. At that point you must consider the evidence against you, and it's overwhelming. Your "knowing" is delusional no matter what the reason for your delusion. Since the above scenario is possible, Craig could also be deluded in claiming to know God exists because of a purported veridical experience of God. The difference between my suggested "murder" scenario and Dr. Craig's scenario for believing in God is that there is hard objective evidence for the "murder," whereas there is no hard objective evidence for Craig's claim. But precisely because there isn't hard evidence for us to debunk Craig's claim, he can go on his merry delusional way all he wants to. But I believe he is deluded, contrary to his claim not to be.

What about third person outsiders who consider Craig's argument? To the outsider this is circular reasoning, although if Dr. Craig is right it's not at all circular [See, "The Outsider Test For Faith…"]. But what an outsider thinks, he says, has no relevance to what Craig believes. This might be true in his own personal experience, except for the fact that as soon as he argues on behalf of the self-authenticating witness of the Holy Spirit, he has invited outsiders to take a look at this claim. Paul Feinberg sees a problem with this approach: "Persons are in a privileged position with regard to their own experiences. The problem arises with this approach in apologetics because the task is not simply to defend believer's epistemological rights to believe, but to convince those who are not believers that the Christian understanding of God and reality is true. That requires the third person perspective." [Five Views on Apologetics (p. 72)].

It seems as though it would be akin to a person claiming to have personal experiences of an intelligent alien being from another part of this universe through a wormhole, although actually touching and seeing such a being would be empirical evidence, something Craig does not have. Yet, this person knows there is such an alien from personal experiences, and yet he cannot convince anyone else that he had these experiences, nor can he replicate such experiences for anyone else. If I had such experiences I would probably believe in the existence of that alien being too, although, I would initially be skeptical about it until proven otherwise. Once I believed this alien existed, no one could convince me otherwise, until they could prove to me that wormholes cannot exist, or that some description of the alien or something he said is simply implausible.

If this were to be shown to me I would be forced to rethink my experiences of this alien being. And at that point I would have to choose between, 1) Accepting my personal experiences anyway, and continuing to believe in spite of the skeptical questions that such an alien really exists, because of a faith that places personal experiences above my inability to answer my critics, or, 2) I would have to reject my own personal experiences in lieu of the skeptical questions. At that point no one can answer for another person which to choose, can they?

Consider first the content to this inner self-authenticating witness. That is to ask, what things did this alien being tell you? Does his inner witness of the Holy Spirit lead Craig to believe that all of the traditional Christian doctrines are true, as he understands them? Does this entail he has the correct understanding of things like God's foreknowledge, predestination, eschatology, and Calvinism? Are his specific views on the deity of Christ, baptism, the atonement, the bodily resurrection of Jesus from the grave, and his second coming all the correct ones? What is the particular content of this self-authentication from the Spirit? There must be some content to the witness of the Spirit that gives him assurance he's right, and where does he learn this content? At what point does it stop and he's left on his own to work things out from reading the Bible?

So what is the actual content of this God experience? Where did this content come from, and how coherent is this content? That's what I want to know, and I believe Craig will have no real satisfying answer to these questions, at least not to third person outsiders like me.

I don't think a coherent understanding of this purported inner witness can be adequately described, since Christians who claim to have experienced this should've gained some knowledge as a result of it. That is, they should have gained some propositional beliefs about the divine being they experienced, along with some specific beliefs this divine being wants them to have. But since Christians who claim to have had this same experience have theological disagreements, then they should be able to explain why there are so many differing doctrinal beliefs among these Christians. These Christians must also distinguish their purportedly unique experience from the experience of people in all other non-Christian religions, or no religion at all. **Either there is no content to this experience, in which case I seriously doubt it is a personal experience of some divine being at all, or, this witness is so muddled and weak as a religious experience that atheists can deny they have even had one at all.**

Consider next the coherence of the beliefs that the inner witness of the Holy Spirit has led Bill Craig to believe? Which is to ask about the coherence of the things this alien being told you. An eternally uncreated Triune being (3 persons in 1?) who has always existed as he is (with no growth, for he was always perfect), with all power (but doesn't use it like we would if we saw a burning child), all knowledge (since he never learned anything), and who is present everywhere (a non-embodied being?) is just is too complex of an entity to believe in. And in the New Testament (which surely forms the content of this witness, and not the witness of the Spirit itself) we find an Incarnate Son of God who atoned for our sins (even though no one has yet made any reasonable sense of either an incarnate God or how his death atoned for our sins). Those who disbelieve go to hell (however conceived), making the problem of evil for a good omnipotent God impossible to solve (even though without a belief in hell it's insoluble anyway).

Whether Dr. Craig is correct or not depends entirely on whether traditional Christianity is true, *plus some*. For instance, how can Dr. Craig tell the difference between the witness of the Holy Spirit in his heart from an emotional feeling? We all have had strong feelings about a great many things that turned out to be false. There are Christians who have had strong feelings that God wanted them to do certain things that were wrong. There are Christians who have a strong feeling that God will do something for them in the near future, which may never transpire. There are Christians who feel (or sense) the Holy Spirit in a contemporary (low) church service rather than in an older traditional (high) church type service in an old cathedral, and vice versa. How can he say he really knows that Christianity is true, unless there is some incontrovertible evidence that it is? Why does he trust his feelings when feelings are so often wrong? People of other persuasions may demur. We must constantly test our feelings in case we err, and it is possible that the cumulative tests we use may someday reveal that our feelings were in error, like I did.

What about Craig's doubts? Children who are taught to believe in Christ at an early age might experience their own self-authenticating witness. That's why we refer to something called "child-like faith"—children pray and act like they have no doubts at all. But as they get older, the experiences of life, the questions they ponder, and their own unanswered prayers cause them to have less and less confidence in that witness. Craig would have to admit that he doesn't have that "child-like faith" anymore, too. Maybe these adult doubts are a check on the experience he claims to have had of the Holy Spirit.

Can Craig truly say that he doesn't have doubts from time to time? Os Guiness has argued convincingly that while "an element of faith is indispensable to all human knowledge," "all of us will doubt at some point, whatever it is we believe." [In Two Minds, (IVP, 1977, p. 41). All knowledge comes with some doubt "because we are absolutely certain of nothing." "Since our knowledge is finite, none of us can exclude the possibility of our being wrong." (pp. 42-43.) So how sure can Dr. Craig be about this inner witness of God? Is he as sure of it as he knows he exists, or that he has a mind? Is he as sure of it as the existence of the chair at his desk, or the truth of a simple mathematical formula? Any philosopher knows, along with Rene Descartes, that all sense data can be doubted because they do not allow us to experience the real world in and of itself. But we can *pragmatically* justify our senses in that they help us to get along in life fairly well, and they are the basis for modern science. What then is the basis Craig has for saying that he's surer of this inner witness than sense data itself, when sense data gives us the cold hard facts which science is built upon?

Moreover, how did Craig come to believe that there is a Holy Spirit and an inner witness? Through experience? Hardly. Did this inner witness tell him that his views on the self-authenticating testimony of the Holy Spirit are true? The four respondents in Five Views on Apologetics take issue with Craig's emphasis and on some of his particulars too. Are they not listening to the Holy Spirit here? The fact is that Craig learned this at a later age in life by reading the Bible and trying to come up with a Christian apologetic. This is when he first believed in the inner witness and how it functioned for his apologetic.

While it might take a great deal to change our minds about our faith, we can never say that we "know" Christianity to be true, because we might later come to believe we were wrong. I started with faith in Christianity but I have come to believe I can't understand it, and that I've tested my experience of the purported witness that I had, and found I was mistaken.

17 Was Jesus Born of a Virgin in Bethlehem?

Some skeptics have gone so far as to deny that Jesus ever was a historical person. [See G.A. Wells, Did Jesus Exist? (1986), and The Historical Evidence for Jesus (Prometheus Books, 1988); Earl Doherty, The Jesus Puzzle: Did Christianity Begin with a Mythical Christ? Challenging the Existence of An Historical Jesus (Age of Reason Publications, 2005)]. Robert M. Price claims that if there is a kinship of the NT writers and belief with those of adjacent of cultures "the real issue of debate ought to be whether there was a historical Jesus at the core of all the mythology." [The Empty Tomb, p. 150; See also his Deconstructing Jesus (Prometheus Books, 2000)]. But I'm not that skeptical. I believe there was a person named Jesus. I just don't think he was a Messiah/Christ/Son of God. [See Jeffery Jay Lowder "Independent Confirmation and the Historicity of Jesus" (1997) at: http://www.infidels.org/library/modern/jeff_lowder/indconf.html]. The Gospels and the rise of the church serve as *prima facia* justification for believing the man Jesus really existed. But there is every reason to question who early Christians claimed he was, what he actually did, and what he actually said, since the myths surrounding him exponentially grew.

Was Jesus Born in Bethlehem? Craig Chester, the President of the Monterey Institute for Research in Astronomy, offers a detailed and elaborate understanding of the rising star in the Bethlehem sky at Jesus' birth, in "The Star of Bethlehem" [Imprimis (Dec. 1993)]. He claims it was Jupiter, the planet known to represent kingship to astrologers in the ancient East, which came into conjunction with Regulus, the star of kingship, which is located in the constellation of Leo, also known as the constellation of kings. This may explain some things the Magi saw, but E. P. Sanders asks, "Why take the star of Matthew's story to be a real astral event and ignore what the author says about it?" [The Historical Figure of Jesus (p. 55)]. How is it truly possible for the star that Chester describes to lead the Magi from Jerusalem to a specific inn located in Bethlehem less than five miles away? [see Matt. 2:9-10]. H. R. Reimarus (A.D. 1768) observed long ago that even if it were some sort of comet with a tail, "it is too high to point to a specific house." If it were a miraculous star then why didn't everyone in the vicinity see it? Pope Leo I (A.D. 461) proposed that the star was invisible to the Jews because of their blindness. But then why did it appear to pagan astrologers?

Jesus was not born in Bethlehem, if Luke is taken literally, according to E. P. Sanders [The Historical Figure of Jesus (Penguin Press, 1993, pp. 84-91)]. What husband would take a nine-month pregnant woman on such a trek from Nazareth at that time when only heads of households were obligated to register for a census when the census would've been stretched out over a period of weeks or even months? But if he did, why did he not take better precautions for the birth? Why not take Mary to her relative Elizabeth's home just a few miles away from Bethlehem for the birth of her baby? According to Luke's own genealogy (3:23-38) David had lived 42 generations earlier. Why should everyone have had to register for a census in the town of one of his ancestors forty-two generations earlier? There would be millions of ancestors by that time, and the whole empire would have been uprooted. Why 42 generations and not 35, or 16? If it was just required of the lineage of King David to register for the census, what was Augustus thinking when he ordered it? He had a King, Herod. "Under no circumstances could the reason for Joseph's journey be, as Luke says, that he was 'of the house and lineage of David,' because that was of no interest to the Romans in this context." [Uta Ranke-Heinemann, Putting Away Childish Things, (p.10)]. The fact is, even if there was a worldwide Roman census that included Galilee at this specific time, there is evidence that Census takers taxed people based upon the land they owned, so they traveled to where people lived.

According to Robin Lane Fox, "Luke's story is historically impossible and internally incoherent." But he says, "Luke's errors and contradictions are easily explained. Early Christian tradition did not remember, or perhaps ever know, exactly where and when Jesus had been born. People were much more interested in his death and consequences." "After the crucifixion and the belief in the resurrection, people wondered all the more deeply about Jesus' birthplace. Bethlehem, home of King David, was a natural choice for the new messiah. There was even a prophecy in support of the claim which the 'little town' has maintained so profitably to this day." So, "a higher truth was served by an impossible fiction." [The Unauthorized Version (Knopf, 1992), p. 31-32]. "Luke's real source for the view that Jesus was born in Bethlehem was almost certainly the conviction that Jesus fulfilled a hope that someday a descendant of David would arise to save Israel," because the Messiah was supposed to come from there (Micah 5:2). [E. P. Sanders, The Historical Figure of Jesus (p. 87.)].

Matthew's account of Jesus' birth fares no better. Robin Lane Fox: "Bethlehem was not Jesus' birthplace but was imported from Hebrew prophecies about the future Messiah; the Star had similar origins (Numbers 24:17). Matthew's story is a construction from well-known messianic prophecies (Bethlehem; the Star), and the Wise Men (Magi) have been added as another legend." "Where the truth had been lost, stories filled the gap, and the desire to know fabricated its own tradition. Luke told a tale of angels and shepherds, bringing some of the humblest people in society to Bethlehem with news of Jesus' future. Instead of shepherds, Matthew brought Wise Men, following a star in the East and bringing gifts...In one version, there are simple shepherds, the other, learned Wise Men: the contrast sets our imaginations free, and perhaps like the Wise Men we too should return by 'another way." [The Unauthorized Version: Truth and Fiction in the Bible (Knopf, 1992), pp.35- 36].

A bigger problem is that Matthew and Luke contradict each other. Luke has Joseph and Mary living in Nazareth from where they traveled to Bethlehem for the Roman census (Luke 1:26; 2:4). After Jesus was born, Joseph took his family from Bethlehem to Jerusalem for up to 40 days (Luke 2:22), and from there straight back to Nazareth (Luke 2:39). But Matthew has Joseph's family living in Bethlehem for up to two years after the birth of Jesus (Matt 2:16)! And after the *Magi* leave, Joseph is warned in a dream to flee to Egypt and stay there until Herod died (Matt. 2:15). After Herod died, Joseph was told in a dream to return to the land of Israel, and he headed for his home in Bethlehem of Judea. But since he was afraid to go there, he settled in Nazareth (Matt. 2:21-23), for the first time!

Was Jesus Born by a Miraculous Virgin Birth? "If we wish to continue seeing Luke's accounts of angelic messages and so forth, as historical events, we'd have to take a large leap of faith: We'd have to assume that while on verifiable matters of historical fact Luke tells all sorts of fairy tales (just mentioned above) but on supernatural matters—which by definition can never be checked—he simply reports the facts. By his arbitrary treatment of history, Luke has shown himself to be an unhistorical reporter—a teller of fairy tales." [Uta Ranke-Heinemann, Putting Away Childish Things, (p.14)].

When Mary first hears from the angel Gabriel that she is to give birth she objects by saying, "How shall this be, since I know not man?" (Luke 1:34). According to Ranke-Heinemann, "psychologically this sentence can never be spoken, because it states that Mary has relations neither with her husband nor with any other man. She does not say the only thing that she could have said: 'since I have no sexual relations with *my husband.'* Instead she says, 'with man,' meaning with any man. This proves that Mary's objection to the angel is a literary invention." [Putting Away Childish Things, (p.16-17)]. The way it's phrased is to justify her virginity to the reader rather than historically retell what might have actually been said.

David L. Edwards in Evangelical Essentials, (pp. 190-193): "Paul's surviving letters do not refer to the virgin birth. Mark's gospel also does not mention this miracle. John's gospel is also silent about a miraculous conception, except that all Christians are 'born' not through sex but 'of God' (1:13). The story of the Messiah's birth—of the miraculous star or the appearance of the angels to the shepherds—is said to have been known widely in Jerusalem (Matt. 2:3; Luke 2:17-18). Yet the story is apparently not known by anyone who meets the adult Jesus. The adult John the Baptist, for instance, doubted whether Jesus was the Messiah (Luke 7:19), although we are told that his own mother had fully shared Mary's experiences before the miraculous birth (Luke 1:39-45). Herod's massacre of 'all the boys in Bethlehem...' is not mentioned in the indignantly careful list of Herod's atrocities given by the Jewish historian, Josephus. But it is suspiciously like the story of Pharaoh's massacre of Hebrew boys in Exodus 1:22. In Luke's narrative the characters, sayings and experiences of John the Baptist's parents (1:5-25; 57-80) are suspiciously like those of Abraham and Sarah in the book of Genesis, and Mary's song (1:46-55) resembles the song of Hannah (I Sam. 2:1-10)."

"My own answer is that the virgin birth story is probably fictional. While Mary says, "nothing is impossible with God" (Luke 1:37), we have to consider what is probable. Many legends of miracles surrounding the births of heroes exist in the world's literature. It is striking that within the Christian Church itself the legend developed that Mary was a perpetual virgin, even though Mark's gospel speaks plainly of four brothers of Jesus, and sisters (6:3). It seems clear, although tragic, that births avoiding human sex were thought of as being purer and more wonderful than the mystery of the sexual creation of a new human being." [David Edwards, Evangelical Essentials, p. 194].

In Matthew 1:20-23 the author claims that Isaiah 7:14 refers to Jesus' virgin birth: "Immanuel with us." The context for the prophecy in Isaiah tells us that before any "young woman" (not virgin) shall conceive and bear a son who grows to maturity that Syria, the northern kingdom of Israel, along with the southern

Israelite kingdom of Ahaz would all lie devastated. The prophecy in the original Hebrew of Isaiah says nothing whatsoever about a virginal conception. And it says nothing about a messiah, either. God will indeed be with Ahaz, but not in salvation, but in judgment.

In the original Hebrew of Isaiah, we find the word, *'almah*, which means any young woman, not necessarily meaning virgin in the strict sense. But the Greek translation of the Hebrew word in the Septuagint is *parthenos*. According to James Barr, "Here there is no question of a mistranslation in the stricter sense, nor was the text miscopied. What happened was a shift in the semantic identification of the word. When the Septuagint translators rendered it *parthenos* they did not mean 'virgin'; they meant the Greek word in the general sense of 'girl'—this usage if found in a majority of cases in the Greek Genesis, as well as in Maccabees. The Greek of Isaiah is well known, in any case, to be rather free in its renderings and to make little attempt at exact correspondence between Hebrew words and Greek words." "For the Christians, however, it was a different matter. Given the conviction of the mysterious origin and birth of Jesus, the word *parthenos* leapt out of the page at them: surely it must be used in the stricter, narrower, and more technical, and also more common and characteristic, sense of 'virgin.' They thus understood the Isaiah passage in this sense and used it so." [After Fundamentalism (Westminster Press), 1984, p. 144].

"Clearly, somebody went seeking in the O.T. for a text that could be interpreted as prophesying a virginal conception, even if such was never its original meaning. Somebody had already decided on the transcendental importance of the adult Jesus and sought to retroject that significance onto the conception and birth itself. I understand the virginal conception of Jesus to be a confessional statement about Jesus' status and not a biological statement about Mary's body. It is later faith in Jesus as an adult retrojected mythically onto Jesus as an infant." [John Dominic Crossan, Jesus: A Revolutionary Biography, (Harper, 1989, pp. 16-23)]. "The traditional Christian interpretation, which points to the Messiah Jesus, is not tenable as an exegesis of Isaiah 7.14." [U. Luz, Das Evangelium nach Matthaus I Mt 1-7 (EKKNT, 1.1; Zurich and Neukirchen-Vluyn: Neukirchener Verlag, 1985), p.107].

Today, with the advent of genetics, Christian thinkers try to defend the virgin birth on the grounds that the humanity of Jesus was derived from Mary, and his sinlessness and deity were derived from God. They do this because they now know that Mary must have contributed the female egg that made Jesus into a man. [Jesus, being a male, could not have been her clone, otherwise he would be a woman, and if cloned purely from Mary's genes would nullify the claim that he was God's son, too]. But the ancients commonly believed that the woman contributes nothing to the physical being of the baby to be born. The mother was nothing but a receptacle for the male sperm, which grew to become a child. The ancient and medieval church believed that Jesus' humanity was a new creation, and therefore sinless. Modern genetics have forced Christians today to take a new view of the virgin birth based upon genetics. But even with that new view, it doesn't adequately explain how Jesus is a human being, since a human being is conceived when a human male sperm penetrates a human female egg. Until that happens you do not have the complete chromosomal structure required to have a human being in the first place.

17 Was Jesus God Incarnate?

Here I can do little better than to share the arguments of John Hick. His published books are: The Myth of God Incarnate, ed. (1977), The Metaphor of God Incarnate (1993), and his summary in Stephen T. Davis, ed., Encountering Jesus: A Debate on Christology (1988). His argument has three major points. We'll briefly summarize and illustrate them in order.

One) The traditional view that Jesus was literally God in the flesh was not something he himself believed or taught, but was written into the Gospels after the Easter event. For Palestinian Jews living in the first century, a close encounter with Jesus "would be a conversion experience." For someone to see the conviction in his eyes as he preached that the kingdom is at hand, the authority of his words and deeds, the way he expressed love, the "miraculous" healings and providential circumstances that surrounded his life, and his apocalyptic conviction of living in the last days of the present age would lead one to think God is indeed in this person.

How this conversion experience led up to John's claim in his Gospel that Jesus was "the only begotten Son of God" (John1:18) is a large and complex topic. In Mark's Gospel, Jesus says to a man, "Why do you call me good? No one is good but God alone." (10:17-18). According to James Barr, "This only makes sense if Jesus is *not* claiming to be God." Because "it fits with the fact that Jesus fully accepted Jewish monotheism." [Beyond Fundamentalism, 1984 (p. 58)]. "Few...will contest that Jesus' message was essentially Jewish." [Geza Vermes, "Jesus the Jew" in Jesus' Jewishness, ed. James H. Charlesworth Crossroad, 1991), p. 113; see also his Jesus and the World of Judaism (SCM Press 1983)]. By contrast, John's Gospel, dated conservatively at 100 A.D., thirty (to forty-five) years after Mark, reveals a very exalted view of Christ.

This process of the deification of Jesus took at least 70 years among ancient superstitious people. Paula Fredricksen summarizes the different cultural milieu that this deification took place, in contrast to the original locus of the events: "from oral to written; from Aramaic to Greek; from the end of time to the middle of time; from Jewish to Gentile; from Galilee and Judea to the Empire." [From Jesus to Christ, (Yale University Press, 1988, p. 8.)].

Marcus Borg points out the progression of thought from Mark's gospel to Matthew's later gospel. [in The Meaning of Jesus: Two Visions, with N.T. Wright (Harper, 1999]. Borg points out that in Mark, the earliest Gospel, "a messianic self-claim is not part of Jesus' own message." Only once did Jesus deal with this issue in his public ministry, at Caesarea Philippi. When Jesus asked his disciples "Who do you say that I am?" Peter gives the answer, "You are the Messiah!" (Mk. 8:27-30). Borg: "The story then concludes on an enigmatic note: Jesus neither accepted nor rejected Peter's affirmation but instead sternly told him to say nothing about it." (p. 56). But when Matthew used Mark and constructed his own account, two things were added. "To Peter's exclamation, 'You are the messiah,' Matthew adds a second christological affirmation: 'The Son of the Living God.'" And, rather than ending it as Mark's gospel did, "Matthew adds a response from Jesus strongly commending Peter and explicitly affirming Jesus' own special status." (Matt. 16:16-17, p. 56-57). Borg also points out the difference between Mark and Matthew when it comes to the story of Jesus walking on the water. Mark's story concludes with "the disciples being confused about what they had experienced." ("They were utterly astounded" NRSV, Mark 6:45-52). But "as Matthew copies this story from Mark, he deletes the disciples' lack of understanding and replaces it with a Christological affirmation: 'Truly you are the Son of God.'" Matthew also adds, "and those in the boat worshipped him." (Matt. 14:32, p. 57). Beyond Matthew's gospel, John's gospel provides "further evidence that early Christian communities projected post-Easter understandings of Jesus back into the ministry itself." (Borg, p. 57).

One huge piece of evidence that leads most scholars to believe John's Gospel was written very late is his usage of the phrase, "the Jews." It occurs about seventy times, in contrast to five occurrences in the other Gospels. In John's gospel it is a stereotype for Jesus' opponents. Compare 7:13: "for fear of the Jews no one spoke openly of him (Jesus)" (See also John 2:18-20; 5:15, 18; 7:1; 9:18, 22; 10:31; 12:9; 18:28; 19:38; 20:19). But they were all Jews! How do Jews fear the Jews? The Gospel writer himself was a Jew, if it was John! Such a usage reveals the complete break between official Judaism and Christianity, which occurred after the destruction of Jerusalem in 70 A.D. by the Roman army. It is a very odd use of the phrase, leading some to believe John the Apostle didn't even write this gospel, because he himself was a Jew. At the minimum it reveals that the author was not so much interested in historical facts, but in elaborating on history, and even creating history. [Someone might object that the phrase "the Jews" merely meant those people who lived in Judea, but several of these occurrences could not be just about people in Judea: John 2;13; 4:22; 5:1; 6:4, 41; 18:20, 33; 19:3,21,19,40].

Conservative scholar James Dunn, in The Evidence for Jesus, tells us the specific problem. It's "whether we can use John's Gospel as direct testimony to Jesus' own teaching." "This problem was not invented by modern scholarship; it was rather discovered by modern scholarship." (p. 31). John's Gospel is "obviously different" from the other three earlier Gospels in terms of style and content. In the other three Synoptic Gospels (so named because they see the same things) Jesus speaks in proverbs, epigrams (cf. Sermon on the Mount for example, Matt. 5-7) and in parables, whereas in John's Gospel Jesus often speaks in long involved discourses (John 6, 14-17). In the three Synoptic Gospels Jesus speaks often of the "kingdom of God" and hardly anything about himself, but in John's Gospel he speaks often about himself ("I am the light of the world...the bread of life...the way the life and the truth."), but he hardly says anything about the kingdom of God.

At best, scholars see these differences as indicative of the fact that John's Gospel is a theological elaboration of history, while still others see them indicating it is wholly theological in nature with not much historical value at all when it comes to what Jesus taught. Case in point is the question of the high view of Christ revealed in John's Gospel. Even Dunn acknowledges that the number of times Jesus speaks of God as his "Father" or 'the Father' in John's gospel (173 times—Dunn's count) when compared to all three earlier Synoptic Gospels (a sum total of 43 times, many repeated between them) leads him to say that John's Jesus is "the truth of Jesus in retrospect rather than as expressed by Jesus at the time…it is expanded teaching of Jesus." (p. 45). And yet it is mostly because of John's Jesus that we get a very high Christology. John's Jesus is quoted as saying: "I and the Father are one," (John 10:30), and "He who has seen me has seen the Father." (John14:9). But, based on what we've just seen, he never said those things. This is John's Jesus speaking, not the historical Jesus.

Furthermore, Dunn asks a very important question with regard to the "I am" claims of Jesus: "If they were part of the original words of Jesus himself, how could it be that ONLY John has picked them up, and NONE of the others (emphasis his)? Call it scholarly skepticism if you will, but I must confess that I find it almost incredible that such sayings should have been neglected HAD they been known as a feature of Jesus' teaching." [Evidence For Jesus (Westminster Press, 1985, p. 36). John Shelby Spong, an American Bishop, goes farther by claiming: "I do not believe I can make a case for a single word attributed to Jesus in the Fourth Gospel to be a literal word actually spoken by the historic Jesus." [Rescuing the Bible From Fundamentalism (Harper, 1991, p. 191)].

Wolfhart Pannenberg argues that the belief that Jesus claimed anything like this "has been demonstrated with growing certainty by critical study of the Gospels to be the work of the post-Easter community. Today it must be taken as all but certain that the pre-Easter Jesus neither designated himself as Messiah (or Son of God) nor accepted such a confession to him from others." [Jesus—God and Man (Westminster, 1968)].

John Hick: ""Among mainline NT scholars, both conservative and liberal, Catholic and Protestant, there is today a general consensus that these are not pronouncements of the historical Jesus but words put into his mouth some sixty or seventy years later by a Christian writer expressing the theology that had developed in his part of the expanding church. To create speeches in this way for famous or revered figures of the past, embodying the writer's sense of the real significance of the past figure, was standard practice in the ancient world; and the discourses attributed to Jesus in the Fourth Gospel are seen today by most contemporary scholarship as examples of this." [in More Than One Way?: Four Views on Salvation, eds, Okholm & Phillips (Zondervan, 1995, p. 53)]. This is the issue of re-writing texts by pseudonymous authors, as we've already seen earlier. Hick provides additional quotes to support his view here:

C.F.D. Moule, "a pillar of orthodoxy": "Any case for a high Christology that depended on the authenticity of the alleged claims of Jesus about himself, especially in the 4th Gospel, would be precarious." [The Origins of Christology, p. 136]. Another "pillar of orthodoxy," Michael Ramsay: "Jesus did not claim deity for himself." And, "the title 'son of God' need not of itself be of high significance, for in Jewish circles it might mean no more than the Messiah…and in popular Hellenism there were many sons of God, meaning holy inspired men." [Jesus and the Living Past, p. 39, 43]. "Distinguished conservative" James Dunn: "there was no real evidence in the earliest Jesus tradition of what could fairly be called a consciousness of divinity." [Christology in the Making, p. 60]. Brian Hebblewaite: "It is no longer possible to defend the divinity of Jesus by referring to the claims of Jesus." [The Incarnation, p. 74].

Robert W. Funk summarizes the four stages of Christology in the New Testament [in Honest to Jesus (Harper, 1996), pp. 279-296]. **Stage One**: Exaltation

Christology. This is an evaluation of Jesus that "assigns him the role of a son of Adam at his death and resurrection." "In this view, Jesus became, or was elevated to, son of God by virtue of his resurrection" (Rom. 1:3-4; Acts 2:36). **Stage Two**: Adoptionistic Christology. "The first stage of Christology did not require the creation of a gospel because the words and deed of Jesus were not essential to his function; the real role of Jesus was to return as the messiah in the very near future. When that he did not return immediately as expected, his followers began to review what they remembered of him and decided that his life, after all, had exhibited some unusual traits. Now they started to fashion another version of his story in which he was designated son of God, not at his resurrection but at his baptism." (Mark 1:10-11). **Stage Three**: "The next step came with the gospels of Matthew and Luke, and these gospels "moved the messianic status of Jesus back to his birth." If there was someone who had a noteworthy life, he must have had a noteworthy birth. "If a hero is human, as in the case of John the Baptist, the miracle is that of a barren woman…If the hero is considered superhuman, as in the case of Hercules and Alexander, the male parent is a god." **Stage Four**: "The gospel of John's prologue (1:1-18) makes Jesus pre-existent from the beginning."

Two) We can trace how Jesus was deified by his followers leading ultimately to the Nicean/Chalcedonian view of Christ as a way of expressing the Lordship of Jesus over the gods and goddesses of the Roman Empire. John Hick: "In general it seems that the early Christians, seeking to understand and communicate the significance of their Lord, grasped at concepts and titles within their culture and that the usage of these developed under the pressures of preaching and controversy." [Encountering Jesus, p. 14].

[Three excellent books that deal with this progression of thought in the early centuries: John Dominic Crossan, The Birth of Christianity (Harper, 1998); L. Michael White, From Jesus to Christianity (Harper, 2004); and Paula Fredricksen, From Jesus to Christ, (Yale University Press, 1988)].

Jewish tradition in Jesus' time had three major images of the redeemer who would bring in the coming new and glorious age. One was the "**Messiah**" (Hebrew for "King"), who was to reign in a new kingdom in which Jerusalem would be the center of the world, and where God's will would be done on earth. The second was that of the "**Son of man**" prophesized in Daniel 7:13-14. Hick reminds us that "with a view to the later Christian doctrine of the incarnation, that neither the Messiah nor the Son of man was, in Jewish thinking, divine…it was emphatically not equivalent to being God incarnate." [Encountering Jesus, (pp. 7-9)]. When you think about it, it just couldn't be!

A third image was "**Son of God**," which was common in the ancient world as well as in Biblical literature. Oscar Cullman: "The origin of the 'son of God' concept lies in ancient oriental religions, in which above all kings were thought to be begotten of gods…. In the N.T. period one could meet everywhere men who called themselves 'sons of God' because of their peculiar vocation or miraculous powers." "In the O.T. we find this expression used in three ways: the whole people of Israel is called 'Son of God' (Hosea 11:1); kings bear the title (Ps. 2:7; II Sam. 7:14); persons with a special commission from God, such as angels (Job 1:6; 38:7), and perhaps also the Messiah, are so called." [The Christology of the N.T., (pp. 271-273)]. James D.G. Dunn: "Some of the legendary heroes of

Greek myth were called sons of God," like Dionysus and Heracles, who were sons of Zeus. "Famous philosophers also, like Pythagoras and Plato, were sometimes spoken of as having been begotten by a god (Apollo)." "The language of divine sonship and divinity was in widespread and varied use in the ancient world and would have been familiar to the contemporaries of Jesus, Paul and John in a wide range of application." [Christology in the Making (Westminster Press, 1980), p, 17). For more on these titles see the Anchor Bible Dictionary].

According to Geza Vermes the title, "'Son of God' was always understood metaphorically in Jewish circles. In Jewish sources, its use never implies participation by the person so-named in the divine nature. It may in consequence safely be assumed that if the medium in which Christian theology developed had been Hebrew and not Greek, it would not have produced an incarnation doctrine as this is traditionally understood." [Jesus and the World of Judaism (SCM Press 1983), p. 72.].

But the Apostle Paul seems to be the exception to this Jewish thinking (see Romans 1:3-4; 8:3; I Cor. 15:23-28; Phil. 2:5-11; Gal. 4:4; Col. 1:15-20). In these passages, Hick admits, "his language moves in the direction of deification." But, Hick asks, "the question is, of course: what did this language mean to the writer and his readers in the first century?" Paul's language suggests "the subordination of the son to the father. And in Paul's writings God and God's Son cannot be said to be co-equal, as Persons of the Holy Trinity were later declared to be. The notion of Jesus as God's Son is indeed pre-trinitarian. Paul's carefully stated theological view, in the Epistle to the Romans, seems…to be that Jesus was a man who was raised by God in his resurrection to a special and uniquely important status." [John Hick, The Metaphor of God Incarnate (Westminster, 1993), p. 43)].

Anchor Bible Dictionary, (Paul): "What kind of education Paul may have received growing up in Tarsus (Acts 21:39; 22:3) is entirely a matter of speculation, although as Acts 22:3 presents it, he had an ideal Jewish education: "I am a Jew, born at Tarsus in Cilicia, brought up in this city [Jerusalem or Tarsus?], educated at the feet of Gamaliel, according to the strict manner of the law of our fathers." This claim suggests that Paul's family moved from Tarsus to Jerusalem, where he received his secondary education (26:4). But this claim must be weighed carefully because it corresponds with the tendencies in Acts to emphasize the apostle's regard for his Jewish heritage (13:14ff.; 14:1; 15:23–29; 16:1–3, 4, 13; etc.) and to link him with Jerusalem (7:58–8:1a; 8:1b–3; 9:1–2, 26–29; etc.). This latter tendency, together with Luke's attendant assumption of Paul's familiarity with Jerusalem, clashes with Paul's own testimony about his visits to the city (Gal 1:22). The fact that Paul acted as an international envoy, first on behalf of Jewish authorities (Acts 8:3; 9:1–2, 21; 22:4–5, 19; 26:10–11; Gal 1:13, 23; 1 Cor 15:9; Phil 3:6), then as a Christian missionary, means that he must have received a good Hellenistic education."

We also may rightly wonder about the gospel that Paul was preaching, for he said: *"the gospel that was proclaimed by me is not of human origin; for I did not receive it from a human source, nor was I taught it, but I received it through a revelation of Jesus Christ….when God, who had set me apart before I was born and called me through his grace, was pleased to reveal his Son to me, so that I might proclaim him among the Gentiles, I did not confer with any human being, nor did I go up to Jerusalem to those who were already apostles before me, but I went away at once into Arabia, and afterwards I returned to Damascus. Then after three years I did go up to Jerusalem to visit Cephas and stayed with him fifteen days; but I did not see any other apostle except James the Lord's brother. In what I am writing to you, before God, I do not lie! Then I went into the regions of Syria and Cilicia, and I was still unknown by sight to the churches of Judea that are in Christ...*" (Galatians 1:11-22). He claims he was taught the gospel by a revelation. Did this objectively happen? And if it was only a vision, how can we be sure of the truth of everything he preached? Fifteen days with Cephas, Peter, may not be enough to sort out all of his theological views. They clearly had debates about some things (Galatians 2:11-21; Acts 15), which has led some scholars to see a major divide in the churches between those associated with Paul and those associated with Peter.

Besides, we know that Paul tried to reach people in the Roman Empire who thought it possible that the gods could take up human form. In Acts, when the crowd in Lystra saw how Paul had healed a man, *"they shouted in the Lycaonian language, "The gods have come down to us in human form! Barnabas they called Zeus, and Paul they called Hermes, because he was the chief speaker."* (Acts 14:11-12) In addition, in Acts 28:6, Paul is called a "god" on the island of Malta. Perhaps Paul was using the language that only they could understand when he preached to them about Jesus, since they might only be interested in the gospel of Jesus if he were a god, or a son of God. And didn't Paul say, "I have become all things to all people, that I might by all means save some." (1 Co 9:22). He was an evangelist that sought to communicate to his hearers in ways that they would understand, and he simply wanted them to know of the greatness of Jesus over that of their gods and goddesses.

According to John Hick: "It is not in the least surprising that Jesus, as a spirit-filled prophet, a charismatic healer, perhaps as Messiah, believed to be of the royal line of David, should have been thought of and should have thought of himself as, in this familiar metaphorical sense, a son of God. What happened, as the gospel went out beyond the Hebraic milieu into the Greek-dominated intellectual world of the Roman Empire, was that the metaphorical son of God was transformed into the metaphysical God the Son." [Encountering Jesus, (p. 14)]. Pannenberg: "At first the 'Son of God' concept did not express a participation in the divine essence....Only in Gentile Christianity was the divine Sonship understood physically as participation in the divine essence." [Jesus— God and Man (p. 117)]. The progression of this train of thought led up to the very strong affirmation of Nicene/Chalcedonian Christology of the 4th–5th centuries. John Hick: "It could well be that its deification of Jesus helped the early Christian community to survive its period of intermittent persecutions and that subsequently, if the church was to be the spiritual, moral, and cultural director of the Roman Empire, and thus of Western civilization, it needed the prestige of a founder who was none other than God, in the person of the eternal Son." [in Encountering Jesus].

Three) The belief that Jesus was fully man and fully God has never been shown to be consistently defined, explained or defended. The Council of Chalcedon (451 A.D.) finally defined the orthodox doctrine of the incarnation. The problem is that the council "merely asserted that Jesus was 'truly God and truly man' without attempting to say how such a paradox is possible." "Merely to assert that two different natures coexisted in Jesus 'without confusion, without change, without division, without separation' is to utter a form of words which as yet has no specific meaning." [John Hick, The Metaphor of God Incarnate, p. 48]. Many attempts before and after Chalcedon were made, but "they all failed," from Docetism, Adoptionism, Apollinarianism, Nestorianism, Arianism, and Monophysitism.

Here then are four conceptual problems with an incarnate God, that is, how can one person be truly and fully God, and at the same time truly and fully a man: 1) God is necessarily an uncreated being. Humans are essentially created beings. Therefore Jesus is both created and uncreated; 2) God is necessarily omniscient—he knows everything. Human beings are not omniscient beings. Therefore, Jesus is both an omniscient and also not an omniscient being. But in the New Testament Jesus didn't act omniscient. He said he didn't know the time of his own return; 3) God is a morally perfect being, and as such could not be tempted to do wrong. Human beings however, can be tempted to do wrong, and are imperfect. Therefore, Jesus could not be tempted, nor do any wrong, and yet we're told that he was tempted to do wrong. 4) God is omnipresent, but Jesus as a human being, was not.

Thomas Morris' Theory of Two Minds.

One modern attempt has been made by Thomas Morris, in The Logic of God Incarnate (Cornwell Univ. Press, 1986), in which he defends the proposition that "Jesus of Nazareth was one and the same person as God the Son, the second person of the Trinity." (p. 13). Initially, such a view raises certain questions. Christians like Morris have three successive periods and persons to reconcile with each other: 1) The 2nd Person of the Trinity who existed before time; 2) Jesus, who is God-in-the-flesh; a unique and new being; and, 3) The resurrected and glorified Jesus "sitting at the right hand of God."

Now keep in mind that Jesus was a fully human being, so any resurrected Jesus must have a body in keeping with his humanity, otherwise he ceased to exist, died, or his humanity was simply discarded. But that cannot be, that God would destroy a sinless man, the man Jesus. Therefore, the resurrected Jesus, being a God-man, is a new and unique being, and this dual natured being is unlike the previous 2nd person of the Trinity. So, did God's nature change? When I asked about this problem of the glorified Jesus, my former professor, Dr. Ron Feenstra, had no trouble accepting the conclusion that the 2nd person of the Trinity took on a human form and now must keep it for all of eternity. [He edited, along with Cornelius Plantinga, Jr., Trinity, Incarnation, and Atonement (Univ. of Notre Dame Press, 1989)]. I just find this whole thing troublesome and implausible, even if it may not be logically contradictory. If the human nature of Jesus is forever linked to the 2nd Person of the Trinity, then the full Trinity now includes a man, that is, the human side of Jesus, the man. In heaven the 2nd Person of the Trinity must now forever live encapsulated within a human body (a glorious body, nonetheless, but a body). Now we have an embodied God—forever! We now have a God who chooses to live within the body of his own creation. This is believed, even though Jesus himself says that God is a spirit (John 4:24). This whole thing seems contrived and is the result of believing that Jesus was fully God and fully man.

The other possibility is that after the resurrection and ascension events of Jesus, there are now two beings rather than one. In heaven there is the human

Jesus, and then there is the 2nd person of the Trinity. There are now two beings who exist and arose out of one being, one person, here on earth. That is, the 2nd person of the Trinity discarded his human form to live for the rest of eternity unhindered, letting the human part of him to exist as a separate person in heaven with him. But incoherence sets in at this point, because the Chalcedon creed speaks of their being a "union" such that the result is "but one and the same Son and Only-begotten God the Word, Lord Jesus Christ." How can such a metaphysical union be separated into two beings? The traditional orthodox doctrine is that Jesus is one person!

But this union is exactly what Morris is trying to defend. To do this he proposes a two-minds theory: "In the case of God Incarnate, we must recognize something like two distinct ranges of consciousness. There is first what we can call the eternal mind of God the Son with its distinctively divine consciousness... And in addition there is a distinctively earthly consciousness that came into existence and grew and developed as the boy Jesus grew and developed." (p. 102). In this way the second person of the trinity could know what was going on in both the conscious and unconscious mind of Jesus although Jesus could be totally unaware that he is even there. [Paul Copan also claims Jesus had "two consciousnesses," in "That's Just Your Interpretation (Baker, 2001), pp. 127-137].

Morris has some major difficulties when he tries to work out this theory involving two minds, even though he uses the results of modern psychology. In the first place, if there are two separate minds, each with its own separate consciousness, then the first question is this: Was the earthly Jesus conscious of the second person of the trinity, or not? If not, then this might describe any human being, and God may be incarnate in them too. If so, then why didn't he exhibit the attributes of deity, like omniscience (Mt. 24:36, Lk. 8:45-46), and omnipotence (Mt. 14:3-13; 26:53)? Stephen T. Davis, answers, "At any point in his earthly ministry, I suspect, Jesus could have called on his omniscience (or omnipotence, for that matter), but had he done so, it would have been tantamount to his no longer being truly human." [Logic and the Nature of God (Eerdmans, 1983), p. 126]. If Jesus had a divine consciousness, then the question can be reformulated: how does having a divine consciousness make him "just like us" as human beings? Doesn't having divine consciousness eliminate the possibility that he was fully human?

When it comes to a unitary "one will" of one person, Morris has additional problems. How can one person have two minds but one will? Does the "divine will" over-ride the "human will"? Jesus himself said that human beings could sin in their thoughts alone (Matt. 5:22,28). Was Jesus able to fully act as a human being, or was his will to sin always restrained? Morris suggests that Jesus had free will, but that if he ever acted to sin the second person of the trinity would have stopped him from doing so. If Jesus' will was restrained in this way, then was Jesus truly like us in that we have the freedom to do what we want? Being restrained from sinning is not praiseworthy at all, because being praiseworthy demands that we acted on our own accord and we thought and did good things, not bad things. But apparently Jesus couldn't totally act freely, so there's nothing praiseworthy about what he thought and did as a human being.

We're told that Jesus was temped (Matt. 4:1; Heb, 4:15). To be temped would entail having thoughts about sinning. One cannot be tempted to do something if there is no desire to do it. If someone tries to temp me to rob a bank, it cannot be done, because I do not have that desire, and never will. This is no temptation for me at all. Theologians have been trying to make sense of this whole idea of the distinction between temptation and the sinful thoughts that Jesus condemns, I think unsuccessfully. But since Jesus was tempted to sin there seems to be some small imperfections in him, since to be tempted means to have desires that do not accord with the nature of God. John Hick: "Even unfulfilled beginnings of evil must themselves count as imperfections; for in order for the divine mind to overrule them there must have been something there that required to be overruled." [1) Jesus exhibited what we'd now call a racist attitude toward a woman (Mark 7:27); 2) Jesus said, "Why do you call me good? No one is good but God alone" (Mark 10:18); 3) he didn't respect his parents like the law would demand (Mark 3:31-5; Luke 14:26), and 4) he used violence in the temple when he cast out the money changers (Matt. 21:12)].

Paul Copan understands the seriousness of this problem, but to solve it he introduces an *ad hoc* theory. Without any Biblical support, he claims Jesus was voluntarily ignorant of the fact that "he was necessarily good," and as such he really was tempted to sin but couldn't, because of his divine nature. ["That's Just Your Interpretation," (2001), pp. 138-143]. Yet, how could Jesus be divine and still lack the recognition that as a divine being, he was necessarily good? Copan answers by saying this is the same problem with how Jesus could know he was divine and yet not know the time of his purported second coming (Matt. 24:36). This doesn't solve either problem. One bad analogy doesn't solve another one.

"What we are left with is…God incarnate in the sense that God singled the human Jesus out for a special role—namely by not allowing him to go wrong. It follows that if God, in addition to being omnisciently aware of the full contents of someone's mind, were to prevent her from making any wrong choices, that person would be another instance of God incarnate." "Those who talked with Jesus were talking to a man whom God the Son was invisibly monitoring and preventing from going astray." This, according to Hick, is the specific problem "that proved fatal for Morris' theory: was Jesus free to commit sin?" [The Metaphor of God Incarnate, p, 58, 60); See also Michael Martin's full critique of Morris' theory in The Case Against Christianity (Temple, 1991), pp.125-161].

Divine Kenosis Theories.

According to Clark Pinnock, "Kenotic Theory is, I think, the most important fresh contribution to Christology since the early centuries." [Theological Crossfire: An Evangelical/Liberal Dialogue (with Delwin Brown) Zondervan, 1990), p. 146.]. This idea comes from Philippians 2:5-11, and claims that the second person of the trinity laid aside his non-essential attributes in order to be a man, like omniscience. It was first proposed by Lutheran theologian Gottfried Thomasius. Thomasius proposed that the metaphysical attributes of the second person of the trinity were temporarily laid aside in the incarnation and the moral attributes were retained, so that Jesus' attributes were divine goodness, love and justice, but not omnipotence and omniscience. Then, what room is there left for God? And how can Jesus be God, according to the Chalcedon Council, without the attributes of God?

According to John Hick, when these Kenotic theologians "come to the apparent contradiction of a being who is God and yet lacks the attributes of God, all that they can do is offer analogies which fail to reach the key issue, and then they appeal to mystery." [The Metaphor of God Incarnate, (p. 62)]. Take for instance Stephen T. Davis, who claims, "If Jesus was God; and if Jesus was non-omnipotent; then being omnipotent is not essential to God." [Logic and the Nature of God (Eerdmans, 1983), p. 72]. And the same is said for his other divine attributes. But after emptying the divine nature of so much, Davis is just left with the properties of "being divine," "being self-identical," and "existing." John Hick argues that, "Existing and being self-identical must indeed be properties of anything that exists, including God." So the only other property is divine existence. But without some characteristics or properties of what it means to have divine existence we are left with nothing specific. Hick: "Thus in making space for divine incarnation, Davis has had to reject much of the traditional Christian understanding of God." [Metaphor, p. 73]. Davis senses the problems of his view and says: "Of course we cannot use kenosis (or any other theory) to remove the mystery of the classical doctrine." Davis continues, "As Brian Hebblethwaite said, 'incarnation is a baffling act of a being whose essence we will never fully understand; it is highly unlikely, therefore, that we will ever completely grasp the incarnation.'" [Encountering Jesus: A Debate On Christology (John Knox Press, 1988, p. 53.]

I had a master's class with William Lane Craig called the "Concept of God." In this class, we read and discussed Stephen T. Davis' book, Logic and the Nature of God (Eerdmans, 1983), very thoroughly. It was a good book for discussion since there was so much room for it. I remember the analogy that Dr. Craig proposed to help solve the problem of the incarnation at the time. He drew a square, and then he drew a circle next to it that connected with the square at one corner. He proposed to suggest that the square would represent the attributes of a man, and a circle would represent the attributes of God. The point at which they touch each other is the person of Jesus Christ. But what does this analogy show? Not much as far as I can tell at this point. Because the question is still begged as to how many properties God can lose and still be God, and how many properties a man can gain and still be a man.

P.T. Forsyth is quoted as saying, "We cannot form any scientific conception of the precise process by which a complete and eternal being could enter on a process of becoming, how Godhood could accept growth, how a divine consciousness could reduce its own consciousness by volition. [The Person and Place of Jesus Christ (Hodder, 1910), pp, 293-295].

E. P. Sanders, in The Historical Figure of Jesus, sums it up: "**It lies beyond my meager abilities as an interpreter of dogmatic theology to explain how it is possible for one person to be 100 per cent human and 100 per cent divine, without either interfering with the other.**" (p. 134).

It would seem much more likely to me, given these serious intellectual problems in understanding the incarnation that it should simply be rejected. It is based upon historical claims, and as we've seen, history is subject to all kinds of differing interpretations. But if we try to make sense of these historical claims and simply cannot do it, then it's high time we reject those claims.

18 "The Passion of The Christ": Why Did Jesus Suffer?

The major atonement theory among evangelical Christians is the Reformer's **Penal Substitutionary Theory**, which dominates in the conservative churches.

This theory hasn't always been the one Christians adopted from the Biblical texts. The earliest attempt to conceptualize what Jesus did for the world on the cross was first advanced by Irenaeus and developed by Origen. Based upon Mark 10:45, it is called the **Ransom Theory**. According to this theory, human beings fell under the jurisdiction of Satan when we fell into sin, and Jesus' death paid the ransom for our release. John Hick comments: "Ransom had a poignant meaning in the ancient world, when a considerable proportion of the population lived in the state of slavery...Being ransomed, and thus made free, was accordingly a vivid and powerful metaphor whose force most of us can only partially recapture today. [The Metaphor of God Incarnate (Westminster, 1993), p. 114)]. And such a version of the atonement stood for roughly nine hundred years as the generally accepted one.

St. Anselm set forth another theory in a different social climate for the people of his day in the 11th century. Of the Ransom theory, he asked why anyone should believe that the Devil has any valid legal rights over the infinite Creator God to demand a ransom in the first place? Anselm then proceeded to argue for a **Satisfaction Atonement Theory**. According to Anselm, our sins are an insult to God and detract from his honor. Therefore God's honor must be restored and the insult must be undone, but only through the death of the God-Man can God's honor be restored and satisfaction be made, since the satisfaction must be in proportion to the amount of sin, and the amount of sin is infinite.

According to John Hick, Anselm's theory "made sense within the culture of medieval Europe," in that it reflected "a strongly hierarchical and tightly knit society." (p. 117). The whole idea of satisfaction "had long operated in both church and society." "The idea of disobedience, whether to God or to one's feudal lord, was a slight upon his honour and dignity, and required for its cancellation an appropriate penance of gift in satisfaction." "When one did something to undermine the dignity and authority of one's earthly overlord, one had either to be punished or to give sufficient satisfaction to appease the lord's injured dignity." (p. 117). John Hick offers a very brief critique of this view with these words: "In our own more democratic age it is virtually impossible to share Anselm's medieval sense of wrongdoing...The entire conception, presupposing as it does a long-since vanished social order, now makes little sense to us." (p. 118). Leon Morris writes: "In the end Anselm makes God too much like a king whose dignity has been affronted. He overlooked the fact that a sovereign may be clement and forgiving without doing harm to his kingdom." [Evangelical Dictionary of Theology, ed. Walter A. Elwell, (Baker Books, 1984), "Atonement," p. 101]. Michael Martin adds, that "the very idea of God's pride being so wounded and demanding such satisfaction that the voluntary sacrifice of his innocent son is required, assumes a view of God's moral nature that many modern readers would reject." [The Case Against Christianity (Temple, 1991), p.256].

In the sixteenth century, the Reformers introduced the **Penal Substitutionary Theory**, which still holds sway in conservative Christian circles. The Reformers used Paul's understanding of justification as their Biblical backdrop, but according to Hick, they understood Paul "in a legal sense":

> "The concept of justification, and hence of salvation as being counted innocent in the eyes of God, emerged from the background of an understanding of law that had changed since Anselm's time. In the medieval world, law was an expression of the will of the ruler, and transgression was an act of personal disobedience and dishonour for which either punishment or satisfaction was required. But the concept of an objective justice, set over ruled and ruler alike, had been developing in Europe since the Renaissance. Law was now thought to have it own eternal validity, requiring a punishment for wrongdoing which could not be set aside even by the ruler. It was this new principle that the Reformers applied and extended in their doctrine that Christ took our place in bearing the inexorable penalty for human sin—a powerful imagery that has long gripped the Christian imagination." ([John Hick, p. 118-119).

A General Critique of These Earlier Theories.

What I say here will apply in various ways to these theories. If Jesus suffered in my place so that I can go to heaven rather than hell, then apart from Jesus' suffering I should be punished for my sins by being sent to hell when I die. But what has any one of us ever done to deserve the kind of punishment Jesus suffered, much less to deserve hell itself? All through my entire life I have never met, nor even heard of one person, who deserved such a punishment. Never.

In our modern society we punish people in a humane way. We don't flog them or crucify them or put them on the rack, or in stocks, nor do we brand them or tar and feather them for public disgrace. These are things only the most bloodthirsty people would do to their enemies. We put them in jail to keep them from hurting more people, and we do so to deter others from a life of crime. Then there is the motive of simple retaliation--retribution. Some are arguing that such a motive is unethical and unbecoming of a humane society, especially when it comes to capital punishment. Now my point here is to ask which motive is it that God has which makes him a just God when he punishes us, if in fact we deserve it? And how do his methods of punishment compare with our more humane ones? Most all of us wouldn't want our worst enemies to suffer as Jesus did. Even those of us who believe in capital punishment would still want it done humanely.

To say that my sins are an infinite wrong because they are committed against an infinite God, and thus demand an infinite punishment, seems mistaken for several reasons.

In the first place, does justice really demand this much punishment? Can it really be true that justice demands I suffer for all eternity in hell for one little white lie? Who creates the demands of justice, anyway? What judge would think this is a fair punishment? What picture of God lays behind this view of justice... a caring father, or an aloof vengeful medieval potentate? Jesus describes God as the former, a caring father. We see this in the Lord's Prayer (Matt. 6:9-15), and the Parable of the Prodigal Son (Luke 15:11-32), where no one pays any penalty for their sins--they merely have to ask for forgiveness. Asking forgiveness was all a Pharisee had to do to (Luke 18:13-14). Jesus himself said, "I desire mercy, and not sacrifice." (Matt. 9:13).

Secondly, if God became incarnate to relate to us, then why can't he also see what sin is from our perspective, as a finite offense from partly good and partly bad human beings? We intend no infinite wrong against God when we sin. God should know this, especially since it's claimed he related to us by being one of us. To claim otherwise makes God's justice misguided and inappropriate.

Thirdly, did Jesus really suffer an infinite punishment for our sins? If Jesus was merely being punished for all of the wrongdoing of every person who ever lived on earth based on human standards of punishment and not infinite standards, we'd still have to ask whether he was punished enough. After all, if every person who ever lived deserved to be slapped in the face just one time, then the equivalent of 10 billion slaps would surely amount to more punishment than Jesus physically endured. But if it's true to say that each and every one of us deserved an infinite punishment for our sins, then how much less is it true to say Jesus suffered infinitely for each one of us? More to the point, if we were given a choice to suffer as Jesus did or else be cast in hell for eternity (which would be our infinite punishment); we would all choose to suffer as Jesus did. Jesus didn't suffer forever, nor did he stay dead.

But it is said that Jesus endured more than just physical pain. He also endured the pain of being separated from God. How can we make sense of this claim? If it's merely a metaphor for the mental pain of not sensing God's help when we need it, then we have all felt that pain throughout our lives. Otherwise, it must somehow mean Jesus ceased to be God while on the cross. However, Christians cannot believe that. Because if Jesus in fact ceased to be God, then since Christians believe a Triune God exists, that means God also ceased to exist when Jesus ceased to be God.

In the fourth place, in order for someone to be forgiven why must there be punishment at all? We know of victims who have forgiven their assailants even though they have never been punished, and we know of other victims who won't forgive their assailants even after they have been punished. To forgive someone doesn't mean that you must first punish the offender at all. Forgiveness doesn't really depend upon the remorse of the offender, either, although it does help quite a bit. At this point it's not up to the offender at all, but the victim who must find a way to forgive. To forgive means bearing the suffering of what that person has done to you without retaliation. If I stole something from you, then forgiveness means bearing the loss without recompense. If I slandered you, forgiving means bearing the humiliation without retaliating. If the cross of Christ means someone got punished for my sins, then that's not offering forgiveness, that's punishing someone for what I did wrong.

If the cross was needed to pay the punishment for my sins, then how can God really be a forgiving God? Forgiveness doesn't require punishment. To put it bluntly, if I can't forgive you for striking me on the chin until I return the blow back to you, or to someone else, then that's not forgiveness, that's retaliation, or sweet revenge! Revenge is never an ethical motive for action, even if we are led to take revenge on others sometimes. John Hick again: """A forgiveness that has to be bought by the bearing of a just punishment…is not forgiveness, but merely and acknowledgment that the debt has been paid in full." (p. 127).

Fifthly, even if punishment is needed, which I seriously question, then how does punishing Jesus help God forgive us? This Christian theory says God himself bore our punishment on the cross in Jesus. But why is any additional punishment even demanded? The punishment borne by the one who forgives is merely the pain that was inflicted by the offender. That is, if I humiliate God in front of the universe by being self-seeking in all of my ways, then in order to forgive me God merely has to bear the pain of that humiliation and open his arms toward me. There would be no additional pain to bear beyond the pain of being humiliated. There would be no need for the cross until it can be shown, based on this atonement theory, that there is a relationship between punishment (or justice) and forgiveness.

The divine way to forgive us when we sin against him is to turn around and punish his Son? If you see me along the roadway and beat me to a pulp, the divine way to forgive you is to turn around and beat myself up all over again, or my son? This is because "someone's got to pay," and a loving divine guy like myself just shouldn't beat you up in retaliation? It doesn't make any rational sense at all. There's no reason for additional punishment especially to an innocent person like Jesus.

Furthermore, if we die outside of faith in Jesus what kinds of reasons would God have for punishing us when we die? Maybe God punishes us when we die to deter others from doing wrong? But then why is it we don't see any evidence of this punishment while we're still alive? Maybe God punishes us in order to teach us to do better, like a father who corrects a child? How can this be, since hell would be final and horrible? Maybe God punishes us because he is angry with us? That doesn't seem to fit either. If God foreknows everything we do, or, rather, if he knows every background experience and genetic makeup that goes into every decision we make, then we can never surprise him by what we do. I have found that the more I understand someone's background, the easier it is for me to love and have sympathy for that person. By the same reasoning do you think God can ever get angry with us enough to punish us with hell? How can he? What judge would do this? What father would do this? He understands everything about us. But what other motives are there for God to punish us when we die? If there are none, then our only punishment is what we do to ourselves here and now. When we do wrong we hurt ourselves. God doesn't need to punish us. By sinning we punish ourselves.

If, however, being sent to hell is not about punishment for our sins, but rather about God not tolerating sin in his presence, then exactly where does sin reside in us? Can it be located somewhere in our bodies and seen by an X-ray machine, or does it somehow make an actual black mark on our soul? The truth is that sin isn't an existing thing at all, nor is sin something we have. We cannot hold a cupful of sin in our hands. Sin is an action we do. Once we do it, sin becomes a memory of a hurtful deed done. We don't carry sin on us; we do sinful things. So there is no sin to bring with us into God's presence.

In a sermon delivered by Tom Smith, Pastor of the *Presbyterian Chapel of the Lakes*, Angola, Indiana, he said, "for some strange reason God believed the cross was necessary for our salvation." See him struggle with this? There must be a reason why Jesus died on the cross. But what is it? John Hick: "The idea that guilt can be removed from a wrongdoer by someone else being punished instead is morally grotesque." (p. 119). Bishop John Shelby Spong wrote: "I, for example, do not believe in a God who willed Jesus to suffer for my sins. I do not believe in a God whose inner need for justice is satisfied when his son is nailed to a cross. I regard the substitutionary version of the atonement as a barbaric attack on both the truth of God and the meaning of human life." [Rescuing the Bible From Fundamentalism (Harper, 1991, p. 69)].

Richard Swinburne's Relationship Theory.

Richard Swinburne has recently produced a somewhat different atonement theory based upon a modern understanding of relationships between people. [Responsibility and Atonement (Clarendon Press, 1989]. According to him, there is a fourfold way to restore a relationship when we damage it. We must repent, apologize, offer reparations, and do penance. This, he claims, is what we must do when we damage our relationship to God, and the same general conditions for reconciliation apply. Swinburne argues we cannot offer adequate reparations and do adequate penance for our sins, since that would require living a "perfect human life" (p. 157). That perfect human life was provided by Jesus who subsequently voluntarily endured a death, which he intended as a sacrifice, that we can now offer to God as our required reparations and penance. (p. 154).

John Hick claims Swinburne's theory "strikes me as anthropomorphic, parochial and unimaginative to a degree that renders it massively implausible." (p. 121). Some of the same criticisms mentioned earlier still apply to this theory, because now the words "reparation" and "penance" are used rather than "punishment." Why, for instance, do my sins require this much penance or reparations in the torture and death of Jesus on the cross? Swinburne still must circumvent the whole idea of the gruesome nature of the reparations Jesus offered for us, since we live in a more humane modern society in the way we deal with offenders.

John Hick argues correctly that Swinburne cannot take this fourfold way to restore human relationships and carry it over "unchanged into our relationship with God." This is Swinburne's "fundamental error." (p. 122).

"The idea that something further, corresponding to this repentance-plus-penance towards our human neighbour, is required by God for Godself, seems to me groundless. It rests upon a category mistake in which God is treated as another individual within the same moral community as ourselves. For a moral relationship with another person presupposes the possibility of actions that can benefit or injure that other person; but we cannot benefit or injure our creator over and above our actions in benefiting and injuring our fellow creatures." (p. 123).

Even if "a benefit solely to God were possible and required," Hick argues that "a perfect human life would constitute it is, surely, illogical." For a perfect human life is already owed to God by all of us, according to Swinburne, and "therefore could not constitute a reparation-plus-penance for not having lived a perfect life in the past." But even if this were possible, "how would one single perfect human life, namely that of Jesus, count as all human beings having led perfect lives?" (p. 123). Swinburne's answer to this problem is morally repugnant, for he says, "God could have chosen one supererogatory act of an ordinary man as adequate for the sins of the world. Or he could have chosen to accept some angel's act for this purpose." (Swinburne, p. 160). If this is so, then Jesus suffered an agonizing death when other ways to accomplish the same results were available. The cross of Jesus was not required? But if the cross wasn't required, and other less morally grotesque ways of restoring us to him were available, it makes God's character morally repulsive.

Even though I have not considered all of the atonement theories here, none of the ones we've considered actually makes sense of the supposed atonement offered to God on our behalf, in Jesus. And given nearly two millennia of theological discussions, I'd venture to say there will never be a cogent well argued theory that can ever pass muster in the future either. I think the whole idea of Jesus dying for my sins to restore me to God is built upon the beliefs of a superstitious ancient world, where gods and goddesses were pleased with sacrifices, whether they were human or animal ones. This ancient world is long gone now, and it's time to give up believing in an incarnate God who offered a sacrifice for us on the cross to atone for our sins. [For a critique of this and other atonement theories, see Michael Martin, The Case Against Christianity (Temple, 1991), pp. 252-263].

19 Did Jesus Bodily Rise From the Dead?

Let's say you meet a sincere, well-dressed friendly man who seems to enjoy life very much, who's very intelligent, very caring, and very religious. After being convinced of his sincerity, he proceeds to tell you the following story:

"I am a missionary/disciple from Iran. For the past few years I have been a follower of the life and teachings of a man named Achmed, who was born of a virgin, preached a message of love and forgiveness to Muslims, and did many miracles. But Achmed was tortured and then killed by the authorities for sedition." This missionary had been a former persecutor of Achmed's followers and claims to have a vision/revelation/encounter that Achmed was truly a resurrected Son of God. Before leaving Iran he himself was subject to persecution too. But he swears that Achmed arose from the dead and now has ascended into heaven to be with his Father-God and Jesus Christ, as an incarnation of the 3rd person of the Trinity. He tells you that "the 3rd person of the Trinity, Achmed, died for the sins of those who have never personally heard the gospel of Jesus.

God decided to take world evangelism in his own hands because the message of the gospel was not getting out like it should, and too many people were being damned to hell. The only people who now will ever receive punishment in hell will be those who personally heard the gospel and obstinately rejected it." This missionary friend came to America because there are many such people to evangelize who have heard the gospel but rejected it. Those who have never heard will now be saved, so he doesn't need to reach them. He would use double-fulfillment type prophetic statements in the Bible to show that Achmed fulfilled the same passages that Jesus did, and he would use a lot of allegory, "pesher" and "midrash" type interpretations, like the N.T writers did to show that Achmed was the Son of God, too. And although the Bible says Jesus was a final revelation to man, "it was meant to the people in his day, not to people in our day," he says. And Achmed did some miracles to back up his claims. The evidence for Achmed's resurrection would be the same, except that you couldn't check any of the facts out yourself.

Now there are no pictures of Achmed, nor any video, either. Just this man's word. And you cannot check out his story, either, since you cannot go there, because Iranian authorities won't allow it.

You would be in the same position as most all of the Roman world who listened to Paul, because like you, they could not check out such a story either. But they believed it. Would you? What would it take for you to believe it? How open would you be to considering it? Pretty skeptical, eh? Why? Because you are a modern person, as opposed to an ancient superstitious person. You might even share some of the same world-view assumptions of this missionary friend, and yet you would still be skeptical.

Today we can check some of the story of the resurrected Jesus out, but not all of it, because we are separated in history by two thousand years. I am skeptical of the Christian claim, just as you would be skeptical of the story Achmed's disciple told you. Neither story fits with the other things you believe, so you begin by being skeptical, both you and I, each from our different perspectives.

What if this missionary told you to have an open mind, "don't be skeptical, but believe," or "pray this prayer with faith and you'll know for sure." Then you'd feel just like I do when Christians approach me that way. The truth is we should approach such stories with a large measure of skepticism. I'll say it this way: **in order for me to believe that a miracle happened in the past (or present) then the evidence should be such that it "requires" a supernatural intervention.** Anything less than that would render my critical thinking faculties null and void.

If there is doubt in some small measure, then I can reasonably reject such an event as miraculous. So this burden of proof is on the Christian, just like the burden of proof is on the hypothetical missionary friend mentioned above. I don't think requiring Christians to have the burden of proof is unreasonable at all here. After all, a miracle would be such a rare event; it would have to have some overwhelming evidence on its behalf for reasonable people to believe it. So if the case I present here is faulty by a 20% to 80% ratio in the minds of the readers, then I still win, because it will take a higher percentage than that to win this debate. The evidence for such a miracle must be simply overwhelming. [On this point see Michael Martin, "The Resurrection as Initially Improbable" in The Empty Tomb: Jesus Beyond the Grave, eds. Robert M. Price & Jeffery Jay Lowder (Prometheus Books, 2005), pp. 43-54)].

I'm not looking for certainty, either. But if there is just a 50-50 chance, or even 70-30 chance that Jesus rose from the dead when I have many other problems with miraculous claims and the inherent problems with Christianity, should this be enough to convince reasonable people? NO! It must be an overwhelming case, not unlike our skepticism regarding Achmed. If, for instance, Christians thought there was a 70-30 chance that Jesus was going to return this week, would that be enough for them to sell everything give to the poor in hopes of converting them, and to wait on a mountain top for him? No? 80-20? It would have to be an overwhelming case, wouldn't it?

Since there are many world-wide claims of miracles, and since not all of them can be true, we should be skeptical of them all, until they are proven correct. If you approach a purported miraculous claim with gullible faith to start with, then you will more than likely end up believing it. The question I would have is this: "What reasons do you have for approaching one purported miraculous claim with faith, and another with skepticism?" Usually, what we approach something with will more than likely end up influencing our final conclusion. It's sort of a catch-22 for us, and yet I have reasons for starting with doubt. Christians do the same thing with regard to other miracle claims. It's just that I am much more consistent than they are, because I treat all purported miraculous claims the same.

What If You Went Back in Time? Let's say that you lived in the time of Jesus and you heard him preach, but you went away totally unconvinced that he was the Messiah for various reasons, including the fact that you believed the Messiah was someone who would throw off Roman rule. Then you learn he was crucified. Later you talk to someone who claims he had risen from the dead, and that several people had seen him too. Would you believe? What if someone showed you an empty tomb and said he was buried here and now he's gone? What if you heard reports that these same people were performing miracles in the name of a risen Jesus to show that he gave them this power from on high (Acts 3, 5:12)? As a modern person, as opposed to an ancient superstitious person, would this be enough to convince you, even if we hypothetically grant for a moment that this was the evidence back then? You know of many reports of miracles by Oral Roberts, and assertions by psychics. Do you believe them? There are religious leaders like Joseph Smith who claimed the angel Moroni visited him, and Sun Myung Moon, whose followers believe he is the Messiah. Do you believe them? The curious fact is that while the book of Acts says many people believed, most people in Jesus' day did not. With rare exceptions, there is no record that Pilate nor his soldiers, Caiaphas nor the Sanhedrin, King Herod nor his court, nor the mob that yelled, "crucify him" were converted to Christianity because of the weight of evidence for his resurrection. Even King Herod and some others were easily convinced that someone could come back from the dead: "At that time Herod the ruler heard reports about Jesus; and he said to his servants, 'This is John the Baptist; he has been raised from the dead.'" (Mt 14:1, Mark 16:14-16)). However, there's no record Herod believed that Jesus himself resurrected, and the gospels would surely point that out, if he did. Why didn't the evidence of this miracle convince most people in Jesus' day, even ancient people who were very superstitious, but that two millennia later the evidence is supposed to convince us?

We do know that according to the New Testament there were other purported miracle/magic/sorcery workers in Jesus and Paul's day (Mark 9:38-39; Acts 8:9; 19:13-14; 19:19). It just wasn't as difficult to believe in miracles for them back then, as it is for us today. According to Richard Carrier, "It is crucial to understand how different the situation was in the first century, in comparison with what we take for granted today. Skeptics and informed or critical minds were a small minority in the ancient world. Superstition and credulity ruled the day. Though the gullible, the credulous, and those ready to believe or exaggerate anything are still abundant, they were far more common in antiquity and taken far more seriously. We are talking about an age of fable and wonder, where magic, miracles, ghosts, and gods were everywhere and almost never doubted." Besides all of this, Carrier asks, "how would a myth be exploded in antiquity? They had no newspapers, telephones, photographs, or access to public documents to consult to check a story. There were no reporters, coroners, forensic scientists, or even detectives. If someone was not a witness, all people had was a man's word, and they would most likely base their judgment not on anything we would call evidence, but on the display of sincerity by the storyteller, by his ability to persuade, and impress them with a show, by the potential rewards his story had to offer, and by his 'sounding right' to them." "In times like these, legends had it easy." ["The Spiritual Body of Christ," in The Empty Tomb, edited by Jeffery Jay Lowder and Robert M. Price, (pp. 171-72), see also, http://www.infidels.org/library/modern/richard_carrier/resurrection].

The Biblical Record. In order to overcome our modern day inclination not to believe in miracles the evidence for the resurrection of Jesus must be extremely strong. Michael Martin (in The Case Against Christianity, (Temple Univ. Press, 1991, p.77) lays down five factors that would affect the reliability and strength of the evidence. "First, if various accounts of an event are consistent, this would tend to increase their evidential weight whereas inconsistencies would tend to lower it." "Second, eyewitness accounts are generally more reliable than accounts that are second or third hand." "Third, if the eye-witnesses to some event are known to be reliable and trustworthy, this should increase their evidential worth." "Fourth, independent testimony that is in agreement should tend to increase our confidence of its reliability; failure of independent confirmation should lower our confidence." "Finally, if an author's purpose in writing a document leads us to believe that the document was not a reliable historical account, then this would lower the evidential weight of the document." This is fair enough of a challenge.

1) Do we have eyewitness accounts? We don't have any eyewitnesses to the actual resurrection itself. According to Willi Marxsen in Jesus and Easter: Did God Raise the Historical Jesus from the Dead? (Abingdon Press, 1990), "There were no eyewitnesses to this event. We do not know anyone in the earliest church who claimed, 'I was there when the dead Jesus came to life.'" (p. 41). What we actually have are N.T. writings that were composed anywhere from 50 A.D. to 100 A.D. None of them were there when Jesus was first seen for them to know precisely what took place, and only does the gospel of John claim John ran to the empty tomb (with Peter). The only eyewitness account we have of a post resurrection appearance of Jesus is from Paul.

According to Keith Parsons, "what we have are, at best, second-, third-, or fourth-hand reports of those experiences as recounted in the Gospels. There is no reason to think that the Gospel records are particularly reliable. On the contrary, how much confidence can we have in documents (1) written by persons unknown, (2) composed forty or more years after the events they purport to describe, (3) based on oral traditions, (4) containing many undeniably fictional elements (5) each with a clear theological bias and apologetical agenda, (6) contradicting many known facts, (7) inconsistent with each other, (8) with very little corroboration from non-Christian sources, (9) testifying to occurrences which, in any other context, would be regarded as unlikely in the extreme." [The Empty Tomb, (p. 439); in footnote # 19 he documents each one of these claims].

All of the gospel writers including Paul spoke of post resurrection appearances of Jesus, except for Mark. But this is very significant! In Mark's Gospel "there was the stunning absence of the risen Lord. Mark's Gospel recorded no picture or vision of the risen Christ. Once the stone had sealed the tomb, in Mark's story, Jesus was never again seen by human eyes. The women who were visiting the tomb were told that Jesus had been raised, but that risen presence was simply not available to them." Bishop John Shelby Spong, Resurrection: Myth or Reality? (Harper, 1994, Pp. 60-61) This is very significant because most all scholars consider Mark's gospel to be written first, and that Matthew and Luke used his gospel when writing their accounts. And on a conservative account, Mark stopped writing at verse eight. At that point the women who went to the tomb didn't see the risen Jesus, and when they left they told no one about what they had seen, because they were afraid.

Those who heard the stories of Jesus' resurrection didn't initially believe them (Luke 24:11), including "doubting" Thomas (John 20:24-29). By them we are led to believe that these people were not gullible—they demanded evidence before they would believe. In the case of the disciple Thomas, when he saw the risen Jesus he "said to him, 'My Lord and my God!'" But we've already seen that John's gospel takes quite a few liberties with what actually was said and done (See "Was Jesus God Incarnate?"). Such a high exclamation coming through the lips of Thomas never happened. So we have reason to wonder if the event itself ever took place. John describes a risen Jesus who appeared to Thomas, even "though the doors were locked," indicating that Jesus either walked through the doors, or just appeared out of thin air. And then Jesus proceeds by asking Thomas to put his finger in his hands, and his hand in Jesus' side. How can both of these descriptions of Jesus be of a flesh and blooded person? The way Jesus appeared to Thomas leads us think that this was nothing but a vision. How then can Thomas touch the flesh of Jesus, which still had open fatal wounds? Did the post-resurrected Jesus still have blood running in his veins? We now know that blood is necessary for the body to function, and that breathing gives the blood its oxygen, which is pumped though the body by the heart. Did he have a functioning heart and a set of lungs? Did the post-resurrected Jesus breathe? To speak, as it's claimed Jesus did, demands a functioning set of lungs. John specifically said that he breathed (John 20:22). But didn't Jesus lose all of his blood on the cross, and didn't the post-resurrected body of Jesus still have open fatal wounds, according to John? These fatal wounds would cause him to lose any remaining blood out of his body. All of this leads me to suspect, at best, it was a vision.

The stories also tell of a post-resurrected Jesus who is usually not immediately recognized by his disciples (John 20:14; Luke 24:16). It's also worth noting that even among those who saw the risen Jesus, "some doubted" (Mt. 28:17). How is that really possible? What is it that made them doubt? The fact that Matthew tells us of this may indicate his honesty in telling the story, or it may be a way of dealing with those doubters out there who told a different story.

2) Are the various Gospel accounts consistent? When comparing the four Gospel accounts there are incompatibilities with how many women came to the tomb (1, 2, or 3 plus "others") when they came ("while it was still dark" or "just after sunrise,") why they came ("to look at the tomb" or "to anoint the body with spices"), who they saw (one angel, two angels, a man dressed in white, or Jesus himself), what was said, who said what, who else came (Peter, or both Peter and John), who saw the resurrected Jesus first (Peter or Mary Magdalene), and what they did as they left the tomb ("they said nothing to anyone" or "they ran to tell his disciples"). Matthew seems to imply that the stone was rolled away in the presence of the women who came to the tomb, while Mark, Luke and John say the women arrived to discover the stone had already been rolled away. Luke's Gospel says the disciples "stayed continually in the temple" because Jesus had told them to wait in Jerusalem until they had been "clothed with power from on high." But John's Gospel has the disciples returning to their fishing trade in Galilee and Matthew has Jesus appearing and commissioning the eleven in Galilee. John's Gospel mentions an appearance of Jesus and says: "this was now the third time Jesus appeared to his disciples" (21:14), but Paul's list and order of appearances (I Cor 15:5-8) doesn't square with John's order of appearances. Paul doesn't mention any appearances to women.

Gleason Archer has made a good but failed attempt at harmonizing the accounts, in his Encyclopedia of Bible Difficulties, (pp. 347-356), as did Simon Greenleaf in The Testimony of the Evangelists Examined by the Rules of Evidence Administrated in Courts of Justice (1847). Most scholars disagree with them. "It has proved impossible to construct a fully harmonized version of the resurrection stories, despite many attempts to do so...the stories as given constitute not a jigsaw puzzle but an insoluble mystery." [David Edwards Evangelical Essentials, (p. 205)]. According to Michael Martin the gospels are either inconsistent, or they "can only be made consistent with the aid of implausible interpretations." [The Case Against Christianity, (p. 81)]. Willi Marxsen: "The conclusion is inescapable: a synchronizing harmony of the different accounts of the Resurrection proves to be impossible." [The Resurrection of Jesus of Nazereth, (p. 74)]. "When we embrace all of their versions in our minds at one time, we discover that all we have in the Bible about Easter is an inconsistent, contradictory, mutually exclusive witness." [Bishop John Shelby Spong, Resurrection: Myth or Reality? (p. 105)].

Looking at these discrepancies one can come away with two different understandings of them. On the one hand, Christian scholars have argued that the lack of consistency in the resurrection stories themselves show that there was no collusion among the authors to create and fabricate an identical story. On the other hand, other scholars see the lack of consistency in the stories as evidence that the stories had a long oral stage of telling and re-telling which lends itself toward exaggerating the claims of what actually happened. According to Michael Martin, "the great differences among post-resurrection appearance stories and the difficulty of reconciling them certainly suggests that oral transmission has generated inaccuracies." [The Case Against Christianity, (p. 83)].

3) Are the eyewitnesses trustworthy? Michael Martin says that we really don't know if they are trustworthy. He writes: "Without independent reason to believe their reliability one must be suspicious. Further, we do not know who reported these stories or how many times they were told and retold before they were finally written down. They were presumably passed down by word of mouth and not recorded until several decades after the event." [The Case Against Christianity, (p. 83)].

Jan Vansina is widely recognized as one of the leading authorities on the subject of the oral transmission of history. Here's what he says about eye-witness testimony: "In the best of circumstances, even the best of witnesses never give a movie-like account of what happened, as all accounts of accidents show. Eyewitness accounts are always a personal experience as well and involve not only perception, but also emotions. Witnesses often are also not idle standers-by, but participants in the events. Furthermore, an understanding of what happened cannot occur through mere data of perception. Perceptions must be organized in a coherent whole and the logic of the situation supplies missing pieces of observation. The classical cases of car accidents or purse snatching document this to satiety. A witness reporting a car accident typically first heard a smash, then saw it, then deduced how it happened—how both cars were traveling before the accident after which he or she built up a coherent account of the incident. Usually he did not see the two cars before the accident drew attention to them. Most witnesses cannot resolve themselves to build up a story starting with a noise and the result of the accident first. If a witness was traveling in one of the stricken cars, much of what took place happened at a speed greater than his own reaction time allowed him to perceive. Such persons often only remember one or two images of the accident. Yet when called upon to tell what happened, they must become coherent and build up a tale in which the logic of the situation makes up most of the account."

"Eyewitness accounts are only partly reliable. Certainly it is true that complex or unexpected events are perhaps rarer than simple, expected events. Yet even here the account remains imperfect. The expectation of the event itself distorts its observation. People tend to report what they expect to see or hear more than what they actually see or hear. To sum up: mediation of perception by memory and emotional state shapes an account. Memory typically selects certain features from the successive perceptions and interprets them according to expectation, previous knowledge, or the logic of "what must have happened," and fills the gaps in perception." [Oral Tradition as History (Madison: University of Wisconsin Press, 1985): pp.4-5].

Certain elements in the stories themselves are hard to believe. Why would the disciples return to their fishing trade after seeing and believing in the risen Jesus (John 21)? Additionally, W.G. Kümmel writes: "In view of the Palestinian climate, it is not conceivable that the women intend to anoint a corpse on the third day after death. Nor is it comprehensible that the women go to the tomb with the intention of anointing the body although they do not know who will roll away the heavy boulder in front of the tomb. Besides, among the Jews it was not the custom to use spices in caring for the dead. In view of these improbabilities, it is hardly possible to regard this account as historically reliable." [Theology of the New Testament, p.100)].

There is also the improbability of the story that the chief priests and elders were reported to have started about the missing body of Jesus. They most likely wouldn't have even heard that Jesus was to rise from the dead, much less believe that Jesus would do so enough to want to post a guard at a tomb in the first place (Mt. 27:62-66). Not even the believing disciples themselves expected it, even though it is claimed Jesus predicted it—which calls into doubt whether Jesus actually predicted his resurrection! But even if the chief priests and elders did want to post a guard at the tomb, Matthew's report of their conversation isn't credible (Mt. 28:11-15). We are told that the guards at the tomb saw the angel of the Lord roll back the stone, and sit on it. The angel's appearance was like lightning and his clothes as white as snow (Mt. 28:2-4). They were so afraid that "they shook and became like dead men." They saw all this, plus the empty tomb, and yet somehow they were paid off to spread a stupid denigrating lie about themselves? Not likely.

In the first place, Matthew tells us that the guard wasn't placed there until the day after Jesus was crucified (Matt 27:62-65). This is one reason that leads Richard Carrier to argue for the plausibility that Jesus' body might have been stolen, because it could've been stolen before the guard was posted. He also suggests that if Matthew didn't have a problem showing these guards took bribes, then it's not that unbelievable to think these guards might have been bribed to allow the theft. ["The Plausibility of Theft," in The Empty Tomb (Prometheus Press, 2005, p. 358).

These soldiers wouldn't have reported to the chief priest and elders, but to Pilate whose soldiers they were (Mt. 28:64). And what was the lie? They are to say; "we were asleep" while the disciples stole the body. Now it's one thing to lie, but another thing for soldiers to spread the word that they were derelict in their duty in order to help people they didn't care for, especially in light of their vivid experience, and with the possibility of being severely punished for it. But again, these soldiers would report to Pilate, not the chief priests and elders. Would they lie to Pilate when brought in by him? Plus, in the face of the soldier's testimony why would the chief priests tell them to lie in the first place? These soldiers would have presented a very powerful witness on behalf of the resurrection.

But the truth is that it's a useless and stupid lie. If they were asleep, how did they know what happened? Anyone who heard them tell the lie would know that they didn't actually know what happened, but rather inferred the disciples stole the body. This inference wouldn't be enough to stop the belief that Jesus rose from the dead. The lie would additionally be unbelievable because rolling a stone back and taking the body of Jesus would surely have woke the soldiers. So why is it easy for Christians to believe the chief priest, elders and soldiers all acted contrary to the intelligent people they were, and not question the historical trustworthiness of the Gospel account itself?

Dr. William Lane Craig maintains that "the real value of Matthew's story is the incidental--and for that reason all the more reliable—information, that the Jewish polemic never denied that the tomb was empty, but instead tried to explain it away. Thus, the early opponents of the Christians themselves bear witness to the fact of the empty tomb. ["The Guard at the Tomb." New Testament Studies 30 (1984): 273-81]. But this demands that the Christian claims of an empty tomb were made very early in the life of the church. According to conservative scholar, Ralph Martin, Matthew's gospel was written "in the ninth or final decades of the first century." [New Testament Foundations, Vol. 1 (Eerdmans, 1975) p. 243. See also G.D. Kirkpatrick, The Origins of the Gospel According to Matthew, 1946; B.H. Streeter, The Four Gospels, 1924; and, F.V. Wilson The Gospel According to St. Matthew, 1960]. If Matthew is late in origin, then when he writes the story of the guards at the empty tomb of Jesus, he's responding to the Jewish opponents of his own day who are reacting to the late church's proclamation that there was an empty tomb. It was not to "the early opponents" that Matthew was responding to, as Dr. Craig affirms.

By that time the preaching in the Christian community did include the story of an empty tomb. If so, then Matthew's gospel is merely responding, as it does throughout the book, to the struggles of the church of his day. Along with the later claims of an empty tomb came the counter-claims by the later Jewish opponents that the disciples stole the body and perpetrated a fraud. And even Stephen Davis admits that if the empty tomb story itself was invented by Mark and "written outside Palestine during or after the Jewish war" then "the location of the tomb could have been forgotten and verification would have been difficult." [Risen Indeed (Eerdmans, 1993), p. 74].

Furthermore, the prophecies used to support the resurrection on the third day, which Paul referred to as "according to the Scriptures" (I Cor. 15:3), don't say anything of the kind. Hosea 6:2 says: "After two days he will revive us; on the third day he will restore us, that we may live in his presence." But this originally was meant as an exhortation to Israel to hope in a forgiving God after being punished by him. Psalms 16:9-10, which is quoted by Peter in Acts 2:26-27, says: "you will not abandon me to the grave, nor will you let your Holy One see corruption." The original meaning of this passage was King David's prayer for recovery from sickness. David Edwards: "The relevance of these passages to a resurrection believed to have occurred about thirty-six hours after a death depends on a method of interpreting Scripture which is ancient rather than modern." [Evangelical Essentials, (p. 202)]. This is Midrash, as we'll explain later.

What doesn't count as evidence for the truth of the resurrection, according to Michael Martin, are eyewitnesses to Jesus' post resurrection appearances who were transformed people willing to die for their beliefs. Many people who weren't eyewitnesses of Jesus were willing to die for their beliefs too, especially since they also believed they would go to hell if they didn't (see my "Hell? No!"). Christian heretics have also been willing to die for their beliefs. "Let us not forget that Muslims, Mormons, followers of James Jones, kamikaze pilots, and many others have been willing to die for what they believed. The fact that people are willing to die for their beliefs can show...strength of character, extreme devotion, and even fanaticism. But it is hard to see that it indicates that what is believed is true or even that the evidential bases of the beliefs should be taken seriously." Furthermore, "if we count Paul's conversion as being evidence for the truth of the resurrection, should we not count Muhammad's conversion to Islam from polytheism as being evidence for the truth of the claim that Jesus was not resurrected (Muslims reject Jesus' resurrection)? The evidential value of Paul's conversion and Muhammad's conversion for the truth of the Resurrection tend to cancel each other out." [The Case Against Christianity, p. 77, 91-92].

4) Is there any independent testimony in agreement with the Gospel record? This is a question that one must ask of any historical event, miraculous or otherwise. However, the problem is a circular one. If the testimony is by a Christian believer then it's not an independent one, but if it is an independent testimony, then it will not reveal the belief that Jesus was resurrected from the dead. Nonetheless, we have no confirmation by either Jewish or pagan sources to show that Jesus rose from the dead. There is a pseudonymous quote inside Josephus to that effect (Antiquities 18:3,3), but even conservative Christian scholars agree that it was a later interposition placed there by Christian scribes. The only other independent testimony is from the *Shroud of Turin*, which is a strip of cloth believers say covered the body of Jesus as he arose from the dead which produced a stunning image of a man who fits the description of someone who had been crucified. The problem is that recent radiocarbon dating of the Shroud reveals it was 99.9% certain the Shroud "originated from the period 1000 to 1500, and 95% certain that the cloth dated from between 1260 and 1390." [See Lynn Picknett & Clive Prince, Turin Shroud (Harper, 1994, p. 8)].

Where is the independent confirmation that the whole land was covered by darkness for three hours (Mk 15:33) or that the Temple curtain miraculously tore in two (Mk. 15:38), or that there was an earthquake (Matt. 27:51), or that "The tombs also were opened, and many bodies of the saints who had fallen asleep were raised. After his resurrection they came out of the tombs and entered the holy city and appeared to many." (Mt 27:52). Surely at least one of these events would have been recorded by Josephus or some other writer at that time. This is not arguing from silence here, because I believe the silences are telling. Where is there any record of these things having occurred except in the gospels? I'll tell you where...nowhere!

5) Do the Gospel writers intend to be historically accurate? There were three groups of people in relationship to Jesus. There were neutral observers, there were his opponents, and finally there were people who had been changed by Jesus, Christians. According to Willi Marxsen, "We do not have any narratives told by neutral observers or by Jesus' opponents. This means that everything that has come down to us is presented from a certain point of view, and that it has been so from the very beginning. Put in a modern way, they wanted to win people for Jesus." [Jesus and Easter, (Abingdon Press, 1990, (pp. 23-25)]. [To see how the Gospel writers were not neutral in dealing with the Pharisees, see the next section]. The gospel writers all had theological and evangelistic aims. From this we don't know for sure if their stories are like preacher's stories today that illustrate truths even though the stories themselves may or may not have happened. Because of this, Michael Martin claims, "we should be suspicious of their reliability." [The Case Against Christianity, (p. 78)].

But what if they never intended to tell the literal historical truth in the first place? The New Testament writers have been mistaken to write the literal truth ever since the gospel left Jewish soil when non-Jewish western European people began to read their writings. What they wrote contained a lot of Midrash. What is Midrash? According to The Jewish Encyclopedia: it is "the attempt to penetrate into the spirit of the text, to examine the text from all sides, to derive interpretations not immediately obvious, to illuminate the future by appealing to the past." (Funk & Wagnall, 1925). It is the ability to tell stories that are illustrative of the truths they believe. We have just seen earlier in this essay the way they used the Old Testament prophecies to illustrate Jesus' resurrection. We've also seen it with regard to the virgin birth of Jesus in Bethlehem (See my study on this). According to Bishop John Shelby Spong, "The question to ask of this Midrash tradition is not, 'Did it really happen?' That is a western question tied to a western mind-set....The proper question is 'what was there about Jesus of Nazareth that required the meaning of his life to be interpreted through the stories of Abraham and Isaac, Moses and Passover, Exodus and wilderness, Sinai and promised land, Hannah and Samuel, David and Solomon, Elijah and Elisha, the servant figure and the Son of man, Pentecost and Tabernacles, and a thousand other choices that served to incorporate the life of Jesus into the meaning of God known in the history of the Jewish people?'" As Christianity was denied its Jewish roots and ignored its Jewish home "it resulted in extravagant literal claims for the historicity of what were in fact Midrashic retellings of ancient themes in new moments of history." [Resurrection: Myth or Reality? (pp. 11-17)].

What Is Meant by "Resurrection"? The only thing all the New Testament writers agree to is that Jesus rose from the dead. Should this unanimous agreement alone be enough of a reason to believe Jesus was resurrected from the dead? It is a reason, no doubt. But there is the problem of knowing exactly what early Christians thought of the resurrected body of Jesus. It was a body that could be touched (Lk. 24:39, Jn. 20:27), could eat fish (Lk. 24:42-43), but sometimes is unrecognizable even to his disciples (Lk. 24:16; Jn.20: 14), it could pass through walls (Jn. 20:19, 26), or appear out of thin air (Lk. 24:36) and then disappear at will (Lk. 24:31, 51). There is also the minor problem of where Jesus got his clothes (rather than angelic robes) that made him look normal to the disciples. What kind of body was this?

The only description we have of resurrected bodies is written by Paul in I Corinthians 15. It is also the earliest written account we have of the resurrection, dated around 55 A.D. From what follows, it seems clear Paul didn't think of resurrection in terms of a physical body. Paul argues that the resurrected body will be a "spiritual body" (v. 44). "There are heavenly bodies and there are earthly bodies" (v. 40). "Flesh and blood cannot inherit the kingdom of God, nor does the perishable inherit the imperishable" (v. 50). Our new bodies will be as different as a wheat plant differs from its seed (vs. 36-37). And while there is some continuity between the seed and the plant, David Edwards reminds us "in the ancient world it was believed that a seed dies in the ground (cf. John 12:24). The continuity pictured by Paul is continuity through death, which is why Paul dwells on the contrast. He compares it with the difference between human flesh and the flesh of fish, or between the sun and the moon." [Evangelical Essentials p. 207]. Elsewhere Paul wrote that "if the earthly tent we live in is destroyed, we have a building from God, an eternal house in heaven, not built by human hands (II Cor. 5:1-8). In Philippians (3:20-21) Paul tells us that someday Christ will "transform our lowly bodies so that they will be like his glorious body."

What little Jesus himself said about the resurrection leads us to think both he and Paul shared the same view. Jesus said there is no marriage in heaven because believers "will be like the angels in heaven" from which they "will shine like stars" (Mk. 12:24-27; Mt. 13:43).

Paul lists six appearances of the risen Jesus to various people in chronological order and then says, "last of all, he appeared to me" (v. 8). The only record we have of Jesus' appearance to Paul is on the Damascus road recounted three times in Acts (9,22,26). He seems to be saying the appearance of Jesus to him was the same as his appearance to the others. But there is no clue what exactly Paul saw. He saw a bright light and heard a voice identifying himself as Jesus. But Paul had never seen Jesus before. Did he see a physical body? We don't know. What scholars lead us to believe is that the word for "appeared" (*ophthē*) used here by Paul is uncertain in meaning. According to Willi Marxsen, "what is being spoken of is a vision." **Paul even says as much (see Acts 26:19, see Acts 9:17)!** What Paul claims in I Corinthians 15 is that the people he listed had "a vision" of Jesus, not that they were witnesses of the physical resurrection of Jesus from the dead. [Marxsen, Jesus and Easter, (p. 69)]. This same word is used in the Greek Septuagint translation of the Hebrew Old Testament (LXX) to describe appearances of God and angels (Genesis 12:7;

Exodus 3:2; 6:2-3). It is also used in the Gospels of Zechariah's vision of the angel Gabriel (Luke 1:22), of Abraham's vision of God (Acts 7:2) and in the Epistles several times to describe Jesus' appearances (I Cor. 9:1). [On this whole point see the excellent argument by Richard Carrier: "The Spiritual Body of Christ," in The Empty Tomb, pp. 105-232].

Some apologists make a big deal about Paul's claim that 500 brethren saw the risen Jesus at the same time (I Cor. 15:6). In the first place, as you saw in "Pseudonymity in the Bible," Robert M. Price makes a good case that such a verse is a later pseudepigraphal interpolation." ["Apocryphal Apparitions" in The Empty Tomb, 2005, pp. 69-104]. But even if not, consider the impact such a statement would have for the Corinthians. Keith Parsons asks, "How many of the Corinthian Christians, probably mostly persons of rather modest circumstances, would have had the means or the disposition to travel from Greece to Palestine to track down the witnesses?" [The Empty Tomb, p. 438]. It would still be Paul's word on it. Did he know them all?

When we realize all of this we can see why Bishop John Shelby Spong summarizes the results of modern scholarship with these words: "there is no sense at all in Paul of a physical resurrection of Jesus back into the life of this world. God did not, for this apostle, raise Jesus from the grave to life on this earth. Rather, for Paul, God raised Jesus from death into God's presence; from the grave to God's right hand." "The essential thing to note about Paul's understanding of the appearances to him is that it was identical with every other appearance on his list. That is, it was not a physical, historical encounter but a revelatory manifestation of the living Christ from heaven…(p. 50, 53). At the very least, David Edwards admits, "…the long dispute of the scholars shows that it is uncertain whether or not Paul believed in the physical resurrection of Jesus." [Evangelical Essentials (p. 202)]. But if it isn't a physical body, then hear what former atheist Anthony Flew said: **"To the unsanctioned eye…seeing spiritual bodies is indiscernible from having visions to which no mind-independent realities correspond."** [Did Jesus Rise From the Dead? (p. 12)].

If what I've just written accurately describes Paul's understanding of the resurrection, then how can we reconcile this with the Gospel claims that the disciples touched Jesus' body, watched him eat, and walked with him? (Although, the Gospels themselves also make us wonder what kind of physical body Jesus had). We could either say that Paul believed in a bodily resurrection as the Gospels report, which doesn't seem to fit Paul's statements at all, or we could say the Gospel writers embellished their stories using the aforementioned writing style of Midrash, or symbolism, or typology, or all three. I believe the evidence points to this second option, but I simply reject Midrsah, symbolism and typological descriptions of such an event. I want to know what happened, and there are discrepancies among the Biblical writers themselves. These are the two options. This is not unlike the problem Biblical scholars have in comparing the tongues experience in Acts 2, with Paul's description of the tongues experiences in the church at Corinth in I Corinthians 14. Do we interpret them to be describing the same tongues experience? If so, do we interpret Acts 2 in light of I Corinthians 14, or do we interpret I Corinthians 14 in light of Acts 2?

Richard Carrier argues that Paul's understanding of Jesus' resurrection didn't require a resurrected body, but that independent from Paul and later in time, the author of Mark invented the story of the empty tomb. Mark did this, as other Biblical authors did, making the empty tomb a metaphor symbolizing either the corpse of Jesus or the ascension of Jesus. "On my theory," he writes, "the empty tomb story originated as a symbol, not a historical fact. It then became the subject of legendary embellishment over the ensuing generations, eventually becoming an essential element in the doctrine of a particular sect of Christians, who spurned Paul's original teachings, and insisted on a resurrection of the flesh instead." ["The Spiritual Body of Christ" in The Empty Tomb (Prometheus Books, 2005), pp. 158-59)].

The Empty Tomb. This brings us to the empty tomb. There is more to the evidence for the bodily resurrection of Jesus, as Stephen T. Davis tells us: "spiritual resurrection theories do not require an empty tomb." [Risen Indeed (Eerdmans, 1993, p. 60)]. What about the empty tomb? Several major mainline Christian scholars, both Catholic and Protestant, argue against the empty tomb like C.H. Dodd, Rudolf Bultmann, Raymond Brown, Reginald Fuller, Hans Küng, Karl Rahner, D. H. Nineham, along with many others.

But listen to Uta Ranke-Heinemann: "The empty tomb on Easter Sunday morning is a legend. This is shown by the simple fact that the apostle Paul, the most crucial preacher of Christ's resurrection, says nothing about it. Thus it also means nothing to him, that is, an empty tomb has no significance for the truth of the resurrection, which he so emphatically proclaims. Since he gathers together and cites all the evidence for Jesus' resurrection that has been handed down to him, he certainly would have found the empty tomb worth mentioning. That he doesn't proves that it never existed and hence the accounts of it must not have arisen until later…. The belief in the resurrection is older than the belief in the empty tomb; rather, the legend of the empty tomb grew out of the faith of Easter." [Putting Away Childish Things, (p. 131)].

It's argued that the belief in the empty tomb was just presupposed by Paul (I Cor. 15:3-5; cf. Acts 13:29-31), as well as Peter on the Day of Pentecost (2:29-33; 3:15). It's true that Peter's Pentecost sermon in Jerusalem, the city where Jesus' tomb was supposedly located, is a shortened summary written by Luke. But why didn't Peter say, "see for yourselves, the tomb where he laid is empty?" While it can still be argued that Peter presupposed the empty tomb because it may have already been known to those people, it has much less plausibility with regards to Paul. Just compare their emphasis on the empty tomb when preaching to convince people Jesus was resurrected, **which is nothing,** with evangelistic writings today that all emphasize it as the number one piece of evidence needing to be explained, and you'll know what is meant. If it's so important to a Christian apologetic, why didn't the Apostles emphasize it?

Richard Carrier argues that Matthew and Luke embellished on Mark's metaphor of the empty tomb. Mark tells a simple story, but by the time we get to Matthew several things are added: Joseph of Arimathea is now "a disciple of Jesus" (Mt. 27:57), who buried Jesus' body "in his own new tomb" (Mt. 27:60). The boy in Mark has now become an angel (Mt. 28:2-3,5), and now there was "a massive earthquake" (Mt. 28:2), along with "a guard at the tomb" (Mt. 28:4). Also added are the women who meet Jesus (Mt. 28:9). Carrier: "There can be no doubt that we are looking at extensive legendary embellishment upon what began as a much more mundane story." ["The Spiritual Body of Christ" in The Empty Tomb (Prometheus Books, 2005), p. 165)]. We see further embellishment in Luke and John. The same trends can be seen in the appearance narratives: From none in Mark, to "clasping Jesus' feet" in Matthew (28:9), to handling and eating with Jesus, and a description of Jesus' body in Luke (24:37-43), to the doubting Thomas story where Jesus "proves" his bodily presence (John 20:24-29). According to Peter Kirby, "Since all accounts of the empty tomb are dependent on Mark, the story hangs by a slender thread." ["The Case Against the Empty Tomb" in The Empty Tomb (Prometheus Books, 2005), p. 237].

The Pseudepigrapha shows us that any telling and re-telling of a story gets expanded as time goes by. We can actually trace such things in the case of a virgin birth story to the Immaculate Conception story, to the story that Mary was a perpetual Virgin, even though the N.T. said Jesus had siblings (Mark 3:31-35). And since there was an oral tradition before such things were put into the Gospels, then we have reason to believe the same kind of expanded story telling took place before all of the gospels were compiled, and even before the New Testament itself was canonized.

Mark's gospel ends with these words from "a young man" at the empty tomb: *"But go, tell his disciples and Peter that he is going ahead of you to Galilee; there you will see him, just as he told you." So they went out and fled from the tomb, for terror and amazement had seized them; and they said nothing to anyone, for they were afraid."* (Mk 16:7-8). [The longer ending is now rejected as a pseudepigraphal later addition and not part of Mark's original gospel. See Bruce Metzger, A Textual Commentary on the Greek NT (United Bible Societies, 1971), pp. 122-26)].

The original ending of Mark is inconclusive. No one had seen Jesus, and the women said nothing about what they had seen. No wonder later Christians wanted to write out the further details and add more verses to Mark's gospel. But why Mark ends it this way is a subject for debate. It could be to explain why the story of the empty tomb did not exist before Mark's gospel. It's because the women "said nothing to anyone." Now in his gospel Mark is telling their story. Peter Kirby: "If the story had been known far and wide, from the beginning of Christianity, ending with the women conveying their message, I would suggest that the author of Mark would not have received it in the form he tells it. For that reason, the story is probably of recent origin in the Gospel of Mark." ["The Case Against the Tomb" in The Empty Tomb (Prometheus Books, 2005, p. 240)]. [Richard Carrier looks at Plutarch's biography of Romulus, the Founder of Rome, and claims that it is "so obviously a parallel to Mark's ending of his Gospel that nearly anyone would have noticed—and gotten the point. It certainly looks like the Christian passion narrative is a deliberate tranvaluation of the Roman Empire's ceremony of their founding savior's incarnation, death, and resurrection." [The Empty Tomb, p. 180-181].

Richard Carrier: "Mark's 'empty tomb" account cannot be regarded as historical with any more confidence than his claim that at Christ's death the whole land was covered by darkness for three hours or that the Temple curtain miraculously tore in two. Neither claim is corroborated in other texts, which could not have failed to record them, and so neither claim is credible." "But like the empty tomb, these two 'wonders' have obvious symbolic and metaphorical meaning, so it is not even necessary to suppose Mark imagined himself as writing history when he added them. As easily as he could add them, he could add the empty tomb, and for all the same reasons. And as later Christians began to believe Mark was reporting those events as history, they could just as easily come to believe the empty tomb was history, too." [The Empty Tomb (Prometheus Books, 2005), p. 176-77].

There is the further problem with the fact that Jesus' empty tomb was not venerated by early Christians. James D.G. Dunn: "there is no evidence whatsoever for Christians regarding the place where Jesus had been buried as having any special significance," with pilgrimages and veneration. Dunn claims this was "because the tomb was empty." But even Dunn admits "that it was quite customary at the time of Jesus for devotees to meet at the tomb of the dead prophet for worship (Matt. 23:29). And it continues today in the veneration accorded the tombs of Abraham in Hebron and of David's tomb in Jerusalem." "Christians today of course regard the site of Jesus' tomb with similar veneration, and that practice goes back to at least the fourth century." [The Evidence For Jesus (Westminster Press, 1985), p. 67-68].

Peter Kirby argues that Dunn's "conclusion is highly illogical." "It is plain to see that the site of the tomb of Jesus would become a site of veneration and pilgrimage among early Christians regardless of whether it was occupied or empty." "The fact that there was no tomb veneration indicates that the early Christians did not know the location of the tomb of Jesus, neither of an empty tomb nor of an occupied tomb. The best way to avoid this conclusion is, I think, to assert that there was tomb veneration despite the silence of any first-, second-, or third-century writers on such an interest." ["The Case Against the Empty Tomb" in The Empty Tomb (Prometheus Books, 2005), p. 255-256)].

On the Christian side, Stephen T. Davis in Risen Indeed, and William Lane Craig in Apologetics: An Introduction, along with many others have all presented strong arguments for an empty tomb. But even so, Davis himself suggests the remote possibility that Jesus was "buried in an unmarked or even a mass grave by a Roman functionary and two underlings who three days later, without having told anyone how they had disposed of the body, were transferred back to Rome," although he clearly doesn't believe that scenario (p. 80). David Edwards suggests the possibility that "the corpse of Jesus was thrown into the same grave as the corpses of other crucified criminals and was beyond recovery and recognition by the time that the story of the resurrection reached the ears of the authorities—a time which may have been months or years after the death." [Evangelical Essentials, (pp. 200-201]. Although, Edwards doesn't believe this scenario, either. But what about the possibility that someone or some people (Roman soldiers?) perpetrated a fraud on the disciples making them suppose the tomb was empty for a good laugh?

According to Davis, the question in the minds of the people in Jerusalem was not "Was the tomb empty?" But rather "Why was the tomb empty?" (p. 72). Even if this is the question, and I doubt it, then along with Luis M. Bermejo we can still affirm the empty tomb but deny Jesus' bodily resurrection, in Light From Beyond Death, (1985). And even if Jesus did rise bodily from the dead, that doesn't prove that he's God, or that the Christian interpretation of his life and death are correct. Jewish theologian Pinchas Lapide in The Resurrection of Jesus: A Jewish

Perspective (Augsburg, 1983), accepts that Jesus arose, but still denies Christianity in favor of Judaism.

Upon finished arguing for an empty tomb, Davis concluded: "The empty tomb, by itself, does not prove the resurrection. It is a necessary but not sufficient condition for the bodily resurrection of Jesus.... Perhaps the tomb was empty because of quite natural circumstances that are now unknown." (p. 84). Later in his book Davis admits that an unbeliever, atheist or naturalist can rationally respond to the evidence for the empty tomb and the resurrection by saying, "The rationalistic explanations do seem weak, and I don't claim to know what in fact happened, but one thing I do know is that it wasn't a resurrection." These people, he claims are not guilty of ruling out the evidence before examining it "only if the evidence for the resurrection of Jesus is very strong indeed—so strong, in fact, as to outweigh the commitment virtually all rational people have made to the notion that dead people do not get up and walk around again. It seems to me perfectly possible for the naturalist to examine the relevant evidence objectively and carefully and still decide that no miracle occurred." (pp. 170-171).

In debating the resurrection of Jesus, former atheist Anthony Flew does just that: "Confronted with testimonial evidence for the occurrence of a miracle, the secular historian must recognize that however unlikely it may seem that all the witnesses were in error, the occurrence of a genuine miracle is, by definition, naturally impossible." [Did Jesus Rise From The Dead, 1987 (p. 6)]. There are several Biblical scholars who have examined the Biblical evidence and concluded Jesus did not physically rise from the dead. This is just what Biblical critic John Dominic Crossan has concluded: "I do not think that anyone, anywhere, at any time brings dead people back to life." [Jesus, A Revolutionary Biography, (p. 95)]. Robert Funk and the scholars in "The Jesus Seminar" reached a fairly firm consensus: "Belief in Jesus' resurrection did not depend on what happened to his corpse" [in Honest to Jesus, 1996 (p. 259)]. Thomas Sheenan writes, "Jesus, regardless of where his corpse ended up, is dead and remains dead." First Coming, (Pp. 172-173). Marcus Borg takes a liberal Christian approach: "The discovery of Jesus' skeletal remains would not be a problem. I see the empty tomb and whatever happened to the corpse of Jesus to be ultimately irrelevant to the truth of Easter." [The Meaning of Jesus: Two Visions, with N.T. Wright (Harper, 1999), pp. 130-31].

What Really Happened?

Episcopal Bishop, John Shelby Spong, of New Jersey, offers a speculative reconstruction of what might have initially happened soon after Jesus' death. He emphasizes that it is just conjecture, too:

Simon Peter felt depressed after the crucifixion of Jesus. He had placed years of his life in Jesus' hands and heard him and seen his beautiful life, and now his hopes were all gone. He went back to Galilee to fish again, and the events of the last few years replayed themselves over and over in his mind. Then it all became clear to him in a vision he had in which he realized that Jesus' whole life and death was a parable of divine love for mankind, and at that moment he felt resurrected—"he saw Jesus alive." "It was as if scales fell from his eyes." This vision was indeed real, but not objectively so. So "Peter rallied his mates with his vision, and together they decided that now they should go up to Jerusalem for the feast of Tabernacles, and in this setting they must share this vision with others so they also might see." This vision came "as much as six months after the death of Jesus." Peter then "opened the eyes of his fellow Galilean disciples so that they, too, could see Jesus risen." In Jerusalem and "inside the liturgy of the celebration of Tabernacles, the story of Easter unfolded." In a subsequent chapter Spong grounds his speculation in the way the disciples used the midrashic understanding of the feast of Tabernacles, Psalms 16, 22, 118, passages from Zechariah, Moses and the Passover, and so forth, to point to Jesus. [Resurrection: Myth or Reality?]

Now it's not uncommon for someone to feel dejected when some hope is dashed and then to see something new in order to continue what they had started. The Seventh Day Adventists, for instance, began interpreting much of the Bible differently once they experienced a failed prediction of Jesus' return. What were they to think now? The answer came in a vision. Jesus entered a "heavenly sanctuary." Likewise, the Jehovah's Witnesses experienced a failed prediction of Jesus' return, and again, the answer came in a vision. Jesus did in fact return after all—he just returned "spiritually." [See Walter Martin The Kingdom of the Cults]. Plus, given the nature of the hallucinations surrounding the Salem witchcraft trials, Michael Martin reminds us, "Surely, it is not beyond the realm of psychological possibility, that in first century Palestine, among the unsophisticated people who believed in the divinity of Jesus, one disciple's hallucination of Jesus could have triggered corresponding hallucinations in the others." [The Case Against Christianity (p. 95)].

Bruce Malina and Richard Rohrbaugh discuss the nature of visions in their excellent book, Social Science Commentary on the Synoptic Gospels [Augsburg Fortress; 2nd ed. 2003) pp. 327-329]. Malina and Rohrbaugh consider the postmortem appearances of Jesus to be "visions." They show that visions of a holy man are in altered-states-of-awareness, and that during the time before and after the Gospels were written visions were widely reported in antiquity. This provides, I believe, the social-scientific basis for claiming that Christianity originated with a series of visions.

After this possible initial "vision" of Peter, several scenarios of viewing the progress from vision to resurrected body are possible, and they all involve the belief that Jesus did not physically rise from the grave. The appearances of Jesus were merely visions or hallucinations, or "revelatory encounters" [Reginald H. Fuller, Formation of the Resurrection Narratives, p. 49). Then with the belief that Jesus was still alive, the original stories were embellished. Paul thought of Jesus' resurrected body as a spiritual one, but beginning with Mark's invention of an empty tomb, the storytellers started to emphasize the physical nature of Jesus' body. According to Robert Funk, "as time passed and the tradition grew, the reported appearances become more palpable, more corporeal." [Honest To Jesus (Harper, 1996), p. 260]. With the later church conflict over Paul's view and the gospel's different view, the followers of Paul lost out, and from then on Christians believed in the bodily resurrection of Jesus. Robert Funk argues that there were other rivalries in the early church that helped formulate the final resurrection doctrine. For instance, "the concern over appearances as the gospel took shape has to do primarily with apostolic right and succession, or, as we would say, with empire building and office politics." Furthermore, "The move to replace a disembodied, supernatural figure with a more tangible, material bodily resurrection was actually triggered by a conflict with Gnostic views." [Honest To Jesus (Harper, 1996), p. 269, 272] [For other similar conjectures see the following books: John Hick, The Metaphor of God Incarnate, pp. 23-26; Marcus Borg, The Meaning of Jesus: Two Visions, (with N.T. Wright), pp. 130-35, Gerd Lüdemann, What Really Happened to Jesus? (Westminster, 1995), and the authors in The Empty Tomb book, just to mention a few].

Conclusion –At every juncture of this study of the resurrection there is some doubt about the bodily resurrection of Jesus. It would seem as though if our eternal destiny were at stake based upon the evidence of the bodily resurrection of Jesus, then God should have made the evidence much stronger for those of us who hear about it centuries later. While it does convince some, it didn't convince most people in Jesus' day, and it doesn't convince most people in our day. It's not an airtight case by any stretch of the imagination. The sum total of my entire modern life experience is that truly dead bodies stay dead. Dead bodies don't get up and walk around again. Until I experience people bodily rising up from the dead—and why wouldn't God do that once in a while just to show that it's a possibility?—I will continue judging the past by the present.

Three further problems arise if Jesus arose bodily. **One) If he did, then so shall all believers.** This raises further philosophical questions of the kind of bodies we shall have, how we will know others, how will we know ourselves, how old will we be mentally, and where will we live? For instance, what kind of resurrected body will a missionary have after been eaten by cannibals, since their physical bodies are now part of someone else's? What about believer's bodies that have been burned up, or eaten by sharks, or decomposed in the deepest parts of the ocean? There are some pretty strong arguments against this possibility, philosophically speaking. [See John Hick's Death and Eternal Life; see also Terence Penelhum's Survival and Disembodied Existence. Also, Anthony Flew's God, Freedom, and Immortality, and The Logic of Mortality].

Two) We need our bodies. Our bodies have a great influence on our abilities to think. "Indeed, the limits to what we are able to think at all are set by our genetic environment; so that one man's physicochemical equipment enables him to be a brilliant mathematician, while another's lack condemns him to lifelong imbecility." [Linda Badham, Death and Immortality in the Religions of the World (Paragon Press)].

Three) What about animals? Will they live on in a resurrected life? Any theory of a resurrection of the dead needs to deal with the death of animals and the possibility of them experiencing life after death. Rene Descartes argued that animals were *automata*; machines of sorts, having no souls and experiencing no pain. But they obviously do have feelings. So where will my dog Franklin (Franky) spend eternity? Does he have to believe in Jesus' resurrection too?

[Some have criticized my use of Bishop John Shelby Spong here, since he's not a scholar, but if William Lane Craig can debate him on the resurrection of Jesus (Easter Sunday 2005, at Bethel College, and aired on CBN), then he's worthy to quote from].

19:1 The Pharisees: Were They That Bad?

The purpose of this section is to see the obvious bias that the NT writers had when it came to the facts, in this case, the Pharisees. Virtually all of our knowledge of the Pharisees comes from three sources: 1) Josephus (c. 75-101 AD); 2) Various Rabbinic compilations (c. 200 AD); and, 3) The New Testament (55-95 AD). Josephus' account is brief and superficial (he likens them to the Stoics). Rabbinic sources are too late to be helpful. The New Testament is generally antagonistic toward the Pharisees. What we read in the New Testament is a one-sided argument against the Pharisees. So, our three sources "provide neither a complete nor a straightforward picture of the Pharisees." [Evangelical Dictionary of Theology: "Pharisees"]. "We cannot assume the church's traditional view of the Pharisees is necessarily correct at every point; a genuine effort must be made to understand whatever evidence is available to us." [Baker Encyclopedia of the Bible: "Pharisees." To better understand them see Joachim Jeremias, Jerusalem in the Time of Jesus, C.K. Barrett, The New Testament Background: Selected Documents, F.F. Bruce, New Testament History, and Alfred Edersheim, The Life and Times of the Messiah, and "Pharisees," in the Anchor Bible Dictionary].

The Pharisees are largely presented in the New Testament as legalistic, hypocritical, ostentatious, traditionalists, and self-righteous men. (See Luke 7, 12:1; 18; Matthew 5-7; 23). But have you ever wondered what the Pharisees would have said in response? They are not as bad as a group that the gospel writers make them out to be. In the first place, Jesus' criticisms were not leveled at all Pharisees, but just to those who were acting hypocritically. But two good things can be said of them generally.

First) They were patriots. This sect arose among those who fought for Jerusalem's independence in earlier years. They called each other "neighbors" and were a close-knit group of largely middle class laymen who looked after each other. Many were ordinary businessmen, some priests, and many were scribes. They numbered about 6,000 in a nation of 500,000 people, and their political power and influence varied depending upon who was king. They were social conservatives, and known as the people's party—highly respected by the masses. They were committed to living clean separate lives, and to resisting the corrupting influence of a pagan Gentile society. They longed to have their nation purged from pagan culture. Hence, they were known as "separatists"—the meaning of their name. They defended and upheld the law, traditions, and the ceremonies of their forefathers. This distinguished them from pagan influences.

Second) They were men of the book. They recognized the authority of the Old Testament. They knew it well and sought to obey every detail. The leaders and influential Pharisees were scribes—experts in the law—who interpreted the laws and oral traditions of the fathers. Josephus tells us that they were known for the precision with which they interpreted the law and the strictness with which they kept it (Antiquities of the Jews, 18:15).

Example: **Handwashing**. (Mark 7:1-5). Mosaic law required bathing to remove certain impurities before entering the temple. The Pharisees thought that it would therefore honor God to do so before the Sabbath and festival meals, for these days are special too. "This reveals how carefully people thought about the law and about observing the will of God. The law in principle covers all of life. Pious first century Jews thought through every detail, so as to observe God's will in every possible way." (E.P. Sanders, "The Historical Figure of Jesus, 1993, p. 45). "The written law is very incomplete; in theory it covers all of life, but it often lacks details. Consequently, it had to be extended and applied in all kinds of ways…"(p. 209).

Example: **The Sabbath Day**. The Bible forbids working on the seventh day. Various passages specify some of the things that count as work, such as lighting a fire, gathering wood, or preparing food (Exodus 16:32; Numbers 15:32-36). There is, however, no systematic definition of work. When it came to treating people with illnesses or healing people on the Sabbath, the Pharisees forbad the work involved in the treatment of minor ailments, so they found ways to achieve desired results without actually working. "On the Sabbath one could not treat a toothache by applying vinegar, but one could put vinegar on food and eat it, which would achieve the same result." While it was generally agreed that transgressing the Sabbath was permitted if human life was at stake, the question remained how serious must an illness be to justify treatment on the Sabbath." [See E. P. Sanders, The Historical Figure of Jesus, pp. 208-209]. When it came to traveling on the Sabbath, they could only walk $3/5^{th}$ of a mile (unless they took a mat and laid down for a while).

There were purification laws, food laws, tithing and fasting laws. "Practically every area of human life came to be included and regulated by an abundance of individual prescriptions…believing as they did that God had provided for every circumstance that could arise." [New International Dictionary of N.T. Theology: "Pharisees"]. **It would be a mistake, however, to think that the Pharisees were consciously trying to make life more burdensome for people.** Evidence suggests they had a passion for ceremonial righteousness, and a strong desire for their nation to be a separate people from the error of paganism, which was what they believed caused God to send their people into Babylonian Captivity.

Three areas of conflict between the Pharisees and Jesus:

One) The authority of the written law over against the oral law and the traditions of the fathers. "Adherence to the oral tradition, with its rules for interpreting the law, was seen by the Pharisees as the way to the fulfillment of the written law." (New International Dictionary of N.T. Theology). It was a way of honoring their fathers (and the 4th commandment) whom they respected. But the oral law also led them to the belief in the resurrection from the dead, with a final judgment of rewards and punishments, along with the belief in a cosmic struggle with Satan and his cohorts [See my sections, "The Devil Made me Do It!" and "Hell? No!"). In this sense the Pharisees were theological liberals as opposed to the Sadducees who rejected the belief in the resurrection. The odd thing is that Jesus (and Paul) also believed these things—things that stemmed from the oral law! This makes Jesus somewhat inconsistent in his view of the relationship of the two laws. And in this sense he too was a theological liberal! [See James Dunn, The Living Word, Fortress, 1987, pp. 44-55). Jesus condemned the neglect of the written law when it was in conflict with the oral law. But the Pharisees just didn't think there was any conflict between the two!

Two) According to the New Testament, some of the Pharisees focused on ritual purity whereas Jesus focused on a purity of the heart (Matthew 23). The charge is that they had a misplaced focus. This was none other than a debate over spirituality, and the Pharisees were unprepared (not unlike the Roman Catholic Church in the time of the Reformation). Because of this, Jesus charged these Pharisees with hypocrisy. According to The International Standard Bible Encyclopedia: "Hypocrisy was a new sin, a sin only possible in a spiritual religion, a religion in which morality and worship were closely related. The prophets had denounced the insincerity of worship, but even they did not denounce hypocrisy, i.e., religion used as a cloak to hide treachery or dishonesty." (p. 2364). The question remains then, were the Pharisees hypocritical? How can someone judge another's motives, which is what it is claimed that Jesus did? Most all of the Pharisees would certainly deny it, although, just fulfilling ritual ceremonial rites to the letter cannot reveal the heart of the person performing them, either way.

Three) The Pharisaical brotherhood ("neighbors") disassociated themselves from the common people, whereas Jesus was a friend of outcasts and those deemed to be sinners (Matthew 9:11; Mark 2:16; Luke 4:16; 5:30; 7:34). In contrast to the masses, "the Pharisees considered themselves to be true Israel." Eventually this "grew to the dimensions of a caste distinction on the part of the Pharisees." [J. Jeremias, Jerusalem in the Time of Jesus]. But in their defense, they just wanted to associate with people who desired to fulfill the law. Poverty, and sickness were both seen by the Pharisees to be signs of God's judgment (Luke 7; 18). Whereas health and righteousness were signs of God's pleasure. And as separatists they disassociated themselves from sinful lifestyles (tax-collectors, prostitutes, and enemies), and few people throughout history have done any better.

The Pharisees and the Death of Jesus. There are several books published that explore who killed Jesus. E. P. Sanders boldly writes: "The High Priest and the chief priests are the primary actors, and the Pharisees play no role at all." "The stories of Pilate's reluctance and weakness of will are best explained as Christian propaganda; they are a kind of excuse for Pilate's action which reduces the conflict between the Christian movement and Roman authority." [The Historical Figure of Jesus, p. 269-274; See also, John Dominic Crossan, Who Killed Jesus? (Harper, 1995), Crossan's, The Historical Jesus (Harper, 1991), and Uta Ranke-Heinemann, Putting Away Childish Things (Harper, 1992, pp. 97-121)].

20 The Devil Made Me Do It!

"**Satan:**" Hebrew word for "adversary." "**Devil:**" Greek translation of "satan," also means "accuser." For two book length treatments on Satan, see Walter Wink's Unmasking the Powers, (Fortress Press, 1986), from whom much of the following was taken, and Elaine Pagels, The Origin of Satan (Random House, 19950.

In the Old Testament Satan is seen as a Servant of God. "The original faith of Israel actually had no place for Satan. God alone was Lord, and thus whatever happened, for good or ill, was ascribed to God. "I kill and I make alive," says the Lord, 'I wound and I heal.' (Deut. 32:39; Isaiah 45:6-7; I Sam. 2:6-7). It was not inconsistent, on the one hand, to believe that God might call Moses to deliver Israel from Egypt, and on the other hand, for God to want to murder him on the way, (Exod. 4:24-26). When Pharaoh resisted Moses it was not ascribed to his free will, but to God's hardening of his heart (Exod. 4:21; 7:3; 9:12; 10:1,20,27; 11:10; 14:4,8,17; Joshua 11:20, etc). Likewise, it is God who sent an evil spirit on Saul (I Sam. 16:14-16,23), and it was God who sent a lying spirit to enter the mouths of the four hundred prophets of Ahab (I Kings 22:22; see II Sam. 17:14)." [Walter Wink's Unmasking the Powers, pp. 11-44].

"The one instance where śātān describes a celestial figure who is not in any way hostile to God is Num 22:22, 32. The Angel of Yahweh is sent to be a śātān to sinning Balaam. The angel performs his task first by blocking the path so that Balaam's ass may not proceed, then by rebuking Balaam. Only when Balaam's eyes are opened does the angel śātān become visible to Balaam. The angel is both adversary to and accuser of Balaam, and is dispatched on his mission by Yahweh. [The Anchor Bible Dictionary].

"One possible translation of 'Yaweh,' God's name, is "He causes to happen what happens." If, then, God has caused everything that happens, God must also cause evil. But God was also the God of justice (Gen 18:25). So how could God be just and still be the one to cause evil? This was the terrible price Israel had been forced to pay for its belief that God was the primary cause of all that happens. Gradually God became differentiated into a "light" and a "dark" side, both integral to the Godhead. The bright side came to be represented by the angels, the dark side by Satan and his demons. This process of differentiation took a long time to complete so that Satan makes only three late appearances in the O.T." [Walter Wink's Unmasking the Powers, pp. 11-44].

In II Sam. 24:1 an angry God incites king David to carry out a wrongful census. But in I Chronicles 21:1, which is a post Babylonian captivity revision of Samuel and Kings, it is now revised to read that "Satan" (used here for the first time as a proper name) is blamed as the one who incited David to carry out the census. Of course, if God indeed used Satan to accomplish his purposes here, then why not just do it himself--but such a relationship seems contrived. In Zech 3:1-5, Satan (Lit. "the accuser") is seen in the role of prosecuting attorney who brings a valid accusation against Joshua, which God rejects because of his mercy. While we don't like prosecutors, they aren't evil just because they are doing their job. It does, however, say a great deal about us as people if we greatly fear and greatly dislike the prosecutor. If we think the prosecutor is evil, then it's most likely because we are the evil ones. In Job 1-2, Satan (again, Lit. "the accuser") cannot be an evil being if he is still a fully credentialed member of the heavenly court, one of the "sons of God." "Satan's role here is somewhat like an overzealous district attorney, where in his zeal to uncover injustice steps over the edge into entrapment. In all of this Satan manifests no power independent of God, and there is no condemnation of him by God." "There is nothing in the context to indicate that the angel is evil." [Baker's Encyclopedia of the Bible, "Satan"].

What about the Serpent in the Garden of Eden (Gen. 3:1-15)?

Bernard Anderson: "There is no basis here for identifying the serpent with Satan." Understanding the O.T. (p.169). **John Gibson**: "It was one of the animals named by the man [and created by God] in the previous chapter." "It is clear that one of the reasons the snake has been selected for the role it plays is that like the fox it is universally credited with cunning, and it was slimy and treacherous to boot." The author "doesn't want a Satan or a Devil brought into the picture, in case that would be thought to detract from man's responsibility for his own sin.....Paradise is lost to humankind through its own fault...No one else was to blame." "The serpent is temptation personified." "This is of course fantasy...animals only speak in fables, but fables contain much wisdom." Genesis Vol. 1 (pp. 121-125). **Donald Gown**: "The curse on the snake (Gen. 3:14-15) clearly shows that the author is thinking of a real snake"—it is condemned to crawl on its belly from henceforth. The author "clearly rejected the belief in evil deities or spirits, which his polytheistic neighbors would have offered as an easy explanation, for his God is the Creator of all that is, and he made it all to be good. So he chooses one of God's creatures to become the source of temptation, and the snake is the best candidate. It had an ambiguous reputation in the ancient East... The instinctive human hatred for snakes made him a logical choice for the one who initiated the human grasp for independence." "Eventually, when the concept of a personal tempter, the source of evil, had developed, interpreters found it easy to identify the serpent with the devil...But this happened long after the O.T. period (see Wisdom 2:24; Rev. 12:9; 20:2)." Genesis 1-11 (pp. 51-52). **Gordon J. Wenham**: "Within the world of the O.T. animal symbolism, a snake is an obvious candidate for an anti-God symbol, notwithstanding its creation by God.... [anyone] familiar with the symbolic values of different animals, a creature more likely than a serpent to lead man away from his creator could not be imagined." "The serpent symbolizes sin, death, and the power of evil." [Word Biblical Commentary: Genesis 1-15 (pp. 72-80)].

The only way Isaiah 14:12-17 and Ezekiel 28 can be seen as referring to Satan is by reading him back into the text. The Jews never saw Satan in these texts. Even the conservative NIV Study Bible says of the Isaiah text that, "the passage clearly applies to the king of Babylon."

The Concept of Satan Evolved

from that of a heavenly public prosecutor to the leader of an angelic host at war with God and man. The original model for the figure of Satan may have been an oriental spy, who in the absence of a state police served as the eyes and ears of the king. The whole notion of a "devil's advocate" is that of a lawyer "who has the job of being an adversary in the interests of discovering the truth." [Uta Ranke-Heinemann, Putting Away Childish Things, (p. 59)]. Logic supports this view too. "If God is really all-powerful, no devil would have a chance against him. So if a devil really exists, it must be because he's secretly in cahoots with God." -- Sidney Harris.

Satan was transformed into the "Evil One" by two trains of thought, according to Walter Wink. 1) Since in Job we see Satan provoking God to bring on sickness, catastrophes, pillage and death, it would not take long for the popular imagination to turn Satan into the N.T. "god of this world" (II Cor. 4:4). 2) Then there was the need to explain the origin of evil. The sheer massiveness of evil in the world pointed to a more malevolent source than puny human beings. The allusion to a fall of angels through supposed intercourse with women (Gen. 6:1-4) provided the seedbed of a whole new set of ideas that led to that of Satan and his fallen angelic host.

"Not until the post-O.T., late Jewish Scriptures (see Enoch 6:14), that is, in the last 200 years before Christ, are God and Satan directly pitted against each other. The accuser is turned into the adversary of God and the head of a God-hating kingdom, hence an evil principle pure and simple." [Putting Away Childish Things, (p. 58)]. In the Dead Sea Scrolls (c. 150 B.C. to 68 A.D.) we finally see "Satan as the leader of the evil forces and attacker of the righteous. This development was probably influenced by the evil god of Zoroastrian religion…" [Baker's Encyclopedia of the Bible, "Satan"]. "In the N.T., Satan bears all the negative, God hating features…Satan is now a superhuman power of evil. In other words, human fantasy is putting more and more distance between God and Satan, in order to free God from the burden of evil." In the process "man has invented the Devil to get himself off the hook," too. "Man doesn't want to be responsible for his actions, but he remains the only responsible party. He and nobody else is the Prince of Hell on earth." [Putting Away Childish Things, (p. 58-59)].

The bottom line is that if Satan was the brightest creature in all of creation, and he knew of God's immediate presence and omnipotent power like no one else, then to rebel against God makes him dumber than a box of rocks! How is it really possible that any creature in the direct unmediated presence of God would want to rebel against the absolute goodness and love of an infinitely all-powerful being? Even if a creature wanted to rebel, he would know that such a rebellion would be absolutely futile. If Satan is supposedly the wisest creature of them all, then he's stupid. But since no one can be that stupid, he doesn't exist at all.

21 Prophecy and Biblical Authority.

Predictive prophecy is used as a support to Biblical authority. In order to predict the future God must have foreknowledge. Can he predict the future, especially of free-willed human beings? What is the basis of God's foreknowledge? There are philosophical as well as Biblical considerations.

Philosophical Considerations.

What would be the basis of God knowing the future? That is, how is it logically possible for God to know with absolute certainty that a specific kind of event performed by a free-willed human being would take place?

1) Theological determinism. God sovereignly decrees/determines what happens (i.e. Calvinism). [For a critique of this, see my section on "Calvinism"].

2) God is outside of time so he sees everything as present. If this were so, God would have no problems predicting the future because it is not actually in the future. He's merely seeing the present from his perspective. Stephen T. Davis, in his book, Logic and the Nature of God (Eerdmans, 1983), argues against this view by claiming that such a timeless being is "probably incoherent." If God created this universe, then there was a time when it didn't yet exist, and then there was a later time when it did exist. So he argues: "it is not clear how a timelessly eternal being can be the creator of this temporal universe." It would also make 2005 B.C and 2005 A.D. simultaneous in God's eyes. But they are not simultaneous in human historical space and time. Davis argues, "We have on hand no acceptable concept of atemporal causation, i.e., of what it is for a timeless cause to produce a temporal effect." (pp. 8-24).

The notion of a timeless God can be traced to Greek philosophers. Plato argued that God must be an eternally perfect being. And since any change in an eternally perfect being must be a change for the worst, God cannot change. Aristotle argued that all of God's potentialities are completely actualized. Therefore, God cannot change because he cannot have unactualized potentialities. Christian thinkers like Augustine, Boethius, and Aquinas brought these concepts to the Bible. Boethius: "God lives in an everlasting present." According to Aquinas God has no past, present or future since everything is "simultaneously whole" for him.

However, Plato's argument, for instance, "is straightforwardly fallacious, because it rests on a false dichotomy. It rests on the assumption that all change is either for the better or for the worst, an assumption that is simply false." We want a watch to reflect the correct time, and so it must change with the time of day. The watch that stays the same all day long, and didn't change, would be imperfect. Likewise, "when God began to create the universe he changed, beginning to do something that previously he had not done." Such a change implies no imperfection in God. [(From William Hasker, in, The Openness of God, IVP, 1994, pp. 132-133). See also Thomas Morris, Our Idea of God, and the late Ronald Nash, in The Concept of God].

The whole notion that God doesn't change seems to imply that God never has a new thought, or idea, since everything is an eternal NOW, and there is nothing he can learn. This is woodenly static. God would not be person, but a block of ice, a thing. To say he does nothing NEW, thinks nothing NEW, feels nothing NEW, basically means he does nothing, thinks nothing, feels nothing, for it's all been done. What would it mean for a person not to take risks, not to plan (for it's already been planned), or to think (thinking involves weighing temporal alternatives, does it not?). But if God cannot have a new thought then he cannot think--he is analogous to a block of ice.

3) The Inferential View. God figures out from the range of options which choices we will make. He does this because he knows who we are completely and thoroughly as the "ultimate psychoanalyst." He can take us in our present state and know with certainty what we will do next, and next, and next, and so on, and so on. He knows the future because he deduces it from who he knows us to be now. This option actually means, however, that what we do is somehow "programmed" into us. The determinist claims that it's all in the genes and environment, so this viewpoint commits the believer to the same position as the determinist. If God can predict future human actions 500 years from now, based upon what he knows about people living today, then we are merely environmentally and genetically programmed rats. There is no human freedom.

4) The Innate View. God just has comprehensive knowledge of the future. He just "sees it" because he is omniscient. But this isn't an explanation at all! When I asked Dr. William Lane Craig in class how it is that God has foreknowledge, Craig, who would normally have elaborate arguments and defenses for his views, merely said, as if this is all that needed to be said, "It's innate, God just has it." What? How? Eventually this answer led me to reject God's foreknowledge of future human free-willed choices.

From these philosophical considerations, I just don't see any real basis for believing that a good God can have absolute and certain foreknowledge of future truly free-willed human actions. Therefore, along with a great many recent Christian philosophers, I do not believe God can predict the future of human history with certainty. And since I also reject theological determinism, then there is no basis for predestination either, whether due to God's supposed foreknowledge of what we will do, or in God's decrees.

Biblical Considerations of God's Timelessness. The Bible does say that God is eternal. (Psalms 90:1-4; Psalms 102:25-27; Revelation 22:13). But this only means that God has always existed and will forever exist. The Bible never says God is timeless, experiencing no past, present or future. The Bible does say that a thousand years is as a day to God (Psalms 90:4), but this verse cannot support the weight of a timelessly eternal view of God. The passage is merely contrasting God's everlasting existence with man's temporal existence. That is, unlike people, God always has existed and will forever exist. [See Nicholas Wolterstorff, "God Everlasting," in God and the Good, eds Clifton Orlebeke and Lewis B. Smedes (Eerdmas, 1975)]. "If God is truly timeless, so that temporal determinations of 'before' and 'after' do not apply to him, then how can God act in time, as Scriptures say that he does? How can he know what is occurring on the changing earthly scene? How can he respond when his children turn to him in prayer and obedience?" [William Hasker in The Openness of God, (p. 128)].

The Bible does say that God is unchanging (Exodus 3:14-15; 34:6-7; Numbers 23:19; Psalms 33:11; Malachi 3:6; Hebrews 13:8; James 1:17). But this only refers to God's nature, character and purposes. God is described as changing in several passages in the Bible (Genesis 6:6-7; Exodus 32:10; Deuteronomy 9:13; I Samuel 15:11; Psalms 106:44-45; Jeremiah 18:8-10; Joel 2:13; Amos 7:3, and Jonah 3:10). According to Clark Pinnock, the Bible presents "a God who responds to us like a dancer with her partner" [in Predestination and Free Will, p. 158]. He answers prayer, directs his people, and redirects his people.

The impassibility of God is the weakest link and the most dubious of the doctrines that follow from a timeless view of God. One would have to deny almost every book in the Bible here, for nearly all of them speak of God's pain and grief over human beings (Genesis 6:1-5; Judges 10:16; Psalms 95:10; Jeremiah 3:1-3; 13:26-27; 31:20; Hebrews 5:7). Jesus felt the same way (Matthew 23:37; John 11:35), especially on the cross.

Biblical Considerations of Predictive Prophecy.
God is described as declaring what will happen in the future (Psalms 139:4,16; Isaiah 46:10-11; Hebrews 4:13). But these verses do not demand that God has absolute certain foreknowledge of what we humans will do. Just as God does not have the power to do an absurdity (Can he create a rock so large that he cannot lift it? Can he ride a horse he isn't riding?), neither can God know our future free-willed choices because they simply cannot be known. The Bible speaks often as if God doesn't know the future (Genesis 22:12; Deuteronomy 13:3; Jeremiah 3:7, 19-20; 26:3; 32:35; Ezekiel 12:3 and Jonah 3:10).

Even from a Biblical perspective predictive prophecy can be explained in one of three ways: 1) God is announcing ahead of time what he plans to do (Exodus 6:6-8; 7:3; Isaiah 46:10-11). 2) God offers predictions based upon his exhaustive knowledge of the past and present (Exodus 3:19-21). Knowing people as intimately as God does he can pretty much predict what they will do in certain limited situations, although, the further into the future human history moves then the more it becomes impossible even for God to predict. 3) Prophecy can also be understood as a warning, and is thus conditional and based upon human responses (Jonah 3:2,5,10; Isaiah 38:1-6; and Jeremiah 18:7-10). [See Richard Rice, "Divine Foreknowledge and Free-Will Theism," in The Grace of God, The Will of Man (Zondervan, 1989, pp. 121-139)].

How the New Testament Writers Used Predictive Prophecy.
One of the major things claimed by the New Testament in support of Jesus' life and mission is that Jesus fulfilled Old Testament prophecy (Luke 24:26-27; Acts 3:17-24). But if not even God can predict the future as it moves farther and farther into the distance, then neither can any prophet who claims to speak for God. As we have seen with regard to the virgin birth of Jesus, the claim that he was God Incarnate, and of his resurrection, none of the Old Testament passages in the original Hebrew prophetically applied singularly and specifically to Jesus. Early Christian preachers simply went into the Old Testament looking for verses that would support their view of Jesus. They took these Old Testament verses out of context and applied them to Jesus in order to support their views of his life and mission. None of the ones we've discussed proves anything of the sort of what was written about Jesus. [See "Did 'Top Psychics' Predict Jesus? (1999) by Robert M. Price at http://www.infidels.org/library/modern/robert_price/psychics].

Many of the claimed prophecies came from the book of Psalms. But the Psalms are simply devotional prayers. Among other things in the Psalms we find prayers for help in distress, for forgiveness, and wisdom, and so on. They declare praise to God, and they express hope that their enemies will be defeated. There is nothing about them, when reading them devotionally, that indicates they are predicting anything at all! But the New Testament writers quoted from several of them and claimed they predicted several things in the life, death and resurrection of the Messiah, Jesus (i.e., Psalms 2, 16, 22, 40, 69, 110, and 118).

Psalms 2 expresses hope for the Messiah, the anointed one. But any Jew writing about his hope for a future Messiah could have said these same hopeful things. A hope is not a prediction. Besides, Psalms 2 and 110 were most likely to be read at the coronation of·Jewish kings. Psalms 110:1 reads: "The Lord says to my lord: 'Sit at my right hand until I make your enemies a footstool for you feet." The New Testament writers make a big deal out of the fact that David wrote this Psalm in which he calls someone else "lord." This supposedly refers to David's future Messianic son, Jesus--his divine nature and mission. But it's fairly obvious that if David wrote this Psalm he did it on the coronation of his son Solomon, whom he subsequently called, 'lord." He did this because of Solomon's new status, which placed him as a ruler even above the aged David himself.

The other Psalms do not predict anything at all. They are prayers to be interpreted within the range of the writer's experiences alone. Any extrapolation of them to Jesus is reading Jesus into the text, and not justified by the text itself. It is more probable that the New Testament writers were influenced in the construction of their stories about Jesus by making his life fit some of these details. That may explain Luke's concoction of a census in order to get Mary to Bethlehem so that Jesus could be born there, according to "prophecy" (Micah 5:2, Matthew 2:6).

Notice that Matthew 21:2 has Jesus requesting both a donkey and also a colt to ride into Jerusalem on, based upon a misunderstanding of Zechariah 9:9, which reads: "Rejoice...your king comes to you...gentle and riding on a donkey, on a colt, the foal of a donkey." Zechariah's prophecy is an example of Hebraic parallelism in which the second line retells the point of the first line. There is only one animal in Zechariah, but Matthew thinks he means there is a donkey and also a colt, so he wrote his story based upon this misunderstanding in order to fit prophecy! [Mark (11:1) and Luke (19:30) both say it was a "colt." John (12:14-15) says it was a "donkey", and then quoted Zechariah 9:9 as saying: "your king is coming, seated on a donkey's colt."

How Matthew's gospel uses the Old Testament is a case in point for us. We've already seen how he uses Isaiah 7:14 to predict the supposed virgin birth of Jesus (Matthew 1:23), and it's simply fraudulent. Let's just look at three more from Matthew. What exactly does the word "fulfill" mean in Matthew 2:14-15: *"Then Joseph got up, took the child and his mother by night, and went to Egypt, and remained there until the death of Herod. This was to fulfill what had been spoken by the Lord through the prophet, 'Out of Egypt I have called my son.'"* According to the conservative The Bible Knowledge Commentary : An Exposition of the Scriptures, "This is a reference to Hosea 11:1, **which does not seem to be a prophecy in the sense of a prediction**. Hosea was writing of God's calling Israel out of Egypt into the Exodus. Matthew, however, gave new understanding to these words. Matthew viewed this experience as Messiah being identified with the nation." "The total disassociation of that the quotation from its context is completely at odds with our own exegetical preferences." [J. Gnilka, <u>Das Matthausevangelium I Kommentar zu Kap 1.1 – 13.58</u> (HTKNT, 1.1; Freiburg: Herder, 1986), p. 55]. "Matthew naturally understand his quotation from Hosea as prophetic; he did not share the insight, common since Zwingli... and Calvin... that his interpretation does not correspond to the original meaning." [U. Luz, <u>Das Evangelium nach Matthaus I Mt 1-7</u>, p. 129].

When Herod the king ordered all boys two years old and younger in Bethlehem to be killed, Matthew sees this as a *__fulfillment__* of Jeremiah 31:15. Jeremiah is mourning for those who will be cast into Babylonian captivity. According to R. Schnackenburg, "it seems far-fetched to quote this text as fulfillment of prophecy." [<u>Das Mathausevangelium 1.1 – 16.20</u> (Die Neue Echter Bibel, 1.1; Wurzburg: Echter Verlag, 1985), p. 27].

Look at Matthew 2:22-23: *"Then after being warned by God in a dream, he left for the regions of Galilee, and came and lived in a city called Nazareth. This was to __fulfill__ what was spoken through the prophets: 'He shall be called a Nazarene.'"* Again, according to the conservative <u>The Bible Knowledge Commentary : An Exposition of the Scriptures</u>, "The words 'He will be called a Nazarene,' were not directly spoken by any Old Testament prophet, though several prophecies come close to this expression. Isaiah said the Messiah would be "from [Jesse's] roots" like "a Branch" (Isaiah 11:1). "Branch" is the Hebrew word *nezer*, which has consonants like those in the word "Nazarene" and which carry the idea of having an insignificant beginning."

Contextually Matthew's use of Scripture is an apologetic to the Jews. Therefore, in some way his contemporaries must have seen such a use of Scripture as evidence of the nature or mission of Jesus. The question we must ask is how does his interpretation confirm these facts? What is the point of the quotations? What does it add to Matthew's narrative? What does it confirm about Jesus? Contextually there is simply no way on grammatical-historical lines that Hosea 11:1 could be used as evidence of the nature or mission of Jesus in Matthew 2:15. It just isn't there. Matthew uses the verse so loosely that it would show evidence of nothing at all to us today were we the ones weighing the claims of another Messiah. It teaches us nothing at all about the Messiah that he hasn't already told us. We today would be extremely puzzled by Matthew's interpretation of it. Matthew's claim that Jesus is a "Nazarene" isn't specifically quoted from any OT source, and even if the Messiah was to be a "branch" from David, that only could mean to the OT reader that he would be from David's blood line, not that he would live in Nazareth!

It sure seems like Midrash to me. In one sense preachers do this all of the time in retelling some of the events of the Bible. Our methods for discerning correctness have changed. If we were to judge them by our standards of hermeneutics, they wouldn't measure up—that is, we would be laughed at by our contemporaries if we employed the same methods in scholarly studies—try it and see!

What was Matthew's intention? Matthew's gospel reads as if he was making a case for Jesus as the Christ. Dunn stated in <u>The Living Word</u> (Fortress Press, 1987) that Matthew's use of the sayings of Jesus is similar to the way he used the

O.T. in that: "the texts used were often significantly different in sense from the original. It was evidently quite an acceptable procedure in Matthew's time to incorporate the interpretation into the saying itself by modifying the form of the saying." (pp. 115-122). Today we think this way of interpreting the OT is wrong. Paul Copan even admits this: "We should not seek to imitate the Jewish methods of interpretation (of the NT)." ["That's Just Your Interpretation" (2001), p. 194].

On the nature of O.T. fulfilled prophecy there are several options available. 1) One might be that the N.T. writers were simply wrong in many of their interpretations. Hence, maybe the Messiah hasn't yet come, or that no Messiah exists. 2) A second option is that the way they interpreted O.T. prophecy is correct and it serves as a model for interpreting all texts since the authors were inspired interpreters with inspired methodology. Once we claim the N.T. writers were correct in their interpretations then it's extremely difficult not to canonize their interpretive methods, including some Midrash, pesher, etc. 3) A third option is possible based upon the fact that the methods for interpretation have changed over the centuries, some for better, some for worse. God foreknew what the methods of interpretation would exist at the time of Jesus, so when God prophesied of Jesus he knew in advance which hermeneutical principles would force people of that day to the conclusion that Jesus was the Messiah. A particular difficult N.T. interpretation might be incorrect based upon the grammatical-historical method, and yet still be a confirmation that Jesus was its intended object for N.T. era people. But I've already argued earlier here against the third option, and the second option is not a live option to me.

The Prophetic Paradigm. Paul J. Achtemeier in The Inspiration of Scripture (Westminster Press, 1980): "It is precisely because the prophet is the one into whose mouth God placed his own words that the prophet became the model for an understanding of the inspiration of Scripture. This way of understanding the inspiration of Scripture was then applied to the other books of the Bible, and to other literary forms: poems, songs, histories, wisdom sayings and all the rest. Behind the books of the Bible stand the inspired authors, each of whom wrote down what God wanted to be written down." (p. 30-32).

But the model of the prophet receiving the very words of God is not a good paradigm for understanding the Bible as a whole. In the first place, prophetic speech claiming "thus says the Lord" is not seen much at all in the Old Testament, although it is true that it is common in the prophetic books. We don't read, for instance, "the priests, who were heads of families, numbered 1,760," '**thus says the Lord**' (I Chronicles 9:13). Or "I am the rose of Sharon, a lily of the valleys," '**thus says the Lord**' (Song of Songs 2:1). According to James Barr, in his excellent discussion on this whole subject, such a prophetic paradigm "is not applied to the total literature of the Old Testament by that literature itself. Large tracts of Old Testament material are not in any normal sense 'prophetic' and these tracts make no pretension to possessing the features of being words directly given by God such as we find in the speeches of the prophets themselves." [Beyond Fundamentalism (Westminster Press, 1984), p. 21-23].

But when we do look at those passages where the prophets use phrases like, "thus says the Lord," what do we find? "For the most part the content concerns the divine judgment and the divine promise upon Israel, Judah and other peoples (See Amos)." "It is a warning of disaster that will come unless one's ways are mended. What a prophet says, then, is characteristically not an absolute. What the prophet says is conditioned. It may be affected by repentance of the persons affected, or by the pleas and prayers of the righteous on their behalf." (Barr, p. 23-24). **Jeremiah 18:5-10** describes this best. It reads: "The word of the Lord came to me: 'If at any time I announce that a nation is to be uprooted and destroyed, and if that nation I warned repents of its evil, then I will relent and not inflict on it the disaster I had planned. And if at another time I announce that a nation is to be built up and planted, and if it does evil in my sight then I will reconsider the good I had intended to do for it." [Contrast this with **Deut. 18:21-22!**].

Isaiah prophesied that Hezekiah would die, but because he prayed to live, God gave him an additional 15 years (Is. 38:1-6). Technically speaking, what the prophet Isaiah predicted was not fulfilled. But that didn't bother Isaiah because "his utterances were not absolute statements of fact, past, present or future; they were warnings, threats, appeals." (Barr, p. 25). Jonah obeyed "the word of the Lord" by prophesying to the people of Nineveh, "forty more days and Nineveh will be overturned." They repented and God did not destroy them (3:2,5,10). But didn't Jonah prophesy that Nineveh would be overturned? We see this throughout the prophets. Barr: "Prophecy was not concerned with accuracy, but with communicating the will and judgment of God. The belief that the prophetic paradigm supports ideas of accuracy and inerrancy can be maintained only if the actuality of what the Old Testament prophets were like is ignored." (p. 29).

Where the prophets do predict the future, according to Barr "the vast majority" of them are fairly short term ones, and as we've seen, most all of these are conditioned upon the responses of the hearers. The prophets did describe a future ideal messianic age in which pain and suffering would be eliminated (Isaiah 11:6-9), but "these are not really 'predictions.' They are expressions of aspirations and ideals which, the prophet is confident, God will bring to realization. They do not 'predict' how or when or in what degree these expectations may be realized." (pp. 101-102). Furthermore, "it is not the case that prediction is possible only with supernatural aid or guidance. People do it all the time. A number of the predictions which Old Testament prophets make could have been made by a capable newspaper columnist of the period." [Barr, p. 102).

If a foretelling God were truly behind the Bible, then in Sam Harris' words, "Why doesn't the Bible say anything about electricity, or about DNA, or about the actual size of the universe?" "You would expect it to contain a passage such as, 'In the latter half of the 20th century, humankind will develop a globally linked system of computers...and this system shall be called the Internet.'" [Letter to a Christian Nation (Knopf, 2006), p.p. 60-61].

From what I've said it will be clear that I do not believe Michael Drosnin's claims in his 1997 book, The Bible Code, that there are any hidden meanings or prophecies in the Bible. [See Jeffery L. Sheler's book, Is The Bible True? How Modern Debates and Discoveries Affirm the Essence of the Scriptures (Harper, 1999), pp. 233-252].

22 Hell? No!

The traditional doctrine of hell "is one of the chief grounds on which Christianity is attacked as barbarous and the goodness of God impugned." [C.S. Lewis The Problem of Pain, "Hell"].

"The God that holds you over the pit of hell, much in the same way as one holds a spider, or some loathsome insect, over the fire, abhors you, and is dreadfully provoked; his wrath towards you burns like fire.... You hang by a slender thread, with flames of divine wrath flashing about it and ready every moment to singe it, and burn it asunder.... Consider this, you that yet remain in an unregenerate state. That God will execute the fierceness of his anger, implies, that he will inflict wrath without any pity...you shall be tormented in the presence of the holy angels, and in the presence of the Lamb.... There will be no end to this exquisite horrible misery.... So that your punishment will indeed be infinite." [Jonathan Edwards, "Sinners in the Hands of an Angry God"].

So here's a question: "What would we think of a human being who satisfied his thirst for revenge so implacably and insatiably?" [Hans Kung, Eternal Life, 1984 (p. 136)]. "If this were true" (i.e., the traditional view) it would make Hitler "a third degree saint, and the concentration camps...a picnic ground." [Nels Ferre, Christian Understanding of God (p. 540)].

"As the Church's threat against all sinners and all its enemies, hell serves the holy purpose of cradle to grave intimidation." [Uta Ranke-Heinemann, Putting Away Childish Things, "Hell].

"The idea that a fully conscious creature would undergo physical and mental torture through endless time is plainly sadistic and therefore incompatible with a God who loves humanity." "In terms of justice, the traditional view of hell is simply unacceptable. It is a punishment in excess of anything that sinners deserve....Besides, no purpose is served by the unending torture of the wicked except vengeance." [Clark H. Pinnock & Robert Brown, Unbounded Love, "Hell"].

"Is it not plain that sins committed in time and space cannot deserve limitless divine retribution? Hell is the ultimate big stick to threaten people with...this monstrous belief will cause many people to turn away from Christianity." (p. 39) "What human crimes could possibly deserve everlasting conscious torture?" (p. 140) "Surely the idea of everlasting conscious torment raises the problem of evil to impossible heights." (p. 150) Any doctrine of hell needs to pass the moral test....The traditional belief....is unbiblical, is fostered by a Hellenistic view of human nature, is detrimental to the character of God, is defended on essentially pragmatic grounds, and is being rejected by a growing number of biblically faithful, contemporary scholars." (p. 165) [Clark Pinnock in Four Views of Hell, ed, Wm Crockett, Zondervan, 1992].

Three Options On Hell (the traditional literal view is not a live option): **1) The Biblical Language of Heaven and Hell is Figurative Not Literal**. Just like depictions of heaven are figurative describing a place of pleasure and rest, so also depictions of hell describe "a place of profound misery where the wicked are banished from the presence of God." [Wm. Crocket, Four Views of Hell, (p. 57)].

Heaven is described as 1st century people would picture perfect bliss. Before the use of gunpowder, thick walls surrounded ancient cities for protection, with sturdy gates. In Revelation (Chapter 21) heaven is described as the most safe and beautiful city ever, even though there can be no use for walls in heaven. Every conceivable precious stone was used in the heavenly city, except the diamond, because it was too difficult to cut and polish back then. Platinum was unknown until the 16th century, so it's not in the heavenly city either. Since pearls were known in antiquity and were extremely important adornments, the heavenly city gates were made from one single pearl! When people worked from dawn to dusk simply to feed themselves, a heavenly rest (Heb. 3-4) beginning with a sumptuous feast (Rev. 19:6-9) was the perfect picture of heaven to laborers in Jesus' day. To people who lived in one room dark houses, heaven could best be described as filled with light and space (John 14:2; Rev. 21:10-27). When only kings could wear a few trinkets of gold, heaven could best be described as having "streets of gold." (Rev. 22:1-3). God was communicating truth to people "in ways they can understand at their particular time in history." [Wm Crockett, Four Views of Hell (p. 56)].

By contrast, Hell, or in the Greek, *Gehenna*, is a valley outside Jerusalem where rubbish was burned. I actually visited this place called hell, and rubbish is still burned there today. So when the Jews wanted to talk about punishment in the afterlife what better image could they use but *Gehenna*? It was a garbage heap. In a garbage heap fire and worms (maggots) consume the trash. To literally say that sinners who die go to hell would quite frankly mean they end up in this valley. But how can that be? Hell is described as a place where there are fire, worms, and darkness (Matt. 8:12; 22:13; 25:30; etc). But fire gives light, not darkness. Furthermore, do the damned get eaten by maggots or are they burned? The wicked are to weep and gnash their teeth while some are beaten with many blows (Matt. 13:42; 24:51; 25:30, Mark 9:48; Luke 12:47). The wicked person's teeth could be knocked out if beaten with many blows. How then can they gnash their teeth if they don't have any? What is meant by "the worm never dies?" Do worms live forever in hell? Physical fire and worms can only cause pain to earthly physical bodies. The picture of heaven and hell here is not literal, but metaphorical and figurative.

2) Conditional Immortality or Annihilationism. We should not confuse the reality of hell with its images. The images of hell are of: 1) "everlasting punishment" (Matt. 25:46); 2) "eternal destruction" (Matt. 10:28); and 3) banishment into the "darkness" (Matt. 22:13; 25:30). How we interpret these images depends on other Bible verses. In the O.T. the wicked will cease to exist (Psalm 37, Mal.4: 1-2). Jesus in the N.T. shows us that the purpose of fire in punishment is to destroy or burn up the wicked (Matt.3:10-12; 13:30,42,49-50). According to John R.W. Stott: "The main function of fire is not to cause pain, but to secure destruction." [Evangelical Essentials, (p. 316)]. Paul likewise emphasized destruction (2 Thess. 1: 9; I Cor. 3:17; Phil. 1:28; 3:19). Peter likewise stressed the sinners' fate as that of destruction (2 Pet. 2:1,3, 6; 3:6-7). Even in John's book of Revelation, the lake of fire will consume the wicked (Rev. 20:14-15). G.B. Caird: "John believed that, if at the end there should be any who remained impervious to the grace and love of God, they should be thrown, with Death and Hades, into the lake of fire which is the second death, i.e., extinction and total oblivion." [Commentary on Revelation, (p. 186)].

"The Bible uses language of death and destruction, of ruin and perishing, when it speaks of the fate of the impenitent wicked. It uses the imagery of fire that consumes whatever is thrown into it." But "linking together images of fire and destruction suggests annihilation. One receives the impression that 'eternal punishment' refers to a divine judgment whose results cannot be reversed rather than to the experience of endless torment (i.e. eternal punishing)." [Pinnock, Four Views of Hell, p. 144].

L.E. Froom claims that conditional immortality was generally accepted in the early church until its thinkers tried to wed Plato's doctrine of the immortality of the soul to the teaching of the Bible." [The Conditionalist Faith of Our Fathers, Herald Pub., 1966]. Biblically speaking, human beings are not immortal. God alone has immortality (I Tim. 6:16); well doers seek immortality (Rom. 2:7); immortality is brought to light through the gospel (2 Tim. 1:10); those in Christ will put on immortality (I Cor. 15:54), so that they now partake of the divine nature (2 Pet. 1:4).

3) Hell is a Non-Existent Mythical Place—My View. The whole notion of a punishment after we die is sick and barbaric. The whole concept of hell developed among superstitious and barbaric peoples, and tells us nothing about life after death.

The concept of life after death mostly developed in the Apocryphal literature during the intertestamental time between the OT and the NT (from passages like Isaiah 26:19, and Dan 12:1–3). "The return to life of the dead did not really come to the fore until the 2nd century B.C.E., in the days of the Maccabean crisis." [The Anchor Bible Dictionary. "Resurrection"]

The whole concept of Hell developed during the Hellenistic period. There was "the notion of a fiery judgment (1 En. 10:13; 48:8–10; 100:7–9; 108:4–7; 16:17; 2 Bar. 85:13), a judgment usually in a fiery lake or abyss (1 En. 18:9–16; 90:24–27; 103:7–8; 2 En. 40:12; 2 Bar. 59:5–12; 1QH 3). The Valley of Hinnom (*gehenna*), often referred to simply as "the accursed valley" or "abyss," then came to represent the place of eschatological judgment of the wicked Jews by fire (1 En. 26–27; 54:1–6; 56:1–4; 90:24–27)."

"The judgment of the wicked occurred either as a casting of their soul in Gehenna immediately upon death or as a casting of the reunited body and soul into Gehenna after the resurrection and last judgment (2 Esdr 7:26–38; 4 Ezra 7:26–38; Ascen. Is. 4:14–18; cf. Sib. Or. 4.179–91). This understanding divorced Gehenna from its geographical location, but retained its fiery nature. Gehenna had become hell itself." ["Gehenna" The Anchor Bible Dictionary].

Paul Copan on Why God Would Send People to Hell. [From "That's Just Your Interpretation" (Baker Books, 2001), pp. 101-109]. As an evangelical, Copan takes the conservative position (1) above, that the biblical language of heaven and hell is figurative not literal. What do these images depict according to Copan? Hell is "the ultimate, everlasting separation from the source of life and hope: God." Therefore, "the pain of hell should not be seen in terms of something physical but rather as pain within a person's spirit." "Hell at its root is the agony and utter hopelessness of separation from God." However, here I must wonder if Copan has done any deep thinking about what it might mean to be separated from the source of life here. There are many evangelicals who conclude that this means the damned cease to exist [position (2) above]. And while it appears Copan is trying to soften the horrors of hell, if correct, such a view of hell is still a horrible fate for a loving God to inflict upon human beings. The punishment does not fit the crime, period. No thinking person should believe this is what our so-called "sins" deserve.

Copan further argues that "hell is the logical outcome of living life away from God." Those who find themselves in hell have committed "not simply a string of finite sins," but "the infinite sin," for unbelievers have resisted "the influence of God's Spirit" and "refused to honor God as God" by "not lovingly responding to God's kind initiative." However, I find this almost absurd that the Christian God blames us for living our lives as if he didn't exist, because there simply isn't enough reason to believe in him over any of the other gods, or no god at all, especially when we usually adopt the religion we were born into! I furthermore find it absurd that God is so upset that we don't acknowledge him in this life that he will punish us forever for it, as if it hurts him that much for us not to acknowledge him. If he is omniscient, then he knows why we do what we do and why we believe what we do, and I fail to see how such a God cannot empathize with how we live our lives. We all do the best we can do given our environment and brain matter.

Copan continues to argue that "to force someone into heaven who would hate the presence of God...would be horrible," and he agrees with D.A. Carson, that "heaven would surely be hell for those who don't enjoy and desire the blessing of God's presence." [How Long, O Lord? (Baker, 1990, p. 103]. "Hell is getting what one wants (and deserves)—no God." Copan also quotes with approval C.S. Lewis that "the doors of hell are locked on the inside." [The Problem of Pain, p. 127]. Copan claims even though the damned are in anguish "they still choose to remain in it," than to prefer "a God-centered existence in heaven." And so "resistance to God continues in hell."

If this is the best answer an evangelical can offer, and it probably is, then it is simply absurd. To claim that the damned prefer the anguish of hell over the bliss of heaven through repentance is simply absurd. Anyone in such anguish would repent of their "sins" if they could experience the purported joys of heaven. Every single person in hell would willingly desire to change if they could escape the torments of hell for the joys of heaven. Every single one of them.

Christians might claim such repentance wouldn't be true repentance. However, *repentance* (Greek: *metanoia*) is "a change of mind." People would automatically change their minds if they could know the truth about God with this kind of certainty. Once someone believes something different, he automatically changes his lifestyle in keeping with that new belief. This is undeniably true and non-controversial. Socrates went so far as to argue that once someone knows the truth, he will then automatically do good.

The parable of "The Rich Man and Lazarus" (Luke 16:19-31), for instance, shows that the rich man in hell (*Hades*) was now a believer. The rich man now knew the truth about God and hell. The whole difference between the rich man and those of us still alive is the fact that his fate was sealed. The rich man, along with the "demons who believe," will all go to hell, and that is the only difference between them and Christians who believe here on earth, according to the Bible. Their new belief is that everything in the Bible is true, except that there are no promises from God to them about a change of lifestyle leading to heaven. Their final destiny is sealed, and that makes all the difference in the world.

Copan's claim is that the rich man doesn't want to "repent" or change his lifestyle. What possible lifestyle did he have in hell that was preferable to a heavenly existence? Just picture yourself in the rich man's shoes. If you were in hell would you be willing to change your lifestyle for a lifestyle in heaven, especially if you now believed the Bible was true? If someone finds himself in hell, his fate is purportedly sealed. The rich man did not ask to be admitted into heaven because in this parable Jesus reflects the common belief that this was impossible. So the rich man requests the only two other things he could: 1) for relief, and 2) he asks on behalf of his family.

This parable doesn't show that the doors of hell are locked from the inside to me at all. It's exactly the opposite! The doors of hell cannot be locked from the inside if it's painful to be there. But if they are truly "locked from the inside," contrary to this parable, there is the very strong possibility that everyone would change their minds (or 'repent") in hell and be admitted into heaven, based on Copan's own argument!

What if the Muslim God Allah exists? Since no one can be absolutely sure when it comes to God, it's possible that *Allah* exists, correct? The Muslim God could exist and the Koran could be his word. As an atheist I admit this possibility, so I suspect that Christians who are not absolutely blinded by their faith would agree with me here. With that possibility, let's say you die and you stand before Allah's judgment and he sends you to hell. Christian, what do you say in response? You say "I didn't know." "I thought Christianity was true." Then the Muslim God simply says: "Ignorance is no excuse, I gave you many clues." "I even spoke through the atheist John W. Loftus in his book when he suggested this possibility....now off you go into hell's eternal flames."

Think of the shock of it all! You would be completely and utterly dumbfounded, wouldn't you? And this is exactly what you believe that Muslims and atheists, Jews and Deists will face on the *Day of Judgment* with YOUR Christian God? No intelligent Being would demand we must believe the right things about him in order to gain entrance into heaven, even if he did exist. This Christian God parallels the barbaric "thought police" in ancient civilizations. This is a democratic age we're living in. We all have various opinions on everything, and these opinions are sincerely held ones. We are tolerant of diverse opinions because educated people realize we will have intelligent differences. But to send people to hell because they disagreed, well, that's barbaric, plain and simple.

I know, I know. Christians will respond that what sends us to hell are our sins. I find that repugnant too, of course. But even if so, and our sins do send us to hell, then the remedy is to believe the correct things, isn't it? In a democratic society we can believe whatever we want to. We are only judged and/or condemned for what we do. So likewise, it's barbaric to democratic loving people to be judged by God (or Allah) based upon what they believe, period.

23 The Problem of Evil.

The problem of evil is known as "the rock of atheism." Michael Martin considers this problem so significant that out of 476 pages of writing and defending atheism, there are 118 pages on this one issue, which is ¼th of his book! [Atheism: A Philosophical Justification (Temple, 1990)].

Dr. James Sennett has said: "By far the most important objection to the faith is the so-called problem of evil – the alleged incompatibility between the existence or extent of evil in the world and the existence of God. I tell my philosophy of religion students that, if they are Christians and the problem of evil does not keep them up at night, then they don't understand it." [Forthcoming book: This Much I Know: A Postmodern Apologetic].

I'm arguing here against the theistic conception of God, who is believed to be all powerful, or omnipotent, perfectly good, or omnibenelovent and all-knowing, or omniscient. The problem of evil (or suffering) is an internal one to these three theistic beliefs which is expressed in both deductive and evidential arguments concerning both moral and natural evils.

There is Moral Evil: suffering as the result of the choices of moral agents. Examples: The holocaust, terrorist bombings, rape, molesting, slavery, torture, beatings, kidnappings. Drunk drivers across America regularly slam their vehicles into other cars instantly killing whole families. There are witchdoctors in Africa who tell men who have AIDS to have sex with a baby in order to be cured, and as a result many female babies are being taken from their mother's arms and gang-raped even as I write this. Is this not horrendous? In sub-Saharan Africa nearly four million people die from AIDS each year! Just watching a re-enactment of the holocaust as depicted in Spielberg's movie, *Schindler's List,* is enough to keep Christians up late at night wondering why God doesn't do much to help us in this life. Nearly 40,000 people, mostly children, die every day around the world, due to hunger. Then there was Joseph Mengele, who tortured concentration camp prisoners; atomic bombs that devastated Hiroshima and Nagasaki, Soviet gulags, 9/11 twin tower terrorist attacks, Cambodian children stepping on land mines, Columbine shootings, Jeffery Dahlmer, Ted Bundy, gang rapes, and brutal slavery. The list of atrocities done by people to each other could literally fill up a library full of books.

There is Natural Evil: suffering due to nature's tragedies (whether animal or human). Natural disasters like floods, tsunamis, droughts, fires, famines volcanic eruptions, earthquakes, tornados, monsoons, and shipwrecks. There are heat waves, blizzards, and hurricanes. Poisonous species like the black widow spider, brown recluse spider, European earth salamander, rattlesnake, cobra, copperhead snake, scorpions, and many parasites, some of them are lethal and kill one person every ten seconds! Poisonous plants: There are 58 poisonous plants, some milder than others (it depends on which part is eaten, roots, leaves, seeds, flowers, fruits, etc.). Possible fatal ones include: Autumn crocus, Castor bean, Daffodil, Hyacinth, Hydrangea, Jimson Weed, Lily of the Valley, Mistletoe, Morning Glory, wild Mushrooms, Poinsettia, Hemlock, Sumac, Rhubarb, White Snakeroot (which was one of the most common causes of death among early settlers in America), Yew (eat it and you die within minutes), and so on. If they don't kill you they may cause diarrhea, convulsions, paralysis and even comas. There are Chronic Diseases: cancer (lung, breast, prostrate, throat, brain, etc), emphysema, leukemia, cardiac problems (many varieties), diabetes, lupus, arthritis, diabetes. Other Diseases and Conditions: Allergies, colds, migraines, Alzheimer's disease, anemia, asthma, bronchitis, colitis, Crohn's disease, manic depression, epilepsy, gall stones, gastritis, glaucoma, gout, high & low blood pressure, lead poisoning, kidney stones, Chicken pox, small pox, Polio, Parkinson's disease, psoriasis, stroke, sudden infant death syndrome, thrombosis, tumors, typhoid fever, ulcers, Lou Gerig's disease, Lyme's disease, malaria, rabies, rickets, Rocky Mountain spotted fever, strokes, typhus, tuberculosis, diphtheria, hepatitis, herpes, leprosy, measles, meningitis, mononucleosis, mumps, pneumonia, rubella, syphilis, AIDS, gonorrhea, shingles, scoliosis, whooping cough, Down's syndrome, hemophilia, Huntington's disease, rubella, muscular dystrophy, sickle cell anemia, Tay-Sachs disease, West Nile, Mad Cow, salmonella, obesity, infertility, anorexia, bulimia, and so on. There are birth defects: midgets, people born with two heads, deformed limbs, blindness, deafness, dumbness, mental deficiencies including dementia, paranoid schizophrenia, and so on.

Some Major Epidemics have decimated peoples in the past:

162 Possibly measles and small pox in Eurasian world.

542 Bubonic plague in the Middle Eastern world

1331 Bubonic plague in China, Asia and Europe.

1494 Global epidemic of syphilis that started in Italy

1520 Small pox in the Americas

1556 Influenza in Europe and the Americas

1648 Yellow fever in South America

1817 Cholera spread all over the world

1918 Influenza killed 20 million

Future? Asian Bird Flu Virus, H5N1 (it could kill 180-360 million people!).

There is also a non-moral category of evil due unintentional accidents which are the result of human neglect and inaction. Consider these: A man on the line at Ford in a rush to keep his quota for the day may inadvertently do something wrong which will cause a fatal car crash on the road later on. Another person may simply fall asleep at the wheel, intent on getting to an appointment on time by driving longer than he should. The war on poverty during the 60's was an attempt at alleviating human suffering but the consequences were disastrous to the families we tried to help. A coroner may not properly assess the death of a person, who is subsequently buried alive. And so on, and so on.

A very significant portion of human suffering is created by people who didn't know the consequences of their actions and did not believe they were doing wrong. The founding of New Orleans, LA, in a bowl below sea level by French explorer Rene-Robert Cavelier is one of them when Hurricane Katrina (2005) ripped through that city. No one can make the case that he did this on purpose. He had benign reasons. Furthermore, why do we have to re-learn our mistakes over and over again? My question with this kind of suffering is why couldn't God have just created us with better memories?

The Problem of Evil Stated. Here is the argument as stated by David Hume (Philo): "Is he (God) willing to prevent evil, but not able? Then he is impotent. Is he able, but not willing? Then he is malevolent. Is he both able and willing? Whence then is evil?" [Dialogues Concerning Natural Religion, Part X]. But I want to be more precise. If God is perfectly good, all knowing, and all powerful, then the issue of why there is so much suffering in the world requires an explanation. The reason is that a perfectly good God would be opposed to it, an all-powerful God would be capable of eliminating it, and an all-knowing God would know what to do about it. So, the extent of intense suffering in the world means for the theist that: either God is not powerful enough to eliminate it, or God does not care enough to eliminate it, or God is just not smart enough to know what to do about it. The stubborn fact of evil in the world means that something is wrong with God's ability, or his goodness, or his knowledge. I consider this as close to an empirical refutation of Christianity as is possible.

Christians believe God set the Israelites free from slavery, but he did nothing for the many people who were born and died as slaves in the American south. These theists believe God parted the Red Sea, but he did nothing about the 2004 Indonesian tsunami that killed ¼ million people. Christians believe God provided manna from heaven, but he does nothing for the more than 40,000 people who starve every single day in the world. Those who don't die suffer extensively from hunger pains and malnutrition all of their short lives. Christians believe God made an axe head to float, but he allowed the Titanic to sink. Christians believe God added 15 years to King Hezekiah's life, but he does nothing for children who live short lives and die of leukemia. Christians believe God restored sanity to Nebuchadnezzar but he does nothing for the many people suffering from schizophrenia and dementia today. Christians believe Jesus healed people, but God does nothing to stop pandemics which have destroyed whole populations of people. There are many handicapped people, and babies born with birth defects that God does not heal. As God idly sits by, well over 100 million people were slaughtered in the last century due to genocides, and wars. Well over 100 million animals are slaughtered every year for American consumption alone, while animals viciously prey on each other.

Let me tell you two specific cases of suffering. The first comes from a man named **Robert Permara**, who for 4 ½ years heard cruel voices in his head. The cruelest voice said that Satan was going to force him to murder his daughter. You may say that these voices were all lies and should have been treated as such. If you say that, then you don't understand the horror or schizophrenia. You wholeheartedly believe these voices. He was so convinced Satan was going to force him to murder his daughter, that he fought the urge to commit suicide on a daily basis so he wouldn't be the instrument of his daughter's death. Nothing that he tried helped him either, and he tried it all: exorcisms, repentance from every known sin, medications, and counseling. His wife eventually divorced him in fear he may have been a threat to his daughter, leaving him to live alone in a psychotic state. He's recovered a great deal. But why didn't God care?

Then there's former American slave, **Frederick Douglass**, who described how his Christian master whipped his aunt right before his young eyes. "He took her into the kitchen, and stripped her from neck to waist. He made her get upon the stool, and he tied her hands to a hook in the joist. After rolling up his sleeves, he commenced to lay on the heavy cowskin, and soon the warm, red blood came dripping to the floor." "No words, no tears, no prayers, from his gory victim, seemed to move his iron heart from its bloody purpose. The louder she screamed, the harder he whipped; and where the blood ran fastest, there he whipped longest. He would whip her to make her scream, and whip her to make her hush; and not until overcome by fatigue, would he cease to swing the blood clotted cowskin." [Narrative of the Life of Frederick Douglass: An American Slave (1845, republished by Oxford Univ. Press, 1999)].

Why didn't the Christian God ever explicitly and clearly condemn slavery? Paul Copan defends the notion that Biblical slavery was different than American slavery in the antebellum South and shouldn't have been used to justify it. ["That's Just Your Interpretation", pp. 171-178]. Even if this is true, the Bible was still used by Christians to justify the brutal slavery in the American South. Distinguished Princeton professor Charles Hodge defended American slavery in a forty page essay written in 1860, just prior to the civil war. Just read the debates over this issue in Willard M. Swartley, Slavery Sabbath War & Women (Herald Press, 1983), pp. 31-66. Then you'll see just how unclear this issue really was to them. So again, why didn't God tell his people, "Thou shalt not own, buy, sell, or trade slaves," and say it as often as he needed to? Why was God not clear about this in the Bible? Just think how Copan's own arguments would resonate with him if he were born into the brutal slavery of the South! Speaking of American slavery, Sam Harris claims, "Nothing in Christian theology remedies the appalling deficiencies of the Bible on what is perhaps the greatest—and the easiest—moral question our society has ever had to face." [Letter to a Christian Nation (Knopf, 2006), p. 18].

Some Theistic Solutions:

G.W. Leibniz (1646-1716) taught that this is **the best of all possible worlds**. The reasoning went like this: A perfect God has the power to create any possible world. Being perfect, God would create the best possible world. No creaturely reality can be totally perfect, but must contain some evil. So God created a world possessing the optimum balance of good and evil--this is the best of all possible worlds! But it's clearly not the best possible world I could envision, because with just one less murder or one less drought this would be a better world.

Norman Geisler has instead claimed that this world is the best possible way to get to the best possible world. [Philosophy of Religion (Zondervan, 1976). But again, such a claim is suspect, given the amount of evil in our world. And it's clearly not the best possible way to get to the best possible world either, because with just one less murder or one less drought this would be a better world leading up to the best possible world.

There is **Theological Determinism, or Calvinism.** [For a critique, see my section on "Calvinism"]. According to Clark Pinnock, "One need not wonder why people become atheists when faced with such a theology. A God like that has a great deal for which to answer." [Predestination and Free Will , ed Basinger, (IVP, 1986, p. 58).

There are Three Global Theistic Theodicy's:

1) **Augustinian**. The traditional Christian answer is that natural and moral evil entered the world as the result of an angelic and then a human fall into sin--freely chosen. God gives us free will in a neutral world, and will allow us to reap the full individual, societal, and global consequences of our own free choices.

"All evil is either sin or the consequences of sin." God sent Christ to overcome that which brought evil into the world--sin. God will eventually be victorious over evil in the end. Sin that is justly punished is thereby canceled out and no longer mars the universe. [See the summary of this view by John Hick in Philosophy of Religion 4th ed. (Prentice-Hall, 1990), pp. 41-44].

2) **John Hick's Irenaean "Soul Making" Theodicy**. [in Encountering Evil, ed. Stephen Davis]. Two stages of creation are involved: a) first humans were brought into existence as intelligent animals, then, b) through free choices human beings are gradually being transformed into God's children. Perfection lies in the future of our existence through successive reincarnations. [He introduces the concept of reincarnation because he's trying to come up with a theology that harmonizes the various religious viewpoints]. This Theodicy requires an "epistemic distance" from God that allows us to exercise free choices without the direct presence of God to restrain us. It also requires that we reject a historical fall from innocence, and accept a universal salvation of all people.

3) **Process Theology of David Griffin** [in Encountering Evil, ed. Stephen Davis.] He argues that God has not finished creating the universe—it is still in process. The world is God's body. The natural evil we see in the world is simply a part of the ongoing creative act of God through the evolutionary process--he's not finished yet. In this view, God only has the power to persuade moral agents like us to do well. God cannot intervene to help us, only persuade us. He cares; it's just that he cannot directly intervene because he cannot completely control his creatures. God does not need to be justified for permitting evil, since it is not within his power to prevent it. According to William Hasker, with *Process Theology* "the problem of evil, as an objection to belief in the existence of God, virtually disappears." (in The Openness of God (IVP, 1994), p. 139), but you no longer have a Christian God, either.

[There are many books and many more journal articles discussing the various issues around the problem of evil. Almost every philosophy anthology textbook, and every philosophy of religion book will deal with this issue in varying degrees. Here are just a few additional books to consider: David Hume, Dialogues Concerning Natural Religion, Parts X-XI; Daniel Howard-Snyder, ed., The Evidential Argument From Evil (Indiana University Press, 1996); William L. Rowe, ed., God and the Problem of Evil (Blackwell, 2001), A.M. Weisberger, Suffering Belief: Evil and the Anglo-American Defense of Theism (Peter Lang, 1999), and the essays in The Improbability of God, eds, Michael Martin and Ricki Monnier (Prometheus Books 2006), pp. 231-336. From a specifically Christian viewpoint see C.S. Lewis, The Problem of Pain (Macmillan, 1962); Henri Blocher, Evil and the Cross (IVP, 1990); John W. Wenham, The Goodness of God (IVP, 1974); Michael Peterson, God and Evil: An Introduction to the Issues (Westview, 1998); John S. Feinberg, The Many Faces of Evil: Theological Systems and the Problems of Evil (Crossway, 2004).

The Logical (Deductive) Problem of Evil is an argument whereby it is claimed that there is a logical (or deductive) inconsistency with the existence of evil and God's omnipotence, omnibenelovence, and/or omniscience. J.L. Mackie's argument was that God is either not good, not omnipotent, or evil doesn't exist. He argues: 1) a good being always eliminates evil as far as it can; and 2) there are no limits to what an omnipotent being can do. Therefore such a

God cannot exist--it is a logically impossibility. He asks: 1) "Why couldn't God have made people such that they always freely choose the good?" And, 2) "Why should God refrain from controlling evil wills?" ["Evil and Omnipotence" Mind, Vol. LXIV, No. 254, April 1955.]

Planting's Free Will Defense seeks to answer this problem in his book, God Freedom, and Evil (Eerdmans, 1974). He argues that it is logically possible that there is a state of affairs in which humans are free and always do what is right. But he argues God cannot bring about any possible world he wishes that contains free agents with significant choice making capabilities. Plantinga introduces the concept of *transworld depravity*: it is logically possible that every free agent makes a wrong choice, and that everyone suffers from it. This is crucial for the free will defense to work. But as I will argue later, the whole notion of free will has many problems. Plantinga also suggests that it is logically possible that fallen angels cause all of the natural evil in our world! According to Richard Swinburne, such an explanation for natural evil is an *"ad hoc* hypothesis," [The Existence of God (Oxford, 1979), p. 202], and as such, according to J.L. Mackie, "tends to disconfirm the hypothesis that there is a god." [The Miracle of Theism (Oxford, 1982), p. 162)].

Most Christians claim the logical problem has been solved, but there are still versions of the logical problem of evil that have not been sufficiently answered. There are those written by Quentin Smith, "A Sound Logical Argument From Evil;" Hugh LaFollette, "Plantinga on the Free Will Defense;" Richard La Croix, "Unjustified Evil and God's Choice" [all to be found in The Impossibility of God, eds. Michael Martin and Ricki Monnier (Prometheus Books, 2003)], Richard Gale's, On the Nature and Existence of God (Cambridge, 1991), pp. 98-178, and Graham Oppy's book Arguing About Gods (Cambridge University Press, 2006), pp. 262-268, who argues at length for the thesis that Plantinga's treatment of the logical problem of evil is inconsistent in several respects. See also A.M. Weisberger's critique of Plantinga's free will defense in her book Suffering Belief (Peter Lang, 1999), pp. 163-184. Just because Plantinga answered Mackie's formulation, and just because Mackie admitted it, doesn't mean that all formulations have been answered, or that others agree with Mackie's admission.

Even if there is no logical disproof of the existence of God because of intense suffering in this world, that doesn't say much at all. The reason is that there are very few, if any logical disproof's of anything.

Consider this deductive argument from Richard R. La Croix: "If God is the greatest possible good then if God had not created there would be nothing but the greatest possible good. And since God didn't need to create at all, then the fact that he did create produced less than the greatest possible good." "Perhaps God could not, for some perfectly plausible reason, create a world without evil, but then it would seem that he ought not to have created at all." "Prior to creation God knew that if he created there would be evil, so being wholly good he ought not to have created." [The Impossibility of God, pp.119-124]. After analyzing La Croix's argument, A.M. Weisberger argued that "contrary to popular theistic opinion, the logical form of the argument is still alive and beating." [Suffering Belief, 1999, p. 39].

Why did God create something in the first place? Theists will typically defend the goodness of God by arguing he could not have created a world without some suffering and evil. But what reason is there for creating anything at all? Theists typically respond by saying creation was an expression of God's love. But wasn't God already complete in love? If love must be expressed, then God needed to create, and that means he lacked something. Besides, a perfectly good God should not have created anything at all, if by creating something, anything, it also brought about so much intense suffering. By doing so he actually reduced the amount of total goodness there is, since God alone purportedly has absolute goodness.

The Evidential (or Inductive) Problem of Evil, according to Richard Swinburne, is "the crux of the problem of evil." "It is not the fact of evil or the kinds of evil which are a threat to theism; it is the quantity of evil--both the number of people (and animals) who suffer and the amount which they suffer." [The Existence of God (Oxford, 1979), p. 219]. Here the skeptical challenge is that theism is not logically inconsistent, but rather it is implausible. That is, given the quantity of evil in our world, it is improbable that a good, all-powerful God exists. Additionally, given the fact that there is pointless or meaningless evil in our world, and there are compelling reasons to think there is, then it's unlikely that a good, all-powerful God exists.

William L. Rowe, is the leading proponent of this evidential argument: (1) There exist instances of intense suffering which an omnipotent, omniscient being could have prevented without thereby losing some greater good or permitting some evil equally bad or worse. (2) An omnipotent, omniscient, wholly good being would prevent the occurrence of any intense suffering it could, unless it could not do so without thereby losing some greater good or permitting some evil equally bad or worse. Therefore: (3) There does not exist an omnipotent, omniscient, wholly good being. According to Rowe, we cannot know with certainty that instances of (1) take place. But it is one thing to prove that (1) is true and quite another thing to have rational grounds for believing (1) to be true. In light of our past experience and knowledge it is very probable that such events have occurred, thus making (1) reasonable to believe. (1) Taken together with (2), can rationally lead us to the conclusion (3).

Rowe offers two specific instances of evil that support his argument, one involving **moral evil**, and the other involving natural evil. The moral evil case came from a *Detroit Free Press* story on January 3, 1986, in which a little girl from Flint Michigan was severely beaten, raped and then strangled on New Year's Day. Then he goes on to argue that "no good state of affairs we know of is such that an omnipotent, omniscient being's obtaining it would morally justify that being's permitting it." [Philosophical Topics 16, no. 2, (1988): 119-132]. The **natural evil** case he described was of a fawn which was badly burned and slowly died from a forest fire, without any human observer. Rowe argued that an omnipotent, omniscient being could've "prevented the fawn's apparently pointless suffering." A wholly good omnipotent being could have stopped the lightning, diverted it, kept the tree from starting a fire, or kept the fawn from being burned, or if burned could have spared it the intense suffering for days by quickly ending its life. But since God didn't, such a God doesn't exist, for he would not allow this fawn to suffer if it doesn't serve some outweighing attainable good, and not even a theist can come up with a good reason why such a fawn suffered. ["The Problem of Evil and Some Varieties of Atheism," in the American Philosophical Quarterly, Vol. 16, No. 4, October 1979].

Rowe brings up the problem of gratuitous (or pointless evil) with these two cases. According to theistic scholar Terence Penelhum: "Although one cannot require God to do anything, in calling him good one is necessarily expressing the conviction that his behavior will satisfy a certain set of moral standards. In calling God good a theist is committed to saying that God's reasons for permitting evils must be reasons that are acceptable to the believer's own set of moral standards." And since this is the case, "any evils that a Christian will admit to being in the world, he must also say that these evils were allowed by God because their presence is at least compatible with the Christian's own moral principles, and that these evils help with the furtherance of bringing about good in the world. A Christian theist, when faced with what he admits to be an evil, must therefore hold that God allows it because the existence of it brings about good in the world. To admit the existence of an evil which demonstrably cannot have this function would be to admit a proposition inconsistent with Christian theism. For such an evil would be pointless. **It is logically inconsistent for a theist to admit the existence of a pointless evil."** ["Divine Goodness and the Problem of Evil," [Readings in the Philosophy of Religion, ed. Baruch Brody, (Prentice Hall, 1974), pp. 214-226]. Gratuitous human suffering, which serves no point, is logically inconsistent with Christian theism, he claims. Why? Simply because it's pointless. It didn't need to happen for some greater good, and hence is inconsistent with a kind omnipotent God.

<u>Now I will argue my case</u> with all of the above as a background. As I do so, keep in mind two things. Keep in mind what Dr. Corey Washington said in a debate with Dr. William Lane Craig: "We've got to hold theists to what they say…if they say God is omnibenelovent, God is omnibenelovent, if they say God is omnipotent, God is omnipotent. We can't let theists to sort of play with these words. They mean what they mean. And if God is omnibenelovent, God will not have any more harm in this world than is necessary for accomplishing greater goods."

Also keep in mind what Dr. Andrea Weisberger wrote: "any proposed solution to the problem of evil which does not account for all kinds of evil in the world, both moral and natural, is deficient in some way, since evil is then not shown to be necessary. And if some evil is not necessary, God's goodness and/or power is called into question." [Suffering Belief, p.102].

I'll begin by assuming for the sake of argument that God exists. **Then why didn't God just create a heavenly world with heavenly bodies in the first place?** Theists typically believe that a heaven awaits faithful believers when they die, where there will be no "death, or mourning or crying or pain" (Rev. 21:4), where believers will have incorruptible bodies (I Cor. 15:30ff), in a perfect existence. So why didn't God just create such a perfect existence in the first place? If there's free will in heaven without sin, then God could've created such a world. To say God initially did create such a world but that there was an angelic rebellion in it merely places the problem of evil back in time. How is it possible to be in the direct presence of a being that has absolute goodness and unlimited power and still desire to rebel against him? Even if this is possible, why didn't God prevent such a rebellion? Pierre Bayle argued: "One might as well compare the Godhead with a father who had let the legs of his children be broken in order to display before an entire city the skill which he has is setting bones; One might as well compare the Godhead with a monarch who would allow strife and seditions to spring up throughout his kingdom in order to acquire the glory of having put an end to them." [Historical and Critical Dictionary (1679) "Paulicians"].

Paul Copan offers three possibilities with regard to free will in heaven [in "That's Just Your Interpretation", pp. 106-108]. 1) That through our truly libertarian free actions on earth we gain access to heaven where we no longer have this freedom to sin. But if heaven is a place where we longer have the freedom to sin, then God could've bypassed our earthly existence altogether. If there is no free will in heaven then why not just create us all in heaven, as I've argued? What does it matter what we did or didn't do on earth? Furthermore, why reward someone by taking away their free will? If free will can be taken away without a loss of goodness, then why create us with it in the first place? 2) That God foreknows that no one who enters heaven will freely choose to sin. But if God has that kind of foreknowledge then again, what is the purpose of creating this particular world? It appears to be a cruel game of hide and seek, where God hides and we must find him, and only the few who find him will be rewarded while the many who don't are punished when they die. If God has foreknowledge then why didn't he just foreknow who would find him even before creating them, and simply place them in heaven in the first place?...then there'd be no one punished for not finding him. If heaven is a reward, then "it seems absurd for a wholly good God to force humanity into a position of ignorance regarding correct moral choice and then hold people accountable for such a choice." [Weisberger, Suffering Belief, p. 136]. Furthermore, if this world is to teach us the virtues of courage, patience, and generosity in the face of suffering, then most all of those virtues are irrelevant in a heavenly bliss where there is no suffering or pain. 3) That those who enter heaven will be in "the unmediated presence of God" such that "not sinning will be a 'no brainer'—even though it remains a possibility." But if this is the case, then as I've already argued, why do Christians think the Devil rebelled against God, since he was supposedly in the direct unmediated presence of God?

I could end my argument here. But let's say God decided to create a fleshly world with free creatures in it anyway, even though there is no good reason to do. **If so, God should've had three main moral concerns:**

Moral Concern One: that we don't abuse the freedom God gave us. The giver of a gift is blameworthy if he gives gifts to those whom he knows will terribly abuse those gifts. Any mother who gives a razor blade to a two year old is culpable if that child hurts himself or others with it. Good mothers give their children more and more freedom to do what they want so long as they are responsible with their freedom. And if children abuse this freedom, their mothers will discipline them by taking away their opportunities to make these choices. It's that simple. Paul Draper wrote, "we would expect God would behave like a good parent, giving humans great responsibility only when we are worthy of it." [Evidential Argument From Evil, p. 24]. Besides, why should we as human beings have to learn the consequences of our actions by such draconian kinds of sufferings when we err? When my children misbehaved or didn't understand the consequences of their benign actions, I didn't send a proverbial hurricane their way. In fact, as a parent I sought to protect them as much as I could from the extreme consequences of their actions. A little pain was a good thing, so they could learn from their mistakes. But no caring father would let them suffer the full brunt of their mistakes—no father.

Furthermore, if my mother sat by and did nothing while my brother beat me to death, and if she had the means to stop him and didn't, then she is morally responsible for letting me die. She could even be considered an accomplice.

God could keep us from abusing our freedom, too. He could've created us with a stronger propensity to dislike doing wrong just like we have an aversion to drinking motor oil. We could still drink it if we wanted to, but it's nauseating.

God could also implant thoughts into a person's head to prevent him from doing evil; much like in Robert Permara's case above, except these thoughts would be good ones, from God himself.

God has many other means at his disposal here, **if we concede for the moment the existence of this present world**: One childhood fatal disease or a heart attack could have killed Hitler and prevented WWII. Timothy McVeigh could have had a flat tire or engine failure while driving to Oklahoma City with that truck bomb to blow up the Murrah Federal building and the people in it. Several of the militants who were going to fly planes into the Twin Towers on 9/11 could've been robbed and beaten by New York thugs (there's utilitarianism at its best).

A poisonous snakebite could've sent Saddam Hussein to an early grave averting the Iraq war before it happened. The poison that Saddam Hussein threw on the Kurds, and the Zyklon-B pellets dropped down into the Auschwitz gas chambers could have simply "malfunctioned" by being miraculously neutralized (just like Jesus supposedly turned water into wine). Sure, it would puzzle them, but there are a great many things that take place in our world that are not explainable. Even if they concluded God performed a miracle here, what's the harm? Doesn't God want us to believe in him? [David Hume first suggested such things as these in his book, Dialogues Concerning Natural Religion, Part XI].

Moral Concern Two: that the environment God places us in will not cause us excessive suffering. If the Christian God wants us to believe in him, then he should've made it a priority to prevent religious diversity by clearly revealing himself in this world such that only people who refuse to believe would do so. In this way he'd prevent all religious wars, Crusades, Inquisitions and witch burnings. There'd be no religiously motivated suicide bombers, no Muslim terrorists, and no kamikaze pilots.

God should prevent all natural disasters too, like the 2004 Indonesian tsunami that killed a quarter of a million people. If God had prevented it, none of us would ever know he kept it from happening, precisely because it didn't happen. Any person who is supposed to be good would be morally obligated to prevent it, especially if all it took was a "snap" of his fingers to do so.

God should not have created predation in the natural world, either. The amount of creaturely suffering here is atrocious as creatures prey on one another to feed themselves. There is no good reason for this and every reason against it. Something must die so that something else can eat. The spider will wrap its victim up in a claustrophobic rope-like web and inject a fluid that will liquefy its insides so he can suck it out. The Mud wasp will grab spiders and stuff them into a mud tunnel while still alive, and then places its young larva inside so they can have something to eat when they hatch. The cat will play with its victims until they have no strength left, and then will eat them while still alive. The boa constrictor will squeeze the breath out of its victims crushing some of its bones before swallowing it. Killer whales run in packs and will isolate a calf and jump on it until it drowns in salt water, whereupon the bloody feeding frenzy begins. The crocodile will grab a deer by the antlers and go into a death spiral breaking its neck and/or drowning it before the feeding frenzy begins. Nature is indeed "red in tooth and claw."

And creatures do experience pain in proportion to the development of their central nervous systems. Look at any mammal who is being physically assaulted and see for yourself. Take for instance the mouse, while being attacked by a cat. See him grimace, listen to his squeaks, look at his increased breathing rates, and if you can monitor them, check out his increased heart and brain waves. Even when you spray a spider, a cricket, or an ant with Raid you see the convulsions, and the futile attempts to run away from the source of the pain. To say these creatures do not feel pain is to say we cannot know anyone beside ourselves who feels any pain. I can imagine a movie scene of "Planet of the Apes" where the Apes are prodding someone with red-hot pokers all the while claiming he doesn't feel any pain, even though he screams like there is pain. If it looks like pain, it is pain, despite Rene Descartes' claim that animals don't feel pain!

All creatures should be vegetarians. And in order to be sure there is enough vegetation for us all, God could've reduced our mating cycles and/or made edible vegetation like apples trees, corn stalks, blueberry bushes, wheat and tomato plants to grow as plenteous as wild weeds do today. [See Quentin Smith, "An Atheological Argument from Evil Natural Laws," in The Improbability of God, pp. 235-249] Paul Copan has an excellent argument using the Bible to show that there was animal death before Adam and Eve's sin (See Psalms 104; Job 38:39-40; 39:28-29; 41:1, 10, 14), and that God did in fact originally create us as meat eaters (See Genesis 1:28; 4:2-4; 7:2, despite Genesis 9:3). [See his "That's Just Your Interpretation" (Baker, 2001), pp. 150-152]. Even if Christians believe we were originally created as vegetarians, why should animals suffer because of the sins in Noah's day (Genesis 9:3)? What did animals do wrong?

God didn't even have to create us such that we needed to eat anything at all! If God created the laws of nature then he could've done this. Even if not, since theists believe God can do miracles he could providentially sustain us all with miraculously created nutrients inside our biological systems throughout our lives, and we wouldn't know anything could've been different.

The truth is, as Paul Draper has argued, "the theory of evolution of species by means of natural selection explains numerous facts much better than the alternative hypothesis, that each species of plant and animal was independently created by God." [Evidential Argument From Evil, p. 25]. Specifically Draper argues, "Both pain and pleasure contributes to two central biological goals of individual organisms, namely survival and reproduction." [Evidential Argument From Evil, p. 15] But since God doesn't need the biological usefulness of pain and pleasure in attaining these twin goals, and since God additionally needs good moral reasons for allowing for pain, theism is antecedently more implausible than say, atheism. This is particularly persuasive when we consider how long sentient animals had to suffer through this evolutionary process before the arrival humans.

In fact, there is no good reason for God to have created animals at all, especially since theists do not consider them part of any eternal scheme, nor are there any moral lessons that animals need to learn from their sufferings. As a result, William Rowe's argument about a fawn that is burned in a forest fire and left to die a slow death without any human observer is gratuitous evil, plain and simple. It serves no greater good. [Also to be found in Evidential Argument From Evil, pp. 1-11, with discussion].

Animals are grown for human consumption under horrible conditions in intensive factory farms, abused in experimental labs, by abusive owners, and they are left to die slow deaths after being hit by cars or in being trapped. The extent of animal suffering cries out against the existence of a good God.

Moral Concern Three: that our bodies will provide a reasonable measure of wellbeing for us. All that seems to be required here is that we have rational powers to think and to choose, the ability to express our thoughts, and bodies that will allow us to exercise our choices. So we could've been created much differently…easily.

God could've created all human beings with one color of skin. There have been too much killing, slavery, and wars because we are not one race with one language.

God could've created us with much stronger immune systems such that there would be no pandemics which have decimated whole populations of people. At the very least, he could've given us the knowledge to cure these diseases the day after he created us.

God could've created us with self-regenerating bodies. When we receive a cut, it heals itself over time, as does a sprained ankle, or even a broken bone. But why can't an injured spinal cord be made to heal itself, or an amputated leg grow back in a few weeks? If that's all we experienced in this world we wouldn't know any different.

We find a lot of things in nature that God could've done for us. He could've made us all vegetarians, as I mentioned, given us wings on our backs so we could fly to safety if we fell off a cliff, and gills to keep us from drowning.

Only if the theist expects very little from such a being can he defend what God has done. Either God isn't smart enough to figure out how to create a good world, or he doesn't have the power to do it, or he just doesn't care. You pick. These are the logical options given this world.

Theistic responses. Theistic Christians will not concede God's omniscience, or God's omnipotence, or God's omnibenevolence, since they are entailed from many Biblical statements and from Anselmian philosophical considerations.

Some theists like C.S. Lewis, in Mere Christianity, will argue from the start that there can be no evil with out absolute goodness (God) to measure it against. "How do you know a line is crooked without having some knowledge of what a straight line is?" In other words, I need some sort of objective moral in order to say something is evil. But the word "evil" here is used both as a term describing suffering and at the same time it's used to describe whether or not such suffering is bad, and that's an equivocation in the word's usage. The fact that there is suffering is undeniable. Whether it's bad is the subject for debate. I'm talking about pain...the kind that turns our stomachs. Why is there so much of it when there is a good omnipotent God? I'm arguing that it's bad to have this amount of suffering from a theistic perspective, and I may be a relativist, a pantheist, or a witchdoctor and still ask about the internal consistency of what a theist believes. The dilemma for the theist is to reconcile senseless suffering in the world with his own beliefs (not mine) that all suffering is for a greater good. It's an internal problem for the theist.

Other than that, the theist has two responses to my argument. The first response is what I call the **"God Can't Do It Defense,"** and the second response is what I call the **"The Ignorance Defense."** On the one hand, God can't remove the suffering in this world because of such things as the independent and neutral laws of nature, or because of "greater goods" like human free will, or that suffering is part of God's plan for "soul-making" which requires "epistemic distance." On the other hand, God is so omniscient that we simply cannot understand God's reasons for allowing for suffering in this world. I'll take them in turn.

The "God Can't Do It Defense." 1) "Good cannot exist without evil, and/or pleasure cannot exist without pain." But this is obviously false, since the theist believes in the goodness of a heavenly existence without pain. Even in this world where disease causes suffering, I can still experience the pleasure of good health without knowing disease. Besides, if suffering is needed to experience pleasure, then isn't pleasure needed to experience suffering? But this too is obviously false, since someone can suffer a horrible short life and then die without any pleasure. [This is a point that H.L. McCloskey, makes in "God and Evil," in Readings in the Philosophy of Religion, ed., Baruch A. Brody (Prentice-Hall, 1974), pp. 168-186.] And how does this apply to the sufferings of animals? Weisberger argues: "This type of explanation only serves to account for natural evil among beings who can appreciate its absence in some cognitive fashion." (Suffering Belief, p. 107). Furthermore, if it's true that we need some suffering to help us experience pleasure, then why do we need so much suffering? That's the whole point. Why all of the senseless suffering?

2) "Evil is necessary as a means to good." Even if this is so, God could've created a world with far fewer evils, which is my point. Besides, how does this solve the problem of animal suffering? What good do they get out of their suffering? Nonetheless, such a solution assumes a good God initially created the world with the proper balance of suffering. If so, the question becomes whether or not we should try to alleviate suffering. On the one hand, a theist is the first one to say we should alleviate suffering wherever we can, even though God is not obligated to do the same. But if we do, then aren't we also reducing the total good created by God, since suffering is good for us? Maybe we should rue the day that someone found a vaccine for Tuberculosis, or Polio? Maybe our real duty would be to increase human suffering, since it molds character? On the other hand, if suffering can be alleviated by modern medicine without making it worse off for us as a whole, then those very evils we eliminated were not necessary for our good in the first place. Can the theist have it both ways? [This is a point that H.L. McCloskey, makes in "God and Evil," in <u>Readings in the Philosophy of Religion</u>, ed., Baruch A. Brody (Prentice-Hall, 1974), pp. 168-186].

3) "It's not God's fault that we bring a great deal of suffering on ourselves." After the Hurricane Katrina hit New Orleans, LA, someone suggested that people shouldn't have lived there in the first place. But where on earth can we escape from all of the potential evils out there? We may instead move into a tornado zone, or one prone to earthquakes, floods, fires, or the like. While we try to escape from one evil we run smack dab into another. By escaping a hurricane we get bit by a black widow spider, or fall prey to a parasite, or a poisonous plant, a poisonous creature, a ravenous wolf, a fire, and so one. And even if there might be one safe place on earth, then such a place would become overcrowded which would result in other kinds of suffering because of the overcrowding.

We have also created some diseases and viruses because of the use of chemicals to produce crops, or because of some scientific experiments. But we don't always know in advance that we are creating these diseases. We are only attempting to make life more comfortable and to save more lives. The diseases are inadvertently created. Our reasons are benign. So it would still be God's fault if we attempt to use the faculties he supposedly gave us in the environment that we have been given. When humans have created such things on purpose, as in chemical warfare, that's a question for why God doesn't control our choices.

4) "Evil is the punishment for wrongdoing." The supposed fall of man in the Garden of Eden is supposed to account for the sheer amount of our natural suffering in our world. This cannot be, since some of it must have been in the garden itself, as Paul Copan has argued. Besides, the whole story is mythical in nature, much like one of Jesus' parables. Even if the Genesis story describes a real event, the punishment is far worse than the crime. The crime was not rebellion, but curiosity, selfishness and ignorance—**the very things God created in them!** The whole idea that this world is the result of Adam & Eve's sin is sickening. In Richard Gale's words: "The whole idea of a deity who is so vain that if his children do not choose to love and obey him he will bring down all sorts of horrible evils on them and their innocent descendents is horrendous." [<u>The Evidential Argument From Evil</u>, p. 215].

Furthermore, how could Adam and Eve know that God was telling the truth? The serpent questioned this, didn't he? So there wasn't enough evidence for Adam & Eve to know for sure that what the serpent said was not true. Why not? Since God is supposedly omniscient, then he knows how much evidence they needed. So if they sinned, he knew in advance that he didn't give them enough evidence to believe and heed the warning. If God didn't give them enough evidence to know he was telling the truth, then God shares the blame for their sins. Why? Because if they knew for sure what would happen, they wouldn't have sinned, and this is a good philosophical argument against the existence of the Devil too.

People in Biblical times defended God against the problem of evil by blaming themselves and their own sins for the natural disasters that God sent on them. They believed God controls all natural happenings (Ex. 12:23,29,30; 32:35; Num. 11:33; 16:46-50; 25:18; 2 Sam. 24:15-16). Why don't very many Christians today use this same response to exonerate God from natural disasters? In ancient times, disasters were usually explained in only one way: God was upset with people because of their sins. And that's the explanation we find most often in the Bible, although there are a few notable exceptions (Job; Luke 13; John 9). But even here we see a God who could do anything with the world of nature that he wanted to do without regard for the ordered world and laws of nature.

In Job for instance, we see the Biblical answer for the problem of evil in the first two chapters. The answer was that God is testing us with disasters and he allows Satan to do us harm so that he might be glorified from our actions. That is a sick answer to the problem of evil, and here's why: Medical ethics will not allow us to experiment on human beings with life threatening procedures, nor with procedures that might cause other serious complications. And they certainly don't allow us to experiment on anyone involuntarily. The other people in the story don't even matter to God at all, like Job's family. But this is what we find God doing to Job and his family, presumably because he can. What we really want to know is if Job's God cares for him and his family, and he doesn't.

In Luke 13:1-5 we find Jesus commenting on why a couple of disasters took place. Were these people worse sinners than those who escaped the particular disasters? Jesus' answer is an emphatic, "No!" His point says nothing at all against the culturally accepted view that our sins cause disasters. He only says that these people were no more guilty than those who didn't suffer these disasters. So apparently everyone deserves the disasters that occur, it's just that some do not experience what their sins deserve.

In John 9 Jesus' disciples asked him who sinned that a particular man was born blind. His answer was that neither he nor his parents sinned. But even so, his being born blind still had a purpose, "that the work of God might be displayed in him," and then it says Jesus healed him. So his "purpose" in being born blind was for him to later be healed by Jesus.

Many Christians would agree with Rabbi Daniel Lapin who tried to explain God's goodness in light of the Indonesian tsunami that killed a quarter of a million people. In the process of arguing his case he said: "God runs this world with as little supernatural interference as possible." Now how does he know that? Such a belief was not shared by most all ancient people before the rise of the repeatable results of modern science. So why don't they argue the way Biblical writers would argue? Let me suggest that it's because they are modern people after all! And let me also suggest that early Christians would have condemned modern Christians who simply say, "bad things just happen." For them, even the very dice cast from a man's hand is controlled by God. (Pr. 16:33).

Surely, the punishment for sin by God cannot account for everyone who ever died from a tornado, a hurricane, a fire, a flood, an epidemic, or a famine. Many innocent people have died. The distribution of disease and pain is not related to the virtue of those punished. The so-called punishments simply do not fit the "crimes." Just look at our own "selfish" system of punishments, and compare that with the God's punishments in the Bible. Our punishments are kinder and gentler. They're civil. The punishments of God in the Bible are barbaric. We simply put criminals in jail. We don't break both arms of an infant because her father lied at the office. According to Weisberger: "It is far from clear how infants who die of diseases or are born terribly deformed with paralyzing ailments such as spina bifida, or with other defects such as blindness, deafness or retardation,

can be believed to have sinned so that they are deserving of punishment."
(Suffering Belief, p. 114). Furthermore, this solution does nothing to answer the
question of why animals suffer. What did they do wrong?

**5) "Evil is necessary for building character, or 'soul-making,' which is a
higher good."** Again this does not explain the sufferings of animals, and it's
difficult to see how this explains senseless evils. Theistic scholars such as Kelly
James Clark [http://www.calvin.edu/academic/philosophy/writings/ibig.htm]
Eleonore Stump ["Providence and the Problem of Evil," in Christian Philosophy,
ed. Thomas P. Flint (Univ. of Notre Dame Press, 1990, 51-91)] and others argue
that "a perfectly good God would not wholly sacrifice the welfare of one of his
intelligent creatures simply in order to achieve a good for others, or for himself.
This would be incompatible with his concern for the welfare of each of his
creatures." [William P. Alston in The Evidential Argument From Evil, p. 111].
Therefore, the theist has the difficult task of showing how the very people who
suffered and died in the Nazi concentration camps were better off for having
suffered, since the hindsight lessons we've learned from the Holocaust cannot be
used to justify the sufferings of the people involved. It's implausible that their
sufferings did more to teach them the virtues of character and cooperation than
from banding together to win an athletic contest, or in helping someone to build
a house.

6) "The purpose of intense suffering is to cause us to turn to God." If so,
God has done a poor job of this. The pain and the question of human suffering
account for more defections from theism than probably any other cause. What
else can explain why the problem of evil is the most serious one for Christians?
God would be found to be building heaven for the millions on the screams of
billions of people who will supposedly wind up in hell.

William Lane Craig and J.P. Moreland have argued against this when
arguing that the chief purpose in life is not happiness, but "the knowledge of
God" "which can bring eternal happiness" to his creatures. Then by using the
statistics in Patrick Johnstone's Operation World [(Zondervan, 1993), pp. 164,
207-8, 214], they attempt to show that "it may well be the case that natural and
moral evils are part of the means God uses to draw people into his kingdom."
They report that following disasters in various countries around the world the
number of Christians have increased. They also make the argument that the
number of committed Christians in the world has grown significantly across the
centuries when compared to the percentage of people in the world, and is
growing faster today than ever. Craig and Moreland write, "It is not at all
improbable that this astonishing growth in God's kingdom is due in part to the
presence of natural and moral evils in the world." [Philosophical Foundations for
a Christian World-view (IVP, 2003), pp. 536-546].

This whole argument reminds me of Jeff Lowder's comment: "It's like saying
in order to get my wife to love me I have to beat the crap out of her."
[Lowder/Fernandez debate on Theism vs Naturalism]. In an online article titled
"Human Suffering and the Acceptance of God "(1997) by Michael Martin [found
at www.infidels.org], Martin argues against such an idea. He questions their
statistical facts, of course, but then continues to argue that: "1) If God's aim was
to have the maximal number of people believe in God, as Craig has argued, He
has not been successful. Billions of people have not come to believe in the theistic

God. 2) There are many better ways God could have done to increase belief in Him. For example: God could have spoken from the Heavens in all known languages so no human could doubt His existence and His message. God could have implanted belief of God and His message in everyone's mind. In recent time God could have communicated with millions of people by interrupting prime time TV programs and giving His message. 3) Why is there not more suffering, especially in America, since unbelief is on the rise? 4) There is also the ethical issue. Why would an all good, all powerful God choose to bring about acceptance in this way since God could bring about belief in Him in many ways that do not cause suffering? Not only does suffering as a means to achieve acceptance conflict with God's moral character, it seem to conflict with His rationality. Whether or not suffering is a cause of acceptance is one thing. The crucial question is whether it is a good reason for acceptance."

7) "Evil is due to free will." I've already suggested ways God could restrict our freedom to commit senseless evils, and this solution likewise does nothing to solve animal suffering. If God gave us more freedom than we can be responsible for, then he's mainly responsible for the horrible deeds we do. J.L. Mackie asks, "Why would a wholly good and omnipotent god give to human beings—and also, perhaps, to angels—the freedom which they have misused?" [The Miracle of Theism (Oxford, 1982), p. 155)] Pierre Bayle exposes this difficulty [in "Paulicians" in his Historical and Critical Dictionary (1697)]. "It is in the essence of a benefactor to refrain from giving any gift which he knows would be the ruin of the recipient." "Free agency is not a good gift after all, for it has caused the ruin of the human race in Adam's sin, the eternal damnation for the greater part of his descendants, and created a world of a dreadful deluge of moral and physical evils."

Theistic scholar William P. Alston argues that "for all we know, God does sometimes intervene to prevent human agents from doing wicked things they would otherwise have done." [Evidential Argument From Evil, p. 113]. My response: 1) This is unfalsifiable. 2) Its implausible God has done this at all, since there are obvious cases of senseless suffering in this world he could alleviate. 3) This is known as the fallacy of the beard. To ask us to draw a line here is like asking us to pluck out whiskers until we can say which whisker when plucked, no longer makes it a beard. 4) Such an objection doesn't say anything about this particular world with the suffering in it. Bruce Russell: "We can know that some penalty (say, a fine of $1) is not an effective deterrent to armed robbery even if there is no sharp cut-off point between penalties that are effective deterrents and those that are not." [The Evidential Argument From Evil, p. 205] 5) If there was no intense suffering or there was an adequate explanation for suffering, my whole argument would fail.

William P. Alston again: But if God were to act to intervene in every case of incipient wrongdoing…"Human agents would no longer have a real choice between good and evil." [The Evidential Argument From Evil, p. 113]. Eliminating intense cases of suffering would still allow humans with significant real choices. Besides, there's a difference between having a real choice, and being able to actualize our choices. For all we know God could turn bullets into butter and baseball bats into a rolls of tissue paper whenever they are to cause harm, for God can surely judge us by our intentions to do wrong alone.

But there is more. If having real free will is a good thing, then "it would seem that we should possess it perfectly," as Weisberger argues. [Suffering Belief, p. 165]. That is, we should not be arbitrarily constrained in what we can choose to do, like we are now. Most women do not have the upper body strength needed to stop a would-be attacker, while some people don't have the rational capacity needed to spot a con-artist. Gender, race, age, brain matter, where we're born and how we're raised all limit the free choices available to each of us. Both our genes and our environment restrict what choices are available for us to make.

I dare say that if God exists and created a different soul inside my mother's womb at the precise moment I was conceived, and if that organism experienced everything I did and learned the exact same lessons throughout life in the same order that I did at the same intensity, then the resulting person would be me, even given free will. And if you won't go that far, the limits of our choices are still set by our genetic material and our environment. We don't have as much free will as we think. All of us have a very limited range of free choices anyway, if we have any at all. So, theists should have no objection to God intervening when someone chooses to do horrible deeds, especially since theists also believe God can restrict our choices just like he purportedly hardened Pharaoh's heart against Moses.

Then there is also the whole debate between Incompatibilism and Compatibilism. **Incompatibilism** is the view that free will and determinism are incompatible because having free will means the ability to do otherwise than one has done. Whatever we choose to do, we could have done otherwise. If we couldn't have done other than we did at the time, then we were not acting as free human being. **Compatibilism** is the determinist's view of human freedom in which free will and determinism are compatible, because having free will merely means the ability to choose what one desires. [To see what it actually means to have free will, see Richard Carrier Sense and Goodness Without God (2005), pp. 97-118, and the short bibliography afterward].

8) **"Evil is a necessary by-product of causal natural laws."** The theist objects that by making these suggested changes to this world it might go against the laws of nature and/or upset our fine tuned ecosystem. Theistic philosopher Peter Van Inwagen claims: "(...For all we know) only in a universe very much like ours could intelligent life, or even sentient life, develop by the nonmiraculous operation of the laws of nature. And the natural evolution of higher sentient life in a universe likes ours essentially involves suffering." (p. 160). However, the theist faces a dilemma here: if God created the laws of nature in the first place, then he could've created a different set of laws, and if he didn't create these laws, then where did they come from? Why then did God choose to create this universe rather than a different one, or not create at all?

Besides, since this present ecosystem is causing so much intense suffering, the question for the theist is why this ecosystem is more important to God than one without so much suffering that constantly needs divine maintenance. People should matter more to God than a fined tuned ecosystem. If changing the environment in any of these ways requires some adjustment that does not accord with any known laws of nature, what's the problem? The ordering of the world by general laws "seems nowise necessary" to God, as David Hume argued. The theist typically believes God created the universe out of nothing, and if he can do that, he can do anything in his world. Christian scholar Richard Swinburne agrees in his book, Is There a God?: "What theism claims about God is that...he can make planets move in quite different ways, and chemical substances explode or not explode under quite different conditions from those which now govern their behavior. God is not limited by the laws of nature; he makes them and he can change or suspend them—if he chooses."

God could even perform one or more perpetual miracles here. As far as the theist knows, the whole world operates by perpetual miracles anyway. Are all things possible with God, or not? Why is it that God could not cause us to levitate whenever we thought about levitating, much like how Superman flies through the air by thinking of flying without any known mechanism for propulsion? Why can't God do this miracle? He could miraculously do anything in the physical world regardless of whether he could create a different set of natural laws.

Peter Van Inwagen further asks us to consider whether or not the actual sufferings of beasts are a "graver defect" in our world than massive irregularity would be: "...massive irregular worlds are not only massively irregular but massively deceptive (i.e., a world created 5 minutes ago, or a world where beasts feel no pain). He claims "it is plausible to suppose that deception, and a fortiori, massive deception, is inconsistent with the nature of a perfect being." (p. 161). And he considers these two states of affairs "morally equivalent" such that "a creator could not be faulted on moral grounds for choosing either over the other." However, any philosophically trained person already knows this universe is massively deceptive. We naively think we see and hear reality just as it is, but that is patently false. What we see and hear is filtered by our particular five senses. If we could see and hear the whole electromagnetic and sonic spectra we would basically see and hear "white noise." Physicists also know that the ground we walk on is actually moving on the microscopic level like swarming bees, even though we're deceived into thinking its still. Given this massively deceptive universe it's simply not incompatible with the nature of a perfect being. Therefore, to say that a "massively irregular world" might be "morally equivalent" to the massive sufferings of animals is nonsense.

William P. Alston argued that a "conceptual possibility is by no means sufficient for metaphysical possibility...it is much more difficult to determine what is metaphysically possible or necessary than to determine what is conceptually possible or necessary," in our world. [The Evidential Argument From Evil, p. 117]. However, in response: 1) If this is the case, then as I've already argued, why create anything at all? 2) I see no metaphysical impossibility for many of the suggestions I've made, even within our particular set of natural laws....like creating all humans one color of skin, with better immune systems and without the law of predation, since we already find instances of these things in the natural world. 3) Even if this is the case, the question still remains, why did God create these particular natural laws in the first place? 4) Finally, why doesn't God do perpetual miracles to avert senseless suffering?

I maintain that the burden of proof is upon the Christian to argue why certain things were metaphysically impossible for God to do. Anything less than this would mean such a God could have done these things. I am suggesting there are things that the Christian God could have done to reduce the amount of human suffering in the world without creating chaos in the world, without inhibiting our character development, and that would help draw (rather than repel) humans to him. If he could have done that but didn't, then there is pointless suffering which serves no purpose. It must be metaphysically impossible for God to eliminate this suffering otherwise God is to be blamed for this gratuitous (or pointless) evil.

The "Ignorance Defense." The Christian theist will finally punt to mystery, with what I call the "ignorance defense," when he says, "we just don't know why bad things happen, but we can trust God knows what he's doing." Theists claim everything will work out from the perspective of eternity. They claim that the sufferings of this present life are not worthy to be compared with the joys of eternity (Rom. 8:18, 28). But this presupposes what needs to be shown. We are on this side of heaven and hell, and from here we want to know if there really is a heaven and a hell. From here we just don't know. David Hume: "Look around this universe. What an immense profusion of beings. How hostile and destructive to each other! How insufficient all of them for their own happiness! How contemptible or odious to the spectator! The whole presents nothing but the idea of a blind nature, impregnated by a great vivifying principle, and pouring forth from her lap, without discernment or parental care, her maimed and abortive children!" [Dialogues Concerning Natural Religion, XI].

Furthermore, what about the damned? No matter what conception of eternity without God the Christian proposes, the fact that most all human beings will suffer this fate is incompatible with the theistic conception of God. Such a punishment simply does not fit the crime, just like the punishments from the supposed fall in the *Garden of Eden* don't fit the crime. [See "Hell? No!"].

Besides, even for those who enter heaven, Madden and Hare argue this is very much like "a torturer telling his victim on the rack that he need not be concerned, for by and by he will be sent to a luxurious spa. To be sure, the victim is delighted to hear that he has such a future ahead of him, but he still cannot understand why he need be tortured before he goes. The torture remains gratuitous for anything the spa argument shows to the contrary." [Madden and Hare, Evil and the Concept of God, 1968, p. 65]. In the absence of good reasons for the torture itself, the final eternal state, even if it's pleasant for all of us, only compensates us for the evils experienced in this life. But compensation for suffering cannot justify the suffering endured; otherwise anyone could be justified in torturing another person so long as the victim is later compensated.

Theists like Alvin Plantinga, and others claim we just don't know how the future will make up for present evils, but that God does, since he's omniscient. Alvin Plantinga wrote: "Say that an evil is inscrutable if it is such that we can't think of any reason God could have for permitting it. Clearly, the crucial problem for this probabilistic argument from evil is just that nothing much follows from the fact that some evils are inscrutable; if theism is true we would expect that there would be inscrutable evil. Indeed, a little reflection shows there is no reason to think we could so much as grasp God's plans here, even if he proposed to divulge them to us. But then the fact that there is inscrutable evil does not make it improbable that God exists." (The Evidential Argument From Evil, pp. 74-76).

Theists are indeed correct that we can't understand the reason why God allows the intense suffering we experience in this world. But are they correct to say that if theism is true we should expect that there would be these particular inscrutable evils? I've already argued that God could've easily done differently.

In response to William Rowe's inductive argument mentioned earlier, Stephen Wykstra offers the CORNEA defense: the "Condition of Reasonable Epistemic Access." "We can argue from 'we see no X' to 'there is no X' only when X has no 'reasonable seeability'—that is, is the sort of thing which, if it exists, we can reasonably expect to see in the situation." "In other words, CORNEA claims that Rowe's noseeum situation justifies his....claim only if it is reasonable for Rowe to believe that a God-justifying good for the fawn's suffering would likely be 'seeable.'" And Wykstra argues that since God is omniscient it's not likely Rowe could see a God-justifying good here. [The Evidential Argument From Evil, pp. 126-150.]

My response: 1) Even if this CORNEA defense works, it must additionally be shown that the theistic God exists, who knows the reason why there are such evils. 2) If it works, it merely argues that it's possible there's a reason for pointless suffering. But we're talking about probabilities here. In Dr. Weisberger's words, there are "many improbable possibilities." ["The Argument From Evil," Cambridge Companion to Atheism, [Cambridge University Press; 2006]. It's possible there are Martians who live beneath the surface of Mars. It's possible that I am dreaming right now. But what we're talking about is plausibility not possibility. 3) Furthermore, if it works, the same defense could justify continuing to believe in God even though most of the available evidence was against God's existence, since it could be argued that an inscrutable God cannot be shown to exist by means of our limited understanding. Again, this is possible, but how likely is it if most of the evidence is against it? 4) The truth is that it seems very likely that we should see God's reasons for allowing suffering since theists also claim God wants us to believe in him. [See Theodore Drange, Nonbelief and Evil: Two Arguments for the Nonexistence of God (Prometheus, 1998), and the essays in The Improbability of God, part four: "Nonbelief Arguments Against the Existence of God," pp. 337-426]. 5) Finally, the theistic response here cuts both ways. **We're told God is so omniscient that we can't understand his purposes, and this is true, we can't begin to grasp why there is so much evil in the world if God exists. But if God is as omniscient as claimed, then he should know how to create a better world too, especially since we do have a good idea how God could've created differently.**

Theistic scholars like Michael Bergmann, Stephen Wykstra and Daniel Howard-Snyder admit they have no expectations of finding a fully adequate solution to the problem of evil. Such a view actually concedes the whole argument from evil. Their defense is that we simply cannot understand God's ways. But this cuts both ways. If we cannot understand God's ways, then there is no reason to think God's ways are good, either. And since that's true, their whole position is also unfalsifiable, because the only way we can test whether or not God is good is by looking at the evidence in the world. If the theist claims God revealed that he is good without any way to evaluate this purported revelation, then how do we know God revealed this about himself? Therefore, the evidence of inscrutable evil speaks loudly against any purported historically conditioned claim of revelation from God, especially if it came from an ancient superstitious people, as I've argued previously.

Theists say God has a higher morality than we do such that God is not bound by the same ethical obligations as we are, because he has "higher purposes." Whatever this higher morality and higher purposes are, we don't have a clue. There are surely specific examples of ethical obligations that should apply to God as well as to us. For instance, it is ethically wrong for anyone, including God, to sadistically kill, maim, or torture innocent people, period. To someone who claims God can do this to any human being because we are all guilty and deserve this kind of treatment, I simply say, as I have already said, that the punishments do not fit the crimes. What they're describing here isn't a higher morality, but a different morality. It's such a different morality that if we treated people like God does in this world through nature we would be locked up in prison.

J.S. Mill (1806-1873) wrote: "In sober truth, nearly all the things which men are hanged or imprisoned for doing to one another are nature's everyday performances. Nature impales men, breaks them as if on the wheel, casts them to be devoured by wild beasts, burns them to death, crushes them with stones, starves them with hunger, freezes them with the cold, and has hundreds of other hideous deaths in reserve. She mows down those on whose existence hangs the well-being of a whole people, with as little compunction as those whose death is a relief to themselves." [Nature and the Utility of Religion, 1871].

So, either 1) God is not bound by the ethical standards he sets down for Christians, or 2) God's ethical code is absolutely mysterious to us. At this point, the whole notion of God's goodness means nothing to us at all, as John Beversluis has argued: "If the word 'good' must mean approximately the same thing when we apply it to God as what it means when we apply it to human beings, then the fact of suffering provides **a clear empirical refutation of the existence of a being who is both omnipotent and perfectly good**. If on the other hand, we are prepared to give up the idea that 'good' in reference to God means anything like what it means when we refer to humans as good, then the problem of evil can be sidestepped, but any hope of a rational defense of the Christian God goes by the boards." [C.S. Lewis and the Search for Rational Religion (Eerdmans, 1985)].

The bottom line is that the evidence of intense suffering in the world is an empirical refutation of the theistic conception of God. There is a group of people who claim the Holocaust is a hoax, apparently including the President of Iran. But the evidence is against this. Likewise, theists believe that a perfectly good all-powerful God exists despite the overwhelming evidence from evil. The evidence is against these two beliefs, period. I think it just goes to show that people can find intellectual reasons to believe what they want to believe, and that they can accept and defend what they were taught to believe based on the "accidents of birth," as I've argued earlier.

Is it ever rational to believe against the evidence? I don't think so. Even though there's a slim possibility that the Holocaust might be a hoax, and that the theistic God exists, what we believe should not be in opposition to the evidence. Now it is quite possible to rationally believe something when there is no evidence one way or another, like for example, that I am not dreaming right now.

But it's not reasonable to have a belief when the evidence is against it, and that's the direction the evidence overwhelmingly points in these two cases. All theistic attempts to fully justify the evil in this world can be likened to a physicist trying to create cold fusion. The naysayers have the weight of evidence behind them.

What if, according to Hume, "I show you a house or palace where there was not one apartment convenient or agreeable, where the windows, doors, fires, passages, stairs, and the whole economy of the building were the source of noise, confusion, fatigue, darkness, and the extremes of heat and cold?" "The architect would in vain display his subtilty, and prove to you that, if this door or that window were altered, greater ills would ensue. What he says may be strictly true. But still you would assert in general that, if the architect had had skill and good intentions, he might have formed such a plan of the whole, and might have adjusted the parts in such a manner as would have remedied all or most of these inconveniences. His ignorance, or even your own ignorance of such a plan, will never convince you of the impossibility of it. If you find any inconveniences and deformities in the building, you will always without entering into detail, condemn the architect." [Dialogues Concerning Natural Religion, Part X].

If God does exist then at best we would be little more than involuntary animals in a grotesque scientific experiment that God finds pleasure from observing how we act under certain controlled conditions. This might please him, but as animals in that experiment we want to know if God cares about us, even if we aren't equals. And from our perspective a perfectly good God should really care about us for us to call him "good."

If the Christian still wants to maintain that there is a good purpose for all human suffering, then let him also consider what Ivan Karamazov, Fyodor Dostoyevsky's character, said: "Tell me yourself—I challenge you: let's assume that you were called upon to build the edifice of destiny so that men would finally be happy and would find peace and tranquility. If you knew that, in order to attain this, you would have to torture just one single creature, let's say a little girl who beat her chest so desperately in the outhouse, and that on her unavenged tears you could build that edifice, would you agree to do it? Tell me and don't lie!" [in The Brothers Karamazov].

In light of all that has been said listen to Voltaire: "The silly fanatic repeats to me. . . that it is not for us to judge what is reasonable and just in the great Being, that His reason is not like our reason, that His justice is not like our justice. What!? How do you want me to judge justice and reason otherwise than by the notions I have of them? **Do you want me to walk otherwise than with my feet, and to speak otherwise than with my mouth?**" Philosophical Dictionary

Let me forcefully conclude with John Stuart Mill, who wrote this: "In everyday life I know what to call right or wrong, because I can plainly see its rightness or wrongness. Now if a god requires that what I ordinarily call wrong in human behavior I must call right because he does it; or that what I ordinarily call wrong I must call right because he so calls it, even though I do not see the point of it; and if by refusing to do so, he can sentence me to hell, to hell I will gladly go." [Reproduced in an appendix in Richard Taylor, ed., Theism (Liberal Arts Press, 1957), pp. 89-96].

24 Calvinism.

How did Calvin (and Augustine before him) come to the conclusion of what is known as Calvinism? They argued for it from the Bible and from outside sources, including Plato. Calvin reasoned that man is totally depraved, God's election is unconditional, Jesus died only for the elect, God's grace is irresistible, and once saved no man can reject his salvation (known as five point Calvinism).

The strict interpretation of Calvinism is what I encounter the most online, in which it's believed Calvin argued that God sovereignly decrees everything that happens—everything--and because of this, God can absolutely predict the future (known as "theological determinism"). Calvin argued God has at least two wills, one is revealed in the Bible telling us what we should believe and do, along with another a secretive unrevealed will in which God sovereignly decrees behind the scenes what he really wants us to believe and do.

All of these doctrines are disputable on exegetical grounds, and I'll let non-Calvinists do that. There are several excellent books that take issue with Calvinism from an evangelical Christian understanding: Grace Unlimited and The Grace of God, the Will of Man, both edited by Clark Pinnock, and What the Bible Says About God The Ruler, by Jack Cottrell. An excellent debate on the subject can be found in Basinger & Basinger, eds, Predestination and Free Will. Calvinistic theology is based upon the exegesis of a historically conditioned set of canonized documents purportedly being from God, even though a proper understanding of history (and the documents that report that history) is itself fraught with so many problems that most all historians now claim we cannot know exactly what happened in the past nor what people believed in the past (see section 13, on the "Historical Evidence and Christianity').

There are many problems with such a theology, but let me briefly mention the two most serious ones. **The first problem has to do with the Calvinist idea that God sovereignly decrees everything we do—that everything we do has been eternally decreed by the secretive will of a sovereign God.**

This Calvinistic God has two wills as I mentioned, one revealed in the Bible and a secretive one...the real one...that decrees the things we actually do. But both wills cannot be true at the same time. If the Bible says, "thou shalt not kill," and then God secretively decrees a man to murder someone, there is a contradiction in what God actually wants him to do. Does God want this man to kill or not? The contradiction is resolved for the Calvinist because he will say God's secretive will is his true will. But this means that on Calvinistic grounds, the Bible cannot be trusted when it tells us what God wants us to do. Calvinists will respond that the Bible is used as a means to get people to do his secretive will one way or another, good deeds or evil deeds. If, for instance, God says "Thou shalt not kill," it might actually lead someone to kill out of rebellion, which is what God secretively decreed all along. And in this way, God needs the Bible to accomplish his secretive will which brings him glory, or honor.

Calvinists believe that because Adam and Eve (and all humanity) have disobeyed him, God has a right to do with us as he pleases and so there can be no complaining about God's dealings with us. We deserve everything bad that happens to us, even hell itself, so why should God be concerned when we suffer through an insignificant hurricane or a holocaust? Any mercy God extends to us is undeserved, since we all deserve the fires of hell for our sins. When it comes to our behavior, Calvinists will argue that human beings desire to do the things that they do, and so God is not to be blamed when we do evil deeds, even if God has also decreed that we should do them. However, if God decrees that we do a deed, then he also decrees that we desire to do that deed. Therefore, God decrees that human beings DESIRE to do everything that they do. We could never have desired to behave differently! So to blame us because of God-implanted desires cannot be our fault anymore than marionettes on strings can be blamed for any of their actions.

The Calvinist will fall back on the idea that God is an artist and he's creating a massive mural painting on a wall. In any painting there will be bright colors and dark ones. There will be highlights and shadows. There will be points of focus, and points that draw attention to the points of focus. God's painting is beautiful, we're told, and he needs all the colors to create it. Some humans will be points of focus while others will be in the recesses, drawing attention to those focal points. We who want to judge the painting simply don't understand what God is doing. We have no right to complain if we are used by God to accentuate the beautiful colors in the mural and are condemned to hell, because after all, we all deserve hell. The end result will be a beautiful painting that brings him glory. Every color is needed, and likewise, every evil deed and every condemned soul is needed, to make this a beautiful painting and to bring him ultimate glory. That's why Calvin describes God's decree as "horrible," and it is.

If we argue that such a God does not care for us and is only interested in himself, the Calvinist will respond that he has a moral right to be concerned with his own glory over everyone else, since he alone deserves all of the glory. We deserve none of it. The Calvinist will claim that we deserve nothing...nothing. And why is that? Because we are "worms," miserable sinners deserving of nothing. Any mercies God may want to offer us by decreeing such things that bring us happiness, including salvation, are undeserved. They will claim we all deserve to be in hell, so anything good we receive is because of God's love and mercy extended toward us. And why do we deserve to be in hell? The bottom line is because it brings God the most glory. This is indeed "horrible." But if God can decree us to desire to do evil deeds, then he can also decree us to desire to only do good deeds. Why does our present world bring more glory to God than a world where God decrees that all human beings completely obey him? At this point the Calvinist punts to ignorance. He doesn't know why. But it's so implausible to think this world brings more honor to God than one where everyone obeys him, which is what the Bible says he desires, that it's much more likely the Calvinist God just doesn't exist. With *glory* like that, who need *shame*? Such a God is duplicitous in his dealings with human beings for his own ends.

The Calvinist answer is that everything God does is good, even if we cannot understand it. Every instance of human suffering brings about a greater good, God's glory. Everything that happens brings God glory. We are not to question this or to complain. He's creating a beautiful painting. God knows what he's doing. We should trust him, they say. But why does a Calvinist think anyone...should trust their God? Why? What reasons are there for trusting such a God? There are none...none!...not on Calvinistic grounds, since according to Calvinists we deserve nothing from God at all! Their God can treat us any way he wants to with complete utter disregard for us as human beings since we are condemned as sinners going to hell. On their own grounds they can't even trust him to be truthful with them, since the Bible tells them one thing and God secretively decrees something different, which brings me to the second problem for Calvinism.

The second problem has to do with the Calvinist idea that God sovereignly decrees everything we believe—that whether or not a person believes Calvinism is true is decreed by their sovereign God. The bottom line here for the Calvinist is that all of these specific Calvinistic conclusions were the ones that God had secretly and sovereignly decreed that Augustine and Calvin should arrive at from all of eternity. They could not have arrived at different theological conclusions.

If so, how is it possible to trust any of these Calvinistic conclusions if we don't have access to God's secretive will? As far as the Calvinist knows, God's secretive will may be that they should be deceived in accepting Calvinism. Based on their own theology they have no reason to trust God...none. Their God is already recognized to be duplicitous. God may be leading them astray, based upon his secretive will, only to cast them in hell for his own glory. For all they know God may turn around and reward those of us who are skeptics, simply because he secretively decreed us into unbelief. For the Calvinist to proclaim that he can indeed trust God just because God says he "doesn't lie," doesn't solve anything, for the Bible is merely God's revealed will, not his true secretive sovereign will. So Calvinism is a theology that leads to total skepticism about everything—everything. Their God could very well be Descartes' evil demon.

All that the Calvinist can say is that "this is what God has led me to believe, and that's why I believe it." Based upon his own theology there is absolutely no guarantee that what he believes is true, or that it's based upon the available evidence. According to the Calvinist I am an atheist because this is what his God has led me to believe, and that's why I believe it. There would be no way either of us could believe differently. Therefore the evidence for or against our respective beliefs could be overwhelmingly against what we each believe but God decrees that we believe what we do anyway.

A Calvinist might object by arguing that even if his God makes him believe against the total available evidence, such an admission still presupposes the very existence of the Calvinistic God. Hence, it still assumes Calvinism is true, even if all of the available evidence was against it. But this is an epistemological problem concerning internal consistency, and the question is whether or not he can know they are correct about their God. If the Calvinist grants that the total evidence could be against his belief, what follows? Epistemologically, he should cease believing. It's that simple. Such a person should reject Calvinistic Christianity...EVEN IF THE CALVINISTIC GOD EXISTS! That's right....even if the Calvinistic God exists! A person cannot continue to believe once it's acknowledged, on his own grounds, that he cannot know whether or not the evidence favors what he believes. Based upon Calvinist grounds he has no reason to say the evidence supports what he believes, and there is way to decide if he believes correctly. If a Calvinist acknowledges this, he should be an agnostic. It's that simple.

Let me personalize this. If God sovereignly decreed that I should be an apostate, then he is his own worst enemy. With decrees like this there must be a great amount of internal conflict within the Trinity itself! Such decrees are contrary to his stated desires (II Pet. 3:9). In fact, that means God decreed I should write this book and start my Blog! Maybe God should just see a shrink. If God is completely sovereign then God decreed what I am doing (and I could not have done otherwise). I'm leading people away from him. If I'm effective, more people will be in hell as a result of my efforts, and I cannot do otherwise.

The Calvinist response is that God purportedly decrees all of this because the people who suffer in hell for all eternity bring him more glory than if they didn't suffer in hell for eternity. But the belief in the eternal suffering of billions of people for slighting God is one of the biggest problems atheists have with God, and one of the main causes to malign him. How could the redeemed ever praise him for this, especially when those who suffer will be their spouses, children, parents, and friends? And God sovereignly decreed all of this? It's plainly obvious that this does not bring more glory to God than having everyone in heaven. Again, with that kind of *glory* who needs *shame*?

People who do lesser crimes get locked up in prison and/or are executed. The fact that he is God and thus more powerful than us makes no difference in the way he should treat us. It just makes him a thug, a despicable potentate. He's a devil in disguise, and unworthy of anything but disgust!

25 <u>The Achilles' Heel of Christianity</u>

According to Greek mythology, when Achilles was born, his mother, Thetis, tried to make him immortal by dipping him in the river Styx. As she immersed him, she held him by one heel and forgot to dip him a second time so the heel she held could get wet too. Therefore, the place where she held him remained untouched by the magic water of the Styx and that part stayed mortal or vulnerable. Achilles died from a heel wound as the result of a poisoned arrow fired by Paris. To this day, any weak point is called an "Achilles' heel".

We live in what has been described as a post-Christian society. There are modern ideas we have come to accept that make us who we are, which we will never give up on. So we must move on, because we cannot go back. From the vantage point of these ideas we must reject the Bible, since we cannot give them up. Genesis does not tell us anything about creation. We do not live in a three-tiered universe, with heaven above, and hell beneath the earth. We also have serious reservations about ancient miracle claims in an age when there were a plethora of such claims. People don't misbehave because they are evil, they may just be sick. Punishment isn't what people need, so much as healing and understanding. A wrathful vengeful hateful God does not exist.

Basically any major social idea that has changed the way we look at the world will necessitate how we look at the Bible too. Male chauvinism is dead. Democracy now reigns in the place of kingship, and all that goes with it. Plus, the whole notion of justice has undergone major revisions, and highlighted by the civil rights revolution. Slavery is abhorrent to the modern ear.

I think this is the Achilles' heel for Christianity. The Achilles' heel for Christianity is the huge difference between the ancient mind and our modern standards of reasoning, our hermeneutical understandings, our moral consciousness, and our methods for understanding history, psychology, and science. We reject the notion of an atoning sacrifice, whether animal or human. We reject the way Matthew, Jesus and Paul interpreted the text of the OT. We have better standards for judging purported historical events. We reject the inadequate moral consciousness of an ancient barbaric Biblical people when it comes to slavery, women and war. And we reject the whole nature of superstitious thinking when compared to modern scientific thinking today.

Christians must either 1) canonize these ancient Biblical standards, and thus perpetuate primitive thinking; 2) come to some half-way house in-between, which satisfies neither house, or 3) reject these particular ancient standards totally, like I do.

I have seen Christians canonize the Biblical standards of slavery for today. They will say slavery isn't wrong, if done the Biblical way. But the Bible says a slave owner can beat a slave within an inch of his life so long as he doesn't knock out a tooth or an eye (Exodus 21: 20-21; 26-27). If the slave owner does kill his slave the only punishment was most likely that he merely lost his property! These Christians are inconsistent on which issues they canonize, which ones they hold a halfway house on, and which ones they reject (like slavery). At least Pat

Robertson is consistent when it comes to explaining why people suffer. He'll argue the way that Biblical writers did when natural suffering takes place. Robertson has said that when evil strikes God allowed/caused it because of someone's sin.

Modern science provides the fatal wound to the Achilles' Heel of Christianity. Science proceeds on the assumption that there is a natural explanation for every event. Every modern person does this, even Christians! When it rains on our parade, modern Christians don't go off thinking God must've sent the rain to spoil their parade. If we cannot have a baby, modern Christians don't go off thinking God must be preventing them from having a baby because they've sinned. These Christians will just go see a fertility doctor, if they have the money. When we hear an unexplainable noise in the night, not even Christians will believe they've been visited by an angel. They will just assume the house creaked, or the wind outside blew a tree limb against the house, or the dog knocked something over. When it comes to prayer, before the advent of modern medicine Christians had to pray with faith when they were sick. Now Christians just take a pill or go see a doctor. Before the rise of the mass production of food in the Western world, Christians had to fervently pray "give us our daily bread," because they didn't know where their next meal was coming from. Now Christians barely even remember to pray before meals, since daily food is no longer a problem.

There is becoming less and less room for God, as we explain more and more. Call it the *God of the Gaps* if you want, but we are less religious today because of science. And while there is no scientific experiment that can show God doesn't exist, or that he doesn't work in this world, we still operate on this scientific naturalistic assumption so often that it makes secularists out of us all. If this assumption works so well and describes so much, then this assumption probably has a metaphysical grounding to it, although such a step cannot be shown from science itself. But it's not a big step.

Since science has been so successful in its own domain, the same standards of rigorous testing have filtered into all the other disciplines of learning. Is a boy demon possessed, or does he have epilepsy? If we continued treating him as if he were demon possessed we may never help such a boy. Is a person sick or oppressed by the devil? Again, by assuming a natural explanation, science helps to fix things. Do we believe an incredulous story about some guy levitating, or do we approach such stories as if there was a natural explanation? In this we are different than the masses of ancient Greek or Roman people.

Empirical testing. Skepticism. Evidence. Proven hypotheses. Technical precision. Specialized languages. Mathematical formulas. Peer reviewed journals and magazines. These kinds of things have infiltrated every major discipline of learning in the modern world. We have more rigorous standards when testing psychological theories, historical conjectures, journalistic investigative reports, and claims of the miraculous. These are the things ancient people lacked, in comparison to our modern scientific communities. It's the rise of modern science that makes us all less religious today, and which causes us to disbelieve the specific claims of superstitious believers in the Bible.

26 Why I'm An Atheist

I know what I reject. I reject Christianity. But after the demolition is done, what could I now believe about how we got here on earth and why? In my letter to Dr. Strauss (written in '96) I said I could be described as a Deist, a theological existentialist, and perhaps a Panentheist (as in Process Theology).

This initial agnosticism of mine was unsettling to me. It simply wasn't an answer. To say, "I don't know," means just that, I don't know. I don't think I'll gain any new information with further research that will help me figure it out. I knew about everything I will know to make a decision. According to William James we must choose. This is the problem he spoke of when it came to *forced options*, and it is a forced one for me. There's no such thing as living like an agnostic. So why couldn't decide? Why? As I pondered this question the answer just hit me like a proverbial ton of bricks. Let me explain.

Faith and Reason Revisited. The relationship of faith to reason is sort of a catch-22 for me. If we initially try to figure it out with reason we cannot figure it out. Take for instance the existence of God. It's undeniable that something now exists, without even trying to come to a common understanding of the nature of that which exists, be it spirit, matter, or a combination of both. That means there are basically two choices for us, or we can just say that it's all completely absurd to the core. Either something has always and forever existed, or something popped into existence out of absolutely nothing. Either horn you grab onto presents us with deep problems. On the one hand, how can we understand what it means for something, let's say God, or the universe for that matter, to have always existed without a beginning? Can anyone say they comprehend that? It's almost absurd.

On the other hand, every attempt to understand how something (either the universe as we know it, or even God for that matter) popped into existence out of absolutely nothing fails. Can anyone say they comprehend that? It's almost absurd. In fact every scientific attempt I've read to describe how our universe began to exist always begins with something—from the "swerving atom" of ancient Greek philosopher Democritus, to Paul Davies' "cosmic repulsion in a quantum vacuum," to what Edward Tryon and Stephen Hawking both describe as a "quantum wave fluctuation" [Tryon in Nature, December 1973, and Hawking in Physical Review (December 1983]. These things are not nothing.

According to Mark William Worthing in God, Creation, and Contemporary Physics (Fortress Press, 1996): "For a true creation out of nothing there can be no scientific explanation. Any theory explaining how something has come from nothing must assume some preexisting laws or energy or quantum activity in order to have a credible theory. It could be claimed, naturally, that there was nothing and then suddenly there was, without apparent physical cause or ground, something. But this would be more a statement of philosophical or theological belief than a genuine scientific theory." (p. 105).

Our choice is between an infinite regress of events, or an uncaused cause. Our choice is between the cosmos having no explanation for its existence, or a final explanation that needs no further explanation. Concerning the origin of our universe, Sam Harris writes, "The truth is that no one knows how or why the universe came into being. It is not clear that we can even speak coherently about the creation of the universe, given that such an event can be conceived only with reference to time, and here we are talking about the birth of space-time itself. Any intellectually honest person will admit that he does not know why the universe exists." [Letter to a Christian Nation (Knopf, 2006, pp. 73-74).

So with regard to the origin of this reality we experience it seems that reason simply cannot help us. The catch-22 here—damned if I do, damned if I don't—is that if I start with reason I may get nowhere, but if I start with faith, the question becomes this: what if I start out by believing the wrong set of things?

The Religiously Ambiguous Nature of the Universe. John Hick is arguably the most important philosopher of religion in the past century, and one of the reasons I quote from him so much. In science there is what is known as the Copernican Revolution, in which our whole understanding of how we viewed the universe changed from the geocentric view (where earth was viewed as the center) to the heliocentric view (where the sun was viewed as the center). Immanuel Kant called for a philosophical Copernican Revolution when it came to our notion of how we experience reality. For him, in short, categories in our minds structure reality, instead of reality shaping our minds (i.e., there is no mind-independent reality).

In 1972, John Hick called for a Copernican Revolution in dealing with world religions. His most important work is titled, An Interpretation of Religion: Human Responses to the Transcendent (Yale Press, 1991), which is an expanded form of the prestigious Gifford Lectures that he gave in 1986-87. According to Hick: "The universe is religiously ambiguous in that it is possible to interpret it, intellectually and experientially, both religiously and naturalistically. The theistic and anti-theistic arguments are all inconclusive, for the special evidences to which they appeal are also capable for being understood in terms of the contrary world-view. Further, the opposing sets of evidences cannot be given objectively quantifiable values." That is, "our environment is capable of being construed—in sense perception as well as ethically and religiously–in a range of ways." Thus, "all conscious experiencing is experiencing—as." (p. 12).

The internationally revered authority on world religions, **Huston Smith**, in Why Religion Matters (Harper, 2001), stated it this way: "the world is ambiguous. It does not come tagged 'This is my Father's world' or 'Life is a tale told by an idiot.' It comes to us as a giant Rorschach inkblot. Psychologists use such blots to fish in the subterranean waters of their patients' minds. The blots approach the patient as invitations: Come. What do you see here? What do you make of these contours? The sweep of philosophy supports this inkblot theory of the world conclusively. People have never agreed on the world's meaning, and (it seems safe to say) never will." (pp. 205-6).

Even though Hick believes that the universe is religiously ambiguous he still chooses the tradition of liberal Christianity to interpret all of the religions—the one he inherited. But if he was correct about the ambiguous nature of it all, then it would also be rational for someone to believe in atheism, and he admits this.

Anglican philosopher **Terence Penelhum** agrees with Hick. He wrote: "An ambiguous world is one in which there are always reasonable grounds for hesitation, and is therefore one in which such hesitation is probably not blameworthy. The world could not be ambiguous if there were no people in it who could reasonably interpret it in more than one way." But we all know that there are such people. [http://www.ucalgary.ca/UofC/faculties/HUM/RELS].

"We appear to be confronted not with a simple theist-naturalist ambiguity, either side of which can justify itself at least in negative terms; we are confronted, rather, by a world that exhibits multiple religious and ideological ambiguity." "It is possible to be conscientiously unable to decide between two or more world-views and life-options. If the world is ambiguous, then it is a necessary truth that this is possible, even though the motives of this or that person may be beyond our powers to determine. Those who insist that unbelief must be willful, and not merely that it may be, have the onus of showing that the world is not ambiguous. Only then can we be sure that unbelief is due to the willful refusal to grant what the accuser thinks is true."

Penelhum concludes: "**I think there is one unqualified obligation for all rational beings, whether they have a faith or not: to remove it—to seek the disambiguation of their world**. To find some truth that eliminates some alternative reading of the world, or a truth that establishes some essential part of a hitherto merely possible reading of the world. But we can't all wait, can we, for the philosophers to determine what it is rational to do before we make life-forming decisions? Of course not; but this is a problem. There are many beliefs we have to go on holding whether philosophers can sustain them for us or not. **But an ambiguous world is a world in which it is rational to go on holding this or that or the other world view...in which the informed thinker knows this**." Therefore, the first thing we must do "is what committed but intellectually responsible adherents of a faith should do," and that is "to try their best to find a disambiguating argument in favor of the position they are living by." [We see him struggling with his faith in "A Belated Return," Philosophers Who Believe, ed. Kelly James Clark (IVP, 1993), pp. 223-236].

I believed that I must try to disambiguate this religiously ambiguous universe, too. In doing this I previously chose to believe in Deism and the philosopher's God who created this universe. This God is not the particular God of Abraham who demands worship and obedience, so much as a God who solves the question of how we got here. While I granted the religiously ambiguous nature of this universe, I struggled to believe in God. It was probably a Kierkegaardian leap of faith for me, which also made me an Existentialist, a Deistic Existentialist. But this wasn't satisfying, for according to Marcus Borg: "There is little difference between a distant and absent God and no God at all." [The God We Never Knew (Harper, 1997, p. 23)].

My Former Position Was Untenable. Since this universe is religiously ambiguous, then there are several religious, or non-religious options available to rational people when they seek to disambiguate this ambiguous universe. But if this is so, why did I existentially choose Deism, and not Atheism, or Panentheism, or Pantheism? Why not even return to some form of Christianity, since Christians too can claim, at least to themselves, to be rational in holding to it. Why not choose as John Hick, Huston Smith or Terence Penelhum does?

This was a tough question for me. All I could do was to say that most Christians welcome reason to examine their beliefs, so that's what I did. They think their faith wins in the marketplace of ideas, and that it's supported by reason. So, in this book I did what they asked me to do. I've examined and evaluated Christianity with the standards of reason and modern science and concluded the Christian faith is not a reasonable faith.

I didn't even think reason applied to ultimacies, so how could I judge anyone else's worldview by the standards of reason? **Then the question hit me. Why is this universe religiously ambiguous capable of being interpreted in various rational and sometimes even mutually and exclusive ways? Why does it all appear absurd when we approach it all with reason? Why must I resort to giving up on reason and punting to the view that I just don't know, or that it cannot be rationally figured out? Why?**

<u>Then The Answer Hit Me</u>. When we seek for a cause of it all we run into absurdities, precisely because blind chancistic events cannot be figured out! Chance events can produce order. We know this. Even if the odds are extremely unlikely for this universe to exist, once there is some order in the universe and someone to look upon the order that's there, it cries out for an explanation. So we try to explain it, but fail time and again. Pascal would be right here to say all over again, "I look on all sides and see nothing but obscurity; nature offers me nothing but matter for doubt." We may even have to say, like I had previously said, that it cannot be figured out with reason, and initially it can't. But when we reflect on why we can't figure it all out, the best reason I can offer is that random chance events can't be figured out hindsight. So in the end, I do have a reason for what I believe. Nature is ultimate. According to the late Carl Sagan, "the cosmos is all there is, was, or ever will be." According to Bertrand Russell the universe is simply "a brute fact." I am an atheist. There is no God. And there is at least one reason for me not to believe in God, and that is because this universe is absurd when we try to figure it out. Any attempt I know of to figure it out fails, except the conclusion that it arose because of chance. According to Jacques Monad, "our number came up in a Monte Carlo game." [See his book, <u>Chance and Necessity</u>].

Even Christians are atheists, in that they don't believe in the other gods and goddesses of other religions. I just deny one more god than they do. I agree with Christian criticisms of other religions and I agree with the criticisms they make of Christianity. My wife Gwen, is an atheist, as I have said. While she's not an intellectual, her argument is quite simple. She asks a very simple question: "If God exists, then why doesn't he show me?" It can be developed into a sophisticated argument, however, and it does have some force to it. Surely if God exists, he knows what it would take for us to believe, so why doesn't he do what it takes?

Michael Scriven claims, "if we take arguments for the existence of something to include all the evidence which supports the existence claim to any significant degree, i.e. makes it at all probable, then the absence of such evidence means there is no likelihood of the existence of the entity. And this, of course, is a complete justification for the claim that the entity does not exist, provided that the entity is not one which might leave no traces (a God who is impotent or who does not care for us) and provided we have comprehensively examined the area where evidence would appear if there was any." [Primary Philosophy (McGraw-Hill, 1966), p. 102]. What I have examined leads me to the conclusion that a divine being does not exist, so I am rational and justified in being an atheist.

Atheism was a very unsettling conclusion to me, in one sense. It means I have no hope in a resurrection, that I no longer have the hope that there is someone outside the space-time matrix who can help me in times of need, or give me any guidance. But on the other hand it's finally a conclusion. I now can believe something, and as I've said, it's better over here. In one sense my intellectual journey is over. It's very relieving to reach a conclusion that I can partially defend. Partially? Yes. I do not have at my disposal all of the ways to defend such a conclusion, since this conclusion is itself based on a cumulative case which includes an irreducible personal element to it. It just seems plausible to me because everything I have examined so far has failed to provide a satisfying answer, except atheism. So ends my attempt to disambiguate this religiously ambiguous universe. Others may seek to do so in other ways.

No matter what position you take on the nature of existence you must start with something seemingly absurd. It's like the Englishman who traveled to India and inquired about the Indian legend that the world rests on the backs of four giant elephants. He asked an Indian man what the elephants rested on, and the Indian man told him a huge turtle. Of course, our traveler then asked the next, rather obvious question: what does this turtle rest on? The Indian man replied, "Oh, sahib, after that it is just turtle all the way down." [See illustration below].

27 What is Life Without God?

Francis Schaeffer has initiated a Christian "cultural apologetic" based upon the human predicament. This apologetic, according to William Lane Craig, "simply explores the disastrous consequences for human existence, society, and culture if Christianity should be false." [Reasonable Faith: Christianity and Apologetics (Crossway, 1994), formerly, Apologetics: An Introduction (Moody Press, 1984, p. 31-53. See also J.P. Moreland, Scaling The Secular City: A Defense of Christianity, (Baker, 1987) Chapter 4].

After noting what Pascal, Dostoyevsky, Kierkegaard, and Schaeffer said about the human predicament without God, Craig offers his own assessment. According to Craig, if there is no God or immortality "then man and the universe are doomed." "It means that life itself is absurd." It means that the life we have "has no ultimate meaning...no ultimate value...and no ultimate purpose." The Biblical book of Ecclesiastes typifies this view. "All is vanity" without God ("under the sun"), in an ultimate sense. I now feel the force of that book like never before. It describes the plight of human existence.

Dr. Craig is careful to point out that arguing for this "cultural apologetic" doesn't prove that the Christian point of view is correct, only that "if God does not exist, then life is [ultimately] futile." I certainly agree that it doesn't prove the Christian faith, but since he considers this argument to have considerable force, let's see what could be said in response.

We can have three options in our lives:

1) A reasoned hope in life after death (belief in a true religion, if one exists);
2) A reasoned despair or pessimism about death (ex. agnosticism, or atheism);
3) A false and/or irrational hope in life (ex. false religions, existentialism).

The despair or pessimism I refer to in option two is due to the idea that life has no "ultimate meaning" beyond this life. That is, our lives have no significant ultimate purpose beyond this life, much like an animal or an insect. When we die, and our children die, and their children die, there will barely be a remembrance of us. How many of us remember much about our great great, great, great, grandparents? When the ever-swelling sun swallows up this whole earth and human life is extinguished, there will be no remembrance of the human species as a whole, unless we can find a way to populate other planets in our solar system, but they too will be swallowed up by the sun, until the sun burns out. But to travel to another inhabitable planet from our solar system seems absolutely remote. Even if we could, this universe itself will expand until it reaches absolute zero degrees where humans cannot survive. So there is no ultimate significance to human beings, and that's what I mean about a reasoned despair. Albert Camus simply asks us, "why not commit suicide?" After all, if there is no ultimate purpose, then at least you can determine the time of your death.

I personally just don't think option one is a live option. I've chosen option two, since option three is no hope at all. According to Michael Martin, "If pessimism is justified by the evidence, then we must be pessimistic. If we are optimistic when pessimism is justified, we are irrational." [Atheism: A Philosophical Justification (Temple, 1990), p. 15]. Yet, this simply does not mean I shouldn't go on living my life as a good person who seeks to be good to other people at all. It doesn't mean that a society that adopts such a position does not have a reason to contribute to the common good either, as I will argue here.

Let me offer six responses to this cultural apologetic. **In the first place,** Schaeffer and Craig point out the moral troubles in Western societies and decry the days when Christianity was a stronger force in western societies. They argue that as Christianity was being rejected our society began to go to hell in a hand basket. Now it is a fact that we have indeed raised many narcissists in our modern western societies, which probably means the West is in moral decline. Many great societies of the past went into moral bankruptcy too. It may just be the natural bent of we human beings. The increase in crime could be partially due to population growth, and overcrowded cities

But remember this, prior to our day and age Christianity was the "myth" that held us together. And since the Enlightenment, scholars are dismantling it piece by piece. With it in decline, pluralism reigns for many people, along with many bankrupt ethical people. There is probably no longer a uniting myth to western societies. And while Schaeffer and Craig are right to point out our moral malaise, the real problem isn't necessarily the loss of Christian truth and values in our society. The real problem is that there is no longer something that unites or binds us together. That may be more of our problem in America today, not the fact that we're rejecting Christianity. I think human dignity, freedom, and democratic-capitalism should unite us as a society, and it does. I also believe we should export these values around the globe; not only because it's good for humanity, but it's also in our own self-interest as an American society at war with Islamic terrorists who seek our demise.

In the second place, let me say that anyone who tries to show that no society can be a good society without Christianity needs a history lesson. They need to study some of the great societies of the past, like Greece during the golden ages, or The Roman Empire, or several of the dynasties in ancient China, or the Islamic Empire under Muhammad, or the historic Japanese culture. None of these societies were Christian ones, but they were great societies by all standards of history. And yes, there was corruption in every one of these societies too, just like any ancient or modern society, even Biblical Judaism and Christian America.

If Christians want to maintain that a Christian society is a better society, then just let them volunteer to go back in time to medieval Christianity and see if they like it. Probably all Christians today would be branded as heretics and persecuted or burned to death. And if today's Christians will say that medieval Christianity doesn't represent true Christianity, which Christian society does truly represent true Christianity? Even in the first few years of the early church there was corruption. There was sin in the camp (Acts 5); grumbling about food (Acts 6); and a major dispute that threatened to split the church (Acts 10-11, 15; Galatians 2). Then there were the constant disputes among these Christians over a very wide assortment of issues (I & II Corinthians). I could go on and talk of Calvin's Geneva, the Crusades, the Inquisitions, witch trials, or any period in the history of America too, with black slavery, the Salem witchcraft trials, Manifest Destiny, and our treatment of women and minorities, to mention just a few.

Christian inclusivist scholar, Charles Kimball, argues that certain tendencies within religions cause evil. "Religious structures and doctrines can be used almost like weapons." (p. 32). Religion becomes evil, according to Kimball, whenever religion: 1) has absolute truth claims; 2) demands blind obedience; 3) tries to establish the ideal society; 4) utilizes the end justifies any means when defending their group identity; or 5) when they see themselves in a holy war. He says, "**A strong case can be made that the history of Christianity contains considerably more violence and destruction than that of most other major religions.**" (p. 27) [When Religion Becomes Evil (Harper, 2002)].

Richard Dawkins, a world-renowned evolutionary biologist, has released a two-part video series in 2006, called "The Root of All Evil?: The God Delusion." Dawkins describes God as the most unpleasant fictional character of all and he attacks religion as the cause for much of the pain and suffering in the world.

I just don't see where a Christian society is a better one. And even if Christianity was the main motivator in starting most all early American universities, most all of our hospitals and many food kitchens, and the like, these things still would have been started anyway, if for no reason other than ·necessity. It just so happened to be that Christianity is the dominant religion in America for a couple of centuries, that's all. Besides, these things were probably not started by Christian churches out of altruism, or any desire for a better society, but as a way for those churches to convert people. After all, who are most vulnerable to the Christian message? They are the sick (hospitals), the poor (food kitchens) and young people leaving home for the first time to enter universities which were mostly started to train preachers.

In the third place, the search for meaning brought about the various religions. We have a great intellectual need to make sense of something that cannot be made sense of, to find purpose when there isn't any to be found, and to find meaning in a meaningless world. This need to make sense of the universe will tend to push us to believe in God, for then we have meaning and security in knowing who we are, why we're here, and where we're going.

In my opinion, this human need may be the reason why people believe in God in the first place, not because of the arguments pro and con. As humans we simply cannot bear to believe we have no ultimate purpose in life, and that our existence is absurd. We think we're more important than that!

Harvard professor and evolutionary psychologist, Steven Pinker, has argued that the mysteries of our existence first provoked the belief in God or gods in the first place. He asked, "who benefits" from the pervasive religious belief in our world? There are the "**consumers of religion**" who are confronted with the mysteries of death, dreams, and questions about existence. Then there are the "**producers of religious beliefs**" who seek to come up with answers to these questions. As these producers come up with satisfying answers to these mysteries, the consumers grant them power, some measure of fame, and money. In this way everyone benefits, but the producers benefit much more, and in this way religion is propagated all over the globe. ["The Evolutionary Psychology of

Religion" (Free Thought Today, Jan/Feb 2005); see also Daniel C. Dennett, Breaking the Spell: Religion as a Natural Phenomenon (Viking 2006); Michael Shermer's, How We Believe: The Search for God in an Age of Science (Freeman, 2000) and Richard Dawkins, The God Delusion (2006), pp. 161-207].

And what better answers are there than that we are significant, and that life does have meaning? These are the answers we desperately want to hear, so it's no surprise to me that there are more religious believers in the world. The producers of religion offer solutions that are very fulfilling indeed, especially the story about a God who cared about us so much that he came down in Jesus and died in our place! The question is how many people would follow a "producer" if his answer were that life is ultimately vain?

When these originating producers of religion gained a foothold of power in a society and that society economically and militarily flourished it validated those religious answers. According to Edward O. Wilson, "All great civilizations were spread by conquest, and among the chief beneficiaries were the religions validating them." [(Consilience: The Unity Of Knowledge (Knopf, 1998), p. 244]. In my opinion, **Christianity is a legendary development from a person named Jesus that lucked its way into political power**.

In the fourth place, we need to consider the dangers of someone who claims to have ultimate values in life. Edward T. Babinski has documented Christianity's "grotesque past" in his book Leaving the Fold (Prometheus Books, 2003, pp. 35-60) and also online, "The Civil War, Slavery, and the Bible," http://www.edwardtbabinski.us/religion/christian_experience), where he discusses some of the atrocities committed by Christian people who claimed to have had ultimate values. Christians don't have a good track record when it comes to slavery, wars, Inquisitions, witch hunts, scientific progress, and so on. [On witch-hunts see Carl Sagan's book, The Demon Haunted World (Random House, 1986), pp. 118-123, 406-413].

The Crusaders had an ultimate reason for slaughtering Muslims in Jerusalem, didn't they? The German church was behind Hitler, claiming ultimate purposes too. There are abortion clinic bombers who claim to have ultimate values. Right now there are American Christian Dispensationalists who support the Jews no matter what they do, because they have "ultimate" knowledge that the Jews are linked with Biblical prophecy. These Christians have actually perpetrated the conflict we now have with the Muslims of the world.

Consider also the harm that has been done by Christians with regard to inhibiting scientific progress through some inaccurate notions about the nature of human beings, forbidding someone by law to follow their desires for a same sex relationship, impeding the progress of feminism, advocating some forms of censorship, intolerance, bigotry, and discrimination to those who are agnostics and atheists.

Militant Muslims have their own ultimate purposes and values, don't they? They are extremely dangerous people because they will die for their ultimate cause and go to heaven to be with 72 virgins (what those virgins did wrong to be in heaven at their service I just don't know). As John Debbyshire comments, "You can point to people who were improved by faith, but you can also see people made worse by it. Anyone want to argue that, say, Mohammed Atta was made a better person by his faith? Can Christianity make you a worse person?

I'm sure it can. If you're a person with, for example, a self-righteous conviction of your own moral superiority, well, getting religion is just going to inflame that conviction." [*National Review Online*, "God & Me." On the dangers of religious faith in a modern world containing weapons of mass destruction, see Sam Harris, The End Of Faith: Religion, Terror and the Future of Reason (Norton, 2005). See also Richard Dawkins, The God Delusion (2006), pp. 279-308].

According to Bertrand Russell, "one of the most interesting and harmful delusions to which men and nations can be subjected is that of imagining themselves special instruments of the Divine Will." "Cromwell was persuaded that he was the Divinely appointed instrument of justice for suppressing Catholics and malignants. Andrew Jackson was the agent of *Manifest Destiny* in freeing North America from the incubus of Sabbath-breaking Spaniards." Of course, such a political program "assumes a knowledge of the Divine purposes to which no rational man can lay claim, and that in the execution of them it justifies a ruthless cruelty which would be condemned if our program had a merely mundane origin. It is good to know that God is on our side, but a little confusing when you find the enemy equally convinced of the opposite." "Belief in a divine mission is one of the many factors of certainty that have afflicted the human race." "Most of the greatest evils that man has afflicted upon man have come through people feeling quite certain about something which, in fact, was false." ["Ideas That Have Harmed Mankind," Unpopular Essays (Schuster, 1950), pp. 146-165)].

In light of Christianity's past it would be better if Christians didn't consider the values that they have to be ultimate ones. Better is a healthy measure of skepticism about such claims.

In the fifth place, while there may be no ultimate reasons for being a good person, as Craig argues, there are plenty of non-ultimate reasons for being good. There is no meaning for human existence beyond the life we humans share on earth. Any meaning is to be found here and now without the help of God, and there is plenty of meaning and purpose to be found here.

Here then, are some non-ultimate reasons for being good. Human beings do not like pain, unless they are testing their own physical endurance level for an upcoming sports contest, in which, the pain is worth the reward. There is mental pain, social pain, physical pain, financial pain, and so on. The avoidance of pain for humans is a huge motivator. Which means the opposite is the seeking of pleasure. Holistic pleasure then, is its own reward, as Aristotle argued.

The values of tolerance, family, and friendship in a political democracy under democratic capitalism provide a society with the best chance to avoid pain for most people in it. According to democratic capitalism, for instance, we receive money from people we serve, so we serve people to get what we want. Anyone who doesn't serve others in this way will not be financially rewarded. And anyone who steals money and is caught goes to jail. If we want fame and power, the same thing applies. We must have something that people want, and so by serving people we get what we want. Furthermore, as social human beings we need approval from others, which is a motivator for doing good deeds, and for contributing to society.

Like most people, my wife and I are good to others. We like the approval of people, and we like knowing we helped out in humanitarian ways. It gives us those Christians on the fringes of our society who think they have an ultimate goal in life and who seek to do others wrong, like the KKK, or Catholic priests who are molesters. They too do harm. The monthly circular <u>Free Thought Today</u>, published by Dan Barker's "Freedom From Religion" organization, (www.ffrf.org) documents many crimes done by Christians, from embezzlement, to rape to molestation. You'll have that on both sides of the fence, whether religious or not. **The real harm is when you place people in power who have ultimate mandates**. These religious people can do much more harm than non-religious sociopaths who are in power, as just noted.

In the sixth place, if I am correct that there isn't a reasoned hope, then no one has any ultimate meaning in this life, precisely because this life is the only one we have to live. **Those Christians who think they have a reasoned hope are living their life based upon a delusion**. They have a false and irrational hope, but just don't know it. They are simply deluded into thinking their lives have some grand ultimate purpose. So who's better off? Someone who lives a life of delusion, doing things because they think it will matter for eternity, along with the daily guilt for not having lived up to those standards, or someone who lives with his or her feet planted squarely on the ground?

Consider the medieval monks, for instance. They lived ascetic lives on the bare bones of existence, spending their lives reading a Biblical text that was false, rather than living the fullest life possible. Consider modern day Catholic priests, who live life without knowing the warmth of an intimate embrace in the arms of a woman, and the joys of being a father and a grandfather. Consider the fundamentalist Baptist minister who never may know what it's like to get drunk. Consider the many nights Christians spend evangelizing others, when those same nights might be better spent with their families or friends. Consider the time many Christians spend reading the Bible, when they could enjoy the great novels of their day. Consider the joy one might have in alleviating the person who is suffering for the pure joy of it, rather than doing it for some false heavenly reward. Consider the money that was spent in building great cathedrals and temples to this false sense of ultimate reality that could be better spent on the needs of people, or with what is leftover, a cruise in the Bahamas.

Contrary to the whole Christian cultural apologetic, **All is vanity when you live a life of delusion**! The Christian life is ultimately in vain, because it is built on a false hope.

[For further discussions on the values and meaning of life without God, see: Albert Camus, <u>The Myth of Sisyphus and Other Essays</u> (Alfred Knopf, 1955); Viktor Frankl, <u>Man's Search For Meaning</u> (S. & Schuster, 1959), Steven Sanders & David R. Cheney, <u>The Meaning of Life</u> (Prentice-Hall, 1980), Daniel C. Dennett, <u>Darwin's Dangerous Idea: Evolution and the Meanings of Life</u> (Simon & Schuster; 1996); Richard P. Feynman, <u>The Meaning of it All</u> (Perseus Books, 1998); J.L. Mackie, <u>Ethics: Inventing Right and Wrong</u> (1977); Kai Neilsen, <u>Ethics Without God</u> (Pemberton Books, 1973); Kurt Baier and Kai Nielsen, <u>The Meaning of Life</u>, E.D. Klemke, ed. (Oxford Univ. Press, 1981); Richard Robinson, <u>An Atheist's Values</u> (Clarendon Press, 1964), Richard Carrier, <u>Sense and Goodness Without God</u> (2005); Michael Martin, <u>Atheism, Morality, and Meaning</u> (Prometheus Books, 2002), and Richard Dawkins, <u>The God Delusion</u> (2006)].

pleasure to please others, so we do. It makes us feel good about ourselves. That not why we do it, but it's what we receive for doing it. And we need no ultima values for this, either. It's just a better life when we have friends that we ca count on in times of need because we were good to them in their times of need When someone is shunned or ostracized as a human being, it's very painful, s it's in our best interests to be good people. And we are.

These reasons may not be enough, but I believe they are values everyone can share. Many Muslims want what we have in the Western world. It was said by Bernard Lewis, who is an authority on Islam, that when American planes were flying over Iran to drop bombs on Iraq, that people held up signs that read, "Drop bombs here!"

You don't need an "ultimate" anything to live life in this world. There just aren't any ultimacies. But there are non-ultimate reasons. And while I don't think what I do in life will matter for all of eternity, it matters very much, both to the ones I love and to me. This life is all there is: a short blip of existence in the cosmos. So it makes what I do here what ultimately matters—it's all there is. I should therefore be motivated to give all I have today, for this is all I have. And while life is ultimately meaningless, I am living life to the hilt everyday. I'm living without the guilt that Christianity threw on me, too! Life is good--very good! I feel better about it now than I ever have!

Here's what atheist Bertrand Russell said: "United with his fellow men by the strongest of all ties, the tie of a common doom, the free man finds that a new vision is with him always, shedding over every daily task the light of love. The life of man is a long march through the night, surrounded by invisible foes, tortured by weariness and pain, toward a goal that few can hope to reach, and where none may tarry. One by one, as they march, our comrades vanish from our sight, seized by the silent orders of omnipotent death. Very brief is the time in which we can help them, in which their happiness or misery is decided. Be it ours to shed sunshine on their path, to lighten their sorrows by the balm of sympathy, to give them the pure joy of never-tiring affection, to strengthen failing courage, to instill faith in hours of despair...let us remember that they are fellow sufferers in the same darkness, actors in the same tragedy with ourselves. And so when their day is over...be it ours to feel that, where they suffered, where they failed, no deed of ours was the cause." This is my goal. ["A Free Man's Worship" in Why I Am Not a Christian (Touchstone, 1957), pp. 104-116].

But what about someone who is self-seeking in all of his ways, and harms people who get in his way? Well, we ostracize these people, and we lock up many of them in our jails and prisons. They are not deemed by any society to contribute to the well being of that society. So the avoidance of any kind of pleasure that leads to the pain of prison is better than unmitigated pleasure. And since we cannot turn our character on and off like a faucet without changing who we are by degrees, we'd be better off being good people in any society we live in.

On the fringes of society we will have some sociopaths, thieves, and sexual predators who seek to do others wrong for their selfish pleasure. This is unavoidable in a free society containing human beings with all of our psychological problems and undisciplined desires. But that isn't what any society considers the norm, and what they do certainly isn't rational, either. We put people in jail for seriously harming others. But this isn't much different from

28 <u>What If I'm Wrong?</u>

What if I'm wrong about Christianity? What then? Well, then I will go to hell, however conceived, when I die. And what did I do to deserve to go to hell? I "sinned," I didn't believe in Jesus' atonement, or in his bodily resurrection from the grave.

Whose fault would this be? Mine? I have honest doubts. Am I to be blamed because I couldn't understand Christianity? I tried with everything in me. I even spent several years earning three master's degrees and studies in a Ph.D. program to understand the reasons for my faith. If I tried to figure it out and I wasn't supposed to try then maybe educated people don't have a chance to be saved? If, however, I'm just not smart enough to figure it out, then only intelligent people who study it out have a chance to be saved. Maybe the only people who have a chance to be saved are those who aren't educated or who aren't very intelligent. But who gave us our mental equipment in the first place? Didn't God create us? Does this mean that when we're born some of us are condemned from the start because of our mental equipment leading us to believe, or not? If God gave it to us, and if only unintelligent people can be saved, then it's set in stone the day we're born what the possibilities for each one of us are.

What if I'm simply deceiving myself? What if my doubts about Christianity and my atheism aren't honest at all, and my claim that they are is disingenuous? Perhaps unconsciously I'm rebelling against God. Well, I'm simply not consciously aware of any attempt to rebel against God, nor am I consciously aware of any attempt to deceive myself at all. I have been a counselor in churches where I served and I know how to dig into my own unconscious mind enough to know that my doubts are honest ones. That's all I can say.

But what if I'm being deceived by the traditional devil to have these doubts? Maybe he is playing tricks on me, making me think my doubts are honest ones, when they are not? If that's so, then I have no chance to win a debate with him. According to the traditional faith he's much too intelligent and powerful for me to overcome. If he deceives me, then I am deceived. The question is why an all-powerful God didn't help me. The devil wouldn't have a chance against God, but why does God do nothing to help me overcome my doubts? While I was beginning to doubt I would pray regularly to God to help me overcome my doubts. Then as my doubts were gaining a foothold on me I was praying that God would help me know the truth. Later I prayed that I'm not being deceived. Now I just think out loud for the most part, by talking to myself. I also know others were praying for me all along my journey. And now with this book I know still more people will pray for me. If prayer overcomes, then why not here with me?

Maybe I was being tested with several experiences like Job but I simply failed the test? So my doubts are now my condemnation, and because of them I'm going to hell when I die. If I failed the test, then I failed the test, and that's all I can say about it. But if God knew in advance (or had a pretty good idea) I would indeed fail the test if certain things happened in my life, then why test me like that? Why let the devil do what he did, if in fact it was a test? If it was a test then it makes me feel like a pawn in a cosmic game of chess. Is this really what happened? God was playing with my life just to win a challenge with the devil, as in Job 1-2? That's disgustingly like experimenting on captive prisoners with new drugs and surgical procedures so that the science of medicine can advance. But if I fail the tough test I'm supposed to go the hell? This is simply immoral on any level.

We humans disagree about all things that can be disagreed about. Some things are much more important than other things. No wonder there are so many different religions, and so many splinter groups of each religion, or no religion at all! According to religious people, whether God is pleased with us and where we will spend eternity are the most important issues of all. And it's no surprise we disagree. But if we cannot agree on lesser important issues, then why is it that we should be any more logical when it comes to religious issues? The more important the issue is to us, the more we cling to it and the more our emotions run wild while we try to defend our viewpoint. It would certainly seem that the more important the issue is to us, the less rational we are with regard to it, and the less likely we are to give it up.

If this is all the case, then it is simply impossible for God, if he exists, to judge anyone based upon what they believe. God cannot judge anyone for not holding to the correct set of beliefs. Whether one believes the Koran or the Bible, whether they are Mormon or Jew, whether they are Catholic or Protestant, there is simply no way God could condemn someone for not believing the correct things about religious issues. Period. Why? Because I'm pretty sure most all of us are wrong about many crucial issues. I could be wrong too. So why should God condemn us for being wrong about religious issues, when we're merely doing the best we can?

If God exists he cannot even judge us for how we behave, because how we behave flows out of that which we believe, and that which we believe flows from the sum total of experiences and thoughts that we have encountered for as long as we have been alive. I believe all of us—every single one of us—does the best we can given our gray brain matter, along with our life experiences. There can be no harsh judgment from God, even if he exists.

If I am wrong about anything I have written, then I am wrong. For me, it is an intellectual matter. I think I am right about what I believe, and I think I'm right about what I don't believe.

If God does exist after all, may he be pleased with me for doing the best that I can, given the nature of that which he has given us to work with—which isn't much. Besides, Dan Barker asks Christians to consider the same question I'm dealing with here. He asks, "Maybe there is a god, but he is only going to reward those people who have enough courage NOT to believe in him." This scenario is no less likely, he says. "What if Christians are wrong?"

A Partial List of My Published Christian Writings:

"The Christian Mind," <u>Christian Standard</u>, August 9, 1981.

"Trade School Mentality and The Christian," <u>Christian Standard</u>, June 27, 1982.

"A Christian Defense of the Gospel in a Twentieth Century Land," <u>Christian Standard</u>, September 19, 1982.

"Views of Freedom And Theories of Inspiration," <u>A Journal For Christian Studies</u>, Lincoln Christian Seminary, Chi-Lambda Fellowship, Summer 1984.

"Effectively Communicating the Gospel to the World of Man," <u>A Journal For Christian Studies</u>, Lincoln Christian Seminary, Chi-Lambda Fellowship, Winter, 1985-86.

"Was Christ Really Misquoted?" <u>Christian Standard</u>, August 17, 1986.

"Does God Still Do Miracles?" <u>Christian Standard</u>, April 17, 1988.

"Jesus and Socio-Political Involvement," <u>Christian Standard</u>, May 22 & 29, 1988.

"Living Together as God's People in Study" <u>The Key</u>, a quarterly magazine of GLCC, June—August 1989.

"The Preacher and Social Issues," <u>Christian Standard</u>, July 23, 1989.

"Do You Believe in 'Freedom of Choice'?" <u>The Seminary Review</u>, Cincinnati Bible College and Seminary, August 1989.

Book Review Essay of J. P. Moreland's apologetics book: <u>Scaling the Secular City</u>, for <u>A Journal For Christian Studies</u>, Lincoln Christian Seminary, Chi-Lambda Fellowship, Vol. IX, 1989-90.

"We Can Fall From Grace According To James," <u>Integrity,</u> Jan/Feb 1990.

"Ten Dumb Myths in the Fight Against Pornography," <u>Christian Standard</u>, February, 4, 1990.

"Tolerating the Tolerable in the Church Today," <u>Integrity,</u> March/April 1991.

"Tongues in the Church Then and Now," <u>Christian Standard</u>, August 4, 1991.

"Moral Truth Always Liberates—Always," <u>Integrity</u> March/April 1992.

"The Bible And Drinking Wine," <u>Integrity,</u> July/Aug 1994.

"Is Baptism Necessary For Salvation?" <u>Integrity,</u> July/August 1995.

"Is Baptism Necessary--One More Time." <u>Integrity,</u> January/February 1996.

My Master's Thesis:

<u>Karl Barth's Doctrine of the Word of God</u>, Lincoln Christian Seminary, May 1982.

Above is a picture of Dr. William Lane Craig and Dr. James D. Strauss together with me at my 1985 Trinity Evangelical Divinity School graduation. Dr. Craig is on the left and Dr. Strauss (in a light suit) is on the right.

I studied under Dr. William Lane Craig when he taught at Trinity Evangelical Divinity School (TEDS). Dr. Craig is considered by many to be the foremost defender of the Kalam Cosmological Argument for the existence of God, as well as the empty tomb of Jesus and his bodily resurrection from the grave. In 1985 I earned my Th.M. degree in the "Philosophy of Religion" with him as my major professor. Half of my hours in that program were under his teaching. Before I attended TEDS I had attended Lincoln Christian Seminary with Dr. James D. Strauss as my major professor. Half of my hours at Lincoln were under his teaching. Under Dr. Strauss I earned M.A and M.Div. degrees in "Theology and Philosophy."

Here's what Dr. Craig said a few years after I graduated from TEDS: "In my former capacity as a professor at Trinity Evangelical Divinity School, I enjoyed the privilege of having graduates of Lincoln Christian College in my classes. I was amazed as one after another distinguished himself as among my brightest and most capable students. What was it about this little Christian school in mid-state Illinois, I thought, that it should be such an academic powerhouse generating good philosophers? The answer was always the same: Dr. Strauss!" [Found on the back cover to Taking Every Thought Captive: Essays in Honor of James D. Strauss, eds, Richard A. Knopp & John D. Castelein, (College Press, 1997)].

I would still like to consider these two professors of mine as my friends. My rejection of Christianity isn't anything personal with them (or any other Christian who treats me with respect). I think very highly of them both. They are both good men. **The arguments just weren't there, period.**

ISBN 1412076811-1

9 781412 076814